# THE
# WILLIAM E.
# BOEING
## STORY

# THE
# WILLIAM E.
# BOEING
## STORY

## — A GIFT OF FLIGHT —

## DAVID WILLIAMS

AMERICA
THROUGH TIME®
ADDING COLOR TO AMERICAN HISTORY

Published by Arcadia Publishing by arrangement with Fonthill Media LLC
For all general information, please contact Arcadia Publishing:
Telephone: 843-853-2070
Fax: 843-853-0044
E-mail: sales@arcadiapublishing.com
For customer service and orders:
Toll-Free 1-888-313-2665

www.arcadiapublishing.com
www.fonthill.media

First published 2022

Copyright © David D. Williams 2022

ISBN 978-1-62545-116-3

All photographs are taken from the Boeing family archive unless otherwise indicated

Typeset in 10pt on 13pt Sabon
Printed and bound in England

*There is no authority except facts.*
*Hippocrates*

A placard outside William E. Boeing's office.

# Contents

# Introduction

The William Boeing story has been told before, but only from the corporate perspective. This book takes a more personal look at Boeing's life. There will be some differences between what you read here and what has been written elsewhere. That doesn't make one version of history right and other versions wrong; the differences arise because this version relies heavily on the Boeing family's extensive archives and the personal insight that they provide. In the end, the Boeing name belonged first to the Boeing family. It is their story told here.

I was lucky enough to become acquainted with Bill Boeing Jr. in the early 1990s, and we enjoyed a friendship that lasted over twenty years. In that time, I heard firsthand many of the stories that appear in this book. In 2014 I began working on the biography of Bill Jr.'s personal pilot, Miroslav Slovak (*A Race to Freedom, The Mira Slovak Story*, 2018). While researching the Slovak book, I taped several interviews with Bill Jr. in which he told me stories about his childhood, including the first time he rode in an airplane with his father. He laughed when he recalled sneaking into the factory with his mother in 1928 to send his father a radio greeting on his birthday. He also told me about being secretly sent to boarding school in far-off Hawaii after a failed kidnapping attempt. Bill Jr. died in 2015, at the age of ninety-two. After his death, I continued my research on the Slovak book, bringing together two of Bill Jr.'s daughters, one of his grandsons, and several cousins for an impromptu family reunion where stories and memories flew around the table. Driving home from that lunch, I realized that William E. Boeing's story was one that needed to be told.

There has never been a full-length biography of Bill Boeing, Sr. When the family members agreed to assist me with writing this book, they also agreed to unlock, for the first time, their considerable family archive of letters, wills, photos, and diaries. This invaluable resource has allowed me to put together a unique and never-before published portrait of a private man who had a profound impact on the world. It is important to note here that the family put no restrictions on me. No areas were to be avoided; no topics were off limits. They wanted, as I'm sure Bill Sr. would have wanted, an accurate, honest account of his life.

I am grateful to the entire Boeing family for their kindness and friendship during this project. Three names stand out: Gretchen Boeing (Bill and Bertha's granddaughter), Jane Paschall (Nathaniel Paschall and Bertha's granddaughter), and Will Rademaker (Bill and Bertha's great-grandson.) All three went beyond the call of duty to answer my questions, provide insight, and guide me through the complex maze of documents. Will Rademaker deserves special credit for convincing his family that I was the right person to write this book. I have tried to tell this story as accurately as possible, and if there are errors in the telling, they are mine.

I remember the wonder I felt the first time I flew on a Boeing airliner. My imagination swirled with excitement as I headed toward a far-off vacation. I can honestly say that the journey I have taken through the life of Bill Boeing is as exciting as any trip I took in one of his company's airplanes.

# Bombs Away
# Seattle, November 13, 1915

A fragile two-seat biplane dove toward the crowded football stadium at almost 100 mph, its stoic pilot staring straight ahead. Directly in front of him, a passenger cradled a bright red bundle in his lap. As the plane approached the stadium, the passenger leaned out of the cockpit and the propeller blast hit him in the chest. He held the package over the edge of the cockpit. "This will wake them up," he thought.[1]

In that autumn of 1915 a great war ravaged Europe, with the Old World's armies mired in a bloody standoff. Massive trenches cut across the heart of France, stretching from Switzerland to the English Channel. Millions of soldiers faced each other across a no-man's-land of mud, burned-out wagons, and smoking bomb craters. Mighty artillery pieces lobbed explosive shells, indiscriminately killing soldiers and civilians at the astounding rate of almost 5,000 per day. Brightly colored biplanes flew across this frightening hellscape to scout enemy troop movements and drop bombs on the miserable soldiers huddled below in their trenches.

In Seattle, Washington, 6,000 miles away from the front lines, people went about their days oblivious to the carnage in Europe. November 13 was a blustery Saturday on the University of Washington campus. The gusty wind swirled yellow maple leaves past students with arms full of books as they hurried toward the library. Towering gray clouds sailed across the blue sky, now blocking, now exposing a magnificent view of Mount Rainier.

Saturdays in Seattle during the fall could be summed up with one word: football. There was an air of excitement as 3,500 fans, many wearing trim straw hats with purple and gold ribbons, headed toward Denny Field to watch Gil Dobie's undefeated University of Washington Sun Dodgers take on their number one West Coast rival: the California Golden Bears.[2]

East 45th Street was backed up with a noisy combination of horse-drawn carriages and Model T Fords. Athletic young men called yell leaders shouted into purple megaphones to excite the partisan UW fans as they filed past the ticket takers and climbed the stadium's wooden bleachers. The fans had plenty to be excited about. Gil Dobie was in his eighth year coaching the Sun Dodgers, and under his direction Washington had never lost a game.[3] Fans roared their approval as Dobie's Dodgers ran onto the field in purple shirts and yellow pants. With the two teams lined up for the kickoff, the referee raised his whistle. Just before he blew it there was a mechanical roar from above. The startled spectators looked toward the sky as a plane dove toward the field. Its snarling engine left a wispy trail of black exhaust hanging behind. Some pointed, others gasped; airplanes were a rarity in 1915. The passenger gestured with his hand, signaling the pilot to go even lower. Some fans thought that the plane was going to land until they noticed it was a floatplane with a wooden pontoon in place of wheels. At the last second, when a crash seemed inevitable, the plane pulled up just enough to circle the field. The passenger leaned out of the cockpit and dropped his red missile-shaped package.

For an instant, panic filled the stadium. There were screams, but the package broke apart to release hundreds of cardboard cutouts that rained down on the crowd. People in the front row leapt over the rail to catch the cards as they drifted to the ground. The plane climbed and flew away to the south, silhouetted against the gray sky and Mount Rainier. Some people thought they saw the passenger give a jaunty wave as he flew out of sight.

The cards were about ten inches long and each was shaped like an artillery shell. "There's a message!" someone shouted.

"What does it say?" one of the yell leaders asked.

The man read out loud: "Protection through Preparedness. This harmless card in the hands of a hostile foe might have been a bomb dropped on you. Aeroplanes are your best defense!!!"

Turning the card over, he read, "Aero Club of the Northwest."[4]

The Aero Club and the bombing stunt were both the brainchildren of William Edward Boeing, a wealthy lumberman who was fascinated with planes and flying. Boeing was thirty-four years old, tall and handsome, with a trim mustache and fine dark hair. He frequently wore brown tweed jackets with leather elbow patches. He had a wry sense of humor, an impish smile, and a thirst for adventure. In August 1915, Boeing had bought a Martin TA floatplane from Glenn Martin of Los Angeles for the astounding sum of $11,863. On the November 13 "bombing mission", Aero Club member Herb Munter had been at the controls of the plane while Boeing tossed out the cardboard "bombs" from the passenger seat.

The Aero Club, founded on August 24, 1915, was an outgrowth of Seattle's posh University Club.[5] Several club members, including Boeing's good friend,

Lieutenant Conrad Westervelt of the U.S. Navy, were interested in flying. Boeing was bankrolling a plan to build two planes designed by Westervelt. Simultaneously, he was taking lessons from Martin's flight school in Los Angeles. After the lessons were cut short when another student crashed the school's only trainer, Boeing bought his own plane and had it shipped to Seattle so he could continue practicing. It arrived in crates by steamship on October 15 and Boeing made his first flight less than a week later.[6]

Bill Boeing believed that aviation was going to revolutionize the world. He wanted to be part of that revolution but wasn't yet sure how he was going to fit in. He was also worried about the war in France and could see that the U.S. was sliding towards it. The European nations had over 7,000 airplanes, while the U.S. had barely more than fifty. Boeing knew enough about airplanes to feel that it was his patriotic duty to alert his countrymen to this deficiency.

Not everyone was impressed by Boeing's bombing stunt. Reverend Dr. Sydney Strong of the Queen Anne Congregational Church preached a fiery sermon condemning Boeing and his message. "I serve notice on the Aero Club that they are encroaching on the territory of Christianity when they drop messages from the sky," he said, pounding the altar and pointing toward Heaven.[7] When Westervelt heard this, he grumbled, "How does the Reverend know we weren't sent by God?" Boeing quipped back, "If God had sent us, we would have had better aim."[8]

The day after Boeing "bombed" the football game (which Washington won by a score of 13 to 7), Herb Munter was giving a ride over Lake Washington to Boeing's friend and fellow Aero Club member John Hull. On this gray, blustery day, Munter was only 70 feet off the water when he saw a dark squall a few hundred yards ahead. He banked the Martin into a tight turn to avoid it, but the fragile plane tilted too far and lost lift. From the shore, Boeing watched helplessly as the plane fell out of the air and hit the water with a tremendous splash. A plume of steam from the hot engine drifted into the autumn sky.

On impact, Munter's head smacked the engine cowl and he was knocked unconscious. Hull grabbed him and held his face above water until a motorboat driven by bystander Paul Howard and carrying *Seattle Post Intelligencer* sports editor Portus Baxter reached the scene.[9] Howard and Baxter pulled the dazed airmen aboard and brought them to shore.[10] Munter quickly regained his senses while Boeing began directing the salvage efforts. He sent Howard and Baxter back to get a line on the broken airplane. Floating on the surface, it looked like a child's kite that had been stepped on.

The rescue boat towed the Martin to the Cascade Boat House in Madison Park, where Boeing rigged a block and tackle from one of its rugged beams to begin righting the damaged plane. Munter was still there, soaking wet and shivering. Boeing wrapped him in a lap robe from the back seat of his Rolls Royce and drove Munter and Munter's brother Archie (who had been waiting for his chance for a ride) to their nearby home. Boeing helped Archie get Herb into the house and then hurried back to the boathouse to remove the plane's engine and begin drying it out.

A short while later, Boeing contacted Glenn Martin in Los Angeles and asked for replacement parts. Martin was in no mood to be helpful. When Boeing had purchased the plane, Martin sent two of his best mechanics, Floyd Smith and Ross Stern, to Seattle to help Boeing assemble it.[11] Smith had long since returned, but Stern was still in Seattle; Martin had heard rumors that Boeing might have hired him to help out on the planes that he and Westervelt were building. Miffed by what he saw as Boeing's poaching of a valuable employee, Martin said that the repair parts wouldn't be ready for a few months.[12] Boeing was shocked by Martin's response. Looking at the broken plane in the dimly lit boathouse, he complained to Westervelt that this was no way to run a business, adding that he was confident that they could do a better job.

"Of course we could," said Westervelt, and a broad smile broke across the naval officer's face.[13] A missing puzzle piece had fallen into place, and Bill Boeing suddenly realized what his role in aviation was going to be. He nodded to Westervelt. Nothing in Boeing's life would ever be the same.

# PART I

## The Beginning
## 1889-1910

# 1. Taconite
## Mesabi Mountains, 1889

There is an old family story about Wilhelm Böing, a German immigrant, and his young, American-born son Bill hiking in the rugged Mesabi Mountains, west of Duluth, Minnesota. The land had once been the home of a Native American tribe called the Ojibwa. Their word for "giant" was "mesabi" and they called this place "Mesabi Wajiw," Giant Mountain.

Böing had purchased a large swath of timber land in the Mesabi Range and had brought his son with him to show him how to "cruise" – a timber industry term for determining the location and quality of a piece of land's timber. It was a warm day at the end of summer 1889; as they walked across a clearing of dry grass, their boots sent a flurry of frightened grasshoppers flying ahead in short hops. Böing was looking for the white pine that was being used to build houses, hotels, and factories across the United States. He had a rifle slung over his shoulder and walked with a map folded open in front of him.

Coming across a narrow stream cutting its way out of the mountains, they frightened a deer, and both smiled as it bounced away with its white tail sticking straight up. They found a place to ford the stream and didn't even notice that the flat stones they balanced on were covered with dark rust stains. If Wilhelm had been a miner, instead of a logger, he would have seen the signs of taconite, an ore that indicates the presence of valuable iron.

They hiked uphill toward a stand of white pine, enjoying the view west across the mountains. Pulling out his compass, Wilhelm was stunned to see that it indicated that he was facing due north. That seemed impossible. Wilhelm checked his pocket watch. It was almost noon. If he was facing north, the sun had to be directly behind him. But when he faced towards the north indicated by his compass, the sun was on his left. He backtracked down the hill. When he checked his compass by the stream, it showed that north was uphill, but as he hiked back uphill, the compass needle spun to left until it was almost 90 degrees off.[1] The confused hikers turned and traced their steps back downhill and joked about the drunken compass.

Neither Wilhelm nor Bill knew that they had just stumbled across the Mesabi Iron Range. With thousands of tons of iron buried just below the surface, the range had a magnetic field so strong that it overrode the earth's magnetic poles. In a few years the Mesabi Iron Range would make young Bill Boeing one of the richest men in America.

Wilhelm Böing had been born to wealthy parents in the Prussian province of Westphalia, in the town of Hohenlimburg, in 1846. After enlisting in the army and serving under Otto von Bismarck during the brief Unification War of 1866, he immigrated to America. By 1868 he had arrived in Michigan, carrying $60 and letters of introduction to prominent members of the German community. Böing had no difficulty finding work: first as a farmhand, then as a hardware clerk, and eventually as a "stapler" tagging wood in a lumber yard.

In 1870 Böing went to work for a German-speaking lumberman named Charles Ortmann in East Saginaw, Michigan. As part of his salary, Wilhelm received room and board, so he moved into Ortmann's crowded house. The Ortmanns had two daughters, Marie and Stephanie, and three sons, Rudy, Charlie, and Edward. Recognizing Wilhelm's potential, Ortmann began to teach him the intricate business of timber, including how to estimate the board feet a stand of trees would yield, how to transport logs from the backwoods to the mills, and most importantly, how to take advantage of the Homestead laws to buy and sell land. In an October 6, 1872 letter, Wilhelm told his father that he and Ortmann had purchased 80 acres of timber for $640 and sold it a few weeks later for $1600.[2] After Congress passed the generous Timber and Stone Act in 1878 it was even easier for investors to snap up large parcels of prime timberland for next to nothing.

With his own family over 4,000 miles away, Wilhelm grew close to the Ortmanns, treating the boys like younger brothers. By 1880 Marie Ortmann was twenty-one years old.[3] She and Wilhelm, who was thirty-four, had fallen in love. They were married on Christmas Day, 1880, and on October 1, 1881, Marie gave birth to a baby boy whom they named William Edward Boeing, using an anglicized spelling.[4] They called their new son Bill.

Bill was a normal, rambunctious little boy. Apparently he had a bad case of the terrible twos, and in an 1883 letter to his sister, Wilhelm wrote, "I would like it very much, Emma, if you could make the acquaintance of my little family here … You'll have to make peace with the youngster, between ourselves he is a genuine pigheaded Böing and if you can get on with that, everything will be all right."[5]

Wilhelm's star rose quickly. His mother had died in 1874 and left him a considerable inheritance. By 1882 he was able to buy 7,544 acres in Minnesota's Mesabi Mountains for about $3 per acre, paying just $22,560 for the land that would eventually make his son a multi-millionaire.[6]

That same year Böing moved to Detroit and spent approximately $35,000 to have an ornate three-story Beaux-Arts mansion built on Woodward Avenue. The massive house was staffed by uniformed servants, including a butler, a cook, two maids, and a laundress who came in once a week. In 1884 the Böings celebrated the birth of a daughter, Caroline, and they added a second daughter, Margaret, in 1887. Wilhelm's friends in Detroit often quipped that he "was all-American in his business life, all-German in his home life." He insisted that his children were raised according to German cultural traditions and that they spoke German while at home.[7]

Wilhelm Böing invested in other businesses as well. Soon he was president of Detroit Edge Tool and vice-president of Galvin Brass and Iron Works. Both companies specialized in manufacturing tools for the logging industry. While his business holdings flourished, his heart still lay with the timber industry, and he made it a point to inspect his lands personally whenever possible.

Hiking in the deep north woods with a rifle slung over his shoulder and a compass resting in the palm of his hand was a tonic for the stress and anxiety that came with building a business empire. According to the *Detroit Free Press*, Böing had "a rugged constitution."[8] He was a skilled bird hunter and passed his love of the outdoors on to his son. It is easy to picture Böing, with a shotgun resting on his arm, walking through the sun-dappled Michigan forest while young Bill struggled to keep up with his tall, robust father. Before long, Wilhelm began teaching Bill how to bird hunt, passing on the skills that generations of Böings had perfected in the pheasant fields of the Ruhr Valley. It was during one of these father-son hunting trips, as they picked their way across an October field of wheat stubble that Wilhelm gave Bill a bit of important advice. Speaking in his native German he quoted poet Johann Wolfgang von Goethe, "It is not enough to know, you must also apply yourself. It is not enough to want, you must also do." This simple advice became the guiding principle of Bill's life.

In the winter of 1887, Wilhelm visited the West Coast and promptly fell in love with the region. He saw tremendous opportunity in the vast wilderness and began making plans to move west.

> It is a great country out there – the timber resources are simply immense – it is to-day a cheap outlay. It is a free lunch and furthermore it is a delightful climate on the whole coast, an even temperature and balmy air and I have concluded that if I can sell out in Michigan I silently will fold my tent and sneak away to that foreign shore on the Pacific.[10]

Wilhelm hired Mr. J. W. Fordney from Eureka, California, to buy timber land in California and Washington. One of his first purchases was 6,000 acres on Grays Harbor in the Washington Territory on February 11, 1887. However, Böing did not live long enough to make the move.

Christmas Day 1889 at the Böing house started the way it did all across America: with the children, Bill, Caroline, and Margaret, shrieking and laughing as they bounded downstairs in their robes and slippers, racing to the parlor to open their colorfully wrapped presents. The room smelled like fresh pine from the large tree decorated with ribbons and glass balls. Stockings bulging with fruit and candy were hung from the mantel over the fireplace. Wilhelm and Marie, celebrating their ninth anniversary, no doubt exchanged loving looks as their children reveled in the joy of the season. Later, a traditional German Christmas dinner of roast goose and bread dumplings with red cabbage was served in the Böings' elegant dining room. After dinner was cleared, Wilhelm kissed each of his children goodbye and told them he had to go to New York on a business trip.

It took Böing all night and most of the next day to travel the 500 miles between Detroit and New York City by train. He checked into the opulent Brunswick Hotel on Madison Square on December 26. Sometime during the journey Böing caught a cold. After a week of too much work and not enough sleep, the cold turned into pneumonia. He convalesced at the Brunswick until Friday, January 5, when he decided that he was healthy enough to travel home. He wasn't. The trip was "trying and painful."[11] Pneumonia turned into pleurisy, and on January 10, 1890, Wilhelm Böing died at home on Woodward Avenue.[12]

A brief funeral service was held two days later. Bill and his sisters sat red-eyed and crying in stiff wooden chairs in front of their father's open casket in the same parlor where the family had celebrated Christmas two weeks earlier. Reverend Dr. C. R. Henderson, of the Woodward Avenue Baptist Church, read a few passages from the Bible, and then Böing's casket was loaded onto a horse-drawn hearse and taken to Elmwood Cemetery for burial. Böing was just 44 years old. Marie was devastated, but she was also extremely wealthy. According to an article in the *Detroit Free Press*, "The estate of the deceased will inventory not far from $4,000,000."[13]

# 2. BOARDING SCHOOL
## VEVEY, SWITZERLAND, 1894

On October 25, 1891, Wilhelm's widow, Marie Böing, was dealt another shock. Her four-year-old daughter, Margaret, died unexpectedly. Grief compounded upon grief, and depression engulfed the heartbroken Marie. Her worried family suggested that she get out of Detroit. On January 31, 1892 she left with Bill and Caroline for an eight-month trip to California, where they spent time at the elegant Hotel Del Monte in Monterey. The spectacular complex was a monument to Gilded Age excess. It included a racetrack, golf course, and private hunting fields. It was North America's first true luxury resort. Bill found peace of mind on the rugged Monterey Peninsula and came back frequently for the rest of his life to walk among the giant old-growth trees or fish in the clear Pacific waters.

The trip did nothing to heal Marie's loss. She returned to Detroit with her children on September 25, 1892 but her depression persisted. Money wasn't an obstacle, so her parents suggested she go to Europe for a "Grand Tour." Her brother Edward was already traveling in Europe, and they could keep each other company. She was reluctant to leave Bill and Caroline behind, so she enrolled them both in Swiss boarding schools. Sometime in 1893, Marie, Bill, and Caroline stood side by side, cheering and waving from the rail of a great ocean liner while steam-powered tugs pointed her east.

A photograph of Bill once he arrived in Switzerland shows him in a sailor's suit with short pants and a "Buster Brown" haircut. It is not hard to imagine young Bill wearing this same suit while exploring every nook and cranny of the massive ship during its passage across the Atlantic. Once in Switzerland Caroline was placed in a girls' school in Geneva, and Bill was enrolled at the prestigious L'Institut Sillig Fréres, a school for boys in Vevey, an impossibly beautiful resort town on the eastern end of Lake Geneva.

L'Institut Sillig Fréres was established in 1836 and boasted a number of famous alumni, including the American financier J. P. Morgan, who put up the money for iconic companies like AT&T, General Electric, and Chase Bank. The school's advertisements claimed that it was in a "splendid and most healthful location" and that its students received a "thorough and practical instruction" with "strict attention being paid to physical development."[1] The school's grounds, which bordered the lake, featured "large gardens and playgrounds" and its students were encouraged to row and sail frequently. Sillig taught classes in French and German, and since German had been spoken in the Böing house on Woodward Avenue, Bill had no trouble communicating with his teachers.

Once the children were settled at school, Marie began her tour, first visiting the famous sites of Europe, then crossing the Mediterranean to Egypt, passing through the Suez Canal, and going all the way to India. She sent dozens of letters back to Bill, each one starting, "To my darling boy," followed by descriptions of her adventures.[2] The pace of Marie's travels made it hard for her to receive mail, although almost every one of her letters ended with a gentle request to write her. The few responses from Bill that survive show the problem: letters addressed to her at the Hotel Beau Rivage in Leipzig arrived too late and were forwarded to her hotel in Cairo and from there to Bombay, on the west coast of India, where Marie finally received months of mail all at once, bundled with a yellow band and brought up to her room with breakfast one morning.[3]

Marie's tour was successful in that it helped heal her broken heart, but at the same time it plunged Bill into a world of loneliness. He went from being the oldest son in a loving family of five to being all alone in a foreign country. To combat his loneliness, he threw himself into stamp collecting. His uncle Edward, traveling with Marie, sent him colorful stamps from each country they passed through. Bill spent many nights carefully working by lamplight to steam the stamps from his uncle's letters and paste them in an album to keep track of his mother's travels.

A photo of Bill at Sillig shows a young boy small for his age and seemingly unhappy. According to the Boeing Company biography, it was while at Sillig that Bill "established an outward correctness that remained with him for the rest of his life."[4] The trauma of losing his father and sister, and then of traveling 3,000 miles from home to live alone in a strange country, may have caused him to erect a formidable wall around his heart. Whatever the reason, Bill became a loner who found it difficult to make casual friendships. As a family friend quipped years later, "Bill listens much better than he talks."

Headmaster Edouard Sillig, oldest son of the school's founder Frédéric Sillig, took a special interest in the quiet, pensive young boy. Sillig personally tutored Bill in the burgeoning new art of photography and taught him how to sail. It was here on the windswept waters of Lake Geneva that Bill fell in love with boats. The Boeing family archives contain a photograph from 1894 that twelve-year-old Bill took of Sillig at the helm of a small sail boat skimming across Lake Geneva with snow-capped mountains behind him.

In June of 1896, Sillig took Bill and several other students to the Swiss National Exhibition in Geneva. For 50 centimes Bill and his classmates were able to spend all day wandering the massive fair. The grounds covered both sides of the Arve River. Three pedestrian bridges allowed fairgoers to stroll back and forth between exhibition buildings on both sides of the river. Bill took special interest in the buildings that focused on science, electricity, and machinery. There was also an amusement park with a log flume ride, a huge merry-go-round with carved horses, and a 1/3-size replica of the Eiffel Tower, including working elevators that whizzed Bill and his classmates to the observation deck in just a few seconds.

Food vendors perfumed the air with the smells of soft pretzels, bratwurst, coffee, and hot chocolate. Bill was on the south side of the Arve exploring a replica of an Alpine village when he saw a colorful balloon with a 60-foot diameter rise into the air. A large wicker basket hanging beneath the balloon was crowded with passengers.

He had heard about balloons big enough to carry people, but this was the first one he had ever seen. He hoped that the crowd in the basket meant that rides were for sale. Bill ran across the nearest footbridge, turned right on the Rue des Sciences, and was out of breath by the time he reached a sign that read, "Ballon Captif. Billet 10F." (Captive Balloon. Tickets 10 francs.) Bill waited patiently, counting the people ahead of him in line and dividing by the number that went up in each flight to figure out if there was enough time to get his ride before the fair closed for the night.

The rubberized silk balloon was filled with hydrogen and carried a wicker basket that could hold between twelve and twenty people. It was tethered by a heavy cable to a powerful steam winch. An attendant walked up and down the line telling anyone who was smoking that hydrogen was extremely flammable and they needed to extinguish all pipes, cigars, and cigarettes. It was late in the day when Bill finally got his flight. After the attendant collected his ticket, Bill rushed to the basket and took a position at the front, holding onto the carved wooden rail. When the balloon was full, the pilot got in, closed a wicker gate, and nodded to the ground crew. They released the safety weights and as the crew began to play out the long cable, the balloon rose smoothly. There was an excited chatter among the passengers, but as the balloon gained height, the voices tapered off and were replaced by the sound of wind blowing through the ropes as the astonished passengers gazed in silence at the shrinking world below. As the balloon rose higher, Bill could see Lake Geneva and its famous water jet shooting 400 feet into the air. It took the ground crew ten minutes to play out the 1,200-foot-long cable so the balloon could reach its full height. At about 1,000 feet, the wind caught it, causing the balloon to rock gently as it sailed past the boundary of the fair and over the city itself. Bill had expected to be scared, but he wasn't; he was thrilled and fascinated.

Eventually he felt a tug as the big winch began to pull the balloon back toward earth. When they touched down and the gate was opened, Bill's first steps felt rubbery and awkward, like when he got off a boat after sailing all day. He was handed a tiny blue and white card verifying that "Mr. W. E. Boeing" rode on "ascension No. 423."[5] Some people search their whole lives for a purpose, but at the age of fourteen, Bill had discovered his.

By the time the Boeing family returned to Detroit, a lot had changed. In 1893 a timber cruiser turned mining surveyor named Frank Hibbing had discovered the iron deposit on Böing's property in the Mesabi Mountains – the same deposit that had caused Böing's compass to behave so oddly in 1889. He immediately made arrangements on behalf of Wilhelm Böing's estate to lease the land to the Oliver Iron and Steel Company, which began extracting the valuable iron. In just a few months the company shipped 10,000,000 tons of ore.[6] The Böing land was eventually combined with as many as 40 other pieces of property to create the Hull-Rust-Mahoning open pit mine, which has been in continuous operation for more than 120 years.

Bill spent 1896-97 attending the Whitton School for Boys in Detroit. He went through a growth spurt at Wilton, gaining well over a foot, and by the time he graduated he had the tall, lanky look of a young colt. In September 1897 he enrolled in Saint Paul Preparatory School, one of the nation's most prestigious prep schools, in Concord, New Hampshire. The 2,000-acre tree-lined campus is larger than most universities, and its picturesque Gothic architecture rivals any Ivy League campus.

Bill chafed under the stern discipline of the school's rigorous schedule and wrote heartfelt letters to his mother, questioning his ability to succeed in such a stifling environment. Marie, meanwhile, rejuvenated from her grand tour, had attracted the interest of a rakishly handsome young physician from Chicago named Frederic Dillard Owsley. She fell in love with him, and they were married on September 11, 1898.

Owsley owned a plantation estate in Virginia called Glooston Manor, which covered 286 acres in the township of Samuel Miller. The mansion, according to the *Detroit Free Press*, "was equipped with hot and cold running water, and furnished with costly and attractive furniture and is lighted with electricity from its own power plant."[7] It also boasted traditional Southern essentials like a stable full of horses and a house full of servants. Immediately after their marriage, Owsley retired from his medical practice and moved to Virginia. Marie sold the house in Detroit and joined him.

During Marie and Frederic's courtship, Bill got along well with his prospective stepfather. The frequent moving that came with switching schools so often had made it difficult for Bill to form important friendships with people his own age, but there was something about horses that resonated with him; he was comfortable around barns and stables in a way that he rarely was with people. Frederic introduced Bill to Thoroughbred horses and he was soon smitten with equestrian sports. He began to take teams of horses to meets throughout Virginia, where he excelled in the driving events. Soon Bill's name was a common item in the sports pages of local papers.

A month after the wedding, Marie filed a peculiar lawsuit against her late husband's estate. When Böing's will was written, Bill was an only child, so the will provided for the estate to be divided equally between Marie and Bill, and "In case, however, I should leave other ... children living at the time of my death ... my ... estate [shall] be divided between my ... wife and children each to share alike." When Wilhelm died, there were three children, but four-year-old Margaret died before the estate could be settled so Marie, Bill, and Caroline each got one third of it. Owsley thought that since Margaret was alive when her father died, she was entitled to 25 percent of the estate, and since she died without a will, her estate should go to her mother. The purpose of the lawsuit was to stop the three-way distribution of Wilhelm's estate and replace it with a four-way distribution, whereby Bill and Caroline each got 25 percent and Marie 50 percent by combining her portion with Margaret's. The lawsuit failed and Bill began to doubt the motives of his stepfather.

There was another ticking time bomb buried in a pile of papers in Owsley's office. Wilhelm Böing's will named Marie as the trustee of the children's portions of his estate.[8] However, if Marie remarried, she had to transfer Bill and Caroline's portions of the estate into a trust managed by Elisha H. Flinn, a Detroit lawyer, within 20 days of her remarriage. Even though Owsley had read Böing's will closely enough to spot the potential loophole regarding Margaret's portion of the estate, Flinn was never contacted and the mandatory trust was never created.

Bill graduated from Saint Paul in June of 1900 and shortly afterward learned that he had been accepted to Yale.

# 3. WHEELS, HEELS AND SAND
## YALE, 1900

In early September of 1900, nineteen-year-old Bill Boeing was sitting alone on a northbound train cutting its way through the humid night, heading from Charlottesville, Virginia, to New York City. There is no way to know what thoughts were occupying his mind as the Virginia countryside rushed past, but it would have been natural for Bill to have felt melancholy and friendless as he sped toward another faraway school and away from a childhood left unfinished by his father's death.

In New York he transferred to an express train that would take him directly to New Haven, Connecticut, and Yale. Compared with the train up from Virginia, the crowd on the express was younger, louder, and almost exclusively male.[1] Many of the well-dressed young men with pomaded hair and dark blazers were fresh-faced and nervous like Bill; others lounged confidently in the smoking car under clouds of blue-gray smoke, calling out boisterously to friends who passed by.

The farther north the train went, the cooler the night felt, and by the time the train pulled into New Haven there was a hint of fall in the air. Bill took a horse-drawn cab past ivy-covered buildings to his new apartment at 150 Grove Street.[2] He was curious about how things worked, so he enrolled in the Sheffield School of Science with the ambition of becoming an engineer.

Abbot Lawrence Lowell, president of Harvard from 1909 to 1933, once asked, "Boys go to Harvard for intellectual reasons, they go to Princeton for social reasons, but why would anyone go to Yale?"[3] Yale men across the nation responded in a loud voice: "To become a success."[4]

Bill quickly learned that there was fierce competition among underclassmen to prove they had "sand," which, in the unique vocabulary of turn-of-the-century Yale, meant "determination – the ability to get things done." The expression came from the railroad: when the driving wheels of a locomotive couldn't get traction on the smooth steel rails, engineers would spread a bit of sand on the rails to give the wheels grip. The way a young "Eli"[5] could prove he had sand was to "heel" for a number of causes and activities. ("To heel" was Yale slang meaning "to work hard," because if someone was working hard you would see their heels as they hurried along.) A successful heeler soon became known as a "big wheel." This was another bit of slang from the world of railroading: the big driving wheels on a locomotive did the work and made the train move, and to be a "big wheel" meant that you were someone who could get things done.

The true worth of a Yale man was not determined by his academic standing or grades, but by how many extracurricular activities he took part in. Yale president Arthur Hadley once quipped, "We need to elevate study to the level of an extracurricular activity."[6] The only extracurricular club that Bill left any evidence of being involved in was the Yale Corinthian Yacht Club. His love of sailing, picked up on Lake Geneva, was still with him.

It was also at Yale that Bill began smoking cigarettes. Most Americans who smoked used pipes or cigars. Cigarettes were hand rolled and unless one rolled one's own, they were expensive; the young dandies at Yale considered them luxurious and sophisticated. Bill began smoking and soon developed a two-pack-a-day habit that would stay with him for life.

Bill made at least one significant friendship at Yale that would prove to be very important later in life. John Borden was a wealthy socialite from Chicago whose grandfather had struck it rich in the Colorado Silver Boom, making the Bordens one of the wealthiest families in the country. The younger Borden seemed to thrive in the active extracurricular culture of Yale, and the yearbooks are full of his accomplishments. He was a member of the Honor Roll, captain of the Gun Club, and even president of the 1905 Yale Senior Society. There isn't any record of exactly when Bill and John met, but the names Boeing and Borden come so close alphabetically, it is likely that they ran into each other often at Yale, where much of an underclassman's life was arranged by alphabet. One can imagine them becoming friends on crisp autumn mornings as they hurried to their classes after mandatory church services at Bechtel Chapel.

At Yale, Bill had more on his mind than the average carefree student. When his father Wilhelm passed away, he had massive land holdings in Michigan and Minnesota, in addition to 25,000 acres of timberland around Grays Harbor in Washington State. In the spring of 1902, newspapers in Washington began to carry announcements from the superior court of what was then called Chehalis County (later renamed Grays Harbor County) that portions of the Boeing property were years behind on their property taxes and would be put up for auction if the taxes were not paid immediately.[7] Bill, who was already uncomfortable with the way that Owsley was handling his father's estate, made hasty arrangements to have the taxes paid. On October 1, 1902, Bill turned twenty-one, and on October 30 he legally discharged his guardianship and took control of over $1,000,000 worth of timber and mining lands.[8]

At the same time, Bill was becoming disillusioned with Yale. He felt that the rich young dandies there, who spent their time hurrying around town organizing dances and parties, were accomplishing nothing. He had inherited real businesses that needed real attention. Early in May of 1903 Bill dropped out of Yale.

The next week, his mother made a peculiar real-estate transaction. In 1900, shortly after her marriage to Owsley, Marie bought a 774-acre Virginia estate called Tiverton. She and Owsley built a mansion on the estate that bore a striking resemblance to the White House. On May 19, 1903, Marie sold the 18,500-square-foot mansion and all of its lands to Bill for one dollar.[9] There are no records about Marie's motives for this extraordinary transaction, but Bill believed that she was beginning to worry that Owsley had designs on his inheritance. If this was Marie's motivation, the fierce lawsuits that would one day rage between Bill and Owsley were proof that her intuition was correct.

After leaving Yale, Bill headed to Europe. He arrived at Bremerhaven in late May when the roads were lined with lilac and rhododendron. He headed toward the Ruhr Valley. Because he had lost his father while still a child, he was searching for a connection with his family.

He found what he was looking for at Lenneufstasse 33, in the tiny village of Hohenlimburg. He nervously knocked on the door of a traditional white stucco "half timbered" house. When the door opened and he introduced himself, he was greeted by a boisterous "Hello" and a big bosomy hug from his corpulent Aunt Emma. She, along with her sisters Ida and Caroline, still lived in Hohenlimburg and happily showed Bill around the picturesque village. Later they cooked him a traditional meal of Kohlwurst (smoked sausage) with sauerkraut while regaling him with stories about his father's childhood. When supper was over, they took him to the old Lutheran cemetery to show him the graves of his Böing grandparents.

The next morning there was a family outing to Hohensyburg, the medieval ruin of a castle perched high atop a wooded crag, overlooking the Ruhr Valley. Adjacent to the castle was the brand-new Kaiser Wilhelm Memorial. After picnicking on the lawn, Bill and a large group of aunts, uncles, and nieces posed for photos at the memorial. Bill's obvious joy at being part of a family, after years of loneliness, shows brightly in the only known photograph from his youth where he is actually smiling.

After the photo session Bill bounded up 132 steps to the top of the Vincketurm, an eight-sided tower, with a spectacular view of the Ruhr Valley. While Bill leaned against the tower walls, gazing at the beautiful scenery, his uncle Edmund, breathing heavily from climbing the stairs, caught up with him. Bill gestured at the peaceful scenery and said, "Es ist schön." Edmund nodded and replied, "Not just beautiful, but bountiful too. Did you know that the Ruhr produces more coal and steel than all the rest of Europe combined?" Bill's memories of this happy trip and his family's homeland on the banks of the picturesque Ruhr would come back to haunt him during the dark years of war that lay ahead.

Bill returned to the United States aboard the SS *Deutschland*, sailing out of Cherbourg, and arrived in New York on June 26, 1903. It was an unseasonably cold day with windswept rain squalls that kept most of the first-class passengers off the decks and in the lounges as the ship docked in New York. Bill must have felt a tremendous impatience as he waited to disembark – not just to get off the ship but to get on with his life. He was twenty-one years old and finished with Yale. Now he was in a rush to start his adult life – to make a fortune, win wars, and more than anything, to make a name for himself.

# 4. WOOD SMOKE AND RAIN
# HOQUIAM, 1903

Late in the summer of 1903, Bill headed to the West Coast to inspect the 25,000 acres of timberland his father had left him in Grays Harbor, Washington. Changing trains in Council Bluffs, Iowa, he caught the Overland Limited to Ogden. The train left Iowa and rolled across an endless sea of grass that was Nebraska. Cloud formations cast immense shadows on the vast prairie. After Nebraska came Wyoming, with its tall aspens and dark tunnels, and then Ogden, where Bill transferred to the Pacific Express for the run across the dry Great Basin to California. Mile after mile of heat-shimmering desert disappeared behind the train until finally, San Francisco, with its cool, windswept bay and dark blue water, came into view. The train was a modern marvel, making the entire 3,000-mile trip in only five days. If Bill could have looked into the future, he would have been shocked to know that one day he would lead a transformation that would make trains seem slow and quaint.

Bill took a small steamer north to Grays Harbor, arriving on a damp, rainy day. 'Grays Harbor is at once both beautiful and awesome,' wrote Robert A. Weinstein in *Grays Harbor 1885-1913*,

> Its color scheme was then, and is yet, gray and green. Its chief green glories are mammoth trees – fir, spruce, hemlock, and cedar that line the … horizon in all directions. Its gray miseries are rain-heavy clouds hanging in leaden skies. It is wet and dank there, the ground is soggy and everywhere the forest drips.[1]

Grays Harbor was surrounded by sawmills that spewed smoke and steam into the air. On cloudy days, it looked like the mills were manufacturing the weather themselves: the gray clouds that billowed from tall brick smokestacks merged seamlessly into low-hanging overcast. Clothes, hands, and hair smelled constantly of wood smoke that no amount of soap and water could wash away.

Grays Harbor is a deep, funnel-shaped harbor on the Washington coast, just a few miles inland from the Pacific Ocean. The harbor is fed by five rivers, each of which was considered "good driving water" (rivers that moved fast enough to carry logs to the harbor). When Bill Boeing arrived in 1903, there were three small towns on the harbor, with more than 50 billion board feet of merchantable timber standing near the rivers.[2]

Bill rented a room at a boarding house at 616 West 6th, Hoquiam, on the north shore of Grays Harbor, where the deep water west of the Hoquiam River made an ideal moorage for the large lumber schooners that were the lifeblood of the region. There he met John H. Hewitt, who, like Bill, was born into a wealthy Midwest family with ties to the timber business. The two men hit it off instantly and stayed friends for the rest of their lives.

By frontier standards, Hoquiam was a big deal. It had a population of 1,500, "with two sawmills, three churches, and one school. Four hotels, a $150,000 electrical lighting plant, two miles of planked streets, five miles of planked sidewalks, and mail delivery once a day."[3] There was also a darker side to Grays Harbor, where the planked sidewalks and electric lighting didn't reach.

Across the Hoquiam River was Aberdeen, and just outside of Aberdeen, on the west bank of the Wishkah River, was a place that the loggers called the "Line." It was a narrow dirt street lined by boisterous saloons offering ragtime piano and 5-cent whiskey, tawdry brothels where men could buy companionship at the rate of 50 cents for thirty minutes, and, wedged between the bars and brothels, cheap boarding houses to sleep it all off. Loggers were paid once a month in cash, and on payday the Line turned into "Hell Street," where every form of sin and vice was openly available for just a few coins.[4]

As impressive as Hoquiam was to the lumber community, it was a far cry from the Gilded Age high-society lifestyle that Bill had enjoyed back East. However, it offered Bill something that he could never find at Yale or Tiverton: a chance to be his own man, to be judged on what he could accomplish on his own, not on where he had gone to school or who his father was. It must have been refreshing to a young man eager to make a name for himself.

Bill's goal in coming to Grays Harbor was to learn the lumber business. He soon met logging expert Daniel McCrimmon, and they joined forces to form the Boeing and McCrimmon Lumber Company.

The logging business hadn't changed much in fifty years. The core of the business was still the logging camp, a collection of temporary shacks that would house and feed about sixty loggers in the woods. Every morning the camp would send out cutting gangs made up of five or six men, whose job it was to find and cut the trees that had been marked by the surveyors.

The first and most important step in the business of logging was "cruising" the land to determine where the best timber was and estimate the value of the timber each tree would yield. Using the knowledge gained from childhood hikes with his father, Bill decided to cruise the land himself. It was difficult, bone-wearying work, slogging up and down deep forest ravines and hacking through thick underbrush. While he was cruising, Bill would spend the nights at the logging camps, sleeping on the rough mattresses and eating rustic breakfasts of corned beef hash, washed down with strong black coffee from an enameled tin cup. He would leave camp at first light wearing a heavy Filson jacket and muddy hobnailed boots and spend hours trudging through the wilderness, taking notes on a pad he carried in a deep coat pocket. Back in Hoquiam, he would sit late into the night, hunched over a tiny desk, fighting off sleep while he copied the notes into a red ledger with a fountain pen. Sometimes the exhausted young man would fold his arms across his desk and lay his head on the book, leaving a faint scent of shaving talc on the page that lingers still and escapes like a benevolent ghost when the modern researcher opens the ledger's fragile pages.

Bill still thought of Virginia as his home, returning to Tiverton just in time to scrub away the mud of the logging camp and take part in the Richmond Horse Show. It was the most important social event of the year. Virginia is horse country, and a gentleman's status was not determined by his income or property, but by how many horses he owned and how well he rode them. Bill entered horses in a half dozen events.

When the show opened on October 13, Bill was in his private box near the judges' stand.[5] Joining him there were two of Richmond's most beautiful and popular debutantes.[6] The women could not have been more different: Matilda Powell was a buxom "Gibson Girl." She wore a flowing pink gown with a bustle and her hair was piled high beneath a floppy hat so big that the people seated behind her were forced to lean to one side to see the events. Bill's other female guest was Gertrude Skelton. Svelte and athletic, she was one of Virginia's best riders, and that day she was to ride in almost every one of the women's events. She cut a dashing figure in tight white breeches, a black shadbelly coat, and knee-high leather riding boots. She had dark brown eyes and thick chestnut hair pulled back and pinned tightly to fit under a black top hat. Bill had invited Matilda because he had a romantic interest in her, and Gertrude because he wanted to see if she would be willing to ride for him in future events.

The show started with a crash of cymbals as the U.S. Marine Band began playing *Stars and Stripes Forever,* while a mounted color guard carried an American flag around the arena. The flag was followed by a parade of the competitors' horses. Everyone rose to their feet and remained standing as the horses trooped by. Matilda chatted, preened and waved to friends. Bill leaned against the rail intently examining his rivals' horses. He was pleasantly surprised when Gertrude joined him and began making expert observations on the competitors. Soon Bill and Gertrude were called from the box to prepare for their events.

Bill was up first, taking second in the "Horse in Harness" competition with a bay named Rajah. Gertrude took second in "Heavy Weight Hunter," riding a powerful gray gelding named Elevator. Between events, Bill and Gertrude would return to the box to relax and get a drink of water. There, Bill was disappointed to find Matilda bored and unhappy, while his heart raced whenever a flush-faced Gertrude swept in, full of excitement about her latest contest.

Eventually Bill finished his events and came back to the box to stay. It was clear to Matilda that Bill's affections had been captured by her athletic and exciting rival. In an effort to rekindle a connection, she asked Bill about his recent trip to the West Coast. Bill's eyes sparkled as he talked about logging, timber, and splash dams. Matilda feigned interest for a while, but when she could fake it no longer she snapped at him, telling him that she couldn't see the point of it all. She even wondered if he was working in the woods because his family needed the money. Bill was hurt. He told her that money had nothing to do with it and explained that he was working for progress and accomplishment, simply to know that the world was a better place because he'd been born.

Bill never heard Matilda's response. Out in the arena, Elevator knocked a rail in a jump and stumbled, throwing Gertrude and then rolling over her.[7] A gasp went around the ring. Bill rushed to the rail, focusing his attention on the motionless young girl. The horse had soon sprung to its feet and walked away. Gertrude slowly rolled to her knees, picked up her top hat and gave a jaunty wave to the crowd as she stood up. The arena erupted in cheers as a groom helped her walk off the field.

It's unlikely that Bill ever saw Matilda again, but he saw Gertrude whenever he was home. Their romance never caught fire, but they remained great friends. In the years ahead she rode several of Bill's horses, capturing many ribbons aboard his magnificent jumper, Taconite.

Two months after the horse show, 235 miles away in North Carolina, events that would one day dominate Bill's life were set in motion.

# 5. TAKING WING
# KITTY HAWK, 1903

The brothers Orville and Wilbur Wright, who ran a bicycle shop in Dayton, Ohio, were obsessed with flying. For three years they had spent the autumn, when it was too cold and wet to sell bicycles, hauling their homemade gliders to Kill Devil Hills, just outside of the flyspeck town of Kitty Hawk, among the wind-sculpted dunes of North Carolina's barrier islands. The brothers wanted to test their gliders at Kitty Hawk because the dunes there were tall enough to launch from, soft enough to prevent injury in a crash, and windy enough to get their gliders in the air.

By the end of their 1902 season, the Wrights were convinced that they could build a powered flying machine for 1903. Gasoline motors were rare, and when the brothers couldn't find one that met their needs, Charlie Taylor, the man they had hired to look after the bike shop when they were at Kitty Hawk, built one for them.

The home-built four-cylinder aluminum engine weighed 152 pounds and produced 12 horsepower. To accommodate the extra weight of the motor, the 1903 airplane was much larger than their previous machines. The Wrights also built two 8-foot propellers to be mounted on either side of the motor and driven by chains and sprockets like a bicycle wheel. The machine had a forward-mounted elevator, a device that could raise or lower the nose of the plane in flight, twin rear rudders, and an ingenious wing-warping system, consisting of cables running from the wing tips to a cradle, where the pilot lay, mounted in the center of the bottom wing. This system allowed the pilot to use his hips to move the cradle from side to side to keep the wings level, while keeping his hands free to operate other controls. On March 23, 1903 the Wrights applied for a patent on their flying machine, including its wing-warping system and rudders.

The Wrights left Dayton for Kitty Hawk in mid-September, but bad weather, broken parts, and a couple of design changes kept them from attempting a test flight until Monday, December 14. The Flyer, as the brothers were now calling their machine, was positioned on a small-wheeled dolly that rested on one end of a 60-foot-long 2-by-4-inch wooden launching track designed to keep the Flyer's sled-like runners from getting bogged in the loose sand.

When everything was ready, the brothers simply flipped a coin to see who would get the first flight. Wilbur won. There was a pause. John D. Daniels, manager of the local Kill Devil Hills Life-Saving Station, described the moment: "After a while they shook hands, and we couldn't help notice how they held on to each other's hand, sort o'like they hated to let go, like two folks parting who weren't sure they'd ever see each other again."[1]

Wilbur slipped in between the taut guy wires and propeller chains to nestle himself into the padded wing-warping cradle. Orville stood in front of the Flyer, holding an 8-volt battery to the ignition system while two assistants from the life-saving station pulled down hard on each propeller. After a couple of tries the motor started with a roar. Orville removed the battery and hurried to the right wing to stabilize the plane. Wilbur advanced the throttle, and the plane began to move. Orville had to run to keep up. After 40 feet the Flyer lifted off the track. Wilbur, not realizing how sensitive the controls were, gave the Flyer too much "up" elevator causing the plane to stall. He over-corrected and dove the plane nose down into the sand just beyond the end of the track. The plane had been airborne for only three and a half seconds, but the brothers knew that their engine, propeller, and controls all worked. It was just a matter of a gentler hand on the controls.

It took a couple of days to repair the damage suffered on the first attempt. December 17 was a cold, windy morning. The water in the wash basin was frozen when they woke up, and the wind was blowing at 21 mph as they positioned the Flyer on the launching dolly. There was a high, solid overcast without noticeable clouds, just a faraway gray that diffused the sunlight so that there were no distinctive shadows. The muffled roar of the surf offered a distant background noise as the brothers and a few helpers from the life-saving station positioned the plane. Shorebirds looking for breakfast circled the beach and battled noisily in the distance over some wave-tossed morsel.

Since Wilbur had flown on the 14th, it was Orville's turn. The motor started easily, and the nearby birds scattered in fright. It was the last time they flew as sole masters of the sky; from this moment on, they would have to share it with mankind. Wilbur took his position at the right wingtip to provide balance, and Orville opened up the throttle. The Flyer accelerated rapidly, and Wilbur had to run as hard as he could to keep up. At 10:35 a.m. the plane lifted off and climbed a few feet above the sand. The 652-pound Flyer hung in the air. Orville fought with the sensitive controls and the plane darted up, then down, then up again, staying in the air for twelve seconds and traveling 120 feet. Wilbur and the life-saving crew chased after the Flyer in celebration. It was a real flight, and they all knew that much more was to come.

The second flight of the day belonged to Wilbur. He went 175 feet. Orville then made a fifteen-second, 200-foot flight. The final flight of the day was Wilbur's. He stayed in the air for fifty-nine seconds and traveled 852 feet. The jubilant brothers telegraphed their father:

> Success four flights Thursday morning all against twenty one mile wind started from level with engine power alone average speed through air thirty one miles longest 57 [2] seconds inform Press home Christmas. Orevelle Wright [*sic*][3]

Lorin Wright, their older brother, was their press agent. He took the telegram to the *Dayton Daily Journal* and showed it to Frank E. Tunison, the Associated Press representative. Tunison took the telegram, read it with a yawn and said, "Fifty-seven seconds, hey? If it had been fifty-seven minutes then it might have been a news item," and handed the telegram back to Lorin.[4] It would be a few years before the world truly understood the significance of what had happened at Kill Devil Hills that cold morning in 1903.

# 6. A City Built of Wood
## San Francisco, 1906

Bill Boeing divided his time between the muddy, pine-scented logging camps of Washington, the rust-stained open-pit mines in Minnesota, and the quiet, sophisticated life of a young country gentleman on a Virginia horse farm with trim green pastures and a staff of uniformed servants. As the Boeing and McCrimmon Lumber Company flourished, newspapers in Washington State made frequent mention of Bill's trips to buy more land. In 1904, the *Aberdeen Herald* reported that Bill had purchased a mining claim in Minnesota for $5,000 and sold it a few months later for $75,000, a profit equivalent to about $1,680,000 today.[1] And his profits were soon to increase in a way he could never have expected.

Eight hundred miles south of Hoquiam, San Francisco, a city of clapboard buildings, was the largest city on the West Coast with a population of around 400,000 in 1906. It was built on top of the San Andreas Fault, the sliding boundary between the Pacific and North American plates. Sometime after midnight on April 18, 1906, the wind shifted and began to blow from the north across the bay towards downtown San Francisco, kicking up whitecaps in the darkness. At 5:12

a.m. there was a faint hint of light in the east; sunrise was several minutes away, and San Francisco was beginning to yawn, stretch, and wake up. Beneath the ground, whatever had been holding the fault line in place for the last three and a half decades broke, and the two plates jumped with a destructive jolt.

In some places the Pacific Plate leapt north as much as 12 feet while the North American Plate moved south 3 feet. The earthquake measured 7.9 on the Richter scale and lasted for forty-two seconds. Across San Francisco, the earth rolled and buckled like the wind-tossed waves on the bay. Shops, hotels, and houses collapsed. The total energy released was greater than the energy released from all of the cannons that had been used in all the wars since gunpowder had been invented. For a moment there was stunned silence, and then the moaning of the injured and dying began.

San Francisco was a modern city. The earth beneath it was crisscrossed by pipes carrying water and gas. Above the streets, power lines stretched from tall poles to almost every house. The earthquake toppled power poles, leaving arcing electrical lines tangled in the streets. Below ground the water mains that fed houses, factories, and fire hydrants were severed. A few great geysers shot into the air, leaving the rest of the system dry. Gas hissed from broken pipes. It didn't take long for the leaking gas to find the arcing power lines, and suddenly there were flames.

Within seventeen minutes of the quake, nearly fifty fires were reported in downtown San Francisco.[2] The gusty wind off the bay whipped the flames, driving them towards each other, and before long there was a solid wall of wind-driven fire marching south from the waterfront, consuming everything in its way. Heroic firefighters showed up with their horse-drawn pumpers, unrolling their hoses and connecting to stubby fire hydrants. But the hydrants were left dry by the shattered water mains, and the firefighters stood by helplessly, holding their flaccid hoses while fire consumed their city.

The navy sent tugboats to the wharf to pump water from the bay onto the flames, saving the piers. Meanwhile, the army sent in demolition teams to blow up buildings in an effort to make firebreaks. It didn't work, and in the end the fire was put out only when it began to rain three days later. An estimated 514 city blocks and 28,000 wooden buildings valued at $500 million were reduced to ashes. Tens of thousands of people were left homeless.

One particular problem for the survivors was money. San Francisco was a financial hub; its gold rush heritage had made it a natural place for banks to locate, but for the most part their cash and ledger books had been locked in vaults now buried under collapsed buildings. Meanwhile, any money stored by individuals at home was gone, either burned to ashes or buried under tons of rubble.

But there was one bank that survived: the tiny Bank of Italy, founded by Italian immigrant Amadeo Giannini. His office was undamaged and held over $80,000 of cash in gold and silver coins in three heavy canvas sacks. Giannini saw billowing clouds of black smoke rolling towards his bank. He commandeered a produce wagon, hid the bank's money under crates of oranges, and raced to his home in the suburbs.[3] Once there he began to formulate a plan.

With the fire still burning, Giannini contacted investors from outside the fire zone and started to assemble large amounts of cash for reconstruction loans. He knew that loans would be pointless unless there was lumber to buy, so he chartered two lumber schooners and sent them north to Washington State. It was a brilliant but risky plan. As soon as the fire was out, Giannini set up shop near the wharf, literally operating from a plank laid across two barrels. From there he loaned money to families and businesses that were desperate to rebuild, and with cash in hand, the new Bank of Italy customers would hurry to the wharf to buy lumber just unloaded from Giannini's charters. Soon the cash would be back in Giannini's coffers, ready to loan out again.

The gamble paid off: the tiny Bank of Italy grew into today's Bank of America. And Giannini's plan also helped Grays Harbor; it is probable that the first two ships he sent north docked there. The *Aberdeen Herald* reported that throughout the rest of 1906 and well into 1907, as many as twenty lumber ships a week sailed from Grays Harbor to San Francisco, carrying, in 1907, over 300 million board feet of lumber.[4] Much of that lumber came from Boeing and McCrimmon Lumber Company. Bill's fortune skyrocketed.

# 7. In the Wake of the Great White Fleet
## Seattle, 1908

In the winter of 1907, Bill was twenty-five years old. He had received a substantial inheritance from his father, and with his shrewd investments in mining and timber, he had more than doubled it. Hungry for a new adventure, he commissioned a yacht to be built in Grays Harbor. It was to be a modern 45-foot hull with a gasoline motor.

On July 22, Bill's yacht was finished. The *Aberdeen Herald* carried the story:[1]

Fine Boat Launched
W.E. Boeing's New Pleasure Boat
Launched at Hoquiam
Hoquiam, July 23 – One of the finest pleasure boats ever built on Grays Harbor was launched last night, the yards being brilliantly lighted and decorated for the occasion. The boat is a trunk cabin cruiser owned by

William E. Boeing a prominent young Eastern capitalist and chief owner of the Boeing McCrimmon Logging Co. Equipped with a 40-horse power gasoline engine, this boat is expected to outspeed anything on Grays Harbor. She was christened the "*Widgeon.*"[2] After the launching a dance and banquet was given by Boeing at the New York hotel.

As predicted, the *Widgeon*, with its white sides and a mahogany cabin, was the fastest vessel in Grays Harbor. Bill motored around the harbor and up and down its many rivers. He also made excursions down the coast to Portland and the Columbia River.

Back in Virginia, there were stress cracks starting to show in the Marie's marriage. She bought the majestic Tiverton Estate back from Bill for $226,000,[3] funneling cash from Wilhelm's estate to her son. A short while later, Bill received a copy of his mother's nine-page will. In the event of Marie's death, it gave Owsley a payment of $35,000, plus an annual income of $10,000 for life. The will gave Tiverton and its opulent grounds to Bill. It then divided the remainder of her estate equally between Bill and Caroline, with the following explanation: "Coming now to my children, I wish to say that the property I own has come to me from their father, the late Wilhelm Böing ... What I have is absolutely mine, and I remember them in my will not only because the property I own came to me from their father, but because they are my children as well, and the benefit I confer on them is a free gift."

Towards the end of the document came an ominous stipulation regarding Owsley and his apparent "threat to challenge the will: "If he ignores my wishes and appeals to the law ... I must state plainly, though I do it with pain, that he shall receive nothing under my will." Who knows what tremendous suspicion and heartbreaking fights were hidden behind this dry, simple language?

That same year, Bill's twenty-three-year-old sister Caroline married a dashing aide to President Theodore Roosevelt, Lieutenant John Hudson Poole. Bill, filling the role that would have been played by his father, walked Caroline down the aisle. In a touching nod to her own parents' Christmas Day wedding, Caroline and Lieutenant Poole were married at noon on December 24th at Tiverton. A special train carried guests from DC to Virginia for the festivities. Washington DC's *Evening Star* called the wedding "one of the most important events in the social world."[4]

\* \* \*

When Bill first came to Washington State, he saw it only as a business opportunity. "I did not enthuse very much about this country," he wrote.[5] He never bought a home in Hoquiam and continued to share rented rooms with his friend John H. Hewitt. But by 1907, the snow-capped mountains, the

endless carpet of green forests, even the gray, moody winters had worked their
way into Bill's heart, and he decided to make the Northwest his home. "I'm
fond of it now," he wrote, "and wouldn't consider leaving."[6]

During a 1907 visit to Seattle, Boeing and Hewitt were befriended by a
steamship magnate named Joshua Green. He showed the two young bachelors
around town, and persuaded them that Seattle had much more to offer than
tiny Hoquiam.[7] They decided to move.

On December 16, 1907, President Theodore Roosevelt stood at the rail
of the yacht *Mayflower*, waving and saluting as sixteen battleships steamed
away from Hampton Roads, Virginia. Roosevelt was famous for his simple
and direct foreign policy, which he summed up with the phrase "Speak softly
and carry a big stick." On this day, December 16, he was watching the "big
stick" putting out to sea for an unprecedented fourteen-month cruise around
the world. The fleet of ships, resplendent in their peacetime paint scheme
with white hulls and gold superstructures, was soon nicknamed "The Great
White Fleet." It arrived in San Francisco on May 8, 1908. After ten days of
celebrating, the fleet sailed north to Puget Sound and Seattle.

As the battleships made their way up the West Coast, Boeing and Hewitt
closed out their apartment at Hoquiam and placed their baggage on board the
*Widgeon*. Decked out in red, white and blue bunting, the *Widgeon* sailed out
with a dozen other spectator boats to meet the fleet. Flags waved and horns
sounded as the battleships steamed past Grays Harbor. When it was over, all
the spectator boats returned to port except the *Widgeon*, which fell into line
behind the fleet, headed for Seattle.

The fleet arrived in Seattle on May 23, 1908. It was a cloudless day with
tens of thousands of spectators gathered on the waterfront. Playful Dall's
porpoises surfed on the bow waves while shore birds wheeled and cawed
above. Steamers and work boats all across Puget Sound greeted the fleet with
bells and whistles.

Bill and Hewitt moored the *Widgeon* in Elliott Bay and headed into town.
It was a madhouse, but just the type of madhouse young men might enjoy.
The city saluted the fleet with dances, fireworks, and a huge parade. Seattle's
normal population of 250,000 swelled to over 400,000, with visitors coming
to see the spectacle from all over the West.[8]

The festivities lasted five days before the fleet left town on May 27. Bill
and Hewitt stayed, first taking rooms at the classy Seattle Athletic Club, and
eventually renting apartments on Seattle's First Hill.[9] According to Seattle
historian Sidney Andrews, the best way to avoid the mud of the city's many
dirt roads was to take the street railways. First Hill, served by three rail lines,
was quickly becoming Seattle's most desirable neighborhood.[10] Joshua Green,
who was about a dozen years older than Boeing and Hewitt, introduced the
young men to the upper crust of Seattle society.

One of the things that made Seattle attractive to Bill was that it combined the best of hardscrabble Hoquiam and Gilded Age high society. Seattle had a society scene with exclusive men's clubs, elegant balls, and exciting theaters, but the rough and tumble logging camps were still just a few hours away. Bill, who loved living with a foot in each world, found it irresistible to be able to put on a top hat and white gloves and go dancing one night, and then slip into his hobnailed boots and Filson jacket to head to the logging camps the next morning. He even bought himself a brand-new Packard automobile so that he could get to the camps faster.

On January 25, 1908 Daniel McCrimmon moved to California and the Boeing and McCrimmon Logging Company was dissolved. Bill re-formed it as the Greenwood Timber Company, named after the community in Virginia where Tiverton was located. On December 11, 1908, newspapers announced that Boeing had purchased a tract of 117 million board feet of timber along the west branch of the Wishkah River, near Hoquiam, for $450,000. The *Morning Oregonian* in Portland called it "one of the biggest timber deals ever."[11] The *Oregonian* calculated that, even when using a low stumpage estimate, the total value of the tract was over $1.7 million, netting Bill $1.25 million in profit.[12]

Bill Boeing was now one of the wealthiest men in Seattle. His name had become a familiar sight on the society pages of local newspapers. He donated to the Seattle Philharmonic Society and the campaign to build an art museum, he entered the *Widgeon* in cruiser races, and he attended many weddings, dances, and galas.

As the wealthy sons of powerful East Coast families moved west to make their own fortunes in places like Seattle and San Francisco, they ran into a problem that their expensive educations had not prepared them for. These young lions of industry had been raised with cooks, maids, and butlers. Then they went to boarding schools and eventually headed to colleges where fraternities and eating clubs provided the basic necessities. When they arrived in boomtowns like Seattle they discovered that, despite being able to quote Homer in the original Greek and perform quadratic equations in their heads, they couldn't cook for themselves.

To fill this gap, they formed men's social clubs, where a gentleman could enjoy stimulating companionship with his peers and be served a well-cooked meal in sophisticated surroundings. By 1908 there were seven such clubs in Seattle, each one serving a slightly different clientele.[13] The University Club, located just a few blocks from Bill's rented rooms on Madison Street, was aimed at East Coast university men: of the club's twenty-three founding members, nine had attended Yale and three came from Harvard.[14] In a simple decision that would have far-reaching effects on Seattle's economy for the next 100 years, Bill applied for membership to the University Club and was quickly

accepted. One of the University Club members whom Bill became friends with
was a hard-drinking young Harvard graduate named Nathaniel Paschall. The
two men would end up playing significant roles in each other's lives.

# 8. Impostor!
# Battle Creek, 1908

James Croft, a successful farmer who lived near Battle Creek, Michigan, had
come to town for the big Decoration Day parade on May 30, 1908, honoring
Battle Creek's Civil War veterans.[1] At some time during the parade, Croft
found himself standing next to a tall, thin man who introduced himself as
William Boeing. The story of Bill's 1904 purchase of a $5,000 mining claim
that later sold for $75,000 had been big news and gained him a reputation
as a business wizard; Croft was thrilled to be standing next to such a well-
known and wealthy businessman.

After the parade, the man claiming to be Boeing asked Croft to join him for a
drink, and over a couple of mugs of cold beer he told him about his vast timber
holdings in Washington State.[2] Croft asked about the famous mining deal, and
the tall man said it was easy, if you knew the right people. Croft wondered if he
could be introduced to the "right people." Asked if he had enough money to take
advantage of the introduction, Croft answered that he had $2,500 back at his
farm. The man claiming to be Boeing smiled, leaned forward, and whispered that
he was about to make an investment in timberland which would yield amazing
profits, but he hadn't brought enough cash with him from Seattle.[3] If Croft would
be willing to add his $2,500 to the investment, he said, he would become rich.

Croft hurried to his farm, dug up his cash, and rushed back to the saloon.
He sat down, out of breath, and stealthily removed the bundle of cash from
under his coat and slid it across the table.

The man thanked Croft and said that he'd like to count the money. It would
be risky to handle so much cash in public, so he was just going to duck into
the washroom where he could count it in private. Croft, eager to please his
wealthy new friend, nodded in agreement.

Croft ordered a drink and waited. How long would it take to count $2,500?
It seemed to be taking a long time; maybe Boeing was counting twice, just to
be careful. After fifteen minutes, he finished his drink and headed to the men's
room. It was empty. Croft's heart sank as he realized he had been swindled.
He rushed out looking for Boeing.

At the same time that this imposter was defrauding Croft of his lifesavings, the real Bill Boeing was facing challenges of his own. While on a business trip to Minnesota, he had received word of a court ruling in Chehalis County that outlawed the use of splash dams on the Wishkah River. The ruling left Bill with no way of getting several million board feet of timber out of the hills and down to the mills.

Splash dams provided a fast and inexpensive means of moving logs. A temporary dam was built across a creek to create a huge backlog of water, and cut logs were then laid in the dry creek bed. The dam was then opened, often with dynamite, sending a flash flood downstream to carry the logs to the main river. The problem was that when the surge of water reached the main river, it caused the river to flood, destroying the crops of the farmers trying to make a living along the banks. The farmers along the Wishkah had sued and won an injunction against the loggers.

Bill caught the next train to Seattle, where he could transfer to Aberdeen and meet with some other loggers to work on a solution. For over 350 miles across the Midwest, the train was battered by wind and rain. Bill tried to read Upton Sinclair's *The Jungle*, but the depressing topic, along with the depressing weather, made it difficult to pay attention. Eventually he put the book down, lit a cigarette, and tried to come up with an answer for the Wishkah River farmers.

Meanwhile, his business trip to Minneapolis had been reported in the papers. According to a June 11 story in *The Seattle Star*, "Croft went to Minneapolis. There he struck the scent. A man named Boeing had taken the train west."[4] Croft boarded a Seattle-bound train that was only a day behind Boeing's and began a chase across the country. By the time he got to Seattle, the trail was cold, but Croft's discreet questioning of bellhops and headwaiters informed him that Boeing had been seen eating breakfast at a downtown hotel. As Croft reached the hotel he saw a tall, thin young man headed south along Second Avenue towards King Street Station. With a knot in his stomach, Croft watched Boeing buy a ticket to Aberdeen. He rushed to buy his own, leaving the counter just as the train pulled away. He ran as hard as he could but he missed catching it by 50 feet.[5]

Boeing arrived in Aberdeen, checked into his hotel, and began setting up his appointments for the following morning. In his room he caught sight of himself in a mirror. He thought that several days of train travel had left him looking a little shaggy and he could use a shave and a haircut. He left the hotel and walked up the street to a barber shop, where he settled into the soft padded barber's chair and relaxed.

Croft, meanwhile, had taken the next train to Aberdeen, arriving just after sunset. Without any clear leads he began walking the streets, hoping for a clue. He passed the barber shop. The darkness of the evening allowed him to stand near the window and get a good view of the young man reclined in a red leather barber's chair. As the barber began to strop the straight razor against a leather strap, Croft went in search of a policeman. He found one and led him back to the shop. The shave was finished and the young man's face was wrapped in a warm towel. Croft and the officer waited outside. The towel was unwrapped, the young man stood up, tipped the barber, put on his hat and walked out the door. That moment Croft said to the policeman, "Arrest this man!" Bill was stunned and asked why. "Impersonating William Boeing!" Croft answered.

Croft's dramatic declaration was met with laughter from the policeman, the barber, and Bill Boeing himself.[6] It only took a few moments for Boeing to explain that yes, he was the real Bill Boeing and yes, he had been in Minneapolis, but no, he had not been to Battle Creek, he had never seen Croft before, and he certainly hadn't taken any money from him. Croft reluctantly admitted that the real Bill Boeing did not look much like the bunko artist who had stolen his money. He apologized and took the next train home, vowing from then on to leave police work to the police department.[7]

For years, the "imposter story" was an interesting anecdote to tell at parties, but it was also the first time that being a public figure had caused Bill problems. It would not be the last.

Bill arranged a settlement of the Wishkah River conflict by taking over management of the Wishkah River Boom Company.[8] His intention was to make "extensive improvements to the Wishkah River" and do everything that could be done "to protect the waterway for the benefit of the farmers." The Wishkah River Boom Company maintained tugboats and log booms on the river, handling the complicated job of receiving and sorting the logs that were swept into the Wishkah from the splash dams of several different logging operations.

# 9. RANCHO DOMINGUEZ LOS ANGELES, 1910

When gold was discovered in Canada's Yukon Territory in 1896, the fastest way to get there from the U.S. was via ship from Seattle. Overnight, Seattle became a boom town as tens of thousands of prospectors converged on the city. The population swelled from 40,000 to 240,000,[1] and as each prospector needed hundreds of dollars of supplies, the city's economy surged.[2]

In 1909, to commemorate the impact on Seattle made by the gold rush, the city celebrated with a public fair known as the Alaska-Yukon-Pacific Exposition. Much of the University of Washington campus, located in northeast Seattle, was still undeveloped land. The university agreed to let it be used for the AYP fairgrounds provided that the roads and exhibition halls built for the fair could afterwards be used by the university.

The AYP opened on June 1, 1909. On the third day of the festival, thirty-three-year-old James "Bud" Mars flew three exhibitions over the fairgrounds in his motorized dirigible.[3] Seventy thousand fairgoers, who had each paid 25 cents admission, watched in wonder while Mars steered his enormous white machine slowly above the fair. It was the first time that Seattleites had seen a powered airship. At the University Club, Bill and his friends talked excitedly about Mars's flights. Bill's curiosity about flying, which had been smoldering since his balloon flight in Geneva in 1896, began to flame bright.

When the Aero Club of California announced in mid-September 1909 that the nation's first International Aviation Meet would be held in Los Angeles from January 10 to 20, 1910, Bill made plans to attend. He took the train south to Pasadena, checking into the luxurious Castle Green Hotel on January 5.[4] There he met his brother in-law, Captain J. Hudson Poole,[5] and Poole's father, Colonel DeWitt Clinton Poole, a veteran of the Civil War. The Pooles, like many other affluent Easterners, were wintering in warm, palm-shrouded Southern California.

Early on the morning of Monday, January 10, Bill Boeing and the Pooles climbed into Bill's Packard automobile, which had arrived by train from Seattle.[6] It had rained over the weekend and there were puddles of water along the road. As Bill drove the 28 miles south to the aviation meet at Rancho Dominguez, the sun came out, and by the time he parked in a field behind the newly erected bleachers, there was the promise of a clear, cloudless day.

When Boeing and the Pooles arrived, there were already 20,000 spectators in the stands and at least a thousand more milling around the colorful flying machines scattered on the grass in front of the bleachers. With wings reflecting the morning sun, the parked planes looked like gigantic insects perched on fragile legs.

The crowd was watching two graceful dirigibles quietly circle the field when a sudden roar of a powerful engine cut through the morning serenity. French aviator Louis Paulhan and his Farman biplane burst out of a "gully hidden from view of the grandstands, circled the course three times, went out across country [and] came back over the grandstands."[7] According to a *Tulare Advance Register* article entitled "Paulhan Is The Star Aviator,"

... [Paulhan] gave a remarkable exhibition of control of his machine, making sharp turns as gracefully as the sudden wearing of a gull, now dipping almost to the ground to scatter frightened officials ... skimming the grandstand a few feet above the spectators, ascending, descending, and finally approaching from the rear, the tent that houses his aero-plane, just clearing the top, and alighting within a hundred feet of its entrance.

When he had finished ... the Frenchman was given a demonstration such as is seldom witnessed at a public gathering in this country. Men shouted themselves hoarse, while women applauded and waved handkerechiefs.[8]

A crowd of men rushed toward Paulhan to congratulate him and ask questions about his machine. Boeing was amazed by his first sight of a real airplane. It appealed to his sense of adventure and he became obsessed with getting a ride. In his book *Vision*, former Boeing director of PR and marketing Harold Mansfield described the scene:

Boeing was out front. "Monsieur Paulhan, my name is Boeing, I like your machine. I like the way you fly it."

"Merci, Monsieur Boeing." The Frenchman clicked his heels and did a quick bow. Boeing asked more about the Farman. Would it be possible for him to take a ride in it?

"Oui Monsieur," said Paulhan, but added that it couldn't be done until tomorrow, after the endurance competition.[9]

Paulhan flew several more exhibitions, including one flight in which he climbed to over 4,000 feet. The only other plane to make it into the air that first day was flown by Glenn Curtiss, who performed well but never rose above 500 feet.

On the way back to the hotel, Colonel Poole, whose trim white beard and neatly combed silver hair left no doubt that he was a retired Civil War colonel, turned to Boeing and said, "Billy, I've been thinking about those two contraptions, especially that one the Frenchman is flying. If we had only had one of those blasted things in 1861 after we crossed the Potomac into Virginia, old Joe Johnston would never have given us the slip to get into the Battle of Bull Run the way he did."

"You're right, Colonel," Boeing replied, "they'll be very useful some day in war."[10]

Boeing came back to Rancho Dominguez again the next day and waited patiently while Paulhan won the endurance competition, flying forty-seven laps around the 1.6-mile course without stopping. (Curtiss had only been able to manage ten laps.) Again Boeing approached the French aviator and asked for a ride. Paulhan responded that yes, he could get a ride, but there were others ahead of him. Boeing waited patiently while a number of luminaries, including newspaper magnate William Randolph Hearst, got rides.[11]

After a third day missing out, Boeing followed Paulhan to the elegant Alexandria Hotel and tried to get a word with him. Paulhan was twenty-six years old, short, thin, and handsome, with a stylish sense of fashion. He and his pretty young wife were being interviewed by a reporter in the hotel's palm-lined dining room.

Paulhan was in a cheerful mood. So far his plane had dominated the event, setting several world records and winning him $19,000 in prize money. His enthusiastic answers to the reporter's questions were easy to hear over the clink of silver on china and muted conversations in the quiet dining room:

"What a beautiful country! It is stupefying! Such climate, and the flowers and the fruit! We had no idea in France that California was so beautiful, do you see?" Paulhan continued with a thick French accent, "Ah, what will aviation do for man? It will enable us to know the world! Aviation will enable us to fly here, there, everywhere without our caring the least little bit how the reefs of the ocean are charted and which way the currents of the sea are drifting."[12]

The reporter asked, "How long do you think it will be before aviation becomes a practical factor in the affairs of the world?" Without pausing, Paulhan answered, "Five or six years. Why, just look at the progress of a year. Fancy what the future holds for us if you can."

Boeing waited for the interview to end and then approached the table. Using the French he had learned at the Sillig school many years earlier, he asked politely if there would be an opportunity to go for a ride in the big Farman biplane. Paulhan was all smiles and assurances and agreed to a ride the next day.

Boeing was thrilled. He left the hotel with an excited spring to his step and spent a sleepless night like a child waiting for Christmas morning. When he arrived at Rancho Dominguez the next day, he was shocked to see that sometime during the night, Paulhan had packed up his plane, folded his tent, loaded everything onto a railcar, and snuck out of town.

What Boeing did not know, and would not know for years to come, was that Orville and Wilbur Wright had come to the Los Angeles aviation meet too. They had not brought their famous Wright Flyer, but they had brought lawyers who served papers on anyone that the Wrights felt were infringing on their patent for a flying machine. Their main targets at the Los Angeles meet were Glenn Curtiss and Louis Paulhan. Hoping to avoid a lawsuit, Paulhan had left in the middle of the night. It didn't work. The Wrights sued and won, and eventually Paulhan was forced to pay the Wrights a significant portion of the $19,000 prize money that he had received. Glenn Curtiss held out and continued to fight the patent, claiming that the hinged flaps (which he called ailerons) on the trailing edges of his plane's wings were different from the Wrights' wing-warping contraption. The "patent wars," as the dispute would come to be known, cast a pall over American aviation for seven more years and would literally take an act of Congress to resolve.

Boeing returned to Seattle like a young man in love, with visions of airplanes crowding his thoughts.

# 10. THE OXBOW PLANT
## SEATTLE, 1910

In early 1910, Bill made two significant purchases that would have dramatic and unforeseen consequences. First he ordered a new 94-foot gasoline-powered yacht worth $100,000 from E. W. Heath Shipyards on the Duwamish River, south of Seattle. The luxurious new vessel, with dark teak decks and a gleaming white hull, was twice the size of the *Widgeon* and would eventually be known as the *Taconite*. Bill was expecting the boat to be finished early in the fall of 1910.

Ed Heath, a respected shipbuilder from Benton Harbor, Michigan, had been born into the business. His father founded the company on Lake Michigan in the mid-1840s and Ed took it over when his father died in 1898. He relocated the business to Tacoma, Washington, possibly to get in on the boom building "Klondike steamers" for the Yukon Gold Rush. In September 1909, Heath moved again, shifting the company to land he had purchased on the "Oxbow" of the Duwamish River in Seattle. There, on the banks of the Duwamish, he built a large barn-like structure with tall white block letters spelling out "E. W. Heath." It was an exact replica of the building his father had built in Benton Harbor in the 1840s.

In March 1910 Heath ran into financial problems. In an effort to keep him in business and ensure that the *Taconite* would be completed, Bill made his second significant purchase of the year: he bought the E. W. Heath Shipyards on March 23, 1910.[1]

* * *

On December 10, 1910, Bill received the news that his mother was dead. To compound his pain, he was soon swept up in two vicious lawsuits with his stepfather.

Shortly before her death, Marie (possibly while battling tuberculosis) had sent Bill $15,000 and asked him to make arrangements to have a family mausoleum built in the Edgewood Cemetery in Detroit for Wilhelm, Margaret, and herself. The plans were drawn up by a New York architect and Marie approved them, but construction hadn't started.

After Marie had passed away, but before Bill could arrive from Seattle, Owsley had Marie's body moved to the receiving vault at the Congressional Cemetery in Washington DC.[2] Owsley wanted Marie buried in his family's plot in Chicago and he refused to release the body to Bill and Caroline, saying that a husband had the right to decide where his wife was to be buried. Bill and Caroline were forced to go to court to fight for their mother's body, with the details playing out in the pages of the Washington DC papers. It took six months, but eventually they prevailed and were able to lay their mother to rest in Detroit alongside their father and sister.[3]

In the meantime, Owsley came up with another infuriating lawsuit. Much of the land that Marie had inherited when Wilhelm died was in Minnesota, which still maintained an archaic law that allowed a husband to ignore his wife's will if he was unhappy with its terms. Owsley used the Minnesota law to challenge the clauses in Marie's will that gave property to Bill and Caroline. Already disgusted with their stepfather after the fight over Marie's body, Bill and Caroline took him back to court for a long, bruising legal battle that would take three more years to settle.

After Marie's death, there followed a fairly long and uncharacteristic period of inaction for Bill Boeing. Despite the beauty of the Pacific Northwest, its dark winters and rain-swept skies are known to trigger depression. He was grieving for his mother and dealing with the unpleasantness of long, ugly lawsuits with his stepfather. His mother had experienced her own battles with melancholy after the deaths of Wilhelm and Margaret, and Bill may also have inherited a susceptibility to depression.

A few years later, when Bill decided to sell his mother's massive Tiverton Estate. Letters between him and his agent provide insight into his frame of mind:

> I have no feelings or associations of Tiverton but one of horror and of anguish, and every visit I ever made to Greenwood . . . has been one of pain and depression in the thought that my mother was suffering and enduring the most hopeless and most impossible life that was ever inflicted on anyone. And I cannot help but feel that if it had not been for those years, she would have been alive and happy and with her children this day.[4]

On August 20, 1912, Bill, with a crew of nine and several friends, left Seattle on the *Taconite* for a six-week cruise to Alaska.[5] It was a warm, clear day with light winds and temperatures in the mid-70s when the *Taconite* motored past the West Point lighthouse, heading for Canada. North of Vancouver they ran into a fierce summer storm with driving rain and angry waves that forced them to take shelter at Port Etches, in southern Alaska. When the storm passed they resumed their cruise, arriving at tiny, isolated Lefthand Bay in the Aleutian Islands in mid-September.

The *Taconite* refueled from barrels of gasoline that Bill had shipped ahead. He then began to work his way south, fishing, hunting, and sightseeing along the wild Alaskan Coast. The stunning beauty of the mist-shrouded fjords, the soaring eagles, and the native villages with their carved totem poles were a tonic for Bill's injured heart. He found a peace in Alaska that he couldn't find anywhere else, certainly not in the boardrooms of Seattle or the drawing rooms of Virginia. If he had been fighting depression, he wouldn't have been the first to discover that blue water, the whir of a fishing reel and a long battle with a 50-pound Chinook salmon worked magic on his mood and healed the soul-bruising scars that life had inflicted. Bill would be drawn back to Alaska frequently for the rest of his life.

On November 26, 1913, the lawsuit over Marie's will was finally settled. It must have been a day of mixed emotions. The court ruled that Owsley was entitled to all of the property in Minnesota, valued at approximately $2 million, but Bill and Caroline would share the property in Washington and Virginia. The best part of the settlement was that the troubling and disruptive Owsley was out of their lives forever. On the same day as the Boeing settlement, Owsley married his third wife, twenty-three-year-old Baroness Mariska von Eltz of Austria in a small service in New York City.[6]

In 1914 Bill moved into a new 19,000-square-foot Mediterranean Revival home built on a 16-acre estate in the exclusive Highlands community, north of Seattle. He had started planning the new home when his mother was still alive in the hope that she would be able to separate from Owsley and join him in Seattle.[7] The grounds were laid out by the Olmsted Brothers, who had designed the AYP campus. In a nod to the industry that had given him his tremendous fortune, Bill named the mansion "Aldarra." According to *The Seattle Daily Times*, "Aldarra takes its name from a tiny country between France and Spain now called Andorra" and is an Arabic word meaning "a place thick with trees."[8]

Bill was thirty-two years old and, from the outside at least, the only thing missing from his life was romance. He had a plan to change that. Cordelia Lee was a young violin prodigy. Born in South Dakota in 1888, she was sent by her parents to St. Petersburg, Russia, when she was twelve to study under violin master Leopold Auer. By 1913 she had matured into a tall and strikingly attractive twenty-five year old, with auburn hair, brown eyes, and an effervescent personality. She was hailed in Europe as "the most beautiful American girl on the European concert stage."[9]

Bill loved classic music and was a supporter of the Seattle Philharmonic Society. In 1913 he contributed money to help bring Cordelia to Seattle to play with the orchestra at the Majestic Theater. She performed Schubert's unfinished symphony and "played so beautifully and with such authority as to … awaken an outburst of applause which swept over the house."[10] Her performance was so successful that she was asked back for a second concert on February 18, 1914. Two days later Bill invited Cordelia to an elegant lunch cruise onboard the *Taconite*.

Bill must have imagined a crisp, clear winter morning with blue skies and breathtaking views of the Olympic Mountains. He may have even hoped to point out the majestic bald eagles and playful Dall's porpoises that typically make a Hood Canal cruise so magical.

Eager to make a good impression, Bill probably picked Cordelia up from the Sorrento Hotel in his brand-new chauffeur-driven Rolls Royce for the short drive to Elliott Bay, where the *Taconite* was waiting.[11] Unfortunately the day turned out to be a cold and rainy, and Bill and Cordelia were kept inside, looking through rain-streaked windows as the yacht cruised through mile after mile of fog and flat gray water. Bill wasn't much of a conversationalist and was probably counting on the spectacular scenery to give them something to talk about during lunch. Anyone that has ever struggled through an awkward first date can imagine the uncomfortable silences. Cordelia came back to Seattle frequently for the next forty years, yet as there is no record of her ever meeting Bill Boeing again, it is safe to guess that the date was a failure.

Bill still spent much of his free time at the University Club on First Hill. He particularly enjoyed playing bridge and savoring a cigar while sipping whiskey with his friends in the mahogany-paneled cardroom. The club offered free temporary memberships to military officers who were deployed in Seattle, and one of the officers who frequented the club was Lieutenant Conrad Westervelt of the U.S. Navy.

Westervelt was born in Corpus Christi, Texas, in 1879, and after graduating from the Naval Academy, where his pugnacious personality had earned him the nickname "Scrappy," and spending three years at sea, he was sent to the Massachusetts Institute of Technology to study naval architecture.[12] He graduated from MIT in 1909 as an assistant naval constructor and was dispatched to oversee submarine construction at the Puget Sound Naval Shipyards in Bremerton and the Moran Brothers Shipyard in Seattle.[13]

Westervelt was "a short plump man with a stern demeanor." He had a round face and a "slightly aggressive chin and protruding lower lip that gave him a rather foreboding aspect." He was the type of person that "people fear to say 'Good morning' [to] lest they be expected to prove it."[14]

Bill Boeing and Conrad Westervelt made an odd pair. Boeing was tall, thin, and thoughtful, while Westervelt was short, heavy, and confrontational. They met one evening over a game of bridge at the club, and when Bill learned that Westervelt had studied naval architecture he said, "I expect you could give me some pointers. I have a boat … that isn't doing so well right now."[15]

The two became fast friends and spent many an afternoon cruising on Puget Sound, enjoying the type of wide-ranging conversations that cement friendships. Both were bachelors and Republicans. They talked about politics, engineering and women. They also shared a fascination with aviation. Nine months after Boeing had traveled to the Los Angeles aviation meet, the navy had sent Westervelt as an official observer to an International Aviation Meet at Belmont Park on Long Island, New York. At Belmont, Westervelt saw many of the same pilots and machines that Boeing had seen at Rancho Dominguez, and the two friends enjoyed discussing the merits of each. As their friendship developed, they gave each other nicknames. Westervelt became "Westy" and Boeing became "WEB," for William Edward Boeing.

It's likely that Boeing and Westervelt discussed the growing tensions in Europe. On June 28, 1914, the heir to the throne of the Austro-Hungarian Empire, Archduke Ferdinand, and his wife, Sophia, were assassinated by a Serbian nationalist. The Austro-Hungarian Empire threatened war with Serbia. A complex web of mutual defense treaties guaranteed that unless Austria showed some restraint, a small regional conflict would escalate into a worldwide war. As June ended and the people of the United States prepared for their 4th of July celebrations, Europe teetered on the precipice of war.

# PART II

# Aeroplanes Are Your
# Best Defense
# 1914-1918

# 11. First Flight
## Lake Union, 1914

Terah Maroney, "part innovator, part showman, part huckster,"[1] was a thirty-four-year-old carpenter from Helena, Montana, and a pioneer in what would soon become known as "barnstorming." He had built a few homemade biplanes, but it was not until he had arranged to make monthly payments on a $4,500 used Glenn Curtiss pusher (a plane that has its propeller behind the wing) that he set out across the American West, landing in any open field he could find and sleeping under the wing of his plane. He made his living selling rides and putting on flying exhibitions.

Maroney had been hired by promoters in Everett to perform at their 1914 Kla-How-Yah festival.[2] He was scheduled to do two shows on Friday, July 3rd, and a final one at noon on Saturday the 4th.[3] The shows were a big success. Thousands of spectators cheered as he flew over the Everett waterfront, climbing to 2,000 feet, then diving down and pulling up at the last second just a few feet above the waves, and speeding past the crowd at almost 100 mph.

Tradition has it that when Maroney finished his show in Everett, he flew to Seattle's Lake Union to take part in an exhibition along with a biplane flown by California aviator Silas Christofferson. Afterwards, so the story goes, he went to Lake Washington to give a ride to Bill Boeing.

The date of Boeing's first flight has become one of the most hotly debated points among Boeing aficionados. There are a few problems with the idea that it took place on July 4, 1914, but the main issue is that *The Seattle Post-Intelligencer* firmly places the exhibition with Christofferson on July 18, 1914.[4] Additionally, the floats that allowed Maroney's plane to take off and land on water were not installed on his plane until July 17, so Boeing's ride could not have taken place until the 18th. Additional proof that the ride happened on that date comes from Maroney himself, who told the *P-I* that when the exhibition on Lake Union was over, he was going "over on Lake

Washington ... [to] take up some passengers." There are even some historians who place the date of this first flight as late as July 1915, but whatever the date, Maroney was the pilot who first took Bill Boeing up in a plane.

When Boeing heard about Maroney's plan to give rides he told Westervelt, "Let's see if we can get a flight."[5] They met at the University Club and Bill drove them to Lake Washington. It was a perfect summer's day with temperatures approaching 80 degrees, blue skies, and no wind. When they arrived at the lake the plane was nosed up to a plank ramp, with its engine idling loudly. Westervelt had to shout over the noise "Would you like to go first?"

Bill nodded "Yes!"[6]

The biplane had muslin-covered wings and a single laminated wooden pontoon. The engine was slung between the wings with a pusher propeller. Maroney was already sitting in the lightweight wicker seat with his feet on the control pedals. He was short and slight, with a bushy mustache and a broad, ever-present smile.

Bill climbed up on the leading edge of the wing and put on a pair of goggles that Maroney handed him; then he wrapped his left arm around one of the "N" struts that held up the top wing and braced his right arm against the leading edge of the bottom wing while his feet dangled in space.

A mechanic in stained coveralls walked the plane around to point it toward the lake. Maroney advanced the throttle and they roared away. On the dock, Westervelt had to duck and hold onto his hat as the prop kicked up spray. Boeing Company PR man Harold Mansfield tells the story:

> Boeing tightened his grip. The water began to get less bumpy. He felt a shake and a boost; there was a surge of power against the small of his back. The din of the motor filled his ears as the water dropped away.[7]

This was the first time Bill had been in the air since his balloon ride in Geneva. The magic was still there; it was like reuniting with an old friend he hadn't seen in almost twenty years. His heart soared as they rose from the water. He wanted to cheer. He probably did, but his voice was lost against the roar of the motor. This was exhilarating and exciting, so much better than the balloon. Bill had often heard pilots talk about the "religion of flying." He had thought that was just hyperbole, but now he understood what they meant.

> In another minute the whole landscape was tilting up beside him and he realized they were banking and turning away from the lake. Boeing looked down on Westervelt and the tiny group on the shore. They seemed like something detached, a detail in a picture. Maroney was winging straight over trees and housetops, still climbing, attaining an altitude of perhaps a thousand feet. Boeing settled more comfortably in his seat. He felt a certain

mastery he had been seeking. It all seemed right, the hourglass shape of Seattle below, with Puget Sound and the Olympics in the distance, unrolling before him. Man was meant to fly."[8]

Next it was Westervelt's turn to perch on the leading edge of Maroney's fragile wing and be carried into the warm July sky. Maroney gave another perfect ride, just risky enough to be exciting but not so wild as to seem dangerous. Back at the dock, Westervelt was every bit as enthusiastic about the experience as Boeing had been.

Boeing invited Maroney and Westervelt to come back to the University Club for dinner so they could continue talking about flying. As they drove up East Madison Street toward the club, a motorcyclist sped past. Maroney, without any sense of irony, shook his head at the motorcyclist and said, "That's a dangerous occupation."[9]

Boeing and Westervelt became obsessed with "aero planes" and could think of little else. Boeing still had to pay attention to his timber and mining business while Westervelt began to research all aspects of flying. He returned to Maroney's camp on Lake Washington for more flights and took along a tape measure so he could copy the Curtiss's dimensions into a notebook. He sent letters to MIT's aeronautics instructor, Jerome Hunsaker, asking for information on the theory of stability and control. (Hunsaker had been a student at MIT three years behind Westervelt and studied aerodynamics. He built the first wind tunnel for the school and by 1914 he had become an instructor.) Before long Boeing made Westervelt an intriguing offer: if he designed a couple of planes, Boeing would pay to get them built.

Meanwhile, the situation in Europe was spiraling out of control. Austria declared war on Serbia, and the carefully arranged dominos began to topple. Russia mobilized its armies to defend Serbia. Germany, fearing an attack from Russia and its ally France, declared war on both. Not wanting to fight a war on two fronts, Germany decided to attack France first, hoping to defeat the French before Russia could get ready to fight. German strategists determined that the quickest way to capture Paris was though France's unprotected border with Belgium. The German generals expected Belgium to give its armies free passage, but Belgium fought back. This infuriated the Germans, who decided to "punish Belgium" and began a wholesale slaughter of civilians. Britain had been trying to stay out of the war but was outraged by the attack on Belgium and declared war against Germany on August 4.

Newspapers in Seattle covered the war with banner headlines. Boeing and Westervelt's attention surely must have been grabbed by an article on the front page of *The Seattle Star* on July 30 under the headline "France and Germany Will Fight It Out in Clouds If War Comes."[10] The story detailed the air forces of the two major combatants and proclaimed that "France's air fleet, if called on for action, will cross the frontier about 500 machines strong, most of them carrying each a pilot and fighting man and a few crews of three each."[11] At the same time, the U.S. Army only had fifty-six planes.[12]

President Woodrow Wilson declared that the U.S. was going to remain neutral in the "Great War," but Boeing and Westervelt felt that the inferior U.S. position in air power was something that needed to be addressed. They both became avid supporters of the "preparedness" movement dedicated to expanding the U.S. military capabilities.

# 12. Preparedness
# Seattle, 1914-1915

For most Seattleites, the war in Europe was a faraway tragedy that occupied their attention for only as long as it took to read the morning headlines while eating breakfast. For Bill Boeing, because of his family ties and because he had been schooled in Europe and traveled extensively in Germany, it was much more personal.[1]

Boeing was a patriotic American, but he had been raised in a strict German household and was proud of his heritage. He was shocked by the brutal way that Germany had attacked innocent Belgium, and like most Americans, he suspected that eventually the U.S. would enter the war fighting against his father's homeland. It was a troubling thought.

Boeing and Westervelt visited a nineteen-year-old exhibition pilot and aviation prodigy named Herb Munter. Munter's hangar was a 50-foot-long shiplap building on Harbor Island, where the Duwamish River empties into Puget Sound, not far from Heath Shipyard. Boeing and Westervelt picked their way around puddles of rainwater to reach the cramped hangar. As they entered, they could smell wood shavings and paint. Munter was busy working on his newest creation.

Munter had close-cropped red hair and a sprinkling of freckles that made him look even younger than he was. His day job was working at Seattle Construction and Dry Dock as an apprentice machinist, but on weekends he was one of Seattle's best-known pilots. Looking up from his work, Munter recognized Westervelt from seeing him at the dry dock and waved hello. Harold Mansfield picks up the story:

"What type of machine are you building?" Boeing asked.
"It's a Munter."

Boeing looked up uncertainly and then fixed his eyes on a wing rib. "You design this yourself?"

Munter's pride was evident. He brushed back a shock of red hair. "This is my fourth."

"Where are the others?"

"Washed out." [Crashed.]

"You built them all here?"

"No, the first two I built at home in the kitchen. Mother helped me. On those we went by a picture of the Curtiss in *Aerial Age*, but the last two have been my own."

"Did you study engineering?" Boeing asked.

"No, I went to high school nights."[2]

Bill's lumber and mining businesses were taking up the majority of his time, so in early 1915 he hired his twenty-seven-year-old cousin, Edgar Gott, as his business manager.[3] Gott, tall, thin, with bulging eyes and thick glasses, had moved from Detroit to Seattle in 1909. He had a talent for management and was to handle some of the day-to-day decision-making for Bill, so that Bill could devote more of his time to his new hobby of aviation. About the same time, Westervelt asked James Foley, the chief draftsman at Seattle Construction and Dry Dock, to help him draw up full-size plans of the new planes they were now calling "B&Ws," short for "Boeing and Westervelt."

Working together after hours, Foley and Westervelt laid out the wings for the first B&W in Westervelt's downtown Seattle office overlooking Elliott Bay. Before long, Bill had offered Foley a full-time job.

As the war in Europe entered its second year, the massive opposing armies had burrowed themselves into the earth, hoping to find protection from the cruel new weapons of the industrial age. Generals on both sides had been schooled in the antiquated tactics of the Napoleonic era. When they attempted old-fashioned massed charges, their young soldiers were killed in the thousands by machine guns and poisonous gas. Germany was attempting to break the stalemate using its submarines to blockade Great Britain. In February 1915, the German government announced an "exclusionary zone" around Britain, declaring that any Allied ships in this area were subject to attack.

Americans of German heritage continued to struggle with their feelings about the war. American by birth, they owed allegiance to the U.S., but they were proud too of their German roots. As the war went on, the gravitational force of the conflict was pulling the U.S. closer and closer to war with Germany. We don't know exactly when Germany lost Bill Boeing's support, but for the vast majority of Americans it happened on May 7, 1915.

May 1, 1915 was a gray, cloudy day. The *Lusitania* nosed away from Pier 54 in New York, bound for Liverpool. She made a quick crossing and by May

7 was approaching Ireland. At 2:10 p.m. the ship was about 13 miles from the Old Head of Kinsale, where ships bound for Liverpool turn north into the Irish Sea to run between Ireland and Wales.

German U-boats had been adhering to a 1909 international agreement called "The London Declaration Respecting the Laws of Naval War." It required U-boat commanders to surface in front of any unarmed civilian vessel they wished to attack, to allow its passengers to board lifeboats before the U-boat launched its torpedoes. Two days earlier, on May 5, a German U-boat commanded by Kapitänleutnant Walther Schwieger stopped the schooner *Earl of Lathon* and allowed her crew to take to their lifeboats before sinking her. The same Kaptiänleutenant Schwieger spotted the *Lusitania* on May 7; this time he was not feeling so charitable. He shot one torpedo from a range of about 770 yards. Schwieger watched its devastating impact from 36 feet under the waves, through the U-boat's periscope. His factual, almost casual description of the event disguises the brutal loss of civilian life caused by his actions.

Torpedo hits starboard side right behind the bridge. An unusually heavy detonation takes place with a very strong explosive cloud. The explosion of the torpedo must have been followed by a second one (boiler or coal or powder?) ... The ship stops immediately and heels over to starboard very quickly, immersing simultaneously at the bow ... the name *Lusitania* becomes visible in golden letters.[4]

The *Lusitania* sank in eighteen minutes. (By comparison the *Titanic* took two hours and forty minutes to sink.) There wasn't time to launch many of the lifeboats. Banner headlines in *The Seattle Star* on May 8 announced, "1346 Perish on Liner; U.S. Asks Germany To Explain." By May 10 the headlines asked, "What Are We Going To Do About It?"

For a man like Boeing, who had crossed the Atlantic at least four times on ships like the *Lusitania*, it would have been easy to imagine the horror the passengers felt when the torpedo struck and they found themselves tumbling into the cold waters of the Atlantic, screaming for help that would never come.

The German government issued a statement saying that a state of war existed between Germany and England, and all merchant vessels entering the war zone were lawful targets. Germany's dry pronouncement only served to make the Germans look callous. Alongside photographs of fishing boats stacked with corpses of women and children, legal technicalities lost their power.

Boeing was now convinced that war was inevitable, but he was deeply concerned that the U.S. was unprepared. He believed that going to war with Germany would be "opening the door to a darn good thrashing."[5] The

Preparedness movement, with its parades and banners and leaflets, seemed to have been ineffective. Bill Boeing was a man of action and he wanted to make a difference. He realized that he was in a position in which he could do something that no one else in Seattle could do. Using the two planes he was building, he could create a foundation for an aviation militia.

A few seaplanes patrolling the water around Ireland could have easily spotted the German U-boat and warned the *Lusitania*. They possibly could have even dropped a bomb to sink the submarine before it launched its torpedoes. Boeing envisioned an aviation reserve that would fly anti-submarine patrols from bases along the Pacific Coast and protect ships serving Seattle, Portland, and Vancouver. On August 3, *The Seattle Daily Times* ran a story that said, "W.E. Boeing ... will proceed to perfect the organization of an aviation reserve for the country's defense."[6]

Boeing quickly broke the project into three steps. First, he would need a base to operate from. Second, he would need airplanes, at least three to start. Third, he would need to learn to fly. Glenn Curtiss and Glenn Martin were both building and selling airplanes. They also each offered flying schools. Boeing had been impressed by Curtiss at the 1910 Los Angeles Air Show, so he went first to Buffalo, New York, to talk to him about buying one of his planes.

Boeing found Curtiss polite but busy. "Right now all of my aeroplanes are going to the U. S. Navy," he said.[7] But before he headed home, Bill was given a tour of the Curtiss factory by test pilot Forrest Wysong (who in a few years would become the first American pilot to take off in an airplane from a warship). This was his first visit to an airplane factory, and he was fascinated. As he and Wysong walked past a wing under construction, Bill stopped to pick up a spruce rib and balanced it in his hand as if he was trying to guess its weight. Next he paused at the sewing tables where women were stitching together the fabric that would cover the wing. He ran his hand over the seams like a tailor judging the quality of a fine suit. Wysong was struck by the way Boeing inspected every detail. He could tell that this was no ordinary customer, and he wondered if Boeing might start building his own planes when he returned to Seattle.

When he got home, Bill bought submerged waterfront lot No. 52 at the foot of Roanoke Street on the east shore of Lake Union. The underwater lots allowed their owners to build on pylons over the lake. They were created by the state legislature to pay off debt left over from the AYP Exhibition. Next, Boeing asked James Foley to design a seaplane base to be constructed on his unique underwater property.

Westervelt, meanwhile, reached out to the Aero Club of America, a patriotic organization on the East Coast promoting aviation preparedness. Its goals were to "train 1,000 aviators to provide [an] aviation corps for the National Guard and Naval Militia of the States and U.S. Possessions and [to] put 100 aeroplanes in use ..." Westervelt asked for permission to form a Northwest chapter of the Aero Club, and on August 2, he and Boeing were granted that permission.

On August 10, Bill left for California to start his flying lessons. On his way to Los Angeles, he spent the night in San Francisco. The next day, under the headline "Millionaire Turns Aviator," the *San Francisco Examiner* ran the story: "William Boeing, wealthiest and most sought-after of Seattle's bachelors, left here last night for Los Angeles to enter the Martin or Curtiss School and become an aviator."[8]

When he arrived in Los Angeles, Boeing started his flying lessons at the Martin School, flying out of Griffith Park. His principal instructor was Martin's mechanic Floyd Smith. They began in the morning when the air was fresh, cool and full of promise, before the notorious Santa Ana winds picked up and made flying the fragile biplane hazardous. Bill was an attentive student and was soon soloing, but his flight training was cut short when another student crashed Martin's only trainer. Boeing knew he would need more experience to fly his new B&Ws, so he ordered a brand-new Martin TA float plane for $11,863.

Boeing was back in Seattle by August 24, when the Aero Club of the Northwest held its first meeting at the University Club. He was elected president and Conrad Westervelt became secretary. Other club members included Edgar Gott, John Hewitt, Charles Bebb, and Herb Munter. The Northwest Aero Club's birth was announced in an Associated Press story. "Serving for military and naval defense" was its mission.[9]

# 13. SOLOING
## SEATTLE, 1915

Early in October 1915, Boeing took the train to Los Angeles to inspect his new Martin and give it a test flight. Everything went well, so it was packed into crates and shipped to Seattle, arriving on October 15. Floyd Smith, Martin's primary instructor, and Ross Stern, another Martin employee, came up from Los Angeles to supervise the plane's reassembly. They prepared the plane in a tent hangar on the shores of Lake Washington, and it was ready to go on the wet and rainy morning of October 21. Smith took it up first. According to *The Seattle Star*,

On Thursday's flight Smith rose to a height of 1,000 feet from the hangar near Madison Park and headed ... west. He passed over the business section of the city, [then] over Elliott Bay, swung south and then headed northeast for the hangar. The flight drew the eyes of thousands as the new flying machine is the largest [in Seattle], its wings spreading over 50 feet.[1]

The following day it was Bill Boeing's turn.[2] The weather was cold and gray, with rain showers ruffling the lake. Bill paced the makeshift hangar, waiting for a break in the weather while the Martin seaplane, already in the water, rocked gently on the swell.

Bill had taken many chances in his life, but this was different. Most of the risks involved money and business, but he had enough money that even when the stakes were high, he rarely risked significant harm. Flying was different. If it didn't go well he could be hurt, even killed. He was nervous, but there was a hint of exhilaration mixed in with his anxiety.

By midmorning the rain had stopped. Bill climbed into the pilot's seat of his Martin. He tightened the chin strap on his leather helmet, pulled the goggles over his eyes, and waited for the lines that held the plane to be cast off. The controls were sparse. There was a hand pump that he needed to pull back and forth to build fuel pressure, and a magneto switch. The throttle was a foot pedal. A steering wheel was on a pedestal between Bill's legs. If he pulled back on the wheel, the plane's nose would come up; if he pushed it forward, the nose would head down. If he turned the wheel to the left or right, the plane would follow.

Bill worked the hand pump to pressurize the fuel, switched the magneto on, and then pressed down on the throttle to open the butterfly valves in the carburetor. A mechanic in white coveralls grabbed hold of the propeller and pulled down hard. The engine popped and blew out black smoke, and then it started with a roar.

The crew walked the tail around to point the plane toward the center of the lake and then hollered to Bill that he was clear to go. He steered the plane toward the open water and accelerated into the wind. He was too busy to feel nervous now. The engine surrounded him with noise. The single pontoon under the hull began to skim across the surface of the lake. The damp October air rushing past the cockpit turned his cheeks red and caused his nose to run. Bill bounced from side to side as the plane hit a few waves. The speed increased and the bumps became fewer and farther apart. One last bump and he was airborne.

Bill felt a familiar hollowness in the pit of his stomach as he pulled back on the wheel and began to climb. He leveled out at about a thousand feet and began a gentle turn to the left that would take him toward Portage Bay and Lake Union. It was cold and gray, but the view was spectacular. He was proud; he was in his own plane, flying above his own home. A few moments later he made another left turn to fly the length of Lake Union so that he could look down at the foot of Roanoke Street and see his half-constructed seaplane base. To his right was Queen Anne Hill and straight ahead, downtown Seattle. He gained more altitude and flew directly over the city and out toward Elliott Bay. Water droplets from the damp air formed on his goggles. He wiped them away with his gloved hand and made a wide circle above the bay before heading back across Seattle toward Lake Washington. Crossing over the city, he recognized the University Club, and following Madison Street, he flew all the way out to the big white tent that was his hangar.

He set the plane down with a gentle thump and a splash, and taxied back to the dock. He shut off the motor, and as the propeller slowed to a stop, he removed his goggles and smiled broadly. Flying was thrilling and adventurous, but there was more. He knew that flying was going to be important to the military, but there was a place for it in the civilian economy too; he just wasn't sure where.

Bill wanted to share the gift of flight with all of his Aero Club friends. He knew he didn't have enough experience to teach anyone to fly, so a few days later he invited Herb Munter to join him and Westervelt at Seattle's posh Rainier Club for lunch. The Rainer Club, located downtown on Fourth Avenue, a short walk from Bill's office, was similar to the University Club, but with one major difference: whereas the University Club was a luxurious escape from business, the Rainier was a sophisticated venue for conducting it.

Nineteen-year-old Munter, who was from a working-class background, must have felt a little uncomfortable in the club's stylish dining room, with its uniformed waiters serving an elegant lunch on china plates with silver utensils. Boeing's offer, however, was something the young man could savor. He asked him to help build the B&Ws for $150 a month, and when he wasn't working on the planes, to use the Martin to teach Aero Club members how to fly. Munter could hardly talk, but he nodded an enthusiastic "yes."

Munter's first opportunity to fly the Martin came on November 11, another rainy Seattle day. Bill was worried by how far the United States trailed Europe in the development of a real air force. He was also frustrated by the lack of interest most Americans showed towards military aviation. He had thousands of red cards printed at 10 ¾ inches long and 2 ¾ inches wide, cut in the shape of artillery shells. There were eight versions of the card, each carrying a different message about military preparedness. On November 11, Munter took the plane up and flew circles just above the rooftops in downtown Seattle, while Boeing, sitting in the forward cockpit, threw the bright red warnings out of the plane to rain down on the busy Seattleites below.[3]

On the 12th, a foggy day with a low gray overcast, Munter and Boeing flew to Tacoma. On their way south, Munter took the plane over Puget Sound, where he could follow the shoreline without fear of running into a hill. He saw a break in the overcast and climbed through the hole until they popped out into clear blue sky. Boeing knew that the sun would be shining above the clouds, but he couldn't help being caught off guard by the sudden joy he felt when the Martin punched through them into a bright world ringed by snow-capped mountains.

They circled Tacoma, dropping more warnings before heading back to Madison Park, making the round trip in an hour and twenty minutes.[4] The flight was a success, and the next day they leaflet-bombed the UW football game. After Munter and John Hull had crashed in Lake Washington on November 15, Boeing and Westervelt moved ahead quickly on the B&Ws. Space had been carved out at Heath Shipyard, where the talented woodworkers were turning Westervelt and Foley's drawings into real aeroplanes.

On Thursday, November 27 Westervelt received a troubling Western Union telegram:

> Lieutenant Westervelt, you are ordered to conclude all duties at Moran Brothers Shipyard in Seattle and report to the U.S.S. Wyoming at Naval Yard Pensacola, Florida on or before December 18, 1915.[5]

The news hit Bill hard. Of course, he knew that as an officer in the navy, Westervelt was subject to transfer and reassignment as the navy saw fit, but he never expected it to happen so suddenly. Westervelt had to be in Pensacola in exactly three weeks. When the time needed to reach Florida by train was subtracted, they had less than a fortnight left together.

Immediately the friends began to make plans. First, they needed to make final decisions on what types of engines and propellers they would use. They weighed the pros and cons of a couple of different engine manufacturers and eventually decided to buy two 125-hp Hall-Scott A-5 engines at a cost of $2,800 each, including radiators and propellers. Second, Westervelt needed to come to a long-term decision about his naval career. Was he going to stay in the navy or resign his commission and return to Seattle to build airplanes?

December 10 was cold and rainy as Westervelt boarded a train at King Street Station, headed for Florida and its warm, sandy beaches. On December 12 he stopped in San Francisco to finalize the engine purchase with Hall-Scott[6] before heading on to Los Angeles to meet with Glenn Martin to buy hardware and fittings for the B&Ws. As the train left California and rolled across Texas, Westervelt thought long and hard about his future. By the time he arrived in Florida, he had decided that he was going to resign from the navy and return to Seattle to help Boeing build airplanes.

Westervelt was a "naval constructor," which meant that he used his skills in engineering and naval architecture to oversee work done on U.S. naval vessels. With war on the horizon, the navy was moving the battleship U.S.S. *Wyoming* from Pensacola to the Brooklyn Navy Yard for modifications. Westervelt submitted his resignation in writing, and boarded the *Wyoming* for the trip to New York while his resignation worked its way through the proper channels.

Westervelt's letter eventually landed on the desk of Franklin Delano Roosevelt, assistant secretary of the navy. Roosevelt felt that war with Germany was now inevitable, and so naval officers would be extremely valuable to the country. He was therefore refusing to accept any resignations.

# 14. RAIDED!
## SEATTLE, 1916

Bill had made plans to spend the 1915 Christmas season in New York, where there were Broadway shows to attend, classmates to catch up with at the Yale Club, and pretty girls to dance with at holiday balls. He also planned to take a day trip up to the Massachusetts Institute of Technology in Boston to meet aerodynamics professor Jerome Hunsaker, and tour MIT's new wind tunnel.

On December 16 Bill boarded a train at Seattle's King Street Station, headed for New York. Relaxing in the smoking car, he read the newspaper while the snowy Cascade Mountains slipped past his window. He had no way of knowing about the unpleasant events unfolding behind him, which would soon land him on the front page of almost a dozen newspapers.

On November 3, 1914, the voters of Washington State, relying heavily on newly enfranchised women voters,[1] passed Initiative Three, which prohibited the manufacture and sale of alcohol. It also prohibited ownership of more than "2 quarts of spirituous and 12 quarts of malt liquors." The law was scheduled to take effect on January 1, 1916.

Bill's Aldarra mansion had been built in 1914 with a large wine cellar, which he had stocked with a collection wines and spirits amounting to an estimated value of $8,000.[2] The crown jewel of his collection was a case of 1835 Veuve Clicquot Champagne, with a value of $60 per bottle ($1,620 per bottle today).[3] The Champagne, like many of the oldest bottles in his collection, had originally belonged to Bill's father and had been passed down as part of his inheritance.

During the prohibition campaign, supporters of Washington State's dry movement had followed in the footsteps of hatchet-wielding Carrie Nation and the Women's Christian Temperance Union, focusing their attention on closing down saloons that sold rotgut whiskey and nickel beers to the vulnerable working class. Bill never thought that his painstakingly preserved collection of fine wines and liquors would draw the attention of the police. He was wrong.

King County Sheriff Bob Hodge was an ambitious man with an eye on the governor's mansion. The burly sheriff had been born in Scotland in 1875 and immigrated to Tacoma around 1890.[4] When he first arrived in the U.S. he worked in a cracker factory. He then became a prize fighter, a railroad engineer, and a coal miner in Black Diamond, Washington, until finally he joined the police force and became a deputy sheriff. In 1908, running as a Republican, he was elected sheriff of King County.

Hodge's charming Scottish accent and no-nonsense style of law enforcement caught the attention of *The Tacoma Tribune* and *The Seattle Star* newspapers. His story of being a poor immigrant who had climbed to the top with hard work and unflinching honesty resonated with the people of Washington. The *Tribune* and *Star* backed Hodge enthusiastically in his 1912 run for governor on Theodore Roosevelt's Bull Moose ticket, and by late October he was considered a shoo-in.

Just before the election, however, *The Seattle Post-Intelligencer*, which was backing the Republican incumbent Marion Hay, published a sensational story based on interviews with Hodge's ex-wife, Jeannie.[5] She claimed that Hodge's squeaky-clean image was all an act, and described in lurid detail how she had suffered from his beatings and womanizing. She said that he had abandoned her and their sons to gamble on dog fights and chase other women. Hodge and Hay both lost votes and Democrat Ernest Lister squeaked to victory by a slim 622-vote margin.

In 1916 Sheriff Hodge was looking to make a comeback. He figured that supporting prohibition was his ticket to finally attaining the governor's office.

January 19 was cold and clear. The weekend's snow hadn't melted yet. The lawns in the Highlands were blankets of white that sparkled in the morning sun. Sidewalks had been neatly shoveled and salted, but the streets were still rutted and icy as two King County sheriff's cars, their tires crunching over the frozen ruts, eased to a stop in the circular drive in front of Bill Boeing's Aldarra mansion.

Deputy Sheriff Scott Malone, a huge, bulky man, unfolded himself from behind the driver's seat of the first car and put on his black-brimmed police hat. Four other deputies climbed out of the second car, adjusting their dark-blue double-breasted uniforms.[6] Malone took a moment to make sure the address was correct and headed up the sidewalk, walking confidently to hide his nervousness.

The five deputies gathered on Aldarra's porch, their cheeks red from the cold while their breath hung in cloudy wreaths around their heads. Malone rang the bell, waited a moment, and then raised his fist to pound on the wooden door. Just then it opened slowly, revealing a man dressed neatly in a black cutaway coat with white gloves and impeccable posture.

Malone announced himself: "I'm Deputy Malone from the King County Sheriff's Office." Gesturing behind him, he said, "These are my men. We're here to see Mr. Boeing."

The well-dressed man in the cutaway politely replied, "Good morning, sir. I am Mr. Clark, Mr. Boeing's butler. I'm afraid that Mr. Boeing is traveling back East for the holidays. We expect him home in a few weeks. Perhaps you would like to make an appointment and come back then?"

Malone's temper began to rise at what appeared to be a brush-off from this fancy butler. He reached into his coat pocket and pulled out a folded sheaf of papers. He then raised his voice. "See here, Clark. I have a warrant to search this place from top to bottom. We've received a tip that there is illegal liquor on the property and we mean to find it."

Clark was stunned; these men meant to barge in and search Mr. Boeing's house. Nothing in his long career as a butler had prepared him to deal with a situation like this. Clark knew that a false step now could land him, or worse yet, Mr. Boeing, in jail. Butlers are trained to maintain good manners and proper decorum no matter how troubling the circumstance, and after a momentary pause, Clark smiled politely, opened the door wider and said, "Welcome gentlemen, please do come in."

Malone and the other deputies followed Clark through the door. Feeling awkward and out of place in the elegant foyer, the officers clustered together in the center of the room as if they were afraid of knocking over a vase or breaking an expensive piece of furniture. They whispered to each other as the snow melting off their shoes made dark water stains on Boeing's expensive carpets. Eventually Malone asked Clark to lead them on a room-by-room search of the house.

Malone knew that Sheriff Hodge was taking a high-stakes gamble. This wasn't going to be a typical liquor raid where a few burly policemen could knock over a table and break down a couple of doors to intimidate a saloon owner into confessing where his barrels of whiskey were hidden. Boeing was wealthy and powerful.

Clark, with perfect posture and stately carriage, led the police to the kitchen and instructed the cook to open all the cupboards and drawers. Next he led them to the pantry and then to the cold storage. Of course, while Clark was taking the police on a slow, methodical search of the kitchen, the rest of Aldarra's staff was quietly scurrying through the massive home, removing a carafe of burgundy from the dining room, an expensive crystal decanter full of whiskey from the library, a bottle of brandy and tray of snifters from the drawing room, and every other trace of alcohol they could find in the living quarters.

The search took hours and eventually the neatly arranged and well-stocked wine cellar was discovered. Malone confiscated the entire collection and reported back to Hodge, who alerted his friends at the newspapers. The story appeared in headlines up and down the West Coast:

"Officers Seize Liquor Found In Boeing Cellar," *Seattle Star.*[7]

"Liquor Seized in Seattle Homes," *San Francisco Chronicle.*[8]

"Seize All the Liquors at Home of Rich Lumberman," *Anaconda Standard.*[9]

But not all the papers were supportive of the raid. In Los Angeles the headline said, "Not Safe at Home. Rich Men's Palaces Invaded."[10]

When Boeing, still vacationing in New York, heard about the raid, he was "disgusted ... I boiled every time I thought of it and I got madder and madder," he told Westervelt in a letter a few weeks later. He decided that if Hodge wanted a fight, he would give him one. "Of course I am going through the courts to the very bitter end and will spare no expense, as a matter of principle and personal satisfaction. They went through the house from top to bottom, personal effects and all."[11]

Hodge was ready for a public relations battle, and the next day *The Seattle Star,* which billed itself on its masthead as "The only paper in Seattle that dares to print the news," ran a large front-page story under the headline "Bob Hodge Tells What He Is Going To Do Under Search Law – And Why."[12]

The *Star* reported that during an interview "where his voice choked and ... his eyes filmed,"[13] Hodge described in melodramatic detail how he had been playing a card game with friends on Sunday when he received an anonymous phone call from a crying woman. She told him that she had voted for prohibition because her husband had been coming home drunk and beating her. She figured that when the saloons were all closed down, her husband would stay home like he used to, "but it was worse than ever," she said – her husband was still able to find liquor at the Rainier Club.

According to the *Star,* during this call Hodge realized that it was his duty to go after the rich as well as the poor. "Hodge rose – fairly jumped – out of his chair," the newspaper reported. "He moved close up. His jaw clenched tight. You could see the muscles in his face drawn taut ... He punctuated his words with clenched fists jerked up and down." Nothing would change, he said, "until a few of the wealthy ones – influential prominent men who regard themselves as better than the common rabble and above the law got caught."[14]

Hodge singled Boeing out for damning praise during his interview: "Mr. Boeing's tastes were evidently those of a connoisseur. An expert told me some of his liquors could not be duplicated. Some of the brands have been off the market for 40 years. Rich, exclusive stuff."[15]

Boeing was the largest individual taxpayer in King County and had many powerful friends who quickly came to his defense.[16] Seattle Mayor Hiram Gill and Washington Governor Ernest Lister said that they believed the raid was unconstitutional; legal scholars cautioned that Hodge's interpretation of the law seemed to ignore the Constitution's prohibition against "ex post facto laws." An ex post facto law attaches criminal penalties to an action that was legal when it took place but was made illegal at a later date. Boeing, they explained, could be prosecuted for buying new liquor after the January 1, 1916 ban went into effect (something he hadn't done), but not for legally accepting liquor from his father's estate decades before the Washington law was passed.

Hodge reveled in the publicity. *The Seattle Star* and *The Tacoma Tribune* continued to run headlines painting him as an honest crusader for the common man, a sheriff who was standing up against a rigged system that treated rich men differently from the poor.

# 15. Lawyers
# Seattle, 1916

Bill Boeing had been dealing with lawyers his whole life, but so far they had all been civil lawyers handling wills and business disputes. Now, because of the liquor raid, he was facing serious criminal charges and he needed a criminal defense lawyer. Luckily, he knew right where to find one.

In 1911, Bill Boeing had moved the headquarters of Greenwood Timber to the eleventh floor of the brand-new seventeen-story Hoge Building, the tallest building in Seattle at the time. One morning in 1912, while heading up to his office in an elevator, the building's owner, John D. Hoge, introduced Bill to a tall, slender man with erect military posture and wispy brown hair. He was George Donworth, a federal judge. In their short conversation, Donworth told Bill that he was planning to step down from the bench soon to partner with Elmer Todd, a former U.S. attorney, in a new law firm called Donworth & Todd. Boeing became one of the new firm's first clients.

In January 1916, Boeing called Donworth from New York. His first piece of advice was for Boeing to extend his vacation in New York, where Prohibition hadn't yet taken hold and the laws of Washington State couldn't reach him. This would allow his legal team time to develop a strategy. Boeing happily complied.

Charges hadn't been filed against Boeing yet, and just from reading the headlines each day, Donworth would have known that aside from Hodge, no one in King County was very enthusiastic about prosecuting the case. On January 28, in an effort to delay the prosecution, Donworth filed suit against King County, challenging the constitutionality of the search of Boeing's home and the seizure of his liquor collection.[1] Hodge, in an obvious publicity stunt, responded the next day that he was suing Boeing for $100,000 for slander. *The Seattle Star* happily ran Hodge's story on its front page.[2]

Boeing returned to Seattle on February 20, just in time to receive bad news on two separate fronts. The headline "Seizure of Liquors Is Sustained By Courts" dominated the right half of the front page of that day's *Seattle Daily Times*,[3] and the left half featured a large photograph of Boeing's Martin TA stuck nose-first into Lake Union, with the headline "Unruly Wind Plunges Air Flyer into Lake Union." Not only had a superior court judge ruled against Donworth's challenge of unconstitutionality, but Herb Munter had again crashed the Martin while trying to make a tight, low-level, low-speed turn. Fortunately neither Munter nor his passenger was injured, and the plane was virtually undamaged too, for which *The Seattle Daily Times* credited the "excellent repairs given to the machine after its first accident four months ago."[4]

The plane crash and the liquor trial were not the only things on Bill's mind that winter. America was beginning to take the threat of war with Germany much more seriously, and the army and navy were finally beginning to expand their aviation capabilities. The need for aviation reserves led by wealthy men like Boeing no longer seemed so urgent. Between December 1915 and February 1916, Boeing's plans for the two planes he was building evolved. He began to think more about selling them to the U.S. Navy, and he began making plans for another plane, this one to be marketed as a military trainer.

Boeing needed Westervelt's help to design this new plane, and Westervelt wanted out of the navy. Boeing began looking for leverage to influence the navy's decision and soon found it in his good friend from Yale, John Borden. Bill thought that Borden might have just the connections he needed.

Borden was spending the spring of 1916 in Seattle and staying with Boeing at Aldarra, while working with Ed Heath on getting a new three-mast schooner ready for an expedition to the Arctic. Borden was trying hard to convince Boeing to go with him on the trip; he even suggested that Bill bring his planes and attempt to fly over the North Pole. Boeing was tempted, and someone leaked the story to the press; on April 14, the *Los Angeles Times* reported that Boeing was going to the Arctic with Borden.

\* \* \*

In his election campaign of 1912, one of Woodrow Wilson's earliest supporters was Franklin D. Roosevelt, a Democratic state senator from New York State. When Wilson won the presidency in an Electoral College landslide, he rewarded FDR for his support by appointing him assistant secretary of the navy. John Borden was another notable supporter; he donated $6,000 to Wilson early in his campaign, an amount worth almost $150,000 today.

Upon hearing of Westervelt's plight, Borden told Boeing not to worry about it. He would simply reach out to Franklin Roosevelt, remind him of the donation, and ask for a small favor. Borden instructed his personal lawyer, Morgan Davies, who had also been involved in the Wilson campaign, to contact the Wilson administration on behalf of Boeing and make the request. Davies sent a letter to the secretary of the navy, Josephus Daniels, containing a reasoned, lawyerly argument about why Westervelt should be allowed to resign.[5] The letter Davies sent to Roosevelt was shorter and almost blunt:

> During our campaign in 1912, in Illinois and Wisconsin, Borden was perhaps our staunchest supporter. We needed money badly and he contributed in various sums something over $6000.00. I am most hopeful that you will bring about an acceptance of this resignation and in case that is impossible, could not a leave of absence be given to Westervelt?[6]

Davies took a train to Washington and met with Roosevelt on May 23 and 24, a pair of unseasonable cold, rainy days. Roosevelt's response to Davies was every bit as chilly as the weather: he was not persuaded, and Westervelt was to stay in the navy. It is interesting to speculate on whether this first, disappointing interaction between Boeing and Roosevelt laid the groundwork for the bitter enmity that would spring up between the two men in the years ahead.

# 16. *MALLARD* AND *BLUE BILL*
# SEATTLE, 1916

Bill was trying to decide what to do with Herb Munter and the Martin TA. Munter's second crash shook Bill's confidence in his friend. In a letter to Westervelt on March 17, 1916, Boeing explained that Jim Foley had examined the Martin's design and couldn't find anything wrong with it, so they rebuilt it without making changes.[1] Boeing told Westervelt, "I have a theory [about Munter's accident] and he admits the possibility, namely that of stalling on his turn to a point where the controls do not act." In a letter on April 22, Boeing told Westervelt, "It will be necessary for Munter to re-establish himself as far as confidence in him is concerned." In the same letter, Boeing also asked Westervelt, "If you have the opportunity, I wish you would look around and see if you can locate a real capable pilot."[2]

On May 19 Boeing wrote Westervelt, saying, "I'm going to have a talk with him [Munter] within the next day or so and tell him that it is our intention to have someone else fly them [the B&Ws] for the reason that in case he might have another smash we would get such a black eye, that it would be difficult to recover from it."[3]

* * *

The Washington State Supreme Court took up the liquor case on May 24. Donworth argued that the intent of the law, as expressed in its first paragraph, was "prohibiting the manufacture, sale, or other disposition of intoxicating liquors." Since Boeing was not manufacturing, selling, or distributing the liquor, and using it only for his personal consumption, it stood to reason that he was not in violation of the law.

While the Supreme Court deliberated, spring rolled on toward summer and the two planes that Boeing and Westervelt had started in November neared completion. There were now four planes occupying Bill's thoughts: the Martin that was being repaired in the hangar on Lake Union; the two B&Ws also in the Lake Union hangar, going through final assembly; and a new military trainer referred to as the "School Plane." So far, the School Plane existed only as an 18-inch-long model. It had been sent to Hunsaker for testing in the MIT wind tunnel.

Westervelt knew that if he was not going to be allowed out of the navy, Bill would need some help with the aerodynamics of the School Plane. He asked Hunsaker to recommend a student from the MIT Aerodynamics Department, and Hunsaker suggested a young naval officer visiting from China named Wong Tsoo. Wong was to graduate from MIT on June 2 and was planning to go to the Curtiss Flying Boat School in Buffalo, New York. He was to pass through New York City on his way.

Westervelt sent a telegram to Bill about the opportunity. He received a quick reply asking him to arrange an interview with Wong "and if favorably impressed engage him." Since Westervelt was now in New York while the battleship *Wyoming* was being refitted, it was easy for him to meet with Wong on board the ship. During their meeting, Wong told Westervelt that the Curtiss Flying Boat School had rescinded its offer to teach him how to fly (perhaps because Wong was Chinese) and therefore he was available to work for Boeing. He was willing to work for $20 per week plus travel expenses to Seattle. Boeing sent a telegram to Westervelt that simply said, "Engage Chinaman."[4] *

---

* The reader is cautioned not to judge by modern standards the vocabulary Boeing used over 100 years ago. Some researchers have suggested that Boeing's use of the phrase "Chinaman" was racist, but this phrase did not carry the same connotations in 1916 as it does today. Boeing was offering Wong the critical position of chief aerodynamicist in his new company and this, above anything else, demonstrates the value he placed in him.

On June 12, Boeing wrote Westervelt saying that he had found a new pilot named "Knox Martin, pilot license #224, who has had considerable experience in many different machines." He had hired him to become his newest test pilot.

On a warm, clear June 15, Boeing's new plane, *Mallard*, was completed. It weighed 2,100 pounds, was 31 feet long, and had a 52-foot wingspan. While similar to the Martin, the *Mallard* sat on two side-by-side pontoons instead of having one central pontoon and two smaller wing floats. *The Seattle Star*, still siding with Hodge in the liquor case, didn't cover the flight, but the *Post-Intelligencer* ran a quarter-page story the day after the first flight:

A big hydroaeroplane skimmed the surface of Lake Union yesterday afternoon with W.E. Boeing at the controls. The white foam curled over her pontoon and the spray flew in a steady stream. Suddenly the pontoons stood out in sharp relief against the water … the machine was in the air.

It was the first flight of the new hydroaeroplane which was built entirely in Seattle.

*Mallard* was the name given the new machine by Mr. Boeing and a sister craft, almost complete will be named *Blue Bill*. The *Mallard* is appropriately named for her trial flights, [which] showed she is "there like a duck."[5]

Boeing's first flight was a short quarter mile hop, and as he taxied back across Lake Union, the growl of the Hall-Scott engine echoed between Queen Anne Hill and Capitol Hill. No one who heard that sound had any way of knowing that the grumbling roar of Boeing airplanes would become the sound of the Seattle's economic heartbeat for the next hundred years. It seems fitting that Bill Boeing himself was at the controls of the plane the day it all started.

The *Post-Intelligencer* story continued:

Mr. Boeing was pleased beyond compare with the performance of the *Mallard*. He piloted her on two trips about Lake Union and Knox Martin, San Diego Aviator whose services will be used by Mr. Boeing this year, handled her once. Mr. Boeing made the first flight himself as he did not want to endanger any one in case the machine turned out to be defective.

He has reason to be proud of the new craft because she has many distinctive features which were worked out by himself.

The two pontoons on which the craft is mounted catamaran fashion were designed by Mr. Boeing and built at Oxbow by Ed Heath, the veteran shipbuilder. "I'm going to have lots of sport with this ship," exclaimed Mr. Boeing when he alighted after the first flight. "She responds readily to every control. She is very sensitive."[6]

The *Post-Intelligencer*, in what may have been an effort to counter the negative press Boeing had received at the hands of *The Seattle Star*, went on to praise Boeing:

> No one in the Northwest is as greatly interested in developing aviation as a sport as well as a serious instrument for national defense as W. E. Boeing. He has worked as quietly as possible. Since organizing the Northwest Aero Club he has constructed a big workshop and hangar at Lake Union, purchased a $10,000 Martin seaplane, which has since been abandoned, and now has completed two new hydroaeroplanes.
>
> Those that have heard of Mr. Boeing always affix Seattle capitalist to his name. He is called clubman and sportsman by those that have met him, and to his friends he is always "Bill" Boeing.[7]

On June 29, two weeks after the *Mallard*'s first flight, Bill was back at Lake Union in the cockpit of the *Blue Bill* for its maiden voyage, another brief quarter-mile hop. Confident that the plane was working safely, Bill let Herb Munter do the rest of the testing.

The following week, on July 5, 1916, the Washington State Supreme Court voted eight to one in Boeing's favor, stating that the prohibition law was poorly written and did not directly address the issues of private ownership of liquor. Writing for the majority, Judge Wallace Mount said, "If the act intended to make it a crime for a person to keep what he has lawfully acquired, that idea ought to have been, and no doubt would have been expressed in plain words in the statute."[8]

Hodge was forced to return the liquor to Boeing, but the court also ordered Boeing to move his expensive collection out of state. In an elegant solution to the entire problem, Bill loaded all of the bottles on board the *Taconite*, registered the yacht as a Canadian vessel, and moved her north to Vancouver, Canada.

In what may be an example of the old adage "keep your friends close, but your enemies closer," *The Seattle Star* reported that Sheriff Hodge and Bill Boeing had patched up their differences and Boeing was placing his recently repaired Martin TA seaplane and pilot T. T. Maroney at the sheriff's disposal to fly him to campaign rallies in the northern part of Washington State.[9] In the event, Hodge couldn't recapture his popularity of 1912 and didn't even make it onto the ballot for 1916. There isn't any record of how long Hodge used the plane and how many flights he took, but it is clear that he never troubled Boeing about liquor again.

# 17. PACIFIC AERO PRODUCTS COMPANY SEATTLE, 1916

Donworth & Todd drew up articles of incorporation for a new company called Pacific Aero Products Corporation to engage in a wide range of flight-related businesses, including the "manufacture of airplanes or other products, [to] operate a flying school, and act as a common carrier of passengers and freight by aerial navigation." The articles were filed with the State of Washington on July 15, 1916 and were approved on August 3. Bill Boeing was president and his cousin and business manager, Edgar Gott, became vice-president.

As shipbuilding jobs at E. W. Heath were winding down, Boeing began moving the skilled woodworkers into aviation jobs. By the time Pacific Aero Products was incorporated, there were twelve men in the woodworking department of the big Oxbow plant on the Duwamish River building wing ribs and fuselage frames, while another fourteen men worked in the building on Lake Union. The Oxbow plant, which would eventually become known as the Red Barn, was "140 feet long and 60 feet wide, with two floors, the upper floor being used for painting, doping, and varnishing and storage room; and the lower floor for assembling and manufacturing."[1] Access to the building was along a boardwalk that skirted a large dirt lot that was often pocked with potholes and mud puddles. The interior of the building was clean and well-lit from dozens of large windows. It smelled of spruce shavings and varnish.

Boeing kept his business offices at the Hoge Building but made frequent visits to the Oxbow plant. One day, when Bill was walking through the Oxbow plant with Jim Foley, the new superintendent for Pacific Aero Products, they stopped at one of the band saws where a sawdust-covered employee was cutting out wing ribs. Boeing picked up one of the newly sawn spruce ribs and held it close to his eyes like a pool player inspecting his cue stick. He was disappointed by what he saw. The cut must have wobbled off line too much. Without saying a word, Bill dropped the piece to the floor and stepped on it, casually shifting his weight back and forth while he and Foley continued to talk. Eventually the fragile spruce splintered, and the rib became trash. With his point made, Boeing moved off to continue his inspection of the factory. Word quickly spread that Mr. Boeing would only tolerate quality work.

Wong Tsoo accepted the job offer from Boeing and arrived in Seattle near the middle of July. He was twenty-two years old, well dressed and handsome with a slender build. He wore his dark hair combed straight back and held it in place with slick and shiny pomade, just like the dandies at MIT. Most noticeably, he was whip-crack smart.

Wong had entered the Chinese Naval Academy when he was just twelve years old. He graduated from the academy when he was sixteen, and the Chinese navy sent him to Armstrong Technical College in London. He graduated from Armstrong with a bachelor's degree in naval architecture in 1913, at the age of nineteen. After that, the Chinese government sent him on to Boston and MIT to study aeronautical engineering. He spoke English well, but having learned it in London, he had a hint of an English accent, which often surprised people.

When Wong arrived in Seattle, Boeing was faced with a problem he hadn't anticipated. While he may have been open-minded enough to hire Wong to be the chief engineer for his new company, the rest of Seattle wasn't. The city was highly segregated with a strong anti-Chinese bias.

Boeing needed to find a place where Wong could live and work uninterrupted, and where they both could come and go without raising suspicions. The solution was surprisingly simple. The University Club had a few rooms available for rent in the attic, where out-of-town guests could spend the night. Boeing rented one of these rooms for Wong. There was also a meeting room on the second floor with plenty of light and a large table where Wong could work on his drawings. The entire staff at the University Club was Japanese and slept in dormitory rooms in the basement. While there are considerable differences between the Chinese and Japanese cultures, it was likely that passersby who saw Wong coming or going from the University Club would have thought that he was a staff member.[2]

The main drawback to the scheme was that the board of the University Club didn't want its members to know that a Chinese aerodynamics prodigy was being hidden in the attic. So they requested that whenever Wong came downstairs to the main floor of the club he put on one of the white serving coats the staff wore.[3] This must have led to a few confusing situations when Wong was hurrying downstairs to get to Lake Union for a flight test, and a club member, seeing Wong in his serving coat, attempted to order a drink. Without stopping Wong would have replied in his slightly accented English, "Sorry old chap, but I'm just popping out for a moment," and then disappeared out the door.

Wong had a firm grasp of aerodynamic principles and an intuitive understanding that a successful plane needed to find the equilibrium that would come from balancing all the forces that acted against it. In a conversation with Jim Foley he said, "We've learned a lot since the Wright Brothers. Now we know how to make a plane inherently stable so it will return to normal if it is forced off balance in any direction."[4]

According to Harold Mansfield, Wong's explanation continued:

We don't need a vertical fin on the tail to stabilize it because if we tilt the wings up – that's called dihedral – you can tip the plane one way or the other and it will come back to level. We can also do away with the horizontal stabilizer by staggering the top wing ahead of the lower one to give a broad surface. Then we'll balance the elevator, put part of it ahead of the hinge line, so it will catch the wind on the opposite side and help the pilot."[5]

Models of Wong's unique design, with lots of dihedral and no rudder or horizontal stabilizer, were sent to Professor Hunsaker to be tested in the MIT wind tunnel. The model tested well, and Boeing ordered the construction of a full-size plane.

On July 26, 1916 John Borden's Arctic expedition, commanded by thirty-six-year-old Captain Louis Lane, left Puget Sound on the brand-new 223-ton schooner *Great Bear*. Borden planned to take the *Great Bear* on a 5,000-mile journey from Seattle to the Aleutian Islands, through the Bering Sea, skirting Siberia and into the Beaufort Sea, ending up at Coronation Gulf in Canada's Northwest Territories. Along the way they would hunt, fish, and film movies. Borden had asked Boeing to come along and bring the *Mallard* and *Blue Bill* with him so they could explore the Arctic by air and perhaps find a sailing route all the way to the North Pole. Boeing longed to go, but his responsibilities at Greenwood Timber and the newly formed Pacific Aero Products meant that he couldn't be away from Seattle that long. He must have felt a bit of envy as he watched the schooner weigh anchor and sail north.

The *Great Bear* was expected to reach Nome, Alaska, by August 10, but it never arrived. It wasn't uncommon for sailing ships to be delayed a few days by unpredictable winds and harsh weather. Wireless communication was still somewhat unreliable too, so Bill wasn't alarmed when he hadn't heard from his friend. He had also inspected the *Great Bear*'s construction several times and was confident, thanks to its thick skin and closely spaced frames, that it was one of the stoutest and safest ships ever built on Puget Sound.

But day followed day with still no word from Alaska. Boeing must have spent a few sleepless nights worrying about his friends. On August 24, newspapers across the country carried ominous headlines reading "Borden's Arctic Expedition Now Weeks Overdue. Anxiety Caused by Failure of Millionaire's Ship to Reach Nome."[6]

On August 26 news came from Nome that the *Great Bear* was lost, but the crew was safe. Bill immediately sent a telegram to Borden's wife in Chicago letting her know that her husband was alive.[7] The following day, newspapers carried the full story:

On the night of August 9 Borden and his party were approaching Nome when they were caught in a fierce summer storm near St. Mathew Island. They turned to face the wind and were easily weathering the murderous waves, but at midnight their wireless operator picked up a distress signal from a vessel nearer the island. Captain Lane took the *Great Bear* in closer to offer assistance, and in the darkness they ran against the deadly Pinnacle Rocks. The-175-foot ship with its 6-inch-thick planks was smashed to kindling against the sharp rocks. The crew launched lifeboats and was able to reach St. Mathew Island, where they set up a makeshift camp. After two weeks living in tents and eating salvaged supplies, the castaways were discovered by the revenue cutter *Bear* and taken to Nome.[8]

The *Great Bear* was a total loss, but everyone survived. Boeing must have felt relief that his friends were safe and glad also that he had made the right decision not to ship his planes north. If he had, they would have been shattered against the Pinnacle Rocks and sunk to the bottom of the Bering Sea.

# 18. University of Washington Seattle, 1916

The information that Boeing was able to get from Jerome Hunsaker and the MIT wind tunnel was invaluable, but the cost in time and money of travelling the country to Boston was prohibitive. On September 27 Bill Boeing, Jim Foley, and Wong Tsoo drove to the University of Washington to meet with Henry Suzzallo, president of the university, and Mr. Eastwood, professor of engineering, to discuss creating an aviation department complete with a brand-new wind tunnel. Suzzallo loved the idea.[1]

Two days later Bill invited Suzzallo to join him for lunch at the Rainier Club to discuss "the means of financing the original cost of the installation."[2] Suzzallo suggested that they run some type of "public subscription plan" or ask the navy to include funding for the wind tunnel in its next budget. Boeing listened to both proposals but wasn't satisfied with either, and the meeting ended without a conclusion. As Boeing thought about it over the next week, he decided that the easiest solution was simply to donate the money to the university himself, with the stipulation that his new company be allowed to use the wind tunnel anytime it needed. On October 2, Boeing offered Suzzallo a $6,000 donation that was earmarked to build the first wind tunnel on the West Coast.[3] Suzzallo agreed, and the University of Washington became only the second university in the United States to operate its own wind tunnel.

November 23, 1916 was an unexpectedly clear, crisp autumn day. The new Model C, with its steep dihedral and staggered wings, was finished and ready for its first test flight. Bill Boeing, Edgar Gott, Jim Foley, Wong Tsoo, and Herb Munter gathered around the plane at the Lake Union hangar. Everyone seemed excited about the upcoming test. Everyone, that is, but Munter, who was expected to fly the new plane. He kept looking at it and shaking his head, saying, "It doesn't look right."[4]

Munter was still trying to reestablish his reputation after his two crashes in the Martin, and he wasn't helping his cause by voicing his concerns about Wong's radical design. It lacked both horizontal and vertical stabilizers, and didn't even have a rudder. Wong's idea was to reduce weight and drag by using only ailerons and a small elevator to control the plane. Munter pointed at the rear of the plane where the rudder would normally be and said, "You can't fly a plane with … no stabilizer on the tail!"[5] Harold Mansfield described the scene:

> Wong was polite but firm. "The controls have been thoroughly proved out." He turned to Boeing with reassurance, "The model has been in the wind tunnel for six hours. Mr. Munter will feel differently about it once he gets it in the air."
>
> Foley looked sharply at Munter, "You're not the engineer, you're the driver."
>
> Bill Boeing, impatient, interposed. "It's just something new that you've got to get used to. Let's get going."[6]

Reluctantly Munter climbed in, pulled on his helmet and roared away. The plane took off easily and gained altitude smoothly. Back at the dock, Foley and Wong exchanged satisfied smiles.

As Munter neared the western edge of the lake he attempted a left turn. At first the plane refused to respond. He stepped on the pedals harder and the plane banked too far. He tried a bit of left aileron to level out of the turn it didn't help and the plane just banker further.

"Why did I give in?" he thought.[7]

He was on the verge of losing control and slipping into a spin.

He was pushing so hard that he was shaking. Slowly it started to pull out. When he finally got the wings level, he landed abruptly with a splash and taxied across the lake to the hangar, ran the plane up onto the ramp, and jumped out yelling, "Put on some more rudder and some fin."[8]

"You'd better take it out again and get used to it," Ed Gott suggested.

"I'll take it out again when you've made the changes," Munter said.

"But there is no reason to change it." Wong insisted. "You've not given it a full trial."

"I'm telling you, if I'm going to fly it, it's going to stay right here till you do what I say."[9]

Eventually tempers calmed down and a traditional rudder and horizontal stabilizer were added to the Model C. The combination of Wong's exaggerated dihedral and wing stagger with conventional control surfaces made the C a stable plane that was easy to fly. Boeing hoped that it would be exactly the type of plane that the navy was looking for as a trainer, and on December 27, 1916 he received an encouraging belated Christmas gift in the U.S. Navy's order of two Model Cs for testing purposes.

Even with the last-minute navy contract, the fledgling Pacific Aero Products ended 1916 in the red. It would take a while to get the exact numbers, but when Boeing's accountants, Price Waterhouse Inc., gave him the final year-end reports, they showed that in its first year the new airplane company had lost $11,444.34.[10] Bill hoped that 1917 would be more profitable, but he was to be disappointed. This was just the first ripple of what would soon become a tidal wave of red ink.

Boeing decided that he needed to build a land-based version of the Model C with wheels instead of floats, so that he could bid on some lucrative U.S. Army contracts. This new plane was called the EA-4. Up to this point, Boeing's planes had been built at the Oxbow plant and then trucked or barged in pieces to the Lake Union hangar for reassembly. Floats were then attached to allow them to take off and land on water. Now Boeing needed to find a grass field that he could use for his land-based planes.

Boeing must have been overheard talking about his need for a landing field by Nathaniel Paschall, a fellow member of the University Club. Paschall's mother-in-law, Alice Potter, lived south of Tacoma in a community called American Lake. She had a nearby neighbor named Jones, who had a large, flat pasture for sale.

In January 1917, when the first EA-4 was finished, Boeing shipped it to Sand Point, an undeveloped field jutting into Lake Washington, for assembly. Taking off from Sand Point's grass runway, Boeing flew south to American Lake and landed in Jones's field. The noise and excitement caught the attention of Alice Potter's twenty-five-year-old daughter Bertha. She carefully picked her way across the field, lifting her skirt to avoid snagging its hem on the underbrush.

Jones's land was priced at $50 per acre, and Boeing, who had been looking at other properties priced at $5 per acre, thought it too expensive and decided not to buy it.[11] But that day he found something far more valuable than an airfield: he found a soul mate.

Bertha Potter Paschall was slender, with short dark hair and a thoughtful, confident disposition. She rarely smiled, but when she did her face was beautiful. She was married with two young sons: Nathaniel Jr., who was four, and Cranston, who was less than a year old. Boeing's letters and papers make no mention of meeting Bertha that day, while Bertha's diary simply says "Mr. Boeing brought his plane down from Seattle."[12]

Bertha had been born in 1891 to a wealthy family in Tacoma, the eldest of three sisters. Her father ran into financial difficulties and died unexpectedly in February 1896, and her grandfather took over financial responsibilities for the girls. He gave them the type of upbringing typical for wealthy young women in the early 1900s, inclusive of first-rate schools and debutante parties. While Bertha and her sisters were making a tour of Europe in 1910, their grandfather died, and the girls rushed home.

At nineteen, with her father and grandfather dead and the family fortune running low, Bertha must have felt a tremendous responsibility to follow the expectations of the day: to find the right sort of man and get married. In 1910 she met Nathaniel Paschall, a Harvard graduate and wealthy real-estate investor. They married on August 23, 1911. Bertha gave birth to Nathaniel Jr. in June 1912 and Cranston in 1916. By the time of Cranston's birth, however, Nathaniel was fighting a losing battle against alcoholism. Bertha had reached the limit of her patience and would soon be asking him for a divorce.[13]

# 19. The Patent War
# 1917

Wilbur Wright died from typhoid fever on May 29, 1912, and after that, Orville lost interest in aviation. He sold the Wright Company to a group of New York investors on October 15, 1915. In early 1916 the Wright Company merged with the Glenn L. Martin Company to form Wright-Martin. In December 1916, just about the time that Boeing received his first order for two Model C trainers from the navy, lawyers for Wright-Martin began vigorously attempting to enforce the Wrights' patent. They demanded a 5 percent royalty on all airplanes sold in the US, with a minimum annual royalty payment of $10,000 per manufacturer.[1] With only two planes sold in 1916, Boeing's payment to Wright would have amounted to $5,000 per plane. Wright-Martin's effort to enforce its patent and the industry's efforts to fight it became known in the aviation industry as the Patent War.

But with a shooting war looming on the horizon, the U.S. military could not allow Wright-Martin and the Patent War to hamstring American aviation. In January 1917, Franklin Roosevelt, assistant secretary of the navy, addressed the problem. Meanwhile, the navy had promoted Conrad Westervelt to superintending constructor of air craft at Curtiss Aircraft. He therefore he had a ringside seat for much the dealings in the Patent War and was able to send his friend Bill Boeing frequent updates:

> In regard to the Wright-Martin situation, it is at present in the following condition: In one of the appropriation bills now before Congress, a million dollars is appropriated to be paid to Wright-Martin Company for the basic Wright patent ... If this appropriation is approved, as there is every indication it will be, the situation will be very much relieved.[2]

Westervelt vented his frustration about what he felt was an improper decision by the Patent Office to give the Wrights a patent in the first place.

> Personally, I regret that this method of relieving the situation was adopted instead of the much more satisfactory method of a condemnation of the patent.[3]

Westervelt's anger at Wright-Martin spilled over into his letters to Boeing.

> I am so disgusted at the attempt of this company to deliberately sandbag the airplane industry that it would gratify me exceedingly to have the Government force them to prove that they were really in possession of an efficient ... [control system]. This, by the way, is something concerning which there is very active doubt in the minds of a number of people, including myself.[4]

The Curtiss Company had long believed that its method of controlling planes with ailerons was wholly unrelated to the Wrights' technique of wing warping and was prepared to battle it out in court.

> The Curtiss Company have right along professed to feel not the slightest anxiety concerning the outcome of their litigation with the Wright-Martin people, and there has been much in the situation to bear out their contention that they had them beaten.[5]

Westervelt knew that the navy had hired Jerome Hunsaker at MIT to research the Wright patent.

> Hunsaker, who was retained some time ago to make a thorough investigation of the subject, has told me that in a final court of resort, the so-called Wright patent would not hold water as it was anticipated in all of its important features by at least twenty years, there being both documentary and photographic proof of this fact. While this does not in any way detract

from the credit due the Wright Brothers, it is, according to Hunsaker, a fact, nevertheless, that all of the essentials of the present day control were appreciated many years ago, and the actual accomplishment of flight by the Wright Brothers was due to the fact that they succeeded in developing a motor of sufficient lightness.[6]

Westervelt made it clear that his anger was directed at the Wright-Martin Company and not at Orville Wright:

At a dinner in New York a few days back, given by G.C. Loening, I had the very great pleasure of meeting Mr. Orville Wright and of hearing him discuss some of his early experiences in connection with the experiments of his brother and himself. He is a most attractive man, of exceeding simplicity and modesty, and my regret is that the million dollars being appropriated for the "high binding" sandbaggers of the Wright-Martin Company is not being paid to Wright, who is the one who really deserves it.[7]

In the end, Roosevelt was successful in creating a "patent pool" in which all aircraft manufacturers were required to pay a small fee (about $200) for each plane they produced, to be divided between the companies (primarily Wright-Martin and Curtiss) that held essential aviation patents.

* * *

Bill Boeing was a man of many interests and in early 1916 he became involved in a project that for a short while almost eclipsed his interest in aviation. Dr. Benjamin Paschall (no relation to Nathaniel or Bertha) was a Seattle physician who specialized in treating tuberculosis. He ran a small sanitarium on Madison Street, west of the University Club.

In the early 1900s tuberculosis was one of the leading causes of death in the U.S., claiming over 100,000 lives each year. (It is likely that Bill's mother had died of TB.) Dr. Paschall had a theory on how to cure the disease and asked Bill for money to research his idea.

Paschall believed that the "germ" that caused tuberculosis (*Mycobacterium tuberculosis*) was protected by a special layer of wax, which prevented the "natural powers of the blood to digest and destroy [it]."[8] Boeing gave Paschall about $10,000 to conduct his research, and after this investment, Paschall claimed that he had discovered a substance called "mycoleum"[9] that could dissolve the "wax coating" and allow the normal "digestive juices in the blood called antibodies ... to destroy or expel the foreign substance."[10] Paschall then asked Bill for help in getting the medicine mass-produced and marketed.

Bill was excited by the idea of doing something that had such "great benefit to the world" and told Paschall that if he could get a patent on the medicine and was willing to put in his patent at a value of $500,000, Boeing would add $500,000 cash to create a company with a value of $1 million. In addition, Boeing promised to "appoint Paschall as the company president with an annual salary of $15,000 per year and if the company proved successful give him a raise to $50,000 per year,"[11] a salary equal to about $1 million per year in current values.

Boeing had a contract drawn up and gave it to Paschall. Paschall didn't immediately respond to Boeing's offer but made a trip to New York to see what type of support he could find on the East Coast. Before long, Paschall decided to relocate his research to New York. Since Westervelt was already spending a great deal of time in New York for the navy, he took over negotiating on behalf of Boeing. For a while, letters and telegrams between Boeing and Westervelt were full of references to Dr Paschall. At one-point Westervelt wrote

> I am in full agreement with you in your opinion regarding the possible dimensions of the Paschall matter, and if you go into this, feel quite sure that it will be of sufficient importance to deserve your entire attention. As a matter of fact, the possibilities are so absolutely stupendous as to be beyond the imagination.[12]

And a week later:

> I am inclined to believe that the one best bet in the whole world at present is Paschall.[13]

Boeing continued to press Paschall for an answer to his generous proposal. Paschall continued to defer and eventually Boeing came to the conclusion that

> Somehow or other he [Paschall] has gotten the idea that he might not expect fair play from me. I do not know how he arrived at these conclusions excepting that any man who has ... accomplished what he has, has a natural fear that someone is going to take his ideas away from him.[14]

Bill was never able to overcome Paschall's reluctance, and after eighteen months of inquiries without a contract being signed, Boeing and Westervelt lost interest in Dr. Paschall. Considering the fact that Paschall never did produce his new medicine (mycoleum was eventually trademarked in 1929 as a floor stripper to remove waxy buildup from linoleum[15]), it is entirely possible that Paschall's unwillingness to join a million-dollar corporation with Bill Boeing had more to do with his own doubts over the effectiveness of his discovery than with concerns over Bill's trustworthiness.

# 20. THE ZIMMERMANN TELEGRAM
# 1917

The U.S. government's outrage over the sinking of the *Lusitania* had caused Germany to back away from its policy of unrestricted submarine warfare. However, as the war dragged into its third year with the lines of blood-soaked trenches in Western Europe virtually unchanged, Henning von Holtzendorff, a German admiral, argued that a tightening of the blockade around the British Isles and a resumption of unrestricted submarine warfare would starve the British into a quick surrender. Holtzendorff brushed aside concerns that his strategy might provoke the United States to enter the war on the British side, saying that Britain would be defeated and the war brought to an end long before the Americans could get their troops to Europe. It was a gamble that the Germans decided to take.

On January 31, 1917, Kaiser Wilhelm's government announced that Germany would be resuming unrestricted submarine warfare the next day. In a misguided effort to slow down the U.S. response by keeping the U.S. military busy at home, Arthur Zimmermann, the German foreign secretary, sent a telegram to the German ambassador in Mexico, instructing him to offer to support Mexico in a war against the United States, with the promise that, if successful, Mexico could reclaim the lost territories of Texas, Arizona, and New Mexico. British intelligence intercepted the telegram and made its contents public on March 1.

U.S. newspapers responded with banner headlines. The front page of *The Seattle Star* announced, "Wilson Foils Kaiser – Blocks His Plot Against U.S."[1] But in Washington DC, Congress was skeptical. Republican Senator Henry Cabot Lodge worried that British intelligence had fabricated the telegram in an effort to drag the U.S. into the war. Lodge demanded a Congressional investigation, but in any case, the following day the Senate unanimously approved a $535 million naval appropriations bill. The newspapers called it "the greatest national defense measure ever passed by an American Congress."[2]

On March 3, all doubts about the Zimmermann telegram were put to rest when Zimmermann himself told a Berlin press conference, "I cannot deny it. It is true." In Seattle, the headlines announced, "Kaiser Confesses Plot Against U.S."[3]

\* \* \*

Bill's friend John Hull got married on June 26, 1917. It was a small ceremony at the bride's parents' elegant home on Capitol Hill. Bill was the best man. Hull was a member of the University Club and had invited several of his fellow clubmen.

Bill was standing with Hull at the makeshift altar of pink and white roses when Nathaniel Paschall walked in, followed a few seconds later by Bertha. She was looking gorgeous in a form-fitting dusty violet dress with silver lace overlaying the bodice. They made eye contact from across the room and Bill's throat went dry. He hadn't seen her since American Lake, and he felt a confusing combination of longing and guilt.

The ceremony was short and simple, followed by an outside buffet under a tent lit with paper lanterns. A string quartet played softly, filling the night with music.

Bill avoided Nathaniel and Bertha; he didn't want either of them to see that he had a crush on Bertha. Like opposing chess pieces, he moved quickly to the opposite side of the party whenever they came close. Nat was drinking from a silver flask that he tried to keep hidden under his coat. The more he drank the louder he got. Bertha tried to quiet him. At one point he reached under his coat for yet another drink. She placed her hand on his arm, whispering, "Slow down."

"Don't tell me what to do," Nat hissed.

Later, Bill came across Nat, slumped against the hand rail on the bottom step of the stairs leading into the house. Bertha stood on the grass fighting back tears. Bill quietly asked, "May I be of some assistance?"

Relief flooded Bertha's face and she nodded "yes."

Bertha hurried to bring the car around. Bill was impressed that she knew how to drive. She gestured towards the slumbering Nat as if to say, "As often as this happens, I've got to know how to drive." When the car was ready Bill got Nat to his feet and helped him stumble to the back seat where he was soon snoring. While Nat slept, Bertha told Bill that she had asked for a divorce. They soon kindled a romance that would last for the rest of their lives.

\* \* \*

Woodrow Wilson's second inauguration was on March 5. In his speech he pleaded for a new "doctrine of internationalism and world peace" while also warning of war if Germany attacked American ships.[4] Wilson's measured remarks were dwarfed on the front pages of the nation's newspapers by a story about a German plot to assassinate the President. Headlines screamed, "Try To Bomb Wilson."[5]

Fritz Kolb, a thirty-one-year-old German army reservist who had come to the U.S. in 1914, was arrested in a hotel room in Hoboken, New Jersey, with "enough explosives to destroy the entire city."[6] Eventually it was determined that the plot was aimed not at Wilson but at U.S. munitions stores, but U.S. anger at Germany swelled.

On March 12 American newspapers carried another alarming story: "Kaiser Speeds 'U' Boats To The United States."[7] The story warned that "within six days ... German submarines will appear off the Atlantic coast and in the Gulf of Mexico, ready to pounce upon the shipping that attempts to leave American ports."[8] More bad news came on March 14 with reports on the sinking of the American steamer *Algonquin* by a German U-boat. *The Seattle Star*'s banner headline read "U.S. Ship Sunk – No Warning."[9]

Addressing a joint session of Congress on April 2, Wilson pulled a sheaf of papers from his coat pocket and began:

> I have called the Congress into extraordinary session because there are serious, very serious choices of policy to be made, and made immediately ... The present German submarine warfare ... is a war against all nations. American ships have been sunk, American lives taken ... The wrongs against which we now array ourselves are no common wrongs; they cut to the very roots of human life ... I advise the Congress declare the recent course of the imperial German Government to be in fact nothing less than war against the government and people of the United States.[10]

Three days later, on April 6, Congress passed a declaration of war and Wilson signed it. The U.S. was officially at war with Germany. Congress then approved $3.4 billion for defense spending, with much of the money earmarked for new ships, new cannons, and of course, new airplanes.[11] Meanwhile, the secretary of the navy, Josephus Daniels, asked for navy personnel be increased from 87,000 to 150,000.[12]

With the massive increase in naval personnel, Boeing knew that there was no way that Westervelt would be able to return to Seattle to help build an airplane company, so he decided to change the name of the company to reflect his sole ownership. On April 18, Donworth & Todd drew up documents changing the name of the company from Pacific Aero Products to the Boeing Airplane Company. With the U.S. at war, Wong Tsoo left Seattle and headed back to China on May 22.

The Model C planes that the navy had ordered in December 1916 were finished in early spring and loaded into fourteen large wooden crates. They were to be shipped by train to Naval Air Station Squantum, Massachusetts, for an initial inspection before being forwarded to Pensacola, Florida, for flight testing. Boeing waited anxiously to hear the results of the inspection. He knew that the future of his new company was riding on whether or not the navy accepted these planes.

Westervelt used his position as a superintending constructor of air craft to inspect an early copy of the report. On June 1 he sent Bill a telegram with an ominous warning:

> Report very unfavorable ... condition was bad to actual point of danger in several particulars fittings and wire rusted several fittings cracked covering punctured in many places no cotter pins and etc I am afraid you will find a very bad impression has been created planes were incomplete and incorrect.[13]

When Boeing received the full written report three days later, it became clear that Westervelt had not been exaggerating. There were five typewritten pages detailing mistake after mistake. The report ended with a paragraph that hit Boeing hard:

> CONCLUSION: – On account of the fact that these two machines were considered suitable for training purposes and have been found totally unfit for the purpose intended it is urgently recommended that these two seaplanes be replaced with two Curtiss N-9 sea-planes.[14]

Westervelt sent a letter to Boeing that said, in part, "little or nothing could be gained by contesting the statements made ... regarding the conditions found in the machines delivered ... You cannot of course afford to raise any embarrassing points in connection with these machines."[15] Westervelt suggested that the planes be returned to Seattle at the navy's expense.

The planes had not yet gone through their flight tests, and Boeing believed that they would fly so well that they might overcome the negative review. He decided to take a gamble and had the planes shipped to Pensacola. He then sent Herb Munter and the new factory supervisor, Claude Berlin, to Florida to fix the planes. Using the five-page critical report as a road map, they went through the list item by item and made all the repairs and upgrades to ensure that the planes met the navy's standards.

Pensacola in July is hot and humid; mornings are clear with temperatures in the high 70s or low 80s, but by noon it can be well over 90, with dangerous late-afternoon thunderstorms that blow in off the Gulf of Mexico. Munter and Berlin were not prepared for the heat. They were mopping sweat from their foreheads and fanning themselves with their hats as they checked in to their hotel. Floyd Smith, in town demonstrating a new plane for the Martin Company, crossed the hotel lobby to say, "You've got a rough deal ahead of you. These guys are rough."[16]

The repairs to the planes were made quickly; they consisted mostly of replacing fittings and cables that had rusted in the humidity. Once the tests started and Munter took the plane up, the "C" began to impress. It easily passed the 70-mph high-speed test, and at 40.8 mph it was the only plane that came close to the 40-mph low-speed requirement.

Before long Berlin telegraphed Boeing: "Advise you get ready for big business. Everything points to big order. They ask how soon we can turn out twenty machines like these."[17]

# 21. TELEGRAM FOR MR. BOEING
# SEATTLE, 1917

At springtime on the University of Washington campus, the gardens planted by the Olmsted brothers during the AYP explode in a riot of color. Azaleas, rhododendrons, and cherry blossoms turn the campus into a floral wonderland, but in the spring of 1917 this lush beauty formed a discordant backdrop to the war fever that was running through the school.

Among the male students there was a rush to enlist in the military, and many left school early for fear that the war would end before they had got a chance to get into the fight. As graduation day approached, *The Seattle Star* ran a story under the headline "War Dulls Campus."

> There has been a note of solemnity in the commencement program never felt before. Always, after the last examinations, the campus is depopulated by the exodus of underclassmen who are bored by the final exercises. This year the place is doubly deserted ... many of the graduating class themselves are not here to receive their degrees ... sixty-seven members of the class of 1917 have volunteered for service.[1]

Not everyone who had wanted to enlist was able to. Clairmont Egtvedt, a twenty-four-year-old senior in engineering was slated to graduate on June 13. He was feeling downcast. He had tried to enlist but had failed his physical because he weighed less than 120 pounds.[2] He stayed at school while his friends headed off for what looked to be a glorious patriotic adventure. It was a serious blow to his ego. One day after class, Egtvedt was collecting his books when he was approached by Professor C. C. Moore, head of mechanics and masonry at the school of engineering. Harold Mansfield picks up the story:

> "You're wanted in the Dean's office."
> Claire Egtvedt, slight, neatly groomed, a serious student, went promptly.

"How would you like a job working on airplanes?" asked Dean Fuller.

"Airplanes? I don't know."

"William E. Boeing needs two or three engineers. You have a good record. If you're interested be at his office tomorrow morning at nine."[3]

It was common knowledge in Seattle that Boeing was trying to secure military contracts for his new airplane company. Egtvedt must have figured that working for Boeing would be a way he could help out the war effort in spite of his failed physical.

The following morning, Egtvedt, along with a fellow UW engineering graduate, twenty-two-year-old Philip Johnson, met with Bill Boeing and Jim Foley at Boeing's office in the Hoge Building.[4] Johnson was taller and heavier than Egtvedt, with a round face and a twinkle to his eye; he radiated confidence like a fire radiates heat. Boeing liked what he saw and immediately offered to hire both young men as draftsmen at $90 per month. Johnson, who was making about 15 cents an hour driving a laundry truck after school, jumped at the opportunity, as did Egtvedt. Foley chauffeured the two young men down to the Oxbow plant in the back of his car and showed them around the factory. Bill had no way of knowing it at the time, but with this simple decision to hire two young engineers fresh out of college, he had secured the future of his company and changed the trajectory of aviation for the next hundred years.

A few days later, Westervelt telegraphed Boeing to say that he was being sent to Europe for a ten-week inspection tour of the air elements of the British and French armies to see what he could learn that would help the American aviation buildup. Bill was frantic to find a way to join Westervelt on this trip and immediately wrote back.

> Although it will be very difficult for me to leave here, I feel that I would be compensated a thousand fold by the experience and likewise would be in a far better position to do something for the Nation in producing airplanes when I return ... I might also add that the experience itself would be the greatest one that could happen to me in my lifetime ... I certainly hope that you can arrange to have me taken along ... If I could be detailed to go with you in any capacity whatsoever.[5]

Eventually Boeing decided that his best chance of being allowed to accompany Westervelt would be to join the Naval Reserve. At the age of thirty-four he became a lieutenant, junior grade, in the reserve, drilling out of the Naval Training Camp at the University of Washington.[6] However, he was much too late to join Westervelt.

When Westervelt arrived in Europe, military censors prohibited him from writing to anyone back in the States. It was only when he was on the ship headed home that he was able to send Bill a long letter. He started with a tongue-in-cheek reference to the U-boat danger: "We seem to be fairly safely through the danger zone ... and I can write a letter without all the work being wasted."[7] Like the hundreds of thousands of American doughboys soon to arrive in Europe, Westervelt had found the size and scope of the war staggering.

> There is so much to tell ... that it is really quite impossible to start ... The proportions of the struggle going on at this time are much beyond the picture we have drawn of it. It is, I feel sure, quite impossible for one's imagination to ... appreciate.
>
> If it were merely of London in time of war I was to speak of, the job would be an easy one – but to tell you in a letter of Paris, of France in general; of Italy; of Venice; of the airmen; the machines ... of the hundreds of things I've have done that I was supposed to do ... and of the thousand that were not any way on my list, is impossible – I cannot even start on it.
>
> All along, throughout the ten weeks – seeming more like ten years as I look back on them – since I left the States, there stand out like peaks this unforgettable incident or picture or that, but all of them together make the picture of the mountain range of events we have traversed and I cannot at present pick out any one of them and say definitely ... "This is Mount Everest."[8]

Eventually Westervelt got down to airplanes.

> As regards airplanes, we are outdistanced, so far as the period of the war is concerned, I should say hopelessly, and we shall have to simply trail along and do the best we can by copying. We shall not, I believe, produce anything commensurate with the foreign results in any other way, as our designers are without the knowledge and experience on which these results have been based.[9]

Toward the end of his letter, Westervelt made an important observation that Bill would use in the years ahead to set his company apart from the rest of the aviation world.

> More and more one is forced to the conclusion that the engine is the machine and that is what has made it possible for the foreign designer to progress so far and so fast.[10]

In 1917, the fastest and most reliable way to send messages across country was via Western Union. Telegrams could be sent electronically thousands of miles, but delivery depended on young boys in snappy blue uniforms riding bicycles from the Western Union office to the final address to hand-deliver the envelopes.

On the evening of September 20, the last full day of summer, Bill Boeing was alone in his office at the Hoge Building, working late. The sun was setting behind the Olympic mountains, setting the sky ablaze when he heard a faraway knock on the outer door. He opened it and saw a young boy in the familiar blue coat, white shirt, and narrow black tie of a Western Union runner. "Telegram for Mister Boeing," the boy said as he pulled an envelope from the leather satchel slung over his shoulder.

Closing the door, Bill casually slipped a finger under the flap of the envelope to rip it open and pull out the message. This was a pivotal moment. From then on his life would forever be divided into two sections: before he opened the telegram, and afterward.

The sender was Edgar Gott, who was in Washington DC negotiating with the navy. Gott told Bill that the navy had just awarded the Boeing Airplane Company a $575,000 contract to build fifty Model C trainers. Boeing was now officially in the business of supplying the U.S. military with airplanes.

# 22. SPANISH FLU
# SEATTLE, 1918

Boeing's mind shifted into high gear to tackle the challenge of mass-producing airplanes. He began buying and leasing land adjacent to the Oxbow plant to expand his factory. He had Greenwood Timber ship him all the aircraft-grade spruce it could find, and he assigned Foley to draw up a slew of new buildings, including a woodworking shop, a larger assembly shed, a wing covering and painting shed, a machine shop, a brazing shop, and an electroplating and enameling shop.[1] Boeing was adamant that everything that went into his planes, with the exception of the engines, was going to be built at his factory, under his control. Next, he ordered fifty Hall-Scott A-7A 100-hp engines.

But the completed planes continued to have issues with quality. Two EA-4s that were sent to the army for testing at McCook Field in Dayton, Ohio, were rejected. Herb Munter, who had been flying the trials, watched the planes being loaded into shipping crates. He asked where they were being sent and was given a disturbing answer: "We're sending them to the mechanics school in Minneapolis to show how an airplane shouldn't be built."[2]

Later, Boeing and Munter accompanied a couple of "C"s to the Naval Air Station at Hampton Roads, Virginia. Boeing walked alongside the inspector as he examined the planes, telling him, "We've tried to give you a good, quality job of worksmanship."[3] According to Harold Mansfield, the "inspection officer came to an aileron cable that was frayed at the terminal end ... [He] jerked on the cable and it came off in his hand ... [Turning to Boeing, he said,] 'This would have been embarrassing if we'd been flying.'"[4] Boeing was humiliated and angry. Struggling to express himself, he replied, "I don't know how this could have got by. Whoever is responsible will be discharged immediately."[5] He sent a telegram to Gott at once:

> A fine state of affairs. What is the matter with our inspection? If I were judging the machine, I would condemn it for all time. I want a complete report made. For the good of the company the person responsible has to go. Any such laxity is unpardonable and I for one will close up shop rather than send out work of this kind.[6]

Production was overseen by a Mr. Darnell, whom Boeing had hired from one of his East Coast competitors. "I dispensed with Darnell's services for many reasons," wrote Boeing to Westervelt after the inspection fiasco. "He brought nothing to the plant in the way of a single idea and in fact he was in no way equipped to hold down the job he had."[7] In an inspired move that would have a long-lasting impact on the future of the Boeing Company, Bill transferred Philip Johnson, the young draftsman, out of the drafting room and made him assistant production manager. Johnson thrived and the quality control issues disappeared. At the same time, Claire Egtvedt was also working his way up the corporate ladder. Within two months of his hiring, he was promoted to assistant chief engineer.

The navy order was certainly good news, but it didn't mean immediate profit. In fact, it meant more money going out to pay for land, buildings, supplies, and labor. Boeing ended 1917 with a loss of $103,000. With the 1916 and 1917 losses added together, his airplane business had cost him nearly $115,000 so far (about $2.2 million in 2022 values).[8]

In the early 1900s a U.S. military contract for planes was a multi-part process. The military would publish a set of specifications. Each company that wanted to bid on the contract would design a plane to meet the specifications and build a prototype. The particular branch of the service that needed the plane would conduct tests, and a winning design would be selected. Then all the companies that had participated in the competition would get a chance to bid on manufacturing the winning plane. It was common for the company that designed the plane to lose out on the production contract, or sometimes a large order would be split between several manufacturers. This was the case in mid-1918, when Boeing was awarded a contract to build fifty Curtiss HS-2L flying boats.

The war was bringing big business to Boeing, but the tragic realities of it were beginning to sink in around the country. The military's need for soldiers was insatiable: over 2 million men had enlisted and another 2.7 million were drafted. At one point, over 10,000 American soldiers were arriving in France every day. When an American soldier died, the War Department sent a short telegram that said simply, "We deeply regret to inform you that [rank and name] has been officially reported as killed in action on [date]." By the autumn of 1918, over 100,000 of these short telegrams with their life-altering messages had been sent to mothers and wives across America.[9] The country was beginning to weary of the slaughter.

* * *

In October 1918, the city of Seattle was distracted from the war in Europe by its own deadly struggle. The lethal Spanish Flu epidemic was sweeping its way across Europe and the big cities on America's East Coast, killing five times as many people as the war. Seattle had stayed safe from the epidemic, but it couldn't last.

Philadelphia was one of the hardest hit cities. In September Philadelphia held a "Liberty Bond Parade" to raise money for the war. The parade was a huge affair covering twenty-three blocks with floats, marching bands and a military honor guard for the grand marshal, a wealthy philanthropist named Joseph E. Widener. A few days before the parade, Fort Dix New Jersey was hit hard by the Spanish Flu and the army unit detailed to provide Widener's guard had to withdraw. The quick-thinking organizers enlisted a group of young naval recruits from a nearby navy facility to fill in.[10]

The highlight of the parade was a gigantic eleven-minute patriotic sing-along in which band leaders stationed along the route got the tens of thousands of spectators lining the route to sing the Star-Spangled Banner in unison. According to the next day's papers, "Thousands of patriotic Philadelphians lined both sides of Broad Street during the wonderful Liberty Bond parade and sang with splendid spirit the songs that are cheering the American armies overseas to victory."[11] Unbeknownst to anyone in the crowd, loud singing in close contact with others was an excellent way of transmitting the influenza. The next few weeks saw a shocking increase in flu deaths in Philadelphia.

The day after the parade a trainload of young naval recruits, perhaps even the sailors that had marched in the parade, was sent from Philadelphia to the Naval Training Station at the southern tip of the University of Washington campus, north of Seattle.[12] The luckless sailors brought the flu with them. The navy reported two fatalities at the UW station on October 4, and soon

Seattle was overrun by the epidemic. On October 9, *The Seattle Star* reported "Flu Grips 984 Seattle Victims" with "369 New Cases Here Today."[13] The following day there were another 424 new cases. The *Star* ran lists of the dead on the front page and the death toll was climbing fast.

Ole Hanson, mayor of Seattle, took extraordinary steps to halt the spread of the virus. He banned public gatherings and closed theaters, schools, and many types of stores. He issued orders to shorten the working hours of all remaining businesses to between 10 a.m. and 3 p.m. to reduce the crowds on streetcars. On October 29 he made it mandatory for all people who went out in public to wear a six-ply gauze mask.[14] For a while Mayor Hanson's emergency orders seemed to be making a difference, and on November 9, the Health Department announced that "the ban will be lifted sometime next week."[15]

Two days later Kaiser Wilhelm abdicated and Germany surrendered. The war was over. At the Boeing Company, the factory whistle blew and workers poured out into the yard to cheer. Soon an impromptu parade along First Avenue led workers to a loud, joyous celebration in the center of the city, as reported in *The Seattle Star*:

> In gigantic cheering masses, Seattle's army of industrial workers surged through the streets Monday morning ... Seattle was a mad surging, seething, bee-hive as early as 9 AM and growing madder and merrier all the time. Industrial magnates, in opulent automobiles with tin cans and garbage can lids banging and clanging in the rear, traversed the principal pavements driving slowly, while beside them shipyard workers in smaller cars, with sheet metal and corrugated iron and tin attached by means of wire and strings dangling behind, tooted madly up and down.[16]

In a sad irony, the joyous citywide celebration came at a devastating cost for Seattle. With thousands of people gathering in the streets hugging, cheering, and not wearing their masks, the influenza roared back and made December the deadliest month of the epidemic.

Bill Boeing missed the celebration; he was in Chicago on a business trip, but he sent a letter that arrived at the plant by the end of the week. "I look for a splendid future in peacetime," he said,

> but there is going to be a gap of six months to two years when it will be a hard struggle.
>
> In the meantime, we should keep our shop occupied with other work ... comb the field and see what we might get into. I can suggest showcase work and interior wood working.[17]

# PART III

## Growing Pains
## 1919-1928

# 23. The Hard Struggle
# Seattle, 1919

The year 1919 did not start well for the struggling airplane company. Word came from Washington DC that the navy was cutting the contract for the Curtiss HS-2L flying boat from fifty planes to only twenty-five. Reluctantly, Bill made the decision to lay off much of his work force. From a wartime high of 400 employees, they were now down to just eighty.[1] The plant seemed eerily quiet to those who were left.

Based largely on the experience that the young company gained in building the big Curtiss flying boats with their 74-foot wingspan and 360-hp engines, Bill asked his engineering department to begin working on designs for a smaller, 100-hp flying boat to target the commercial market. As the flying boat project was to be the first entirely new Boeing design since the company's name change, it was given the model number "B-1."[2]

On January 8, Boeing and Edgar Gott went to Washington DC to try to drum up Congressional support for a combined airmail and passenger service from Seattle to Alaska using large seaplanes capable of carrying fifteen passengers at a time.[3] Their suggestion seemed to fall on deaf ears. When the new postal appropriations bill was passed later that year, not only was there no money allocated for an Alaska airmail program, but the government's entire airmail budget was cut by $800,000.

About 120 miles north of Seattle, across the Strait of Juan de Fuca, the Canadian government was sponsoring a traveling exhibition of captured war "trophies" called the "Great Official War Exhibit." It was scheduled to open in Vancouver on February 12, and one of the local promoters, a businessman named E. S. Knowlton, thought that adding an airplane exhibition to the show would help generate publicity. He contacted Bill Boeing and asked him to fly up. Bill agreed, and before long plans for the "stunt," as Knowlton called it, grew to include Boeing carrying a sack of mail from Seattle to

Vancouver and trading it with Knowlton for a mail sack destined for Seattle.[4]

The night before the flight to Vancouver, Bill didn't sleep well. A cold front blew through, rattling the windows in his bedroom and making the big firs behind his house sway in the gusty winds. Once more he was taking a risk to advance aviation. February 17 dawned just as cold and blustery as the night had been. Breakfast and several cups of strong coffee helped Bill get his nerves under control. He chain-smoked unfiltered cigarettes as he drove past broken branches on his way to the Lake Union hangar to meet the company's newest test pilot, Eddie Hubbard.

When he arrived at Lake Union, Bill parked in a small gravel lot near the wood-planked walkway that led to the hangar. He looked at the sky and frowned. Just as a farmer walking his fields can note the telltale signs of winter on its way, a pilot reading the sky can see trouble ahead.

Yellow lamp-light came from a small multi-pane window in the back wall of the machine shop. "Good," Boeing must have thought, "the boys are getting the plane ready." He crushed out a last cigarette beneath his heel and walked across the slick pier. He opened the barn-like rolling door into the machine shop. It smelled of cutting oil and kerosene. Turning left, he made his way down a narrow hall to the office where he quickly changed into flannel long johns and a bulky leather flight suit. Bundled against the cold, he slid open another rolling door on the back wall that opened onto the hangar. A gust of cool fresh air hit him in the face and helped calm his nerves. He watched patiently while mechanics in white coveralls guided his Model "C" down the ramp and into the wind-ruffled lake.[5] After a final inspection of the fragile-looking biplane, Boeing and Hubbard climbed into the cockpit. Gusty winds almost tipped them over as they taxied to the center of the lake for takeoff.

Once they were airborne, Hubbard hunted for a break in the overcast. He found one and quickly climbed to 2,000 feet. A pale winter sun, bringing light but no warmth, greeted them as they broke through the cloud cover and headed north toward Bothell. They then corrected to north-northwest and steered toward Everett. The winds stiffened, and after about ninety minutes bucking the headwind, they realized they were burning through their fuel and would not have enough to cross the Strait of Juan de Fuca. They descended towards Fidalgo Bay and the busy lumber port of Anacortes to refuel. A motor launch was headed out to give them a tow to the inner harbor, when according to *The Seattle Daily Times*,

> A sudden and violent gust of wind struck the machine head-on and tipped it up on its tail. It was literally standing on its tail when a great wave smashed in and the rudder controls gave way under the extraordinary strain. Neither

man was spilled nor any the worse for his experience. The launch arrived shortly afterwards and towed the wounded plane into port.[6]

The mission to Vancouver would have to be delayed while the broken parts were replaced. The next day, Boeing and Hubbard made a field repair to get the plane back to Lake Union, where more professional repairs could be made.

Ten days later, Bill and Eddie Hubbard took a second crack at flying to Canada. February 27 was a cold day with a heavy overcast and a drizzle on the verge of turning into snow. They took off from Lake Union around noon, climbed to 3,000 feet, and turned north following the shore of Puget Sound toward Vancouver. Above Everett the weather started to change. Hubbard tapped Boeing on the shoulder to get his attention and then gestured toward a swirling bank of ominous clouds; seconds later a gust of wind hit head-on with a jolt that rocked the fragile plane. The wind was followed by snow, which was whipped into their faces by the propeller blast. Boeing looked back at Hubbard and gestured "down." Hubbard agreed, and slowly began to descend through the clouds. Finally they saw the slate gray water and leveled off. They followed the snow-blurred shoreline, fighting against the wind until they reached Anacortes. When Hubbard finally landed an ashen-faced Bill said, "Good job, Eddie."[7]

The next day, the *Vancouver Sun* ran the headline, "Anacortes Proves Boeing's Waterloo." The story read, "For the second time, Anacortes proved an ill-fated spot for Capt. [sic] W. E. Boeing, Seattle aviator, who has twice attempted the flight to Vancouver on the invitation of the Canadian War Exhibit."[8]

The weather improved, and on the 28th Hubbard and Boeing took off from Fidalgo Bay and made a quick and uneventful passage to Vancouver. They landed at Coal Harbor and were towed in to the Royal Yacht Club by a powerboat.

Boeing turned the mail sack over to the Canadian Post Office. It included the following letter from Ole Hanson, mayor of Seattle, to his counterpart in Vancouver, R. H. Gale:

> To our neighbors across the line. Greetings – The City of Seattle extends to you heartfelt friendship and kind wishes. May the fraternal relations existing between our country and yours last for all time. We all stand for freedom and liberty and law and order. We fight unitedly against ... the Red menace, which threatens all governments of the world. "United we stand and divided we might fall."[9]

Boeing and Hubbard spent two days in Vancouver flying exhibitions, giving rides, and talking about an Alaska passenger and airmail route that would include a stop in Vancouver. At a noon ceremony on March 3, the promoter E. S. Knowlton handed Boeing a Royal Canadian Mail bag loaded with sixty letters addressed for Seattle. Boeing and Hubbard taxied away from the wharf and took off, planting the seed for a brand-new industry. This brief publicity stunt became the first international airmail into or out of the United States.

On the way back to Seattle, the plane again ran low on fuel and they had to set down north of Seattle in Edmonds. Arriving in Seattle later in the afternoon, Boeing turned over his bag of international airmail to the Seattle superintendent of mails. When they were back at the Boeing hangar, Hubbard said, "Mr. Boeing, if we can do this in the Model C, it would be a cinch in the B-1 ... I'd sure like to fly there and back on a regular basis."[10]

The next day, Bill Boeing took a train from Seattle to Washington DC to try to convince Congress that the time was ripe to invest in airmail. At the same time, President Wilson was trying to sell the country on the League of Nations. Both proposals would fall on deaf ears.

As the Curtiss HS-2L flying boat contract wound down, Boeing and his employees began to hunt for any work that would keep the doors open. For a few weeks in May 1919 they ran Boeing Air Taxi from the Boeing hangar on Lake Union, offering sightseeing flights over the city for five dollars. In the spring, Boeing signed a licensing deal with the Hickman Sea Sled Company of Boston to become the exclusive West Coast producer for the company's high-speed wooden boats, which featured a unique twin V-shaped hull and powerful engines that were capable of speeds close to 50 mph. Boeing even entered the furniture business, making plans to build bedroom suites. None of it seemed to help, and Bill had to reach into his personal finances to keep the struggling company afloat.

# 24. WEAVING SPIDERS COME NOT HERE
## MONTE RIO, 1919

In the mist-laced valley of the Russian River, north of San Francisco, is a large grove of California redwood trees. At 350 feet tall and 2,000 years old, they are some of the largest and oldest living things on earth. "The grove itself is a spot that one calls beautiful, with the sense that the word is inadequate," wrote Porter Garnett in *The Bohemian Jinks*. "To see it for the first time is to be filled with wonder that is never lost though one returns to it again and again."[1] In a painful twist of irony, a little more than twenty-five years after

Bill's first visit, this peaceful grove was to play a significant role in creating the deadliest weapon ever known to mankind.

The grove is the summer home to San Francisco's eclectic and secretive Bohemian Club. Formed in 1872 by a group of writers from the *San Francisco Chronicle*, the club holds an annual two-week retreat at a 270-acre wilderness compound on the banks of the Russian River. By the early 1900s the Bohemian Club was opened to the elite of the business world, taking on a mystique similar to Skull and Bones at Yale. Membership in the male-only club was highly sought after; some men waited years to learn whether they had been accepted. Bill joined in 1915 and immediately became an active member.

The 1919 Bohemian encampment attracted over 600 of America's wealthiest men. The goal of the camp was to give members a respite from the worry and care of business. The club's motto, "weaving spiders come not here," taken from Shakespeare's *A Midsummer Night's Dream,* meant that no work was to take place at the camp.

On July 19, Bill caught a southbound train out of Seattle. As it rattled its way down the coast, Bill let his worries about military contracts, cash flow, and red ink fall from his shoulders. By the time he changed trains in San Francisco to an 8:45 a.m. special headed directly to Bohemian Grove, he was looking forward to two weeks of swimming, trap shooting, and relaxing. John H. Hewitt, Bill's friend from his logging days, was coming, and Bill was excited to catch up with him.

As Bill stepped from the train, the scent of coal smoke from the locomotive mingling with that of the pine trees must have reminded him of his logging camps. Bohemian Grove was primitive, with few buildings: the clubhouse and a rustic bar were the only wooden structures. The bathhouse, barber shop, kitchen, and sleeping quarters were all made of canvas tents stretched tight with ropes and poles. The center of activity was the Campfire Circle, consisting of a large cleared area for a nightly bonfire. East of the Campfire Circle, at the foot of a wooded hill, sat the Main Stage.

In 1919 Bill stayed with nine friends in a camp called "Woof," which had tents raised on wooden platforms above the forest floor. Kerosene lamps hung above canvas cots with rented mattresses and pillows. Outside there was furniture carved out of stumps and a charcoal grill for frying eggs and bacon if the campers didn't want to trek down to the kitchen. Bill enjoyed fixing "Bill's Eggs" (a combination of grilled onions and scrambled eggs) for his fellow campers. No matter how primitive the setting, Bill and all the guests at the Bohemian Grove dressed in suits and ties every morning.

There were plenty of activities, including hiking, swimming, and fishing, but cocktails with friends took up much of the day. Bill probably went fly fishing on the river and joined the trap-shooting competition. The highlight of each evening was a late-night campfire where the campers would enjoy singing along with professional performers visiting from San Francisco.

The next several days of camp were spent relaxing, swimming, and going to lectures on current events. The grand finale came on the last Saturday of the retreat. The campers gathered at the Main Stage at 9 p.m. for the High Jinks performance, a piece of serious musical theater, written and performed by professional artists. A full orchestra and professional costumers were brought up from San Francisco.

The 1919 High Jinks was called "Life," written by playwright Harry Wilson. The theatrical reviewer for the *San Francisco Examiner*, Ray Brown, wrote that, in this production, Wilson "has set forth in symbolism the mysterious urge of life – the eternal hunger for knowledge, the restless quest for the unknown."[2] For over an hour the show's simple poetry and haunting score, featuring primitive wooden flutes, wove a series of vignettes about the nature of life. Coming as it did, when almost every member of the audience had lost a friend or loved one to either the Great War or the Spanish Flu, the poignant stories resonated in the hearts of everyone watching. When the play ended, the campers were treated to an elegant midnight dinner in the forest. The next day it was time to return, via private train, to normal life.

The Bohemian encampment had such a profound impact on Bill that he had his own "grove" carved out between a few old-growth Douglas firs on his estate in the Highlands, where he held "grove" parties each summer. These parties were heavily lubricated with bootleg whiskey and open to men and women. Bill enjoyed cooking for his guests: one of his specialties was "Steak Lazarus," – steak marinated in a combination of Worcestershire sauce, olive oil, dry mustard, and garlic.[3] An invitation to one of Bill Boeing's grove parties became one of the most highly sought-after invitations in Seattle.

# 25. TELL THE JUNK MAN TO CART IT ALL AWAY SEATTLE, 1919

On July 17, 1919, Bill received a memo from Ed Gott asking that he loan the company another $10,000 to cover payroll through the end of July.[1] The problem was easy to see, but harder to solve. With the war over, the U.S. military had no need for the huge numbers of planes that had been built during the conflict. Not only had the military stopped ordering planes, but it was selling hundreds of brand-new ones, still in their shipping crates, to the surplus market. The solution for the aviation industry was two-fold: First, the industry would have to design new planes that were so superior to the existing ones that the military would have to buy them or risk using obsolete equipment if another war came along. Second, the government had to be persuaded to assist in developing a civilian aviation market based on an airmail and passenger service. Both solutions would take time, and with Bill underwriting his company with his own money, it wasn't clear how much time the Boeing Airplane Company had.

On August 1, Boeing signed a distribution contract with S. H. MacDonald Company, allowing MacDonald to represent the new Boeing line of bedroom furniture in all states west of the Mississippi and up into Canada. Boeing built 300 bedroom suites, consisting of dressing tables, chiffoniers, and headboards. The stylish furniture came in a choice of three finishes: ivory, walnut, or mahogany. Gott wrote a well-researched four-page letter arguing that the company should move away from the airplane business and devote its full energies to the furniture business, but the Boeing furniture did not sell well.[2]

Boeing also began building ten Hickman Sea Sleds on speculation. The first completed Sea Sled was tested in front of the company's Lake Union hangar on August 30; it was stopped by the harbor patrol and ordered off the lake for breaking Lake Union's 8-knot speed limit. The incident ended up making it into the newspapers and bringing Boeing some unexpected publicity, with *The Seattle Star* calling the Sea Sled "the fastest boat known on Lake Union."[3] But like the furniture, the Sleds, though attractive, did not sell.

The foreman on the Sea Sled project, George Pocock, was a legend in the world of competitive rowing and had become famous building racing shells for the University of Washington. When the Great War halted international rowing competitions, Pocock went to work for Boeing, building laminated floats for Model Cs and then heading up the Sea Sled project. In his biography, *Ready All!*, Pocock tells of how Bill ordered one of the Sleds for himself and came frequently to the shop to watch its progress. Bill was particularly anxious for the boat to be finished because Bertha and Nathaniel Paschall had separated by that stage. Nathaniel had moved to California and Bertha was living west of Seattle on Bainbridge Island. Bill wanted to use the speedy Sea Sled to cross Puget Sound and visit her.[4]

On September 18, 1919 Bill received a copy of a memo that Ed Gott had sent to Claire Egtvedt. It had an ominous title: "Technical Staff – Reduction Of," and the third paragraph opened with "It is not this company's intention, as far as can be seen at present, to go ahead on a large scale with airplane development work ..."[5] Boeing had no choice but to trim the engineering department down to just Egtvedt and his assistant, Louis March. He then approved a small round of raises in an effort to keep morale up for the rest of his employees.[6]

On October 1, Gott sent Boeing another memo under the subject "Funds:"

I quote below from the Auditor's letter dated September 20th,

"Please note the attached cash report shows $5,146.57 in the bank, which is hardly enough to take care of the pay roll coming due on Saturday."[7]

Pressure was mounting on Bill to close the company. In a move that shows just how desperate the situation was, on October 16 the company took a job building umbrella stands for a California restaurant named The Pig and Whistle.[8] Later that month it bid on a job to make display fixtures for the Seattle department store Frederick and Nelson.[9] It did not get the job.

The first week of November 1919 saw a large bank of angry gray storm clouds roll through Seattle. Edgar Gott collected four years' of ledgers and headed to Bill Boeing's office in the Hoge Building.

Boeing sat in a large chair behind a mahogany desk. Gott entered the room and took a seat across from Bill. He opened the 1919 ledger and placed it on the tidy desk, cleared his throat, and nervously announced "We're going to finish the year $90,000 in the red." He paused. Then he asked, "Do you think we should close up shop?"[10]

Boeing shook his head. "I don't know," he replied. He got up and walked across the office to the window and looked down on the snarled traffic below. He rubbed his forehead, turned to point at Gott's stack of ledgers and said, "I'll take these home and review them. I'll have an answer in the morning."

Bill cautiously picked his way through the deep puddles and congested traffic of storm-weary Seattle on his drive to the Highlands, and it was well after dark when the headlights of his car reflected off the entrance to Aldarra. After a quick dinner, prepared by his cook, Bill instructed his butler Mr. Clark to have a fire laid in the bedroom fireplace and to turn down the covers. He retired to his room, carrying the heavy stack of ledgers, and set them on the nightstand as he changed into his night clothes.

Bill's room had several windows overlooking the back yard and a French door leading to the patio. The room had dark wood floors covered with red and blue Persian rugs. Two overstuffed chairs flanked the fireplace. The walls were covered with beige wallpaper and the ceilings were high and white. Photographs of Wilhelm and Marie sat in gilt-edged frames on the mantle, and above the fireplace hung a rugged seascape showing the wind-tossed schooner *Great Bear* approaching Pinnacle Rock. A couple of lamps on tall wooden bases with silk shades and long fringes stood on either side of the bed. Bill rang for Mr. Clark and asked for a glass of warm brandy as he settled into bed, sitting upright against a stack of pillows, ready to read Gott's ledgers.

The brandy was warm and sweet with a slight burn. Bill sipped slowly while he leafed through the ledgers. The company had lost $11,434 in 1916, $103,252 in 1917 and $19,324 in 1918, and it was on track to lose $90,000 in 1919. So far it had lost a total of $224,049 (equivalent to more than $3 million in 2022). The answer was there in black and white: When morning came, he was going to have to "padlock the plant and tell the junk dealers to cart it all away."[11] It was a heartbreaking decision. He had held onto this dream for so long, but he could not dispute the facts laid out before him in the ledgers. And as difficult as the decision was, there was a certain relief that came with setting a new course. With a settled mind, he tossed back the remainder of the brandy, turned off the lights, and went to sleep.

By the time Bill woke up the next morning, things looked different to him. It was the men that he thought about now, not the planes. "On awaking the next morning, the thought of terminating relations with the splendid and loyal group of men who had devoted their best efforts in the study of aeronautics and in the manufacturing of planes didn't seem right."[12] He would give the company a little more time.

As luck would have it, a few days later, on November 19, the company landed an army contract to modify forty-seven de Havilland 4s and replace their fabric-coved wooden fuselages with steel tubing.[13] At $1,363 per plane, the new contract wasn't enough to save the company, but it would provide enough income to keep the doors open until at least May 1920. Now they had six months to try to come up with something else.

# 26. B-1
## SEATTLE, 1919

It was a wet morning in 1919 when the big doors at Boeing's Lake Union hangar opened to reveal a green and silver flying boat: the brand-new B-1. Bill Boeing and Edgar Gott were on hand to watch while workers in rumpled white coveralls eased the 2,400-pound biplane down the planked ramp into Lake Union. Eddie Hubbard climbed into the pilot seat. The plans were to do some high-speed taxi tests. Claire Egtvedt and his assistant Louis March strapped into the back seat. According to Harold Mansfield, they wanted to see if the water would break clean along the sides of the hull.

Water dripped off the upper wing from a near-constant drizzle, and a breeze from the southeast ruffled the lake. The plane pulled away from the ramp and headed into the wind, picking up speed as the engine roared. At over 50 mph, Egtvedt leaned out of the cockpit to watch the water. "It's coming clean," he shouted.[1] Mansfield wrote, "They hadn't expected to fly but the boat popped right out of the water. Hubbard looked around with a grin.

He was continuing to climb. They reached about 300 feet when the engine coughed and sputtered."[2]

The engine-driven fuel pump had slipped out of gear. There was a hand-operated emergency pump. Hubbard took one hand off the control column to operate the pump. The motor re-fired briefly, but without two hands on the control column he was overpowered by the load on the elevator. The plane's nose pitched up and it stalled.

Hubbard immediately let go of the pump to use both hands to wrestle with the controls. He got the nose level, but the engine died. He moved back to the pump to get the fuel flowing, and the controls overpowered him once more, causing the plane to pitch up and stall again. From their seats behind the pilot, Egtvedt and March could see the struggle as the plane bucked and stalled over the lake. They leaned forward to assist and after three or four more cycles of stalling, falling, and re-firing, they landed heavily with a big splash but no damage.

As they taxied back to the ramp, Egtvedt began to diagnose the problem. The fuel pump would be an easy fix, but the controls were a whole different issue. The elevator needed to be big enough to control the plane, but not so big that it would overpower the pilot.

Later, in his office at the Oxbow plant, Egtvedt began to sketch new elevator designs. The floor next to his waste basket was littered with crumpled balls of paper. When he tried drawing the elevators long enough to give him the control he wanted, he realized that no pilot he knew would be strong enough to move them. He was just about to toss his latest drawing into the waste basket when he looked at it from the side and had a moment of epiphany. Instead of making it longer, what if he made it wider? That would give him the increase in area he wanted, but it wouldn't be any more difficult for the pilot to operate.

A few weeks later, Boeing, Egtvedt, Hubbard and the B-1 were back at Lake Union. The new wider elevator worked like a charm. In fact, the B-1 flew so well that Hubbard asked Bill if he could buy the plane. The airmail flight to Canada had inspired him to make a serious effort to run airmail between Seattle and Canada.

Bill Boeing threw significant support behind Hubbard and his innovative plan. He sold Hubbard both the B-1 and the CL-4S on favorable terms. He leased him space in the Lake Union hangar and, most importantly, he provided a personal guarantee to the U.S. Post Office that if Hubbard was unable to deliver the mail, he and the Boeing Company would make good on the commitment.[3]

# 27. WET *vs.* DRY
## SEATTLE, 1920

When the sun came up on the rainy streets of Seattle on Saturday morning, January 17, 1920, the city looked exactly as it had the day before. Overnight, however, something extraordinary had happened. For the first time since the nation had been founded 144 years earlier, the people of the United States had voluntarily given up a right. When the clock struck midnight on Friday night, the Volstead Act, which enforced the 18th Amendment to the U.S. Constitution, prohibiting the manufacture, sale, or importation of alcohol for beverage purposes, took effect. The United States was now "dry" from coast to coast.

Seattle and all of Washington State had been dry since January 1916, so at first the people of Seattle, including Bill Boeing, didn't expect much to change. They were wrong. Local authorities had enforced the law up to this point, and after the significant backlash aimed at Sheriff Bob Hodge over the Boeing raid, an unofficial truce had been reached. The police cracked down on flagrant breaches of the law, but as long as the "wets" did their drinking quietly behind closed doors, they were left alone. With the 18th Amendment, however, Prohibition was now a federal issue, and the Volstead Act provided federal agents to enforce that law. When the government agents arrived in Seattle everything changed.

Roy Olmstead was a well-respected thirty-four-year-old lieutenant with the Seattle Police Department. His round, youthful face belied his intelligence and ambition. Since Washington had gone dry in 1916, Olmstead had been involved in several liquor arrests and understood the risks and rewards of bootlegging.

March 21, 1920 was a foggy night on Puget Sound. At 3:58 a.m. a powerful speedboat cut its lights, throttled back is engine, and rocked gently in the slow-moving swell a hundred yards off Meadowdale Beach, north of Seattle. A light blinked from the bow of the speedboat and was answered by a flashlight on the beach. At this "all clear" signal, the boat engaged its engine, belched dark smoke, and headed to a small wooden dock. With hoarsely whispered instructions, a crew of nine men waiting in the darkness were told to unload ninety-six cases of whiskey, valued at $14,400, into eight waiting automobiles. When the last case was in the trunk of a car, floodlights were suddenly switched on and federal Prohibition officer Captain C. C. Klinger stepped in front of the lights, shouting, "Everybody freeze!"

The speedboat gunned its engine and sped off. A federal agent fired his pistol at the fleeing boat and in the same instant, all hell broke loose. Over fifty rounds were fired as the terrified smugglers dove for cover behind crates and barrels. Miraculously, no one was hurt, and when the Feds rounded up the smugglers, they were shocked to find that the ringleader of the group was Seattle Police Lieutenant Roy Olmstead.[1]

Olmstead pled guilty to smuggling. He lost his job, was fined $500, and released. Prohibition was unpopular with Seattleites, who felt that it had been forced on the city by rural voters. According to Norman Clark's book *The Dry Years*, "The newspapers ... made much of the Meadowdale story, playing up the 'Baby Lieutenant' with the 'brilliant career.'"[2] Instantly Olmstead became something of a folk hero.

With his police career in ruins, Roy Olmstead embraced his role of gentleman bootlegger. He carefully pieced together a sophisticated operation that involved large orders of whiskey bought legally in Vancouver, Canada, for shipment to Mexico. Shortly after leaving Vancouver, the freighters would make an unpublicized stop at a Canadian leper colony on D'Arcy Island, just a few miles across the Haro Strait from Washington's San Juan Island. There the whiskey crates would be offloaded onto the docks of the secluded colony. Then, under cover of darkness, a fleet of smaller speedboats would pick up the crates and bring them to Seattle to sell to a thirsty city. Olmstead frequently cleared over $200,000 profit per month. Clark wrote,

> Olmstead dressed and entertained in a princely fashion and walked the streets of Seattle with a big smile and a pocket full of money. During his walks he might ... spend a few minutes with his friend the Mayor, Dr. Edwin J. Brown. Or as he strolled Olmstead might give personal attention to the needs of his more distinguished customers, such as a millionaire airplane manufacturer.
>
> Public officials, professional men, merchants and bankers waved cheery greetings to him. Twenty men would speak to him in one block on Second Avenue. He had the power that goes with good liquor ... and good money ... He was the toast of parties where popping corks warmed the generous spirit.[3]

Everything Olmstead did was touched with a cheerful sense of excitement.

> He sometimes brought his boats to the docks in downtown Seattle, unloading them in broad daylight into trucks marked simply "Meat" or "Fresh Fish." He would roar with laughter as time and again he eluded the law. And even more than this, his unique code of ethics endeared him to many thirsty citizens. He never corrupted his merchandise. People could trust him. He never allowed his employees to arm themselves, lecturing to them sternly that no amount of money was worth a human life ... Olmstead ... avoided

the sordid behavior of others in the same business – no murder, no narcotics, no rings of prostitution or gambling.[4]

According to Brad Holden's book *Seattle Prohibition: Bootleggers, Rumrunners & Graft in the Queen City,* it wasn't long before Boeing found customers for the speedy Hickman Sea Sleds.

> Boeing advertised the sale of ... Sea Sleds in a Sunday edition of the *Seattle Post-Intelligencer*. Targeting a very specific demographic, the ad placed emphasis on the boat's speed. By the next day, every single Sea Sled had been sold and all had been paid for with cash.[5]

Local legend has long held that many of Boeing's Sea Sleds went to Roy Olmstead. Bill Boeing was one of Olmstead's best customers, and unbeknownst to either of them, federal agents working for William Whitney, assistant director of the Seattle Prohibition Bureau, were tapping Olmstead's phones and compiling a detailed list of everyone who ordered booze. Whitney was patiently building a case, and when the time was right, he would pounce.

Prohibition had an instant and unanticipated impact on the nation. Few people actually stopped drinking. Prohibition simply forced people who used to be law abiding to visit illicit speakeasies with live music, hard cocktails, and mixed company. In *Only Yesterday*, Frederick Lewis Allen's classic study of the 1920s, he writes, "The old days when father spent his evenings at Cassidy's bar are gone and probably gone forever; Cassidy may still be in business ... and father may still go down there ... but since Prohibition mother goes down with him. Under the new regime not only the drinks are mixed but the company as well."[6]

Once the average citizen had crossed over the threshold of drinking illegally, all manner of societal norms were easily cast aside, and short skirts, easy divorce, and jazz music ushered in an era that became known as The Roaring Twenties.

# 28. AIRPLANES, NOT CEMENT SIDEWALKS! SEATTLE, 1920

The army contract to refurbish the de Havilland 4s was going well, but May was approaching quickly and when the last plane was finished the company would be out of money. Edgar Gott pored over the books every day and lay awake at night worrying about how to keep the business afloat. He was on a constant mission to reduce costs. The engineering department was already running on a shoestring, but engineers do not directly generate income. One day Gott told Claire Egtvedt that he had to cut expenses even more.

Egtvedt called his assistant Louis Marsh into his office, closed the door, and told him the depressing news. Marsh looked glum as he shook his head and said, almost in a whisper, "It looks like our chance is running out."[1]

That night, as Egtvedt drove home, Marsh's words kept playing in his head. What had happened to their dreams? "Isn't progress a right thing? If I have the ability to bring it about, is there any power that can keep me from using it?"[2] The next morning he marched into Gott's office, determined to argue his case. Boeing was sitting across from Gott and they were deep in somber conversation. For a moment Egtvedt's nerve faltered. He started to turn away, thinking that maybe this wasn't the right time to speak his mind, but then he turned back. "We are building airplanes," he said, "not cement sidewalks."

If you want to build cement sidewalks and just do the work requiring a minimum of engineering, then you can do away with engineering. Do away with it. Just mix the materials and pour them into a form and collect your money. But if you want to build and sell airplanes, you first have to create them. That takes research and development and testing and engineering. The airplane isn't half what it ought to be. We have a foothold again now. Can't we hire a few engineers and try to build a future?[3]

Gott was caught off guard by Egtvedt's emotional outburst. He started to speak, but stopped when Boeing got to his feet, nodding. "Claire is right," he said.[4]

Egtvedt got his new engineers and the army extended the de Havilland contract, first to 100 planes and then to 354 over the next five years.

\* \* \*

The U.S. Post Office wasn't allocating much money to the fledgling idea of international airmail, but it did say that it would be willing to pay for airmail as long as it didn't cost any more than ground service. The idea behind Eddie Hubbard's airmail service from Seattle to Victoria was as follows:

[To] advance the mails to and from the Far East. On dates of sailing of mail steamers from Seattle, a flying boat would be dispatched in the afternoon to overtake the ship at Victoria and deliver the mail which had come in from the East, on trains, too late to be placed on board. This would advance delivery of the mail from eight to ten days ... On days of incoming steamers, the post office in Seattle would be notified by wireless as to the time the ship would arrive at Victoria and the flying boat would be dispatched to that city to pick up the mail that had arrived by steamer. The incoming mail would then be immediately flown back to Seattle in time to catch the east bound trains.[5]

The Post Office liked Hubbard's idea and awarded him the first scheduled Foreign Air Mail (FAM) contract in U.S. history.[6] His first day of operation was set for October 15, 1920.

October 15 was a wet day with a stiff wind that blew newspapers off front porches and caused autumn leaves to swirl in tiny cyclones. Shortly after noon a dark brown Model T mail truck left Seattle's King Street train station with five bags of mail weighing 150 pounds and rushed to Boeing's Lake Union hangar. By 2 p.m. the mail bags (four destined to connect with the Japanese ship *Africa Maru*, outbound from Canada to Japan, and one to stay for delivery in Victoria) were loaded aboard Hubbard's CL-4S seaplane. Boeing's subtle green and tan paint scheme had been covered over with bright yellow paint and tall black letters spelling out "U.S. MAIL."

A small group of dignitaries and well-wishers was on hand. Bill Boeing, taller than any of the other men, stood on the dock in a long black overcoat while the wind ruffled his hair. He shook Hubbard's hand and wished him luck as Eddie climbed into the cockpit. Hubbard primed the engine with a couple of quick pulls on a hand-operated fuel pump, and the big Hall-Scott engine fired up with a roar. He gave a jaunty wave and pulled away at 2:15 p.m.

The pontoons on his plane kicked up spray that was carried away in the wind as he taxied to the center of the lake and took off. The bright yellow plane stood out against the dark gray clouds as it circled for altitude. Fifty-eight minutes later, Hubbard was over Victoria's Inner Harbour.

In contrast to the small gathering of dignitaries that said goodbye to him in Seattle, there were thousands of Canadians on hand to welcome him. Unable to resist a bit of showmanship, Hubbard made a low, fast circle around the elegant Empress Hotel before landing in the harbor and taxiing up to the outer wharves on Rithet's Pier to deliver the mail. He had intended to turn right around and fly home as soon as he could refuel, but there were so many reporters wanting to interview him and well-wishers vying to shake his hand that he didn't get back in the air until 5:40, landing back in Seattle well after dark with only one lone mechanic on hand to meet him after his historic day.

The following day saw a much larger mail load, with eighteen bags totaling almost 500 pounds, so Hubbard decided to give the big B-1 flying boat a shot. He made the trip to Victoria in record time: only fifty-three minutes.[7]

The service proved to be very popular, and over a million letters were delivered in the first ten months.[8] Boeing felt like a new industry had been born and that he was the doctor who had delivered it.

\* \* \*

In April 1921 the army was taking bids to build 200 Thomas-Morse MB-3A fighters. It was to be the largest military contract for airplanes since the end of the war. The plane was essentially an American copy of the famous French SPAD. All the big manufacturers were bidding, but Boeing had a significant advantage: The MB-3A was a conventional wooden airplane, and Bill Boeing owned a lumber company.

It is unclear whether Greenwood Timber sold the Boeing Airplane Company its aircraft-grade spruce at a discount or if Bill's superior knowledge of the lumber industry simply allowed him to buy the wood at a greatly reduced rate, but when Ed Gott arrived in Dayton, Ohio, on April 21, 1921 to watch the bids being opened, Boeing's bid of $1,448,000 was half a million dollars lower than the nearest competitor. A representative of Curtiss told Gott that he would "lose his shirt" and suggested Boeing back out before it went bankrupt.[9] Gott made a worried phone call to Phil Johnson back in Seattle to find out if they should stand by the quote. Johnson checked again with Bill, and they stood firm on the price.

With 200 new planes on order on top of the 354 de Havillands to modify, the future of the Boeing Airplane Company finally looked secure. Former employees were rehired and the work force swelled to over 270 employees. Buildings locked since 1918 were opened and swept out. Handbills were posted around the factory that said:

> Employees of the Boeing Airplane Company only.
> Finished bedroom suites ... taking up room needed for the ... manufacturing of aircraft, which this company is concentrating on ... offered at sizeable discounts ... Dressers $22.40, chiffoniers $20.00 beds $17.20 net cash delivered or payroll deduction ... P.S. If you have delayed getting married on account of the high price of furniture, now is the time to get a good start.[10]

Boeing was back in the airplane business.

# 29. Dearly Beloved
## Seattle, 1921

The first two decades of the twentieth century saw tremendous changes in the status of American women. The women's rights movement had earned them the right to vote, hold office, and work outside the home. By 1920 women were smoking in public, drinking alcohol alongside men, and bobbing their hair. Fashions changed too. In 1905 it took an average of 19¼ yards of fabric to make an outfit for a well-dressed woman; by 1920 it took only seven.[1] And by the mid-twenties, the knee-length fringed dress worn by daring young "flappers" took much less than that.

Bertha Potter Paschall was not a flapper, but she certainly was a modern woman of the 1920s. Intelligent and well-educated, she was not afraid to speak her mind. She wore fashionable clothes and enjoyed a cigarette with her cocktails. Her thick dark hair was bobbed short, and the lilac perfume she dabbed behind her ears smelled like springtime. She was ten years younger than Bill and several inches shorter. She wrote poetry and dabbled in painting. She had a clever sense of humor and particularly enjoyed the satirical and sometimes bawdy wit of Dorothy Parker; she even copied the following poem into her diary:

> To drink much, I'm not able.
> It's one or two at the most.
> With three I'm under the table
> With four, I'm under the host.[2]

An avid reader, Bertha kept a notebook in which she wrote down new words and their definitions. She was also generous and loved Christmas. During the early days of her marriage to Bill, when the company was still relatively small, she bought Christmas gifts for the children of every single Boeing employee and kept track of her gift-giving from year to year in a thick leather-bound address book.[3] Most notably perhaps, she spoke her mind. She was Bill's equal and not intimidated by his wealth or power. He loved her for it.

Bertha's divorce from Nathaniel Paschall became final in the last week of March 1921. She had to wait six months before she could remarry, and six months and a day later, on Tuesday September 27, 1921, Bill and Bertha had a small civil ceremony at the King County Court House. The ceremony was witnessed by Bertha's sister, Grace Hiscock, and Bill's closest friend, John H. Hewitt. In a move that was uncommon in 1921, the word "obey" was dropped from the bride's vows, with Bertha promising Bill that she would "love him, comfort him, honor and keep him in sickness and in health, and forsaking all others cling on to him as long as [we] both shall live."[4] After they were married, Bertha and her sons moved into Aldarra with Bill.

\* \* \*

Airplane manufacturing was still a new industry. Bill once said, "We are embarked as pioneers upon a new science and industry in which our problems are so new and unusual that it behooves no one to dismiss any novel idea with the statement that 'it can't be done!'"[5]

Midway through the MB-3A contract, Claire Egtvedt was frustrated by the military procurement process. The army would send out detailed specifications and anyone wanting to bid on the project would have to work within those parameters. Egtvedt felt handicapped by the army's specifications. There was no way of trying something new or making a bold leap towards an innovative new plane. He thought there was a better way, and on January 3, 1922, he and Edgar Gott traveled to Bill's downtown office in the Hoge Building.

Egtvedt was a little intimidated by Bill's office. Facing Bill across his huge desk, he nervously cleared his throat and started to speak. "We are in the pursuit plane business now. The pursuit is different from anything we've built before." Too excited to stay seated, he got to his feet so he could emphasize what he was saying. "When you see the young fellows in the Air Service up there, rolling and diving and dogfighting, you realize that they have to have a superb airplane. The MB-3A is far from being what they need. It's based on the old French SPAD. We know how to build a much better airplane than that. When the MBs are finished, we should have a better plane to offer."[6]

Boeing nodded his head but reminded Egtvedt about the army rules that said they could only bid on what the army was asking for. Egtvedt went on with contagious enthusiasm, gesturing with both hands. "What I'd like to do is go out on our own to build the best pursuit we can: The Boeing Pursuit. The design will belong to us, at least till we sell it to the army. It will be entirely up to us to make it the last word in performance, efficiency, and general utility for the purpose – a pursuit airplane."[7]

Boeing, catching Egtvedt's excitement, got to his feet too, walked over to the windows, and turned to face Egtvedt with the stunning view at his back. "That's exactly what we should do," he said. "Do it on our own. Keep it a secret. Develop the best pursuit that can be built, then we'll take it back to Dayton and enter it in competition with the others."[8] It would take eighteen months to design and build this new plane that was dubbed the PW-9,[9] but in the meantime, there were 200 Thomas Morses to build and over 300 de Havillands to modify.

One day Egtvedt and Boeing were doing a walk-through inspection of the Oxbow plant. It was crammed full of airplanes. The productive sounds of saws and sanders made it difficult to talk. Boeing pulled a crisp white handkerchief from his coat pocket. Egtvedt thought that the clouds of spruce sawdust in the air were making Bill's nose run. To his surprise, Bill removed his glasses and dabbed tears from his eyes. After a few moments of silence, he turned to Egtvedt and said, "When we started this business it was kind of an adventure. Look what it has become."[10]

The 200 Thomas Morse MB-3A planes that Boeing was building used a 320-hp Wright water-cooled H-3 engine. Boeing ordered 200 of them. Wright ran into difficulty delivering the large order on time. While other managers may have been tempted to stomp, storm, and threaten lawsuits over the delay, Bill, in what would eventually be one of the most important moves of his entire career, contacted Frederick Rentschler, the president of Wright, and worked out a revised delivery schedule that Wright could live with. Rentschler was impressed and would never forget Boeing's kindness.

As exciting and challenging as the airplane business was, timber and mining were still Bill's main businesses. On April 7, 1922, he sold land that included an estimated 600 million board feet of timber to Harry Miller of Chehalis for over $2 million. This one timber transaction yielded more profit than the Boeing Company had yielded in its first seven years of existence.[11]

On May 3, Bill reorganized the leadership at Boeing, resigning the presidency so that he could move up to chairman of the board. Edgar Gott was promoted to president and Phil Johnson, only twenty-seven years old, became vice-president and general manager.

If the spring of 1922 hadn't been joyful enough, Bill received one more piece of exciting news: Bertha was pregnant. It was a difficult pregnancy, however, and she was confined to bed rest from April 14 to May 6. In a diary entry from June 12, Bertha wrote, "I've been through perfect hell for the last two months and a half. At last, I'm starting to feel human again."[12] Two weeks later, her health took a turn for the worse and she was back in bed from June 23 to July 7. She gave birth on November 22 to a six-pound, two-ounce boy who was named William Edward Boeing Jr. Everyone called him Billy. Due to complications with the delivery, Bertha and Billy stayed at Swedish Hospital, near the University Club, for twenty-two worrisome days, not coming home until December 13.[13]

As Christmas 1922 approached, Bill had much to be grateful for. His new wife was home from the hospital with their son, his timber and mining businesses were performing well, and after seven years in the red, the Boeing Airplane Company was finally showing a profit. Bill wanted to share his joy, so he issued Christmas bonuses in the form of a $500 paid-up life insurance policy to all 278 employees.[14]

The Boeing Company entered 1923 on solid footing, but lumber was still Bill's primary business. The profits that he saw from the airplane company were tiny compared to what was going on in the world of timber. Western hemlock was the most common tree in Washington's forests. American builders didn't care for it and preferred white pine or fir. Hemlock, if it was cut down, was used for crates, pallets, or paper pulp, but more often than not it was just left in the woods.

A few moments before noon on September 1, 1923 a 7.9 magnitude earthquake struck Japan's main island of Honshu. The ground bucked and rolled for over four minutes. When it stopped, the cities of Yokohama and

Tokyo were devastated. Because the quake hit almost at noon and many people were preparing their lunches over charcoal fires, thousands of small fires from spilled coals spread instantly. The fires merged into colossal firestorms that swept through the cities, destroying the wood and paper structures of traditional Japanese homes. Over 100,000 people were killed, 570,000 homes were destroyed, and almost 2 million people were left homeless.

In Japan, hemlock wood was an important building material. There wasn't enough native Japanese hemlock to provide all the lumber needed to rebuild, but the Western hemlock of the Pacific Northwest was close in quality. Immediately after the quake, and for at least five more years, timber companies in Washington State exported 600 million board feet of hemlock to Japan annually. The hemlock market was suddenly worth millions of dollars per year, with much of that lumber was shipped out of Grays Harbor from Bill Boeing's Greenwood Timber. Boeing and his team of accountants were careful not to mix assets from the timber and airplane businesses, but clearly the huge profits that Bill realized by resupplying Japan with lumber after the 1923 earthquake eased the financial pressure on the airplane company.

In a strange and tragic twist of irony, two decades later, these Japanese cities, re-built with Boeing-supplied timber, would be destroyed again with Boeing-built bombers.

# 30. WHISPERING WIRES
## SEATTLE, 1924

By 1924, the Roaring Twenties were in full swing. The skirts were short, the gin was cold, and the music was jazz. Douglas Fairbanks was breaking hearts in *The Thief of Bagdad*, Georgia O'Keeffe was shocking art collectors with her erotically stylized paintings of flowers, and "Silent Cal" Coolidge rode a wave of prosperity to victory in the presidential race.

In the world of aviation, the Post Office was finally waking up to the value of airmail. U.S. mail was carried by a fleet of war-surplus government-owned de Havillands. In 1924 the Post Office asked the airplane industry to bid on a plane to replace its aging biplanes. Much like the military, the Post Office had a strict set of design specifications. From Boeing's perspective, the most frustrating requirement was that they had to use an outdated Liberty engine.

During the war in Europe the government had asked Hall-Scott and Packard to collaborate on an engine that could be mass-produced quickly. The result was the Liberty, a sturdy V-12 water-cooled engine that produced 400 horsepower. Close to 20,000 of them were built before the war ended, but few made it into airplanes. After the war, with a huge surplus of unused engines, the government directed that the Liberty be used to power the planes built for the Post Office.

The Liberty was a wonderful engine when it was built, but its cooling system required a radiator and a water reservoir. At 8.34 pounds per gallon, water added a lot of extra weight.
Boeing built a sturdy biplane called the Model 40 to compete for the Post Office contract. Relying on the Liberty engine, the plane was underpowered and slow. The Post Office bought one, but no more.

* * *

On May 1, 1924 the experimental PW-9 was finished and ready for testing. The army liked what it saw and placed an initial order for twelve planes on September 18.[1] Between 1924 and 1927 the army and navy would combine to order 147 of the maneuverable little planes.

* * *

November 18, 1924 had been an uneventful day for Bill Boeing. He came home after work for a quiet dinner with Bertha in the dining room while Billy and the Paschall boys ate in the kitchen. Then he settled into a comfortable chair in the drawing room to read the evening's newspaper.

Like the rest of Seattle, Bill was shocked to see bold headlines announcing that Seattle's gentleman bootlegger, Roy Olmstead, and seventeen other people had been arrested in a late-night raid led by William Whitney of the Seattle Prohibition Bureau. Boeing was relieved to see that Olmstead and several other defendants had already been released on a $10,500 bond, but deep in the text of the article, he read something that caused a flicker of anxiety in the back of his mind. During the arrest, federal agents had seized "papers and documents relating to the sale and possession of intoxicating liquor."[2] Bill had been buying liquor from Olmstead for almost seven years and could not help but wonder if his name would show up in the seized documents.

A grand jury was immediately impaneled to hear evidence from the Olmstead papers and quickly began handing down indictments. November 27 was Thanksgiving, and Whitney knew that most people would be home celebrating with their families. That meant they would be easy to find, so his federal agents, armed with more than a score of warrants, fanned out across the city to make arrests.

As the arrests piled up, rumors began to swirl through the city. How many more were coming? Eventually Whitney announced that there could be as many as ninety, including at least sixty of Olmstead's major customers. Federal agents didn't visit Aldarra on Thanksgiving, but Bill spent a sleepless night. Each time the wind rattled a window he flinched awake. He was worried about a "grove party" he had held at Aldarra on July 5. He recalled placing a large order from Olmstead on the morning of the party. He tossed and turned through the night, expecting federal agents to burst through his door at any moment.

A few days later, Whitney showed up unannounced at the Hoge Building with a burly deputy. This was several decades before the Supreme Court's Miranda decision, which guaranteed anyone being questioned by the police the right to legal counsel, so Bill had to face the tough meeting without a lawyer. It is easy to imagine the scene: Bill sitting stiff-backed and proper behind his desk, with perspiration rolling down his back; Whitney lounging almost casually in one of the two chairs that faced Boeing's desk; his hulking deputy standing guard near the closed office door, making sure that no one would interrupt the meeting.

Whitney quickly announced that he had been tapping Olmstead's phone calls and had recorded a call on Saturday July 5 at 10:55 a.m. between Bill and one of Olmstead's lieutenants. Bill was overheard ordering five cases of whiskey. Whitney paused for a long time to let that information sink in. Eventually he began talking again, explaining that he was trying to build a case against Olmstead and needed good, reliable witnesses: prominent men who were well known and respected, and whom a jury would believe. He had evidence on sixty of Olmsted's customers, but he didn't have to prosecute all sixty. In fact, he needed a few to testify for the government, and of course, he wouldn't prosecute anyone who was willing to be a witness. Eventually Boeing agreed to testify, and Whitney decided not to bring charges.

Olmstead's case went to trial on January 18, 1926. There were dozens of defendants in a trial that lasted seven weeks. All three of Seattle's papers gave front-page headlines to every new development. The press soon dubbed the trial "The Whispering Wires Case."[3]

There was an audible gasp from spectators in the crowded courtroom when Boeing's name first came up about two weeks into the trial. Federal agent Richard L. Fryant was reading the transcripts of a phone call made at 10:55 a.m. on July 5th, between one of Olmstead's men named Fred Gage and a customer:

"Hello," a man said. "This is Boeing. Can I get any?"

"What do you want?"

(Gage then listed several brands.)

"I'll take five cases, I believe."

"We'll get it out today."[4]

Boeing was called to testify on a blustery February 2. High winds blew heavy rain against the windows while a clearly uncomfortable Bill Boeing made his

way through a silent courtroom to the witness stand. He was wearing a blue
serge suit, bow tie, and horn-rimmed glasses.[5] After swearing in, Boeing sat
awkwardly in the witness box while Olmstead stared angrily at him.

The prosecutor stood up and politely requested, "State your full name."

"William E. Boeing."

"Where is your office?"

"In the Hoge Building."

"And your residence?"

"At the Highlands."[6]

The crowded courtroom was made hot and stuffy by its steam radiators.
The wind was blowing too hard to open the windows. A few of the spectators
fanned themselves. Bill took a handkerchief from his pocket and dabbed at
the sweat on his forehead.

"Do you know Fred Gage [one of the defendants]?"

"Yes."

"Did he ever give you a telephone number from which you might order
whiskey if you wished?"[7]

Instantly the defense attorney, a short, belligerent street fighter of a lawyer
named George Vanderveer, was on his feet with an objection. He claimed that
since it was illegal to own whiskey, the prosecutor was asking Boeing to waive
his 5th Amendment right against self-incrimination and admit to an illegal
act. The judge overruled the objection and Boeing answered with an evasive,
"That is quite possible."

"Did you or did you not?" the prosecutor insisted. Again, the defense
objected, and the prosecutor tried a new question.

"He gave you a phone number, didn't he?"

"He may have, or he may not have."

"Do you recall the number Elliott 6785?"

"I do not."

"Do you recall that on July 5, 1924 you gave Fred Gage an order for one
case of Holt's Decanter, one case of King George [both Scotch whiskeys], and
two [cases] of Old Tom gin?"

"I did give an order but I can't recollect the date."

"Was it delivered to your house in The Highlands?"

"Yes."[8]

Realizing that he had gotten Boeing to admit to receiving alcohol from
Olmstead's organization, which was all he really needed Boeing for, he turned
his reluctant witness over to the defense.

Vanderveer began by asking that Boeing's testimony be thrown out because
Boeing had never clearly identified that it was Fred Gage on the other end of
the phone.

The judge allowed the testimony to stand.

Vanderveer approached the witness, "Was it ever intimated to you that you might be prosecuted?"[9]

The prosecution objected loudly, and the judge sustained the objection.

"Was it ever intimated to you that unless you testified, you might be indicted?"

The prosecutor objected again.

The defense pleaded to the judge, "But your honor, if a man has been paid or promised immunity, his testimony is worthless, and if he has been threatened, it clearly affects the value of his testimony. Testimony given freely and that given under compulsion are two different things."[10]

The court sustained the prosecutor's objection.

The defense continued, "We offer to prove by cross-examination, your honor, that this witness was told that the possession of liquor was an offense for which he would be prosecuted, unless he told his story on the stand."

"That offer is declined," the judge said with finality. "And the witness is excused."[11]

A battered but relieved Boeing left the courtroom without ever making eye contact with Olmstead. Olmstead was found guilty and sentenced to four years at McNeil Island Federal Penitentiary. He never forgave Boeing for testifying and after the trial he tried to trick Boeing into buying more illegal booze and incriminate himself by paying with a personal check.[12] The ruse didn't work.

Olmstead fought his conviction all the way to the U.S. Supreme Court, claiming that the phone taps were a violation of his constitutional rights. A bitterly divided Supreme Court upheld the use of wiretaps.[13]

\* \* \*

As the calendar rolled over to 1925, Edgar Gott decided to strike out on his own. He resigned from Boeing, and in a move that made Bill furious, took a job at Fokker Aircraft of North America. Fokker, a Dutch-based company, had outbid Boeing on a contract to refurbish more of the army's de Havilland 4 biplanes. Fokker couldn't get the contract unless the work was performed in the U.S., so Gott took the knowledge he had gained supervising the de Havilland rebuilds at Boeing and helped open a new Fokker Aircraft plant in New Jersey.[14]

After Gott's departure, Bill turned the presidency over to Philip Johnson, and Claire Egtvedt moved up to vice-president.

# 31. ROUND UP!
# PENDLETON, 1925

Airmail continued to grow, but railroad companies didn't think it was fair that they had to compete against a government-owned airmail carrier. Under pressure from the railroad lobby, Pennsylvania Congressman M. Clyde Kelly introduced the Air Mail Act of 1925, which soon became known as the Kelly Act.[1] The act authorized the postmaster general to contract with private business for airmail service. The act passed on February 2, 1925.

\* \* \*

Bertha Boeing was close to her sister Grace, who was married to Thorp Hiscock, a dashing Renaissance man. He had graduated from Cornell and made his fortune in banking, but was attracted to the "cowboy lifestyle." When his uncle died and his aunt offered him the opportunity to run a large hop farm in Union Gap, near Yakima, Washington, he leapt at the chance. He and Grace moved to eastern Washington and carved out a lifestyle that was a mixture of cowboy and country squire.

Hiscock heard about a festival in southeast Oregon called the Pendleton Round-Up. It was a Wild West gathering full of cowboys on bucking broncos and Native Americans wearing buckskins and camping in teepees. Thorp and Grace invited Bertha and Bill to join them on a trip to Pendleton.

Hiscock, who was fascinated by radio, had given Bill a primitive receiver as a Christmas present. Bill had enjoyed using it to listen to music, but then it quit working. In a simple act that would one day have a dramatic impact on aviation, Bill decided to take it with him to Pendleton to see if he and Thorp could repair it. Early on the morning of September 17, 1925, Bill and Bertha loaded up their Rolls-Royce touring car with a couple of suitcases and Bill's broken radio to head over the Cascade Mountains. Their plan was to pick up Thorp and Grace, and then drive to the Pendleton Round-Up.

There was a narrow gravel road that wound uphill from Seattle into the picturesque Cascades. Bertha, an aspiring writer, kept a detailed diary of the trip.

> We reached the highest point in ... Snoqualmie Pass at 8:37 and made good time down the eastern slope around the shore of Lake Keechelus.
> We followed the sinuous path of the Yakima River from Easton until we reached the canyon it had carved for itself between Ellensburg and Yakima.

It is one of the loveliest parts of the whole trip, the contrast between the barren tawny brown sun baked hills with their outcroppings of black volcanic looking rock and the vivid blue of the river with its fringe of green trees ... [was beautiful] ... We ... reached the Hiscock ranch at noon ... Hop picking is going on now, and there is a whole encampment of Indians just a few hundred yards from [the] house, the teepees looking like a regular mushroom village that has sprung up overnight.[2]

Grace and Thorp loaded up their baggage and they all headed south. While Bertha and Grace leaned close together in the back seat, sharing the latest family gossip, Bill and Thorp sat up front and talked about radio. Thorp saw it as the greatest technological advance since the printing press. As they drove through the rolling hills of southeastern Washington, Thorp impressed Bill with his vast knowledge of diodes, vacuum tubes, and transmitters. Thorp suggested that Bill outfit his planes with radios. Bill made a note to contact Bell Labs when he returned to see if that would be possible.

Bertha's diary captures the beauty of the drive as they passed into Oregon:

Forty five miles of paved road through the wheat fields, some great expanses of yellow stubble since harvest and others lying fallow until spring, a most beautiful patchwork of gold and brown, reaching to the base of the Blue Mountains.[3]

They arrived in Pendleton about noon.

The main street of Pendleton was a gay, colorful holiday crowd, most of the men wearing satin shirts of emerald green, sky blue, and every imaginable shade of pink, yellow, purple, and red. The favorite kind of hat was what is known as the "ten gallon lid" and men, women, and children all had bright silk handkerchiefs tied around their necks a la cow-boy style.[4]

Bertha bought Bill a ten-gallon hat that he wore proudly all through their Pendleton trip. Bertha loved the entire weekend:

The most beautiful spectacle of the whole [event] was the Indian Parade. There must have been 500 of them mounted on gaily bedecked horses dressed in gorgeous vivid colors, reds, blues, magentas. Purples, greens, and yellows, some with magnificent beaded capes, leggings, and bags, and some with elk's teeth sewed in decorative patterns on their clothes. Many of the men wore nothing but a breech cloth, their slender bodies daubed with red paint. Some were draped in furs and blankets, but clothed or not, they all had gorgeous feathered war bonnets and head gear of various shapes and sizes.[5]

When the Round-Up ended, the two couples loaded back into Bill's dust-covered Rolls-Royce and headed north to Yakima, reaching the hop farm a little before noon. Bill and Thorp began working together on Bill's broken radio as the lazy afternoon drifted on toward evening.

The next morning Bill and Bertha got up at 7:30, said goodbye to the Hiscocks and headed back across the mountains to Seattle. They arrived at Aldarra late at night and tiptoed into the boys' rooms to kiss them each good night before tumbling exhausted into their own bed. The day after, Bill went to work and Bertha began sorting through the large stack of unopened mail. She spotted an interesting story on the front page of the September 24 *New York Times*. The headline read "Hoover and New Ask Civil Flying Aid" with the sub-heading, "Airmail Expansion Urged."[6]

Bertha paused in her sorting to read the story. It described how Herbert Hoover, the secretary of commerce, and Harry New, the postmaster general, believed that "it was the proper function of the Government to aid in the development of aviation as an industry."[7] Hoover went on to propose that the Commerce Department be allowed to create a Bureau of Airways to provide services for aviation in the same way that the department was already assisting maritime commerce. Postmaster New advanced the idea that airmail contracts were lucrative enough that they could support the fledgling business of commercial aviation.

Bertha knew this story would be of interest to Bill, but that he could miss it among the week's worth of mail and newspapers he had to sort through. The next morning, when Bill sat down to his breakfast of corned beef hash and eggs,[8] there was a lone copy of the *Times* next to his plate, carefully folded open to reveal the airmail story. Bill read it with interest. When he got up to head to work, he folded that paper neatly, tucked it under his arm, and took it with him so he could give the story more attention once he got to the office. Bertha couldn't help but smile to herself. If Helen of Troy had launched a thousand ships, Bertha had just launched ten thousand airplanes.

# 32. THE ENGINE IS THE MACHINE
## SEATTLE, 1926

In the fall of 1925, Bill began to correspond with his old friend Frederick Rentschler. When Rentschler was president of Wright Aeronautical, he had overseen the production of a small 200-hp air-cooled engine called the Whirlwind. He felt there was a market for a larger air-cooled engine and asked the board of directors of Wright Aeronautical for permission to develop one. The board was narrow-minded and unwilling to take the risk, so Rentschler resigned and began working on his own. He designed a revolutionary nine-cylinder air-cooled radial engine that he hoped could produce the same 400 horsepower of a Liberty, but without the added weight of the radiator and water reservoir. Rentschler took his ideas to the Pratt & Whitney Tool and Die Company, which prior to this had not had any involvement in aviation. He asked them to take a gamble on him and his new engine. The company agreed, and Rentschler got busy building a prototype.

As Boeing read Rentschler's letters, he couldn't help but remember the dispatch that Conrad Westervelt had sent him long ago on his way home from Europe after inspecting the Allied air forces: "More and more one is forced to the conclusion that the engine is the machine ..." Boeing knew that he was right, and that if this new engine was as light and powerful as Rentschler said, it could be a game changer.

On Christmas Eve 1925, Rentschler's first engine was finished. It weighed 200 pounds less than the Liberty while putting out about 10 percent more horsepower. When it started up, it made a snarling noise that Rentschler's wife, Faye, said sounded like a swarm of wasps, so the new engine became known as the Wasp. At Bill's suggestion, Claire Egtvedt began to look at installing the new, lighter Wasp in the PW-9 fighter. The result was the high-performance F2B carrier-based fighter. The navy ordered thirty-two of them.

Eddie Hubbard's Seattle-to-Victoria airmail service had been going well and making money for several years, but he was ready to move on to something bigger. On November 15, 1926 the U.S. government announced that it would be putting the Chicago-to-San Francisco airmail route up for bid. It was the longest and the most lucrative run. The story ran on the front page of newspapers across the country. Hubbard saw it and started to dream. According to the terms of the Kelly Act, the Post Office would allow bids as high as $3.00 per pound for the first 1,000 miles and 30 cents per pound for each additional 100 miles.

Hubbard stopped by the Oxbow plant to tell Egtvedt about it. "This is the opportunity of the century, Claire," he said.[1] Egtvedt responded:

> "You're talking about a huge undertaking. That's a lot of country. The distances are big. You'll have winter blizzards to contend with."
>
> "We could do it." Hubbard answered, "... I've got all the figures on mileage and pounds of mail ... If you can produce some mail planes I know we can operate them successfully."[2]

Egtvedt's thoughts flashed to the Model 40. It was a good plane, but it was handicapped by the outdated Liberty. If they could run their own airmail service, they wouldn't be hampered by the government's engine requirements, and they could use the new lighter P&W Wasp. That would really bring the plane to life. Hubbard and Egtvedt took a few days to formulate a more detailed plan. They gathered all their notes and calculations and headed downtown to Boeing's office in the Hoge Building.

Everyone has good days and bad days, and Bill was having a bad day. Hubbard was just starting his presentation when Boeing interrupted, "This is something foreign to our experience."

"I've logged 150,000 miles on the Victoria route without any trouble and I've made money," replied Hubbard.

Boeing answered grumpily, "But this is over the whole western half of the country. You've got mountain ranges and winter storms to contend with. It would be a mighty large venture, risky."

Hubbard and Egtvedt tried to get the meeting back on track, hurrying through the rest of their presentation, but when they finished, there was an awkward silence. As they rode the elevator down, Egtvedt murmured, "It was a good try."[3]

Bill had trouble sleeping that night. Thoughts crowded his mind. The company was building a lot of planes for the military, and finally making money, but what Eddie Hubbard and Claire Egtvedt were proposing was something different, requiring a whole new business. They would need twenty-five new airplanes and experienced pilots, plus a string of ground crews operating from ten airfields between Chicago and San Francisco. He tossed and turned, keeping Bertha awake long after midnight. She could tell something was bothering him and eventually she propped herself up on her elbow and whispered, "What is on your mind, Bill?"[4]

"Maybe we'll bid for the Chicago to San Francisco route," he replied. He turned to face her. "What would you think of that?"

"Why not? It will develop a market for planes."

"It will be a hazardous thing [and] big."

They talked until morning. Bill got up early and by the time Egtvedt arrived at the plant at 7:30 there was already a message waiting for him. "Call Mr. Boeing right away. He's been trying to reach you for half an hour."[5]

When Egtvedt and Hubbard walked into Bill's office at the Hoge Building, they immediately noticed a change in his demeanor. He was excited and energized. "I want to talk some more about that proposition. It kept me awake all night."[6] They huddled around Bill's desk, laying out charts and graphs. Egtvedt described how well the Wasp was working in the F2B fighter and figured that if they modified the Model 40 to replace the Liberty with a Wasp, they could use the weight they saved to add seats for a couple of passengers.

They also wanted to take a gamble with their bid. When the Kelly Act had passed in 1925, airmail was still a novelty, and the volume of mail being moved was small. In order to break even, companies had to bid a high amount per pound. Hubbard said that during the several years he flew the Victoria mail, he had seen the volume more than double. He told Egtvedt and Boeing not to worry about the Post Office's estimate of volume but prepare the bid on an assumption of at least double the volume.

They looked at the numbers, estimated the cost of the planes and the pilots' salaries, and calculated the fuel consumption on the new Wasp engines. When they were done, they figured they could fly the mail from Chicago to San Francisco for $1.50 per pound for the first 1,000 miles and 15 cents per pound for each additional one hundred miles. They checked and double-checked the numbers. "Let's send them in," Bill announced.[7]

The bids were opened on January 15, 1927. Stout Air Services bid $2.64 per pound,[8] Western Air Express bid $2.24, and Boeing Air Transport, Bill's proposed new company, won the contract with its bid of $1.50. The failed bidders protested bitterly, claiming that "Boeing was out to wreck the whole airway system; that he could not operate safely on such an income."[9] The Post Office wasn't so confident either and required that Boeing post a $500,000 bond to guarantee his company's performance.

# 33. MR. BOEING GOES TO WASHINGTON
## WASHINGTON DC, 1927

News of the successful bid reached Bill on Sunday, January 16, and he decided that he and Bertha would take the train east to Washington to be on hand for the contract award. Bertha kept a meticulous diary of the trip.

Monday Jan 17, 1927 Onboard the Oriental Limited No 2 East Bound.
A hectic day attempting to do everything ... for our sudden trip. I accomplished most of it and here we are settled in the observation car stateroom. The ground was white [with snow] ... and all through the Cascades it was piled in massive [walls] beside the tracks.

Tuesday Jan 18
Early in the afternoon a telegram from George Tidmarsh [Boeing's representative in Washington D.C.] gave us a nasty shock. Apparently our low bid is in danger of being rejected on account of some failure on the part of the bonding company to properly record the power of attorney [for their]

representative in Washington D.C. ... Telegrams began to fly back and forth and though the situation looked serious, the last wires tonight seemed a little more encouraging.

Wednesday January 19th
We were awakened by the porter at 10:30 with a newspaper and a telegram from George, but it was merely saying that things looked a little brighter.

We crossed the continental divide last night ... and now we are down on the plains that stretch away for mile after mile after mile, white with snow and glittering under the sun, their interminable expanses broken only by the telephone and telegraph poles that follow the train track and an occasional grouping of bare desolate farm buildings.

More telegrams during the day ... in spite of our anxiety over the outcome, we have had to admit [that] the situation has made our trip anything but monotonous.

During the afternoon a strong wind blew and though the sky was clear ... the snow swirled as though we were in a blizzard. I spent my time with the time tables looking up stations we stop at long enough to send or receive telegrams.

Thursday January 20th
Breakfasted, read the St. Paul papers, smoked, wrote and slept, aroused by another telegram from George. No detailed news but his telegram sounded more calm and hopeful. The train followed the banks of the Mississippi River which was completely frozen over and in most of the sloughs we saw men at work cutting ice and loading it onto motor trucks that had ... driven out on to the ice.

Another telegram from George saying that no action would be taken by the Post Office Department until Bill's arrival, we feel that is a great help and we were so cheered up, that we had two highballs to celebrate. Arrived in Chicago ... and [rode] in Checker Cabs to the Drake. Our welcoming committee came up to our rooms and we had several scotch highballs and heard much news of our [old] friends.

Friday January 21st
We awoke to a typical grey murky disagreeable Chicago winter morning. While dressing, George Tidmarsh called Bill from Washington D.C. to tell him the wonderful news that the Solicitor of the Post Office had ruled that our bid could not be rejected. Bill was of course delighted beyond words and by way of celebration dashed off to [a tailor he knew in Chicago] to order some new clothes. [We took a cab] to the B and O station [and boarded] the Capital Limited on the last leg of our journey to Washington D.C. The car we were in was the nicest one I have ever seen. Steel of course and with [a] porcelain wash

basin instead of the usual metal ones we have had for ages. We rested, and then at seven we had a deluxe dinner with prairie chicken and champagne ... served in our stateroom by a cheerful, fat, smiling black waiter.

Saturday January 22nd
We arrived in Washington at 9 a.m. and were met by George Tidmarsh and drove over to the Carlton Hotel which is to be our home while in Washington. The trunks arrived and we bathed, unpacked and settled ourselves in the lovely rooms George had arranged.[1]

The next few days were spent sightseeing and going to the theater. On Thursday they went to a party where they met Ralph Williams, vice-chairman of the Republican Party, who promised Bill and Bertha that he would reach out to Wesley Jones, Washington's Republican senator, and try to arrange an opportunity to meet with President Coolidge.

Friday, January 28th
This has been a very thrilling and eventful day. Shortly after we wakened, our friend Mr. Williams phoned to say that he had called on the Postmaster General and from his talk, he felt that we were in a very good position. He said that he could tell us nothing definite, but that he had been told the award would be made within twenty four hours. He also told us that Mr. New (the Postmaster General) had heard so many of our competitors knocking us, that he had reached the point where every new knock was actually a boost for us.

The next exciting thing that happened was a call from Senator Jones's secretary saying that Senator Jones was sending a note down and that [Bill] was going to go and see President Coolidge at 12:30! The note arrived at 12 and to my surprise I saw that my name was included, so I dashed into my clothes and George drove us to the White House.

The man at the entrance told us we were supposed to go to the Executive Offices, so we walked down, and entered a large hallway filled with people. Bill presented his letter to a man at a desk, and we were told to take a seat. In a few minutes this man came dashing past saying "Everyone, step lively please. Single file. This way!" And at double quick we stepped through a small hallway into a room. As I stepped through the door, a hand shot out at my right – which I touched – a voice said "How do you do?" and the next thing I knew the crowd behind had pushed me across the room and out the door in to the same hallway we had entered [from.]

It was the funniest performance I've ever gone through, and Bill's description of [it] as a "Marathon" is not far from the truth. The momentary impression I got of the President was that he was taller than I had imagined him and very much lined in the face, ever so much older in appearance than his pictures show him to be. He stood with one hand behind his back and his right hand worked like a mechanical arm.

Later Mr. Williams phoned and asked Bill if he had enjoyed meeting the President, and when Bill told him about our visit [Williams] said, "I thought Jones would take you there personally!"

Bill said, "No he just sent a letter."

"The god damned fool!" Williams exclaimed.

It was an amusing experience anyway, and Bill and I got a tremendous amount of [laughter] from our first call on the president.[2]

A short while later they returned to the Carlton Hotel and Bill headed to the Capitol to meet with Senator Jones. George Tidmarsh also stopped by:

Less than ten minutes [later] the phone rang and George answered it. After the first few words, his whole expression changed and he fairly yelled into the phone, "You don't mean to say we've got it!?!?" With that [we all] jumped up and down around the room like crazy people. Bill returned soon afterwards and [was] bubbling over with joy.[3]

The next two days were spent celebrating. On Monday Bertha went to lunch with Ralph Williams, the vice-chairman of the Republican Party.

He was incensed at the lack of courtesy shown us by Jones. [He] went to Mr. Saunders, the President's secretary – and then finally to the President himself and was promised that we would get an invitation to attend the big reception given each winter by the President and Mrs. Coolidge. This one is for the Cabinet, Senators and Congressmen, and it is almost impossible to get an invitation, especially as late as this. So I was thrilled by the news.[4]

Frederick Rentschler had come down from Connecticut and Bill invited him to join him and Bertha for dinner in their rooms at the Carlton. Bill was in a delicate situation. He had based his low bid for the mail contract on being able to manufacture a fleet of twenty-five Model 40-A planes with the lightweight Pratt & Whitney Wasp engines. Since he was taking over the route on July 1, he would need to begin building planes right away, but Rentschler had just received an order for 200 Wasps from the U.S. Navy. The navy's order would take all of Pratt & Whitney's 1927 production run. Boeing wouldn't be able to get his hands on the desperately needed Wasps for at least a year, but he had to have his new mail planes ready to fly in five months.[5]

Over an elegant dinner of steak, oysters, and a good deal of rye whiskey, Boeing persuaded Rentschler to bump his order for twenty-five Wasps, at $6,000 apiece, ahead of the U.S. Navy's. Bertha reported in her diary, "Mr.

Rentschler is delighted to get an order for the 25 'Wasp' engines that are to go in the mail planes. Bill says it is the biggest single commercial order that has been given in this country."[6]

Tuesday, February 1 was given over to sleeping late and shopping. They spent the next day at Arlington, placing flowers on the graves of friends that had been lost in the Great War. "We drove up to the white marble amphitheater and walked around the colonnade ... out on a wide terrace to see the Grave of the Unknown Soldier," wrote Bertha.

> He is buried at the edge of the hill and from the steps where we stood, the city of Washington was spread out before us, beautiful in the soft warm sunlight across the gently flowing Potomac River and just in front of us, the simple white marble tomb of the "Unknown Soldier" with a sentry on guard pacing up and down, with his gun on his shoulder.[7]

# 34. Meeting the President Washington DC, 1927

Bertha's diary, Thursday, February 3:

> Bill and I dressed in our best bib and tucker and drove to the East Entrance of the Whitehouse ... We stepped out of our car and walked into a long corridor lined on either side by pigeonholes and booths to check wraps in. Then we passed on with the crowd, up some marble steps and to our right into the beautiful East Room with its huge crystal chandelier, its white walls, gold hangings and mirrors and mantel pieces ... were most beautifully decorated with ferns, roses and carnations ... we heard the fanfare of trumpets announcing that the President and Mrs. Coolidge were coming down the stairs. Immediately people began to line up and pass through ... the East Room ... [and] down the hall to the dining room, through the Green Room to the Blue Room where President and Mrs. Coolidge stood.
>
> In spite of the marvelous system of handling (or maybe I should say herding) the 2,000 guests, it took some time for us to reach the Blue Room.
>
> The President and Mrs. Coolidge received alone, two Secret Service men in evening clothes stood just back of them and the Naval and Military aides stood on either side and as we approached each in turn was asked his or her name by an aide, who turned and repeated it to the President.[1]

Having met the President and Mrs. Coolidge, Bill and Bertha returned to the East Room.

> We milled around and watched the crowd. Mr. Williams introduced ... Herbert Hoover (Secretary of Commerce.) We left about 10 and decided to go to Chanticleer's for some oysters, so off we went and heard that wonderful (jazz) music and ate oysters and drank a couple of drinks and danced and had a wonderful time.[2]

The next morning, Bertha packed for their departure. They didn't head straight back to Seattle but went up to Connecticut to spend time with the Rentschlers. During their visit Mr. Rentschler took Bill for a tour around the Pratt & Whitney factory. After Connecticut, the train journey back home was uneventful except for an emotional stop in Detroit to place flowers on the graves of Bill's mother, father, and sister.

When he got back to Seattle, Bill formed a new company, Boeing Air Transport (BAT). Philip Johnson was made president, Eddie Hubbard vice-president, Bill was chairman of the board, and the general manager was Claire Egtvedt.[3] The articles of incorporation for Boeing Air Transport were drawn up by William Allen, a fresh-faced twenty-six-year-old new hire at Donworth & Todd, who had just graduated from Harvard. By the time he was thirty, Allen would be on the Boeing board of directors, and he would eventually become one of the most important people ever to work at Boeing.

Egtvedt was anxious to get to work on the mail planes. There was a special feeling about this order; even if it was going to another Boeing business, it was still their first large civilian order.

\* \* \*

On the rainy morning of May 20, 1927, Charles Lindbergh, a twenty-five-year-old airmail pilot, took off from Roosevelt Field on Long Island in a tiny monoplane named the *Spirit of St. Louis* in an attempt to fly nonstop from New York to Paris. It had never been done before.

Lindbergh's departure was broadcast live via the new medium of radio, but since Lindbergh did not have his own radio, the broadcasters went silent as soon as he had flown out of view. The world held its collective breath. The next day, sharp-eyed spotters picked out his plane as he approached the coast of Ireland. Radio reports tracked him across Britain, then the English Channel, and finally, all the way to Paris, where a massive traffic jam of 150,000 cars surrounded Le Bourget Aerodrome.

Lindbergh landed at 10:22 p.m. on May 21. When he was safely on the ground, 100,000 admirers stormed past the outnumbered gendarmes and surrounded his plane, forcing him to shut off the engine to protect people from its spinning propeller. The fans pulled him from the cockpit and carried him triumphantly around the field on their shoulders.

Europe and America were swept up in Lindbergh hysteria. In *Only Yesterday*, Frederick Lewis Allen's account of the 1920s, he writes,

> Every record for mass excitement and mass enthusiasm ... was smashed during the next few weeks. Nothing seemed to matter ... but Lindbergh and his story. On the day the flight was completed the *Washington Star* sold 16,000 extra copies, the *St. Louis Post-Dispatch* 40,000 and the *New York Evening World* 114,000. Upon his return to the United States a single issue of a single Sunday paper contained one hundred columns of text and pictures devoted to him.[4]

Western Union delivered over 55,000 congratulatory telegrams to Lindbergh. New York City gave him a tickertape parade along Broadway on June 13. When it was over, the NYC Department of Sanitation swept up 1,800 tons of tickertape and confetti.

The world seemed to be crazy about aviation, and the timing for Boeing couldn't have been better. Three days after Lindbergh's parade, Boeing's first Model 40A flew from Seattle to the Boeing Air Transport headquarters in Salt Lake[5] and BAT announced that it would begin offering transcontinental passenger service from Chicago to San Francisco for $200 per person.[6] On June 21, Boeing allowed one of the new mail planes to be displayed at the Standard Furniture store in downtown Seattle. Over 10,000 people showed up to see it.[7]

\* \* \*

By late June most of the 40As were finished. Bill, Eddie Hubbard, and Phil Johnson flew an inspection tour of the route before meeting up with Bertha in San Francisco for the ceremony marking the official transfer of the airmail service from the government to Boeing Air Transport. Bertha's diary tells the story:

June 30th 1927, Thursday
This has been a most thrilling and exciting day. We were called at seven-thirty ... then as our bags were already, we sat on the front veranda [of the Hotel Del Monte] until the quaint old horse-powered station wagon came to take us to the 9:09 train.

Mr. Herron (a BAT Vice President) met us at the station and took us to the Palace Hotel where Bill and Col. Powers (Postmaster of San Francisco) were waiting. We had quite a discussion about what better be used to christen the *San Francisco*. (The 40A that would carry the first East bound mail.) I held out strongly for champagne but Mr. Herron urged using something like orange juice, as the ceremony was to be held on Army ground. It was left more or less undecided ... [but] Col. Powers ... insisted on taking out some champagne on the chance that we could use it.

Off we went, arriving at Crissy Field we found about one hundred people ... [and] two U.S. Mail trucks, draped with American Flags ... were drawn up in front of our plane. The *San Francisco* had the Stars and Stripes draped over [its] engine cowling.

Shortly after we reached the field, a plane came in ... and the cameras clicked and movies turned as Bill and Col. Powers shook hands and greeted the pilot of the last government plane ... At least he was supposed to be the [last] regular mail pilot, but the west bound plane was late and as the ceremony was all arranged, a mail plane was sent over from Concord with dummy sacks.

The Government pilot handed over his cap, goggles and gun to our pilot ... then we walked up some steps onto the mail trucks ... listened to a few short speeches ... [and] I broke a bottle of orange juice over the center hub of the propeller. Ten minutes later the engine started.[8]

The flight to Chicago wasn't scheduled until the next morning, so the newly christened *San Francisco* gave a couple of scenic flights over the city. Colonel Powers and Bertha went up together:

[We] got in and off we went. San Francisco is perfectly gorgeous from the air. The Golden Gate was hidden by fog and as we rose above it, it looked like a seething milk white sea that completely hid the ocean from us. We could see ... [the fog] pouring over the low hills around Mount Tamalpais like a huge water fall. The city was clear and the inner bay was a lovely blue expanse below us ... Just before we landed it was a little bumpy, but when we were way up, it was smooth and quiet and so very warm that we opened up our windows to get all the air we could.[9]

At 9:25 that evening, a BAT mail plane took off from Chicago with 251 pounds of mail as well as its first paying passenger: Jane Eads, a twenty-six-year-old reporter for the Chicago *Herald and Examiner*. She showed up for her flight in a knee-length business suit, a feather boa, and high-heeled shoes. Shutters clicked and flash bulbs popped as if she were a movie star as she stepped up on the wing and ducked to enter the cabin.

The Model 40A was a typical biplane with a slightly longer than normal fuselage and an open cockpit behind the wings. The passenger cabin was ahead of the cockpit, nestled between the wings. It had rectangular windows on each side and felt much like the interior of a small yacht. There were two side-by-side high-backed leather chairs and a small dome light in the ceiling.

According to Harold Mansfield, "[Jane Eads'] heart palpitated as she began her role of trail blazer in a new form of transcontinental travel."

> The pilot ... seemed far away. Alone with the night, behind the constant vibrant drone of the motor ... Jane found companionship for a time with a thin crescent moon beyond the left wing ... She wasn't sleepy ... this was fun.
>
> They passed over Des Moines without coming down ... a city without buildings, just strings of jewels. She found the leather-cushioned seats just large enough to curl up on, kitten fashion. It was peace.
>
> The landing jolts of Omaha awakened her. Reporters were there to interview her. "I could fly forever," said Jane. "I love it."[10]

At Omaha Jane transferred to a new plane and was back in the air by 1:45 a.m.

> Great flashes of lightning lit up the sky... The plane was being lifted and thrown about. Jane put her head on her knees and tried not to think about falling. Then it ended as suddenly as it had begun. There was a yellow fringe on the horizon ... which grew and flooded the earth with a golden glow. She remembered how a pilot had told her he never knew why the birds sang so sweetly until he saw his first dawn from the sky.
>
> Jane flew on past ... flats of the Great Salt Lake country, the forbidding waterless gulches of Nevada, the ultramarine blue of Lake Tahoe. Suddenly the yellow, razor-topped hills below her opened into San Francisco Bay. Twenty-three flying hours after leaving Chicago, Jane Eads put her foot on California soil, like an explorer who had discovered a new world: air transportation.[11]

# PART IV

# The Great Depression
# 1929-1933

# 35. NEAR DEATH!
## SPOKANE, 1927

Boeing Air Transport made money from its first day in business. By year's end it had moved 230,000 pounds of mail at $1.50 per pound and 525 passengers at $200 each for a gross income of over $450,000. But it almost all came to a shocking end in mid-September.

The Air Derby at Felts Field in Spokane included parachute exhibitions and acrobatic flying. The main event was the 120-mile "Great Race:" twelve laps around a 10-mile course between the army, navy, and marines. Boeing's FB-5 was to be flown by the navy; the army had the Curtiss XP-6A; and the marines were in the Curtiss F6C Hawk.

Bertha, along with Phil Johnson's wife Katie, came over to Spokane on the morning of September 20 by car, while Phil and Bill flew across later in the day in a BAT 40A. They met up at the elegant Davenport Hotel and checked into the State Suite, which they would share while in Spokane. Bertha declared that the suite was "perfectly magical."[1] Grace Hiscock had a room on the same floor and her husband, Thorp, was to arrive later.

The morning of the 21st began peacefully enough. The Boeing party slept in and had room service deliver a late breakfast of Bill's favorite, corned beef hash, at 10:30. When they were finished eating they joined Louis and Verus Davenport in the eleventh-floor owner's suite to share cocktails and watch a flight of twenty or thirty military biplanes fly in a V-shaped formation over the city, dropping leaflets promoting the Air Derby. It was a mild fall day with a crystal-clear blue sky.

At 1:30 Bill, Bertha, Grace, and the Johnsons headed to Felts Field. They parked and walked toward their seats. The air was full of the scent of dry grass, high-octane fuel, and popcorn. In the center of the front row of the grandstands was a "splendid box" reserved for the big Boeing party, who sat together chatting, laughing, and enjoying the pleasant September sun. In the corner of the Boeing box, there was a tall "pole with a loudspeaker on it."[2] Bertha recorded the day's events in her diary:

> It is impossible to go into detail over the things we saw, but I must say that the whole affair went off beautifully for two hours with planes arriving from [all around the country.] We saw parachute jumping, marvelous stunting by the Army in Curtiss Pursuits (the ones we call the *Curtiss – Boeing* type as they are an almost exact copy of our Pursuit).[3]

Her diary then suddenly takes an ominous turn when she mentions "the miraculous occurrence that will never be forgotten by anyone of the thousands of horrified witnesses ... Three Marine flyers in Curtiss [Hawks] were doing stunts in the effort to outdo the Army exhibition ... one, flown by Lt. Towner was too close to the ground."[4] The following is from the *Spokesman-Review*:

> Lieutenant Towner had just about completed a wonderful demonstration of stunt and formation flying with his associates from Quantico – Captain F.O. Rogers and Lieutenant L.H. Sanderson. They had looped together, rolled, flipped and twisted; they had done other maneuvers that made the grandstand crowd gasp and shudder.[5]

Back to Bertha:

> [He] did a half roll and flew up the field on [his] back, and in diving to right [him] self, crashed with a thunderous noise just a few hundred feet in front of the ... grandstand. Everyone thought of course that the pilot was killed – when to our utter amazement and horror we saw the plane zooming straight at us with the landing gear completely torn off and the lower right wing hanging.[6]

Like something out of an awful nightmare, the crippled plane flew at the Boeings' crowded box, shedding parts as it came. A wheel from the broken landing gear hit a man on the field, knocking him unconscious. "[The damaged plane] cleared the big pole with the loudspeaker (right beside us) by literally inches," wrote Bertha. "[We] were as close to death as [we] ever will be before we actually die."[7] The *Spokesman-Review* continued:

> Pilots in the crowd were frantic as it seemed impossible Towner could land the damaged plane without serious, if not fatal injury to himself. They watched him circle ... over the crowd and slowly drop the cripple on the field with a swoosh in a great cloud of black dust. In a moment, Towner stepped out uninjured but for scratches on his nose and forehead as mechanics, pilots and ambulances rushed to his assistance.[8]

Bill, Bertha, Grace, and the Johnsons were all shaken by how close Towner's plane had come to crashing into their box and were horrified at the thought that they all could have been killed. They didn't feel like staying for the rest of the air show, so they returned to the Davenport. Once they were in their suite, Bill mixed gin fizzes for everybody to help calm their nerves before heading down to dinner in the quiet, stately Palm Court restaurant. They discussed their harrowing day while listening to live jazz and enjoying Louis Davenport's famous crab salads, now known worldwide as "Crab Louie's."

The next day Bill took the Davenports up for a ride in his Model 40A. When they were back on the ground, Verus declared that she was "tremendously thrilled."[9] Later that afternoon, ten planes took part in the *Spokesman Review*'s "Winged Victory" air race. The army, flying their Curtiss XP6-As, took first and second place with a winning speed of 201.239 mph. The navy, in Boeing FB-5s, took third, fourth, fifth, and sixth.

Boeing's FB-5s might not have been as fast as the new Curtiss, but its Model 40A mail plane was causing a stir in the airmail business. Word was spreading about how lucrative the 40A was on the Chicago to San Francisco run. When one of Bill's competitors asked him how he could afford to fly the mail over the Rocky Mountains so cheaply and still make money, Bill quipped, "Because we're carrying mail over those mountains instead of radiators and water."[10]

In December 1927, Vern Gorst of Pacific Air Transport (PAT) approached Boeing to ask if he could buy a few 40As. PAT was running the Seattle-to-Los Angeles mail route via San Francisco with a fleet of Ryan M1 monoplanes (a plane that looked like the *Spirit of St. Louis*), and Gorst was losing money hand over fist. PAT had suffered three fatal crashes in its first year and was hanging on by a thread. Gorst had paid $3,700 apiece for his Ryans and couldn't believe that Boeing was asking $25,000 for his Model 40As.[11]

Gorst asked his banker to help him raise the money he would need to pay Boeing. After a thorough examination of the books, Gorst's banker said that he could not loan him the money for the new planes, but he had a better idea: Why didn't he sell PAT to Boeing? It was an idea that made sense to everyone. It would give Gorst enough money to settle his debts with cash left over to buy a Boeing seaplane to begin flying freight and passengers from Seattle to Alaska, and it would also allow BAT to begin flying out of Seattle to San Francisco.

On January 1, 1928, Bill Boeing handed Gorst a check for $94,000. With that move, Boeing took a huge step toward making BAT one of the nation's largest and most profitable air carriers.

# 36. PAINFUL PROGRESS
## NEBRASKA, 1928

Samuel Nesbit Craig was a busy man. At forty-two years old, he was president of Midland Barge and Treadwell Construction, an important business in the hard-working steel town of Midland, Pennsylvania. Tall and thin, with a high forehead and dark hair combed straight back, Craig was also deeply involved with the Shriners and Freemasons in his hometown of Beaver, a quaint, old-fashioned town of shade-dappled streets and wide front porches on the banks of the Ohio River. He and his wife had two sons and a daughter. He was fascinated by flying and for a while he had owned his own airplane, but he had given it up, possibly to devote more time to his growing young family.

On February 25, 1928 Craig left Beaver on a westbound train. His final destination was Los Angeles, where he had an important meeting early the next week. He was supposed to change trains in Chicago but he missed his connection. To avoid missing his meeting, he booked passage the next day on the BAT flight from Chicago to Los Angeles. It was a decision that would cost him his life.

Craig was alone in the passenger cabin of a Boeing 40A when it took off from Chicago on the evening of the 26th. The plane was flown by Frank Yeager, a veteran pilot with many years of experience. It was a cold and cloudy night; sixteen bags of mail were on board, weighing 800 pounds. Yeager was worried about ice forming on the plane's wings, so he flew well below the clouds to find warmer, drier air to keep his wings clear. They made their first stop at Iowa City on time. Omaha was the next scheduled stop, but as there was no mail heading to or from Omaha, Yeager elected to skip it and fly to North Platte.

Pilots navigated via dead reckoning, using a combination of compass coordinates and the airspeed indicator, along with an accurate clock to enable them to figure out how far they had traveled. There were also bright electric beacons every 25 miles along the airmail route to help the pilots stay on track. Yeager would still have to fly over the Omaha Airport, but he wouldn't waste the hour or so it took to land and take off again.

Ordinarily, when a mail pilot stopped he would receive a telegram from his next destination to warn him of the weather ahead. If a pilot was skipping a station, the station attendant was supposed to telegraph ahead to get the weather, and if there was a change for the worse, he was supposed to shoot red flares as the mail plane flew over, indicating to the pilot that he should stop and get the updated weather report.

The station master in Omaha got word from North Platte that there was a heavy storm moving east, and that Yeager was flying straight into it. He grabbed his flare gun and headed outside to warn the pilot. He heard the plane fly over and fired a flare, but the engine just kept droning. He fired a second flare. There was no change in the sound, and soon it had faded into the distance.

One hundred and twenty miles due west of Omaha, near the tiny village of Marquette, Yeager was flying at 95 mph about 100 feet above a flat sea of Nebraska corn. Visibility was poor and the wind picked up dramatically. The small plane was tossed up and down by fierce gusts. There was a small cluster of farmhouses and a row of cottonwood trees ahead. Yeager saw it at the last second and pulled back hard on the stick. The plane began to climb. Just then, a violent burst of wind slammed the plane down. Its propeller chewed into the tops of the cottonwoods, cutting through a five-inch branch. Then its left wing hit the trunk of the next tree, somersaulting the plane onto its back in a nearby corn field.

Yeager was thrown from the cockpit and knocked unconscious. Craig was trapped in the crushed cabin. The engine stopped turning and for just a moment there was an eerie silence as farmers from the nearby houses, awakened by the crash, rushed to the scene. They arrived just in time to see the fuel pouring from the plane's ruptured tanks explode in a fireball and engulf the cabin. Yeager, having regained consciousness but stunned and bleeding from a gash across his forehead, walked toward the farmers. Together, they tried in vain to reach the cabin and rescue Craig. The flames were too hot. Craig burned to death in the inferno. His time of death was recorded as 3:15 a.m., February 27. It was the first fatality in the history of Boeing Air Transport.[1]

Bill Boeing got the news that morning at the Hoge Building. He was stunned. His mind kept playing with all of the "what ifs." What if Yeager had seen the flare? What if the plane had stopped in Omaha? What if there had been some way of warning Yeager about the high winds he was flying into?

Grace and Thorp Hiscock were visiting from Yakima and staying at Aldarra. Before the accident, Bertha had invited Katie and Phil Johnson, who were also friends of the Hiscocks, to join them for dinner. Bill and Phil dominated the dinner conversation with a somber discussion of the accident.

"Everybody knew about the storm but the pilot," lamented Boeing. "If only we had some way to talk with our pilots when they are in the air."

"What's the matter with radio?" asked Hiscock.

Boeing shook his head, "I've put the problem up to all of the big radio companies in the country and they say it just can't be done."[2]

"It can too," Hiscock answered, adding, "With a two-way radio, they [the pilots] could get the weather from each other."[3]

"I wish I knew who could do it," Boeing said.

"I'll do it," Hiscock declared.[4]

Hiscock got to work immediately, bringing over a friend from Yakima named Bill Lawrenz. Behind the Oxbow factory on the Duwamish River, they built a primitive "radio shack" with a large experimental antenna. Hiscock was tall and lanky and Lawrenz short and stocky, so people around the plant began to refer to the pair as "Mutt and Jeff," after the comic-strip characters.

Hiscock outfitted a truck with a short-wave receiver and sent Lawrenz out to drive around Puget Sound while he broadcast from his shack behind the factory. Since they were primarily interested in voice transmission, and Hiscock couldn't talk and work on the transmitter at the same time, he bought an Electrola record player and eight 78-rpm records of the popular comedy duo Two Black Crows. Hiscock would broadcast the records nonstop while he tweaked his transmitter, and Lawrenz would drive all over western Washington to see if he could pick up the signal.

Early on, they ran into intense electrical interference from the spark plugs on the engine. This was the same problem that Bell Laboratories (one of the big radio companies that Bill had asked to research the problem) had struggled with. Bell attempted to solve the issue by shielding the receiver, but any shield that was effective enough to block the engine interference also blocked a good deal of the radio signal and limited the radio's range. Hiscock tackled the problem from the exact opposite end: he experimented with putting metal insulators on the spark plugs.

The idea worked like a charm and by August 16, 1928, Boeing was ready to test the new two-way radio. The *Seattle Post-Intelligencer* carried the story with a huge headline that screamed, "New Mystery Plane Phone To Be Tried Here." The article went on to say "With new equipment cloaked in Mystery, first test will be made today at Boeing Field of a new radio telephone system devised by the Boeing factory which is hoped, will enable a person flying to talk with another anywhere in the United States."[5]

The experiment worked and in a short while all BAT planes were equipped with two-way radios. By January 6, 1930 Hiscock had the shielded spark plugs patented.[6]

# 37. A MILLION ANGELS
## SEATTLE, 1928

When Boeing was building primarily amphibious planes, the Oxbow plant on the Duwamish River worked well. The finished planes could take off right from the river. If Boeing built a land-based plane, it need to be shipped in pieces to Sand Point for final assembly there, so the plane could take off from the grass field north of Seattle. By the late 1920s most of Boeing's new planes were land based, and it was becoming costly to ship them so far away.

At that same time King County began dredging and straightening the Duwamish River. A place was needed to dispose of all the dirt. A mile and a half southeast of Boeing's Oxbow plant was a ramshackle cluster of old farms. King County condemned the farms and 634 acres of adjacent land. They trucked in the dirt that had been dredged from the river and put 18 feet of fill over it all. It was then covered with crushed cinders and named Boeing Field.

On the hot summer day of July 26, 1928, 20,000 people showed up to watch the new airport being dedicated. There weren't any buildings yet, and just one long runway, but the new field, close to the Boeing plant and downtown Seattle, had tremendous potential. At 3 p.m. the Seattle Police Department band began playing patriotic music. It wrapped up with a rousing version of the Star-Spangled Banner as the American flag was raised above the field for the first time.[1] Politicians sweating in their three-piece suits made their way to the platform to give easily forgotten speeches. Finally it was Bill's turn to mount the flag-draped podium. He wasn't used to public speaking, but what he lacked in eloquence he made up for with earnestness. He pulled a speech from his coat pocket, unfolded it, and nervously began.

> This day is just about the happiest one of my life. It gives me a tremendous feeling of pleasure to be so honored.[2]

Bill began to relax.

> I have often wondered ... if I deserve it at all. I then realize that it has been brought about through the ... cooperation ... and efforts of my colleagues who have worked with me. So, my gratitude is not only expressed to the ... Board of County Commissioners ... but also to the entire personnel of the Boeing Airplane Company.[3]

The crowd was full of Boeing workers who applauded. Bill was warming up to his audience.

> Benjamin Franklin [was] in Paris in 1783 [and] witnessed man's first successful attempt to rise from the ground by balloon ... A gentleman standing near Franklin asked him what he conceived to be the use of the new invention. [Franklin] retorted, "What is the use of a newborn child."
>
> The Boeing Airplane Company was our newborn baby. There was a time that even with a father's care ... things did not go so well. It was a very colicky baby.[4]

Laughter rippled through the audience.

> The public ... did not want airplanes, and sustenance ... to nourish our youngster [didn't come.] It seemed so hopeless ... Now it has become a healthy kid and ... it should reach manhood. Benjamin Franklin's remarks can be construed as a prophecy ... with proper care and nourishment, a new baby has all kinds of possibilities. From the bottom of my heart, and with all sincerity I ... thank those who have ... honored me. It is the greatest possible reward I could receive for my faith and belief in aviation.[5]

Bill folded his speech and tucked it back into his coat pocket as the audience cheered and clapped. When the applause died down, five-year-old Bill Boeing Jr. came forward and pulled back the America flag that covered the front of the podium, revealing a bronze plaque with an eagle clutching a propeller in its talons and the name Boeing Field. Right on cue a flight of navy biplanes "came slanting over the field ... in their perfect wild-geese V," reported *The Seattle Daily Times,*

> flying in great circles; and then, dropping so near the field they almost skimmed it. Heads bent back and all the vast crowd stared at an air exhibit which began as a dignified tribute to the field and to the man for whom it is named, William Edward Boeing, and which ended in as spectacular a series of air stunts as ever ripped a crowd into cheers.[6]

Two weeks later, Bertha Boeing arrived at Boeing Field at 6:45 a.m. She and her sister Grace were going to fly to San Francisco. The passenger business was doing so well that Boeing had built their first airliner. It was a twelve-passenger, three-motor biplane called the Model 80.

Bertha loved to fly, and Bill felt that it would be good publicity for her to make this flight; if he had enough confidence to send his wife on an 800-mile trip in this plane, then anybody ought to believe that it was safe to travel in.

"There stood the big plane," wrote Bertha in her diary; "all silver except for the ... Boeing Air Transport insignia on its sides ... and its license number painted in black."

> The engines were running, and it was a matter of just a few moments to transfer our bags from our automobiles to the plane, shake hands with friends who had come to see us off and step into the passenger compartment.
>
> Waving gaily to our friends who had very wisely removed themselves as far as possible from the hurricane of dust raised by our propellers, we were off – moving swiftly down the runway faster and faster, until the very slight bumping ceased – and [we] knew we were in the air ... at 7:00 by the big

clock on the forward wall of the passenger cabin. The altimeter next to it registers 500 feet – then 1000 as we rise with the strength of a million angels and the noise of a million devils through the misty morning air. We're headed south over Puget Sound toward Tacoma. The Kent Valley below on our left is full of thick white fog, but we continue climbing and are now rising above the mist. The sky is clear and blue.

Passing Tacoma we're nearing 4000 feet … We have two of the windows open, as four of us are smoking, so it's a little more noisy, but even so, we can talk.

The Airspeed indicator needle points to 100 miles per hour, and we're sailing along more smoothly than a motor [car] on a paved highway. It's five minutes to eight and I think we're approaching the Columbia River because of a mass of … fog below, that stretches away like a turbulent river of milk [toward] the Pacific Ocean.

Erick Nelson [the pilot] has just walked back and handed me a slip of paper that says, '110 miles for the first hour.' I can see Mount Hood so we must be approaching [Vancouver and] our [first] landing field.

The engines are roaring as though someone has stepped on the accelerator and brake at the same time. We turn once more and dip down over a high railroad embankment along the edge of the river – and now we are headed straight for the runway passing low over a herd of cows, who pay no attention to us and at 8:20 we are standing still in front of the Pacific Air Transport hangar in Vancouver, Washington.[7]

Here, Bertha, whose nickname was Bee, inserted a short poem in her diary.

Plane Rhymes for the Air-Minded

I used to travel near and far
Along the road by motor car
Just like a busy ant I'd go
Through dust and mud, sedate and slow.

But now I hate a car or train,
I simply have to fly by plane
For I'm air-minded as you see
(Perhaps that's why the call me 'Bee').

So after all, as I'm a bee
And claim the rank of royalty
Three captive 'wasps' draw through the air
In queen-like style, my silver chair.

We're off again – leaving Vancouver at five minutes of ten. Good weather reported ahead. We are passing over Eugene at 11:05 and I can hardly believe it, for on March 28th of this year, it took me exactly ten hours driving by motor [car] to cover the distance between Seattle and Eugene that we have done today in two hours and forty-five minutes.

Here and there, far below us float stray clouds that look as if they are searching for a place to hide from the sun. I can see the famous Rouge River far below. The view is magnificent.

Grace, who has been very much worried for fear she would be air-sick, has asked me to write down in black and white the fact that she hasn't been. And to that I'm going to add that she's the first one to ask for lunch.

So we've suggested that Kenneth [Kenneth Knickerbocker – the director of passenger services for all BAT transcontinental flights] try out a few of his best service ideas on us and now he is busily engaged at the buffet getting out the bags and boxes that contain our luncheon ...

> Sing a song of picnics
> Ten thousand feet on high!
> Try hard boiled eggs and coffee
> While soaring through the sky.
>
> Sandwiches and cookies
> Oh! Almost anything
> Will have a perfect flavor
> When eaten on the wing.

Just here, over the mountains, there is a slight rise and fall to the plane which always reminds me of being in a rowboat. It is delightfully cool, and I'm just comfortably warm with my coat on. The upper wing makes a wonderful shade, and if it weren't for the fact that I'm afraid I'll miss something, I could go to sleep.

We are past the mountains and are flying straight down the Sacramento Valley. Slim [Boeing test pilot Harold T. "Slim" Lewis] wanted to know if I'd like to go forward. So here I am right up in the nose of the ship in a glass-enclosed sun porch, feeling exactly as though I am sitting in a gigantic bus with the whole valley as my avenue.

The immensity and beauty of the view before me is indescribable. One has a sensation of space and color and beauty that is impossible to define. The sun baked yellow floor of the valley lies directly below and, on either side, like ocean waves, the distant blue mountains seem about to come tumbling and rolling in beneath us. Patches of snow on the higher crests look like 'white caps' and add to the illusion.

San Francisco bay is in sight! ... We have a gorgeous view of it ... we've
come down to 7000 feet, but the fog bank hides the ocean, Grace and I have
put on our hats and everyone is beginning to tidy themselves up a bit. The
scene is very much the same as ... a transcontinental train nearing the end of
its run. Again, we have that curious sensation of trying to go up hill with all
the power and all the brakes on.

Another turn over the muddy, green wrinkled water of San Francisco Bay,
4:21 and we're 500 feet up. 4: 22 landed in Oakland ... I bet Bill is excited
and thrilled, but he has nothing on us.[8]

Bill had flown ahead the day before on a 40A and was waiting on the ground
for Bertha and the Model 80 to arrive.

# 38. PRATT & WHITNEY
## SEATTLE, 1928

One of most important decisions Bill ever made was to partner with Frederick
Rentschler. The decision was easy, not just because Rentschler had years of
experience in aviation, but also because Bill and Bertha had become close
friends with Rentschler and his wife, Faye. While Boeing was getting ready to
launch his new airmail service in the summer of 1927, he received a heartfelt
letter from Rentschler congratulating him and wishing him "every success in
this interesting venture."[1]

When the first week's mail service to San Francisco had proved to be
a success, and before Bill and Bertha returned to Seattle, Bertha went to
Chinatown and bought Faye Rentschler and her daughter Martha matching
silk kimonos.[2] The kimonos were sent to Connecticut along with a short note
from Bill that said, "Thank you very much for you kind letter ... we greatly
appreciate your good wishes for the future success of our new air transport
company."[3]

Boeing and Rentschler continued to correspond though the rest of 1927. A
simple line at the close of a letter from Rentschler to Boeing midway through
December started a chain of events that would end up dominating the world
of aviation for years to come.

There seems to be good reason to believe that the Aircraft Industry will
considerably expand during the next five years. As this expansion takes

place, it may become advisable for certain groups to work closely together. I believe we are all thinking along the same ... lines in regard to all of this. With kindest regards to Mrs. Boeing and yourself, F. B. Rentschler.[4]

Again, as it had done many times before, Conrad Westervelt's insightful statement came to Boeing's mind: "More and more one is forced to the conclusion that the engine is the machine." Rentschler and Pratt & Whitney clearly built the best aviation engines in the country. Throughout 1928 Boeing and Rentschler talked about the idea of merging their companies, and as the discussion evolved, they decided to bring in two more partners. The first was Chance Vought Corporation, which supplied the navy with fighters and trainers. It had been founded by Rentschler's good friend and Wright Aircraft alumnus, Chance Vought. The second was Hamilton Aero Manufacturing, which was best known for building propellers.

Now Bill needed to find a bank to handle the complex financial aspects of the giant merger. According to *The Seattle Daily Times*, Bill, along with his lawyer Elmer Todd and long-time friend William Calvert, brought together "many of the most prominent businessmen of this city" to create Pacific National Bank.[5] The bank opened on September 17, 1928, just three blocks north of Bill's office on Second Avenue.

On October 28, 1928, the Boeing Airplane Company, Boeing Air Transport, and Pacific Air Transport were merged to form a single new company named Boeing Airplane and Transportation Corporation, with an estimated value of $10 million.[6] The first board meeting for the new entity was held three days later in Bill's office in the Hoge Building. The main purpose of this merger was to combine the stock from the three different Boeing companies into stock from one single umbrella company that could be more easily merged with Pratt & Whitney. Pacific National Bank oversaw the complex process, essentially buying all the shares from the three previous companies and then selling back shares of the newly formed BATC.

On December 15, 1928 the merger of BATC with Pratt & Whitney began when Bill traded 9,190 shares of BATC stock for 318,076 shares of Pratt & Whitney.[7] Pratt & Whitney had its own favorite bank, First National City, of which Fredrick Rentschler's brother Gordon was a director. Large corporations rarely sell stock directly to the public; they sell to investment banks that buy all of the stock at once, at a slightly reduced rate, and then offer the stock to the open market. This process is called underwriting. It benefits corporations because it reduces their risks and lets them get their cash all at once, and it benefits the underwriters because they keep the profit on the difference between the reduced price they paid for stock and the higher rate on the open market. Underwriting the merger of these two huge companies would involve much more risk than Bill's Pacific National Bank was willing to take on by itself, so Pacific, acting as the lead bank, arranged a syndicate whereby part of the risk was underwritten by Rentschler's First National City Bank.

While Gordon Rentschler believed in his brother's new company, he had a responsibility to his shareholders to learn as much as he could about Boeing before investing millions of dollars in the merger. He sent one of his most trusted partners, Joseph Ripley, to Seattle to inspect the books and get to know the people involved.

Upon his arrival in Seattle, Ripley, who had been a few years behind Boeing at Yale, was given a tour of the factory by Boeing and Phil Johnson. Ripley was close in age to Johnson and had a similar disposition, and it quickly became clear that the two men were going to be good friends. Boeing asked Johnson to take Ripley to dinner and give him a tour of Seattle. Over dinner Johnson and Ripley formed a friendship that, twelve years later, would play a dramatic role in the future of the Boeing Company.

The massive merger was completed at Bill's office in the Hoge Building on the morning of December 22. Wind blew a heavy winter's rain against the eleventh-floor windows. The water that dripped down the glass obscured the view, but there was nothing to see besides gray clouds. When the final deal was signed, Bill was chairman of the board of the new behemoth, Frederick Rentschler was president, and Phil Johnson and Chance Vought were vice-presidents.

On January 31, 1929 notices ran in *The Seattle Daily Times* that the newly formed Boeing Airplane & Transportation Corporation would be changing its name to the United Aircraft & Transport Corporation (UATC).[8] And Boeing and Rentschler were just getting started. On July 1 they brought Stout Air Services on board, followed by Sikorsky Aviation and Standard Steel Propeller on September 1, and then Stearman Aircraft and Jack Northrop's Avion Corporation on October 1.[9]

The 1929 UATC stockholders' report, published at the end of the year, stated that "United is composed of fourteen important units, each of which has a record of successful performance and has contributed in a distinguished manner to the progress of aviation." The report went on to list United's key accomplishments and advantages:

– Millions of miles flying over its own routes.
 [The Model 40A] mail plane . . . now in wider use than any other type [of mail plane].
– Engines designed by United are used . . . by ninety per cent of the air transport lines operating in the United States.
– United Aircraft, through a subsidiary, owns and operates the longest regularly daily scheduled air mail line in the world. The length of the line

being two thousand miles. Another United mail line carries 27 percent of all the airmail transported in the United States.

– Another line, devoted exclusively to passengers, has carried its one hundred thousandth passenger and has flown nearly one million miles without a single injury to pilot or passenger.

– Almost fifty percent of the total volume of 1929 aeronautical exports from the United States . . . consist of United products.[10]

United was a financial success as well. Its first year's profit after paying shareholder dividends and federal taxes of over a million dollars was $8,304,781, equal to about $127 million in 2022.[11]

The United merger was so successful that Bill looked seriously at creating a similar gigantic monolith in the timber industry by merging fifteen different logging companies, lumber mills, and railways. Bill brought Joseph Ripley to Seattle to arrange financing for the merger through First National City Bank. The gigantic holding company would have been worth $51,558,000,[12] but the deal fell apart when Frederick Weyerhaeuser (also a Yale man like Boeing and Ripley) inexplicably withdrew from the project.[13] Bill's finances were flying high, but the rest of the world's economy was in shambles.

# 39. DEPRESSION
# 1929

Woodrow Wilson was a "starry eyed idealist"[1] who had led the nation through the horrors of the Great War in Europe and the Spanish Flu pandemic. He also had a vision of the United States at the head of the League of Nations bringing "the truth of justice and of liberty and of peace" to the rest of the world.[2]

By 1920, American voters were tired of Europe, tired of idealism and tired of the Democrats. Warren G. Harding, a "small government" Republican from Ohio, won the presidency in a landslide with over 60 percent of the popular vote. Harding's scandal-ridden administration came to an abrupt end when he died suddenly on August 2, 1923. He was replaced by Calvin Coolidge, who continued Harding's hands-off approach to U.S. business. The economy surged throughout the Roaring Twenties and Coolidge happily took credit for it. He was easily elected to four more years in 1924. By the time of the 1928 presidential election, the U.S. economy had grown 42 percent since the last days of the Wilson administration, and Herbert Hoover sailed to an easy victory, becoming the third Republican president in a row.

Under Republican leadership, the stock market soared. Stocks are supposed to represent the value of a company, and as the value of the company increases or decreases, the value of its stock should rise or fall to match. But in the 1920s things went haywire and stock prices soared so high that they could no longer be traced to the value of the company.

It was much easier to buy on margin then than it is now. Buying on margin meant that one didn't have to pay the full value of a stock in cash. An investor could put down as little as 10 percent. To buy $10,000 worth of stock, all one had to do was pay $1,000 to a broker, who would loan the rest. If the stock doubled to $20,000 (a common occurrence during the bull market of the 1920s) the investor could sell it, pay $9,000 plus interest to the broker, and walk away with $10,000 profit. This seemed like a magic money-making machine, and it was, as long as stock values kept going up.

Under Harding, Coolidge, and Hoover, the Dow Jones went from just about 100 on the day of Harding's election to 380 by September 1929. Prices on all types of stock quadrupled and shrewd investors became millionaires almost overnight. But the rise in prices didn't reflect an increase in the value of the companies; it was driven by more than a million margin speculators getting into the market, using more than $8 billion dollars of credit to out-bid each other for the available stocks.[3] Essentially, there was nothing backing up the inflated value of the stock.

The high-water mark of the Roaring Twenties was reached on September 3, 1929 when the Dow climbed to 381.2. Then prices began to fall, slowly at first. All through September pundits claimed it was just a natural correction, but the "correction" lasted into October, and brokers had to call for payment on the money they had loaned. The bubble finally burst: investors, desperate to sell in order to pay their debts, began to unload their inflated stocks, and with more sellers than buyers, prices dropped further. A vicious cycle started whereby the more the market dropped, the more margin calls were needed, which spurred more sales, which caused the market to drop more. Eventually investors panicked, flooding the market with sell orders. The biggest single loss came on Thursday, October 24, when the market lost 9 percent of its total value. It continued to spiral down for months, and by the time it bottomed out in 1932, the market was down 90 percent.

When investors couldn't sell their stocks for enough to cover their debts, they had no choice but to go bankrupt, which caused the banks underwriting the brokers' loans to fail too. Over 9,000 U.S. banks failed. When the banks failed, people who had money deposited with the bank lost it all. Life savings were wiped out, businesses had to close, and before long unemployment shot up to almost 25 percent. There was tremendous suffering throughout the country, and the newspapers began calling the crisis the Great Depression.

According to F. W. Allen's book, *Since Yesterday*:

> The disaster which had taken place may be summed up in a single statistic. In a few short weeks it had blown into thin air thirty billion dollars–a sum almost as great as the entire cost to the United States of its participation in the World War and nearly twice as great as the national debt.[4]

Congressional Democrats were frustrated and felt that government controls and financial safeguards could have protected the economy from this disaster. Their frustration turned to anger when Hoover refused to take any action to save the sinking economy, saying, "Economic depression cannot be cured by legislative action or executive pronouncement. Economic wounds must be healed by the action of the cells of the economic body – the producers and consumers themselves."[5]

The Democrats' anger turned to outright rage during the winter of 1930, when unemployment topped 15 million and Hoover refused to offer any assistance, instead saying, "This is not an issue as to whether people shall go hungry or cold in the United States. It is solely a question of the best method by which hunger and cold shall be prevented. [I believe that] the American People ... will maintain the spirit of charity and mutual self-help through voluntary giving."[6] The Democrats vowed that things would change when they got back in power.

During the first bleak February of the Great Depression, Dr. Richard O'Shea, who had delivered Bill Jr. and perhaps even saved Bertha's life after her difficult pregnancy, came to visit Bill and Bertha at Aldarra. Dr. O'Shea was deeply involved with Seattle's Children's Orthopedic Hospital, which specialized in treating sick and injured children, and he told the Boeings that the hospital was in a difficult position. It was unwilling to turn away patients, but the economic bust had left so many people destitute that many of the families bringing their sick children could not pay their bills. Bill and Bertha were moved by O'Shea's words and agreed to pay for any family that could not afford its child's treatment.

Bill wanted to make his donation anonymously, so he wrote a check to O'Shea for $50,000 (equivalent to $770,000 in 2022), and O'Shea gave the money to the hospital.[7] Each February, for the remainder of the Great Depression, O'Shea or another representative of the hospital would travel to Aldarra, sit down with Bill and Bertha, and tell them how much was needed; then Bill would write a check.

\* \* \*

Bill's uncle Ed, Marie's younger brother, held a special place in Bill's heart. When Bill had been a lonely twelve-year-old boy in Selig, Switzerland, Ed had made a point to write frequent letters to him, stuffing the envelopes full of exotic stamps for Bill's collection.

Ed's life had been difficult. He struggled with an "illogical melancholic condition."[8] Bill and his sister Caroline worked together to "look after his well-being and his comfort."[9] He lived near Caroline and her husband in Pasadena, and she paid him frequent visits. Bill visited less often, but he sent a monthly stipend to cover Ed's bills.[10]

In May 1930, Ed underwent prostate surgery, which left him "down the banks"[11] and "hysterical[ly] sobbing." Dr. William Elder, a specialist in "nervous and mental cases," examined Ed and determined that "the history of the last ten or twelve years definitely establishes ... Ed as a sufferer of a regularly returning periodic form of melancholia ... the scientific term is manic-depressive." In a June 24 letter to Bill, Caroline's husband, John Poole, worried that Caroline's frequent visits to Ed were "almost like suicide for her own delicately balanced nervous system. Every time she has returned completely unstrung [and] has spent an absolutely sleepless night."[12]

Bill and Poole worked together to arrange long-term care for Ed at the respected Las Encinas Sanatorium, in Pasadena. Ed refused to go, instead electing to enter a Christian Science care facility. Christian Science was a popular religion in the 1920s and '30s for those seeking healing through spiritual understanding.

There is a hereditary element to depression, and Uncle Ed's manic-depressive diagnosis sheds an interesting light on Marie's severe melancholy after Wilhelm's death, and perhaps even Bill's long period of inaction after Marie's death.

# 40. THE MONOMAIL
## SEATTLE, 1930

By 1930, the Kelly Act of 1925, which had spurred the birth of commercial aviation, was outdated. There were three major problems with it.

First, the act called for airlines to be paid strictly by the pound, without any minimum fee per flight. This meant that if there were only a few letters going to a specific destination, the planes still had to fly, so the airline would get paid next to nothing for a long, costly flight. It led to unscrupulous airmail carriers padding their weight by placing each individual letter into its own mail sack, and then making sure that each mail sack was secured with a heavy Post Office padlock. Walter F. Brown, the newly appointed postmaster general, felt it would be fairer to guarantee the carriers a minimum fee per flight to ensure that there would always be a certain volume of cargo capacity available to the Post Office.

The second flaw with the Kelly Act was that it called for bids every four years. This discouraged airlines from upgrading their equipment because no one wanted to spend hundreds of thousands of dollars on new planes if the contract would expire long before the planes were paid off. Postmaster Brown asked Congress for the authority to reward successful carries by converting their contracts into ten-year "route certificates."

The third flaw, and perhaps the most significant, was that when the Kelly Act was written there were not many mail planes capable of flying long distances, so the routes were short and choppy. For example, there wasn't a New York-to-Los Angeles route. Instead, there was a New York-to-Detroit route that connected to a different company that flew to Chicago, which then connected to a third company that flew to San Francisco, which finally connected to a fourth carrier that took the mail to Los Angeles. Brown figured that switching between so many carriers was slowing down the mail, raising costs, and keeping passengers from taking air travel seriously. He wanted the authority to combine routes as he saw fit. He explained his motivation:

> I could think of no other way to make the industry self-sustaining ... than to compel the air mail contractor to get some revenue from the public. Almost all of them were refusing to carry passengers and were depending almost wholly on the Post Office Department. We were getting nowhere in the development of airplanes. They were just using little, light open cockpit ships to move the mail ... but no progress in a broad sense was being made in the art.
>
> I believed that it was my duty to force them, if I could, under the law to get revenues from non-postal sources and obviously one was passengers.
>
> At any rate, I decided to take on the responsibility, and I used the power in the Watres Act ... to compel the carrying of passengers.[1]

Congress gave Brown everything he asked for, and the new Air Mail Act of 1930, also known as the McNary-Watres Act, became law on April 29, 1930. Lost in the complex language of the act was the addition of one single word that represented a simple and sensible idea, but triggered a chain of events that, in 1934, would lead to the breaking up of Boeing's mighty United Aircraft & Transport Corporation and the deaths of more than a dozen Army Air Corps pilots.

While the Kelly Act had awarded contracts to "the lowest bidder," the McNary-Watres Act would award contracts to "the lowest *responsible* bidder." "Responsible" was defined as a bidder "who has owned and operated an air transport service on a fixed daily schedule over a distance of not less than 250 miles and for a period of not less than six months prior to the advertisement for bids."[2]

Brown called a conference at Washington DC of all of the major players in the airmail system for the first week of May 1930. It was an opportunity to explain and discuss the new law and route consolidations, which were intended to speed up the mail and make it more cost effective for the government. Postmaster Brown requested that Phil Johnson come to the meeting to represent UATC.

Just before the conference started, UATC had bought National Air Transport which flew between Chicago and New York with a couple of stops in Ohio and Pennsylvania; United entered the conference, therefore, with the biggest airmail network in the nation. But UATC did not benefit from the conference; in fact, Phil Johnson estimated that the Watres Act could cost UATC as much as 40 percent of its mail volume.[3]

The southern routes were given to a holding company called Universal Air Lines, which would eventually become American Airlines. The central routes were awarded to another conglomerate called Transcontinental Air Transport, which would soon become Trans World Airlines (TWA). The only direct benefit that UATC saw from the conference was that it was awarded the Los Angeles-to-San Diego route as a logical extension of its existing Seattle-to-Los Angeles route.[4] All the existing airmail contracts within the UATC system were converted to ten-year route certificates. In the years ahead, this dry, stuffy conference would become known around the country as the "Spoils Conference."

According to UATC's 1929 annual report, even after the ravages of the stock market collapse, it ended the year with "$27 million in assets including, $15.9 million in cash or readily marketable securities."[5] This meant that for the first time in the history of the Boeing Company, it had enough money to experiment.

Airplane designs between 1919 and 1929 were basically just refinements of the fabric-covered biplanes that had dominated the skies during the Great War. When Boeing gave Claire Egtvedt a free hand to try something new in 1929, Egtvedt jumped at the opportunity. He began designing a revolutionary, all-metal mail plane powered by Pratt & Whitney's latest 575-hp Hornet engine. The streamlined low-winged monoplane also had a retractable landing gear and a top speed of 158 mph.

Midway through the design work on the plane, Egtvedt became ill, likely due to stress and overwork, and was rushed to hospital. Chief engineer Monty Monteith stepped up to take over the job. As part of Egtvedt's recuperation,

Bill Boeing sent him and his wife Evelyn on a trip to Europe to allow him time to rest and relax, but even on vacation, Egtvedt could not stop thinking about airplanes. He visited several factories in Germany and even had lunch with Willie Messerschmitt and Claude Dornier. During this friendly and civilized lunch, it would have been impossible to imagine that in a little over a decade, planes designed by Egtvedt, Messerschmitt, and Dornier would be engaged in fierce battles that would lead to the deaths of tens of thousands of young men.

Boeing's new all-metal mono-wing mail plane was dubbed the Monomail. Technologically it was a giant leap forward, but commercially it was a flop, and Boeing could not even sell one. A second version of the Monomail was built to carry six passengers. When the new passenger plane was tested at Boeing Field on a balmy day in August 1930, Bill took Bertha and Bill Jr. with him in the cozy passenger cabin. He wanted the world to know that he believed in his own products and trusted them with his entire family.

Bill Jr. had vivid memories of this first flight. He recalled the distinctive "new airplane" smell, a combination of new leather upholstery, lacquer, and aircraft exhaust. He held his mother's hand tight as the Pratt & Whitney Hornet began to growl and the plane accelerated down the runway. Once they were in the air, he looked out the windows and saw that the illusion of perspective had turned the ships on Puget Sound into toy boats, small enough to fit in his bathtub. More than anything else, he was aware that he came from an aviation family, and now, at the age of seven, he had finally been initiated into the world of flying.[6]

In the spring of 1930, Boeing's San Francisco district manager, Steve Stimpson, was flying from Reno to San Francisco in a Model 80. It was a rough trip and the copilot couldn't leave the cockpit, so Stimpson decided to lend a hand by passing out boxed lunches and pouring coffee for the ten or twelve passengers on the flight. Back at his office, he sent a letter to Seattle suggesting the airline consider adding a young male steward to the crew. Before he had even received an answer, a petite young woman named Ellen Church marched into his office. She was twenty-four years old and a little over five feet tall, with short, curly hair and an effervescent smile. She had a groundbreaking idea.

Church was a licensed pilot and wanted to fly for Boeing. Stimpson didn't think that the public was ready for a female airline pilot, and he told her so; but she wanted to fly no matter how, so she made a second offer.[7] Church was also a licensed nurse and she felt that having a nurse on board each flight to look after passengers who were afraid of flying would be a big benefit to Boeing. Stimpson was sold on that idea and sent a letter following up on his idea of adding a steward, suggesting using young nurses to act as stewardess instead:

Imagine the psychology of having young women as regular members of the crew. Imagine the national publicity we could get from it, and the tremendous effect it would have on the traveling public. Also imagine the value they would be to us not only in the neater and nicer method of serving food but looking for the passenger's welfare.[8]

Boeing agreed to a ninety-day trial. Church was hired as chief stewardess and asked to help Stimson find seven additional nurses who would be willing to join her. They were put on the Chicago-San Francisco run and earned $125 a month. With a full load of passengers, the Model 80s capacity for luggage, mail, and freight was only 898 pounds, so weight was critical, and the stewardesses weren't allowed to weigh any more than 115 pounds. After Church's first flight there were stewardesses on almost every commercial flight in the U.S.

# 41. THE SILENT QUEEN ON THE UPPER DECK QUEEN CHARLOTTE SOUND, 1930

On April 26, 1929, the Boeing Airplane Company bought a Canadian shipbuilding firm named Hoffar-Beeching in Vancouver, British Columbia. Jimmie Hoffar had been building ships since 1911, and he and his brother Henry had become fascinated with seaplanes. They had started building their own in 1917 from plans they had ordered out of a magazine.[1] Soon, along with orders for tugs and yachts, the Hoffars were getting orders for seaplanes.

In a move that echoes the development of Bill Boeing's famous Oxbow plant, Hoffar outfitted his 30,000-square-foot boatyard to build boats and planes. When Boeing bought the yard, he made plans to double its size and take on a lot more aircraft work. However, before the expansion could be finished, the Depression hit, and ship orders dropped from thirteen in 1928 to just one in 1930. The big yard was virtually empty. To keep its employees working, Bill ordered a brand-new, 125-foot, 289-ton luxury yacht. He named it *Taconite*, after his previous one.

The new *Taconite* cost more than $300,000 to build (about $4.5 million in 2022). It was designed for ten passengers with a ten-person crew and could cruise at 16 knots with a range of over 5,000 miles. It was furnished with an elegant teak interior and equipped with an onboard machine shop that could make or repair any part needed not only for its 200-hp Atlas diesel engine, but also for the four-passenger Boeing 204A flying boat, *Rover*, which accompanied the *Taconite* on most trips.

The *Taconite* was launched on June 11, 1930, and Bertha's sister Grace swung the Champagne bottle at the christening; since they were in Canada, beyond the reach of Prohibition, they used real Champagne. Sea trials were held two weeks later, and the first pleasure trip was taken on July 15. The *Taconite* sailed from Vancouver with Bill, Bertha, Bill Jr., and the Paschall boys on board, along with George Tidmarsh from Washington DC and Charles Beebe (the architect who designed the Hoge Building and Aldarra.) They headed north through the Strait of Georgia toward Queen Charlotte Sound.

The western coast of Canada boasts some of the most dramatic cruising waters in the world. Yachtsmen say that the area's steep-sided inlets rival the famous fjords of Norway for beauty. The plan was for the *Taconite* to stay north in Queen Charlotte Sound for much of July, while guests and supplies came up from Seattle on the flying boat.

The first plane up from Seattle, in mid-July, brought one of the world's most famous pilots, Amelia Earhart. Young, petite, and attractive, she was the "Female Lindbergh" and had flown the Atlantic in 1928. Like Lindbergh, she had written a best-selling book about her adventure and was a media darling. Bertha had met her in San Francisco, and they recognized each other as kindred spirits.

Earhart was in Seattle speaking to the Zonta Club, an international service club whose mission is "empowering women through service and advocacy." Earhart, a member of the Boston chapter, had given a well-received lecture on July 13. *The Seattle Daily Times* quoted her speech:

> The trouble nowadays, as it has been always, [is that] woman is bred to timidity. This is what handicaps them. From the time they first go to school, little girls are taught to be afraid of certain things. In reality, most women are just as strong as men. In fact, they could do most things as well as men if they were only educated the same way.[2]

Earhart caught up with the *Taconite* when it anchored at Vananda Cove, on Texada Island, about 120 miles north of Vancouver.

There was a rhythm to life aboard the *Taconite*. At first light, Bill and any hearty guest who felt like joining him, would dress, grab fishing poles, and slip into one of the work boats for an hour or two of fishing. Bill tried to return in time for breakfast, turning over whatever he caught to his French chef, Carlo, in the kitchen. For everyone else, the days began at 8:15 a.m., when gentle raps on their stateroom doors told them that breakfast was ready.

Breakfast typically started with orange juice (with or without gin) followed by toast, eggs, and muffins, and whatever seafood delicacy the chef could prepare with the results of yesterday's fishing expedition: often smoked salmon, fried trout, or maybe potted shrimp. Once breakfast was served, the *Taconite* would weigh anchor and head for the next destination.

While the boat was moving, guests could read, sunbathe, play cards, work on jigsaw puzzles (cut out of wood of course, never cardboard), or enjoy cocktails and conversations with friends while some of the most beautiful views in North America silently slipped past. Lunch was typically served at around 1 p.m., and the menu depended entirely on the results of Bill's early-morning expedition. Grilled salmon, fried cod, boiled shrimp, and oysters were always possibilities.

While lunch was being served, they would anchor, and when lunch was over, guests were welcome to use the small boats to fish or sightsee. Bill would often arrange for trips on the flying boat: maybe a flight to a pristine alpine lake to fish for trout or to the nearest town for shopping and newspapers. Bill was an excellent fisherman and even though the *Taconite*'s kitchen was well stocked, he enjoyed providing his guests with fresh salmon, halibut, or cod that he had caught with his own rod and reel. The *Taconite* crew also put crab and shrimp pots over the side as soon as they were anchored, so there was always the chance of a seafood delicacy prepared by Carlo.

A formal dinner was served at seven every evening. Men were expected to dress for dinner in suits and ties, and women wore dresses. After dinner, "toddies" were served while guests read, played bridge, or watched the sunset.

Amelia Earhart's arrival on the *Taconite* was like a warm southern breeze. She was beautiful, stylish, and just a bit of a rebel. There is a photograph of her standing next to Bill and Bertha on the bow of the yacht. Bill looks stiff in a gray suit and bowtie, Bertha is bundled against the wind in a heavy coat, with her hair wrapped in a scarf, and Earhart stands just ahead of them, proudly, in thin harem pants of a wild floral pattern, while the wind blows her short, boyish hair straight back.

The years since she had flown the Atlantic had been a whirlwind of action. Not just the flight itself, but the book, followed by the publicity tour, then speaking engagements across the country, and endless newspaper interviews. She was exhausted and enjoyed the quiet time on board the *Taconite*, away from the crowds. She spent much of her days alone on the upper deck, sleeping, reading, and sunbathing. George Tidmarsh wrote in the *Taconite* logbook at the end of his trip that one of the highlights for him had been "the silent Queen reading on the upper deck."[3]

Earhart would come back to visit Bill, Bertha, and the *Taconite* at least one more time. She had often promised to take Bertha flying, but somehow it never worked out. On her final visit, in 1937, just before she attempted to fly around the world, she gave Bertha a copy of her book *20 Hrs., 40 Min.*, and inscribed it, "With the hope that the broken flying engagement may someday be consummated, Amelia Earhart."[4] Earhart disappeared over the Pacific Ocean and never did get a chance to take Bertha flying.

The logbooks of the *Taconite* are full of famous guests, but they also show visits from Boeing's most trusted employees. The frequency with which Phil and Katie Johnson and Claire and Evelyn Egtvedt show up as summer guests onboard the yacht shows that Johnson and Egtvedt were not only Bill's employees, but also cherished friends. Clearly Bill believed that spending a summer morning watching the sun come up over the tree-lined fjords, or playing cards and sipping whiskey late into the night, went a long way toward forging the trust and commitment that was the hallmark of Boeing's management style.

\* \* \*

Something happened in Seattle in early July 1931 that seemed common and inconsequential at the time but would reshape American politics for years to come.

A forty-nine-year-old businessman named James A. Farley decided to travel to Seattle to attend the annual Benevolent and Protective Order of Elks Grand Lodge Convention. Farley was part owner of New York's General Builders Supply Corporation, and to any one of his 23,000 fellow Elks celebrating in Seattle, he was just another middle-aged businessman enjoying himself at the BPOE annual gathering. What none of the other Elks knew, however, was that Farley was deeply involved in Democratic politics and had used his trip to Seattle to visit eighteen states in nineteen days, lining up significant Democratic support for New York Governor Franklin Delano Roosevelt's bid for the presidency.[5]

Bill Boeing hadn't given Roosevelt much thought since he had blocked Westervelt's resignation from the navy back in 1916, but within three years Roosevelt would come to dominate almost every waking moment of Boeing's life.

# 42. DANGERS AT HOME
# 1932

Charles Lindbergh was the biggest celebrity in the United States. His marriage to Anne Morrow, the daughter of the ambassador to Mexico, was covered in the newspapers like it was a royal wedding. The nation rejoiced a year later when Anne gave birth to Charles Lindbergh Jr.

Anne was a writer, poet, and pilot. She and Lindbergh flew around the world together and she wrote magazine articles about their adventures. Their fairytale life came crashing down on the night of March 1, 1932, when the Lindberghs' nurse discovered that baby Charles was missing. Lindbergh rushed to the nursery and found a poorly written ransom note demanding $50,000 for the baby's safe return.

On April 2, Lindbergh paid the $50,000 ransom, but the baby wasn't returned, and on May 12, the infant's decaying body was found. Charles Lindbergh Jr. had been dead since the night of the kidnapping. There was widespread speculation that the kidnappers may have received help from of one of the Lindbergh servants. It would be years before an arrest would be made, but the sensational crime inspired copycats.

In mid-August 1932, Bertha Boeing was looking to hire a new housekeeper for Aldarra. There are no records of how many people she talked with, but when she interviewed a forty-nine-year-old woman from New York named Annie Vermilia, something didn't feel right. She mentioned it to Bill, who called in a favor with King County Sheriff Claude Bannick.

When Bannick ran a background check, he found out that Vermilia had a long record, going back to 1904 in New York. It included arrests for prostitution and larceny, and time spent in an insane asylum.[1] Bannick also found that Vermilia was posing as the older sister of a twenty-four-year-old mobster named John Thompson. According to Bannick's chief criminal detective, R. A. Allingham, "We have what we believe to be reliable information that this mob is in possession of a Thompson submachine gun."[2]

Apparently the plan was for Annie to go to work for the Boeings. Then she would give Thompson and his mob access to Aldarra, where they would kidnap Bill Jr. and hold him for ransom. Detective Allingham went on to say, "This man Thompson, I would say is the only man in the mob that could plan that which they intended to do, as he has quite an extensive criminal record, mostly robbery. The last sentence that he served was [for] robbery of the main office of Western Union in Seattle." Allingham also wrote, "It is rather surprising to the writer to learn that people of this class would resort to such extremes in crime, as we have regarded them as rather small timers."[3]

Bill's immediate concern was keeping nine-year-old Billy out of reach of any potential kidnappers. He already had a long summer cruise to Alaska planned on the *Taconite*, so he decided that Billy and his nanny, an energetic young woman named Lily Olson, whom Billy called "Ole," would stay on board the *Taconite* for as long as it would take him to figure out a more permanent solution.

At first Billy thought it was a grand adventure, a summer vacation that never seemed to end: fishing with his dad and half-brothers every day, playing card games with Ole and working jigsaw puzzles with his mother as the Alaskan

*Above left:* Wilhelm Böing, 1846-1889,
Bill Boeing's father. *Boeing family archives*

*Above right:* Marie Ortmann, 1862*-1910,
Bill Boeing's mother (see endnote 3,
chapter 1). *Boeing family archives*

*Right:* William Edward Boeing, Detroit,
Michigan, *c.* 1889. *Boeing family archives*

AT HOTEL DEL MONTE. AUG. 9. 1892.
C. W. J. JOHNSON, PHOTOGRAPHER, MONTEREY, CAL.

Bill and Caroline Boeing in a pony cart at Hotel Del Monte, Monterey, California, 1892.
*Boeing family archives*

Bill discovered his love for boats at the prestigious L'Institut Sillig Fréres on Lake Geneva.
Note the school's name on the banner on the left side of this photograph, taken in 1895.
*Boeing family archives*

*Above left:* Bill Boeing's first flight took place on board the Ballon Captif at the Geneva National Exhibition, 1896. *Boeing family archives*

*Above right:* Marie Boeing Owsley sitting on the lawn in front of Tiverton Estate, in Greenwood, Virginia, *c.* 1900. *Boeing family archives*

*Below:* Bill Boeing (back row, second from the right in the white hat) visiting his German aunts, uncles and cousins at the Kaiser Wilhelm Memorial, Dortmund, Germany, 1902. *Boeing family archives*

Bill arrives in Hoquiam, Washington, by steamship, autumn 1903. *Boeing family archives*

Bill and probably Daniel McCrimmon riding on a lumber train near Hoquiam, 1903. *Boeing family archives*

*Right:* William Edward Boeing, Seattle, Washington, *c.* 1908. *Boeing family archives*

*Below:* Heath Shipyard, 1911. This was after Bill had purchased the shipyard but before it was converted to airplane manufacturing. *The William E. Boeing Sr. Papers / The Museum of Flight*

*Left:* George Conrad Westervelt, 1879-1956. *Boeing Company archives*

*Below:* Bill Boeing learning to fly in Los Angeles, October 1914. The caption written in Bill's own hand says, "Los Angeles – 10/14 – First 35 min, flight. Quite bumpy good practice –" *The William E. Boeing Sr. Papers / The Museum of Flight*

Bill returns from his first test flight of the *Mallard*, June 15, 1916. The *Mallard* was built by Boeing and Westervelt. Even though the Boeing Airplane Company did not incorporate until 1917, this plane is considered to be the first Boeing plane and Bill its first pilot. *Boeing Company archives*

Claire Egtvedt, 1892-1975. *Museum of Flight archives*

*Above:* Phil Johnson
working on a Boeing Sea
Sled, 1891. *The Museum
of Flight Collection /
Biographical Files*

*Left:* The Boeing
Airplane Company, 1918.
*Boeing Company archives*

Bill Boeing (seated, far right) relaxing at the 1915 Bohemian Club Encampment. *Boeing family archives*

Bill returns from Vancouver with the first bag of international airmail on March 3, 1919. *Boeing Company archives*

Boeing's 19,000-square-foot mansion Aldarra on his 16-acre estate north of Seattle in the Highlands community. *Boeing family archives*

*Above left:* Bertha Marie Potter Paschall Boeing, 1891-1977. *Boeing family archives*

*Above right:* Bertha prepares to christen the Boeing Model 40A with a bottle of orange juice, June 30, 1927. *Boeing Company archives*

The *Taconite* on its way north toward Alaska, 1934. *Boeing family archives*

*Left to right:* Bill, Bertha and Amelia Earhart on board the *Taconite*, July 1934. *Boeing family archives*

*Above:* Bill Boeing and his son Billy on a fishing trip in Canada, 1934. Bill's Douglas Dolphin *Rover* sits behind them. *Boeing family archives*

*Left:* Bill Boeing relaxing on board the *Taconite*, 1934. *Boeing family archives*

*Above left:* Ten-year-old Bill Boeing Jr. and his nine-year-old cousin Jane Paschall arriving in Pebble Beach, California, to attend the Douglas School in 1933. *Boeing family archives*

*Above right:* Bill Boeing Jr. showing off his hula moves at the Halekulani Hotel, 1935. *Boeing family archives*

*Below:* Twenty thousand people showed up to celebrate the opening of Boeing Field on July 26, 1928. *Boeing Company archives*

*Above left:* A clearly unhappy Bill Boeing leaving room 357 of the Senate Office Building after being questioned by Senator Hugo Black during the Special Committee to Investigate Air and Ocean Mail Contracts, February 6, 1934. *Used with permission of Getty Images*

*Above right:* "Unemployed Johnson," former president of United Aircraft & Transport Corporation. Phil Johnson joined Bill Boeing for a fishing trip to Canada after they both resigned from their jobs in 1934. *Boeing family archives*

Bill Boeing lighting a campfire to cook freshly caught fish after his and Phil Johnson's resignations from Boeing in 1934. *Boeing family archives*

President Franklin D. Roosevelt makes a surprise visit to Boeing Plant 2 to see B-17s being built, September 22, 1942. *Roosevelt Presidential Library*

Bill and Bertha's Aldarra Farms, east of Seattle, near Fall City, 1944. *Boeing family archives*

*Above:* Bertha Boeing christens the new Dash 80 with real Champagne (no orange juice this time), while Boeing president William Allen looks on, May 15, 1954. *Boeing Company archives*

*Left:* Bill and Bertha Boeing pose in front of an apple tree on their farm in September 1956, a few days before Bill's death. *Boeing family archives*

scenery sailed by. When August's clear skies gave way to September's clouds, the yacht left Alaskan waters and cruised south through Queen Charlotte Sound, spending the rest of autumn closer to Vancouver. Eventually Cranston and Nat Jr. had to go back to school, and one day they flew away with Bertha on *Rover*.

The *Taconite* was equipped with one of Thorp Hiscock's two-way radio telephones, so Bill was able to stay on top of his business affairs while spending a great deal of time on board, but occasionally he took *Rover* back to Seattle for important meetings. When that happened, it was just Billy, Ole, and the crew left on board, and loneliness would settle over the *Taconite* like a chilly winter's fog.

Late in November, the yacht put into Vancouver and Bill flew up from Seattle to celebrate Billy's tenth birthday. (Bertha wasn't able to come because she had flown to Connecticut to visit an ailing relative.) At breakfast on the morning of November 22nd there was a pile of colorfully wrapped presents at Billy's place at the table.

There was a Mickey Mouse birthday card from the crew of the *Taconite*, and a telegram from Bertha wishing Billy a happy birthday, with a reminder to Bill to give him "ten hugs from me." The highlight of the gifts was a double-barreled shotgun from his parents and a promise that he could go duck hunting with his father. After breakfast, Ole gave Billy his morning lessons. When school was done, she took him to the zoo, where he enjoyed watching a big grizzly bear named Trotsky wrestle with two of its younger cage mates.

When Billy and Ole were back on board the *Taconite*, they headed out from Vancouver for a week-long cruise up the west coast of Vancouver Island. Ole and Billy were joined by Bill for dinner, which was followed by a chocolate birthday cake with ten candles. After blowing out the candles, Billy cut the cake himself and seemed to get a special thrill in serving big messy pieces to his father and Ole. The day was capped off with a "radio telephone" call from Bertha in Connecticut. As Billy was getting ready for bed, he told Ole that when he woke up that morning he had been missing his mother and had expected to feel lonely all day. "My tenth birthday turned out to be my best," he said.[4]

Two days later, Bill, Ole, and Billy celebrated a wet, rainy Thanksgiving Day alone on the boat. Father and son sat together listening to the University of Washington football game, which the Huskies lost to the undefeated USC Trojans, before sitting down to a traditional roast turkey dinner with all the trimmings.[5] They all put on a good face, but the isolation was beginning to wear everybody down.

When January's stiff wind and pelting rain came along, the *Taconite* put into port in Vancouver for the winter. Ole held school for Billy in the mornings, and after lunch she would take him to town to go to the movies or visit a toy store and sometimes the zoo. But after six months of living on board the *Taconite,* life had turned lonely. February was wet and cold. Even with Ole's constant attention, it was only natural that Billy began to feel forgotten and abandoned by his family. Years later a family friend would comment that Billy's time in seclusion led him to grow up "feeling that the world was made up of guards and suspicious strangers."[6]

In an ironic twist that echoed Bill's own childhood, he eventually sent Billy and his governess to live in the exclusive California community of Pebble Beach in Monterey, California, not far from the opulent Del Monte Hotel, where he, Caroline, and Maria had stayed in 1892. Bill felt that Pebble Beach, with its stone walls, wrought-iron gates, and guard houses, would be a safe place for Billy to relax and enjoy being a child. To make sure that he wasn't lonely, Bertha and her sister Grace sent Grace's precocious nine-year-old daughter Jane with Billy and Ole. Aside from being his cousin, Jane was one of Billy's closest friends, and her effervescent personality more than made up for Billy's reserved demeanor.

Life in Pebble Beach was "a dream come true" for the young cousins and a perfect antidote to the cold, lonely months cooped up on board the *Taconite.*[7] They and Ole lived in the Italian-style Villa Hebe, overlooking the 18th hole of the world-famous golf course, and they attended the Douglas School, which had only twenty-seven students. Billy was in fourth grade and Jane was in third. Billy reveled in the outdoor activities that the school offered. According to Jane's diary, "Monday was swimming, Tuesday was horseback riding, Wednesday was golf or tennis, Thursday, back to horseback riding, Friday was riflery [*sic*] or archery."[8] Saturday and Sunday were spent beachcombing, tide pooling, and playing on the beach with their pet dogs, which had accompanied Billy and Jane from Seattle.

Back in Seattle, under pressure from the King County Sheriff, the Thompson gang moved several times in the fall of 1932, and eventually Vermilia and Thompson moved east to New Jersey. Boeing hired additional security and tried not to dwell on the kidnapping threat until it literally came knocking on his door two years later.

# 43. FDR
# 1932

In January 1932, while visiting her fourteen-year-old son John at the Los Alamos Ranch School in New Mexico, Bill's younger sister Caroline was taken ill and admitted to hospital. She died on January 11.[1]

Caroline left behind a will that was as loving and generous as she was. It included a codicil that stated: "Good-bye, all my dear ones – my own, my family my friends … I am deeply grateful to many and go my way in peace and in perfect faith in the new life that awaits me … I leave … a benediction of love upon the hearts of all those dear to me and who have touched my life in passing with a handclasp of strength and love."[2] She left $15,000 to her maid (equivalent to $280,000 in 2022) and $10,000 each to a number of friends and relatives. Her final bequest was a new woodshop to "the boys of Los Alamos Ranch School," to be named after her late father.[3]

The exclusive private college-preparatory school for boys between the ages of twelve and eighteen was located on the starkly beautiful high plateau of northern New Mexico. It offered an educational program modeled after the Boy Scouts of America. Students were expected to wear scout-like uniforms to classes, earn merit badges, and spend much of their time outdoors. One of its most famous graduates was the writer Gore Vidal. A decade later the secluded Los Alamos Ranch School and the Wilhelm Böing shop would play a significant role in World War II.

With Caroline's death, Bill found himself the last of his generation There are no direct records of how this impacted him, but it must have led him to some serious introspection; shortly after his sister's death, Bill began to talk about fifty being the right age for him to retire.[4] But fifty was still a few years off, and in the meantime UATC continued to grow at an astounding rate, finishing 1931 with over $12 million profit and heading into 1932 with $47 million in available cash. This meant that Claire Egtvedt was able continue experimenting.

During his visit to Germany in 1929, Egtvedt had inspected Claude Dornier's twelve-engine DO-X flying boat and had become intrigued with the idea of using multiple engines on larger planes.[5] He pushed for an expanded version of the Monomail featuring two engines mounted on its wings, to be marketed to the U.S. Army as a long-range, high-speed bomber. The new bomber, named Model 214, made its first test flights on April 13, 1931, and it proved to be 5 mph faster than the fastest pursuit planes in the army's arsenal. The army designated the new plane the B-9 and immediately ordered seven of them with a promise of many more orders to come.

Egtvedt then turned his attention to building a high-speed, all-metal mono-wing pursuit plane that could keep up with the new Boeing bombers. The result was the extraordinarily fast and nimble P-26 "Peashooter," which had a top speed of 234 mph. The army ordered 151 of the planes at $14,009 each.

\* \* \*

During the last weekend of June 1932, the weather in Chicago was hot and humid, with temperatures approaching 90 degrees. A few minutes past 3 p.m. on Sunday the 26th, a massive thunderstorm rolled in from Lake Michigan and slammed the city. It rained 1.6 inches in just a few hours. The South Side took the brunt of the storm. Lightning knocked the steeple off the Union Avenue Methodist Church, and a house on Monroe Street was hit too. All across town, branches littered the streets and power lines were down. For the 20,000 Democrats visiting Chicago and waiting in their hotels for the presidential convention to start, the storm was a godsend. Temperatures dropped 16 degrees, and by bedtime, it was a reasonable 75 degrees.

It took all week and a bruising floor fight over rules before Roosevelt finally secured the nomination on July 1. Breaking with tradition, he flew to Chicago from New York and accepted the nomination in person. The new Chicago Stadium that the locals called "The Mad House on Madison" was built to hold 17,000 people, but more than 20,000 were in the stands and the fire marshals had turned away another 5,000. The ecstatic crowd roared its approval when FDR took to the microphone:

> Never before in modern history have the essential differences between the two major American parties stood out in such striking contrast as they do today. Republican leaders not only have failed in material things, they have failed in national vision, because in disaster they have held out no hope, they have pointed out no path for the people below to climb back to places of security and of safety in our American life ... I pledge you, I pledge myself, to a new deal for the American people.[6]

The battle lines were drawn. Roosevelt and the Democrats were laying the blame for the Great Depression squarely at the feet of Herbert Hoover and the Republicans. They were angry after being shut out of power for twelve years and frustrated at being unable to ease the pain of the Depression. They were going to get the presidency back, and they were going to hold the guilty accountable.

Roosevelt won in a landslide, claiming 42 states with 472 Electoral College votes to Hoover's 6 states and 59 electoral votes. At one point an angry man from Illinois addressed a letter to Hoover at the White House, telling him to "vote for Roosevelt and make it unanimous."[7]

In a move that would have a devastating impact on Bill Boeing, Roosevelt tapped James A. Farley, who had attended the Elks Convention in Seattle and was by his own admission "ignorant about air mail," to take over as postmaster general.[7] It was a position of absolute control over the U.S. airmail system and, consequently, the entire airline industry.

# 44. MODEL 247
# 1933

Claire Egtvedt was ready to take everything he had learned on the Monomail and B-9 bomber and use it to design a big, innovative, all-metal transport plane that could carry 400 pounds of mail and ten passengers.

The new plane, called the Boeing Model 247, would be a refinement of the twin-engine B-9 bomber. It had a fuselage that was widened to accommodate two rows of seats with an aisle between them, and it was insulated against cold and noise. The 247 featured an enclosed cockpit, retractable landing gear, a variable pitch propeller, and an autopilot. Thorp Hiscock contributed another brilliant invention: a unique system of rubber bladders that could be expanded with compressed air to knock ice off the wings as soon as it formed. The plane would be 70 mph faster than other planes of its size, and its unmatched standard of passenger comfort would make it universally recognized as the world's first modern airliner.

Egtvedt showed the design to the UATC board that now oversaw both Boeing and United. Its members were thrilled. In fact, they loved it so much that they made an uncharacteristic mistake, immediately ordering sixty planes for United at $68,000 apiece. This huge order would tie up Boeing's production line for at least two years.

At the same time, TWA wanted to place a multimillion-dollar order for a fleet of 247s. Egtvedt suggested building twenty planes for United, then twenty for TWA, and alternating between the two until both orders were complete, but the UATC board said no: all sixty United planes had to be completed before they could begin working on the TWA planes. In frustration, Jack Frye, president of TWA, took his millions of dollars and the 247 design specifications to Douglas Aircraft, asking Donald Douglas to build his own version. The result was the DC-1, which ultimately matured into the DC-3, 10,000 of which were sold over the next three decades.

As UATC grew, Bill Boeing, the board chair, had more business to look after and spent less time at the Oxbow factory. Phil Johnson moved to New York to become president of UATC, while Claire Egtvedt moved up to become president of Boeing Airplane Company.

February 8, 1933 was a clear cold day in Seattle, with temperatures expected to drop into the mid-teens overnight. The bare aluminum of the brand-new Model 247 shone brightly in the weak winter sun. At exactly 12 noon, the 247 prototype took off for the first time, banked smoothly to the west, and sailed out over Puget Sound toward the snow-capped Olympic Mountains. The new plane was more powerful, could climb higher and fly faster than anything Boeing had built before. According to Harold Mansfield, "This was Bill Boeing's hour of triumph."[1] But in Washington DC, trouble was brewing.

The Hoover administration was coming to an end. Postmaster General Walter Brown's plan for the airmail system seemed to be working well. In spite of the deepening Depression, the airline industry thrived, and by the end of 1932 it was "the one sector of the economy experiencing steady growth and profitability."[2] The number of airline employees had tripled since 1929, and the Post Office's average airmail cost per pound had dropped from $1.10 to $0.54 per mile. The air transport system, which in 1929 covered only 14,400 miles, now spanned 27,062 miles and carried more than 500,000 passengers per year.[3]

Louis Fulton, a twenty-nine-year-old reporter, was born and raised into the power circles of Washington DC. Using family connections, he gained juicy inside information that made his syndicated weekly column, *The Washington Sideshow*, one of the most popular items in William Randolph Hearst's Universal News Service. Fulton was charming and handsome, with slicked-back dark hair and a boyish grin that put people at ease during his interviews.

The first two weeks of February saw cold, drizzling rain in Washington. Headlights reflected off the wet pavement and car tires splashed through puddles as Fulton hurried to a DC speakeasy to meet with "an old friend" for a drink. The anonymous informant was a disgruntled former senior "officer" from the recently defunct Ludington Airline. (There is a good chance it was Eugene Vidal, who had been general manager of New Jersey-based Ludington Airlines and lived on the west side of DC, less than 2 miles from Fulton's home.)[4] In a quiet corner of the dark speakeasy, against the backdrop of clinking glasses and late-night jazz, Fulton's contact told a disturbing story about Ludington's meteoritic rise and sudden fall.

Founded in 1929 just before the Depression hit, Ludington was the brainchild of Eugene Vidal and Amelia Earhart. With financial backing from the wealthy Ludington brothers, the airline offered a shuttle service between Washington and New York, with inexpensive $25-per-person flights leaving every hour, on the hour. Ludington made money in its first year and became the first U.S. airline to be profitable without depending on a mail contract.

As the Depression deepened, travelers began opting for cheaper train services and Ludington's profits dropped. By 1932 it was losing money, and in a last-ditch effort to stay afloat, the company, which had never carried airmail and did not fly any farther south than Washington DC, bid 25 cents per mile on Commercial Air Mail contract #25, from New York to Miami.

Ludington's financial problems were well known, and with its bid coming in at less than half the actual cost of moving the mail, Brown worried that

Ludington could not perform the service at the quoted price. He ended up giving the contract to Eastern Airlines at 89 cents per mile. Ludington was soon faced with monstrous debts, and rather than declare bankruptcy, it sold to Eastern for pennies on the dollar.

What the mystery man from Ludington neglected to tell Fulton, or perhaps what Fulton conveniently forgot to include in his story (a habit that would soon earn him a reputation as "one of the most unprincipled journalists ever to practice the trade"),[5] was that Ludington's New York to DC route covered only 230 miles, which meant that the company did not qualify as a "responsible" bidder under the McNary-Watres Act.

Fulton salivated over the story. It was a muckraker's dream: a perfect example of government corruption forcing a worthy business to sell to a competitor. He went first to Hearst, who wasn't interested in publishing it, and then began to shop the story around town. In the politicized climate of Washington at the start of the Roosevelt administration, it did not take long to find an audience for a story that showed the Hoover administration in a negative light.

In a few days Fulton found what he was looking for in Hugo Black, a Democratic senator from Alabama with a slow Southern drawl that made one think of rocking chairs on a front porch on a soft summer night. Black often introduced himself as "a Clay County hillbilly," but in fact he was a brilliant lawyer with more than twenty years' experience at the bar.[6] He believed that the Depression had been caused by greedy Yankees and their Republican allies, and he was determined to put a stop to it.

Events moved fast. On February 25, 1933 Black introduced Senate Resolution 349 "to establish a special investigatory committee to inquire into the government's system of awarding air and ocean mail contracts."[7] The Senate, controlled by Democrats after years of Republican domination, passed the resolution quickly and appointed Black to head the committee.

Roosevelt's inauguration took place on the windswept Saturday afternoon of March 4. According to *The New York Times*, "100,000 of his countrymen saw Franklin Roosevelt swear on the ancient Bible of his Dutch fathers to cherish and defend his country. Five hundred thousand others saw his reassuringly confident smile as he rode from the Capitol to the White House at the head of a parade of 18,000 men and women."[8] Meanwhile, tens of millions of worried Americans clustered around their radios to listen to his inaugural address. All were moved by the confident, earnest way that he spoke:

> So, first of all, let me assert my firm belief that the only thing we have to fear is fear itself.

He outlined the causes of the Depression head on. When he used the phrase "rulers of the exchange," people knew he was talking about Wall Street investors and their Republican supporters:

> Yet our distress comes from no failure of substance. We are stricken by no plague of locusts ... Plenty is at our doorstep, but ... the rulers of the exchange of mankind's goods have failed, through their own stubbornness and their own incompetence, have admitted their failure, and abdicated ... They have no vision, and when there is no vision the people perish.

He ended with a promise: "The people of the United States have not failed. In their need they have registered a mandate that they want direct, vigorous action."[9]

Senator Black, listening to Roosevelt's call, considered himself to be an instrument of that "vigorous action" promised by the president.

# PART V

## The Break Up
## 1933-1938

# 45. NITROGLYCERIN
## CHESTERTON, 1933

The Model 247 entered service for United Air Transport on May 22, 1933. It soon proved to be everything Claire Egtvedt promised it would be. Passengers loved the luxurious new plane, and even with a couple of stops in Salt Lake and Chicago, it set a record for the fastest trip from San Francisco to New York on its first flight. Unfortunately, the UATC Board's short-sighted decision to build all sixty United 247s before building planes for other customers hampered sales. Only ten other planes were sold, including two that were delivered to Germany's Lufthansa Airlines.[1]

The 247 was a great plane for United. Costs went down, profits went up, and everything seemed headed in the right direction until the rainy night of October 10, 1933. A United 247D flying from Newark to Oakland had left Cleveland and was headed to Chicago with four passengers and three crewmembers on board. At 9:14 p.m. they were 1,000 feet above Chesterton, Indiana, traveling at almost 200 mph, when the plane suddenly exploded. The back third, with the rudder and stabilizer, was ripped off and tumbled to earth, throwing two of the passengers to their deaths. The rest of the plane burst into flames and dove into the ground alongside a gravel road a little over a mile from where the tail had landed. Some of the crew survived the crash, only to burn death in the fire.

At least a dozen people witnessed the tragedy and rushed to the crash site. It was horrific. According to the *New York Times*, "the first to reach the scene were driven back by sheets of flame with the screams of the dying in their ears."[2] A few would-be rescuers tried to throw buckets of water onto the flames, but it was hopeless.

News of the crash was telegraphed to United's Chicago office within about five minutes of it happening, and from there on to Boeing, Rentschler, Johnson, and Egtvedt. Stunned, they immediately dispatched a team from Chicago to figure out what had happened. The rest of the population read the story on the front pages of newspapers across America. The first reports stated that an engine had exploded and set one of the fuel tanks on fire. It was United's first passenger fatality.[3]

Something didn't seem right to United's crash team. Even if a motor had blown up and set a fuel tank on fire, there was no reason for the tail to have been blown off. The next day the nascent United States Bureau of Investigation (formed in response to the Lindbergh kidnapping, and soon to be renamed the Federal Bureau of Investigation) sent its top investigator, Melvin Purvis, to look into the accident. Purvis worked fast, and by October 14 he announced that the plane had been brought down by a nitroglycerine bomb on a timer.

> Our investigation convinced me that the tragedy resulted from an explosion somewhere in the region of the baggage compartment in the rear of the plane. Everything in front of the compartment was blown forward, everything behind was blown backward and things at the sides outward. The gasoline tanks, instead of being blown out, were crushed in, showing there was no explosion in them.[4]

The only thing Purvis was unable to tell Boeing was who had done it and why. He speculated that it could have been a murder, or suicide, or maybe the work of union activists or even anarchists, but he had no suspects and no hard evidence for any of his hunches. In early 1934, Melvin Purvis closed his investigation into the Chesterton bombing, and the case remains unsolved to this day.[5]

* * *

While the federal investigation of the 247 crash was in full swing, a separate investigation was being launched into Boeing's finances. On November 6, barely three weeks after Purvis's preliminary announcement on the cause of the crash, Bill received a three-page letter from A. G. Patterson, an investigator for Senator Black. It included thirty-nine questions about Boeing's finances. A few of them were easy to answer, for example:

> Question 1. Who were the original stockholders of Boeing Airplane Company?

Most, however, were long and complicated, reading like something from a final exam for a college accounting class.

> Question 4. If consideration other than cash was accepted as payment for stock, state fully what it was. If it consisted of airplanes or other property

describe it in detail, giving its age; previous use; purchase price; from who purchased and the value at which it was placed on the books.

And:

Question 6. Attach an itemized profit and loss statement for each year since the organization of the company (1916) including a showing in detail of the amount charged off each year as loss in sales of properties and giving details of stock losses in stocks held by the company.[6]

Of the thirty-nine detailed questions about Boeing's finances, only six mentioned anything about airmail. With a company the size of UATC, Patterson must surely have thought that Boeing would turn the questions over to a staff of accountants, but that was not the way Bill Boeing worked. He sat down with a thick pad of yellow ledger paper and a pencil and wrote fourteen pages of answers. If the answers involved math, Bill, like a schoolboy taking an exam, included handwritten worksheets showing the number of shares, their value, and long-hand multiplication or division to yield the final answer. The orderly columns of numbers written in neat handwriting are reminiscent of the stumpage estimates in the old red ledgers from Bill's logging days in Hoquiam. It's impossible to look at the pages and not be struck by his extraordinary aptitude with numbers. He could see and read numbers the way most people read words. A quick glance at an equation would yield an instant answer.

Once the answers were complete, the handwritten documents were handed over to a staff typist to make a clean, typed copy. Most of the answers were written in first person, for example, "I did own 20,810 shares of Preferred [stock]. At present time [I] own none."[7]

Bill hurried to get the complicated answers finished and sent off to Washington, but before he could finish, there was another letter from Patterson, with seventeen more questions about Boeing's finances. This time, not one of the questions mentioned airmail. Once more Bill sat down with his ledgers and a yellow pad and pencil and began writing his answers. On the 29th another letter from Patterson arrived with a dozen more questions about Boeing's finances. A short while later, a fourth letter came, asking about Bertha's finances.

Finally, on December 9, a sixty-page packet with detailed answers to all of Patterson's questions was sent from Seattle to Washington DC via registered airmail. The packet, no doubt having flown on one of Bill's own airmail planes, was signed for by Patterson at 3 p.m. on the afternoon of December 12.[8]

With the Patterson packet finished and dispatched, Bill and Bertha headed south to visit Bill Jr. in Pebble Beach for the Christmas holidays. Billy and

Jane were both taking part in the Douglas School Christmas pageant. They dressed as "Dutch twins" in traditional Dutch Voldendam costumes, complete with wooden shoes. The *San Francisco Examiner* ran a cute quarter-page photo of Billy and Jane in their costumes and identified them in the caption as "Miss Jane Hiscock and her cousin Master Billy Boeing."[9] Boeing would certainly have been proud to see the adorable photo of his son in the paper, but frustrated that all his efforts to keep his son's location a well-guarded secret were now wasted.

With the Patterson questions behind him, Bill was able to relax for a few days. He spent them strolling along the windswept beach with his son, probably telling him about his own visit to Monterey in 1892. On the morning of December 26, while still basking in the joy of his family holiday, Bill received a telegram from Patterson demanding that he "furnish by airmail names and amounts of all stock issued by Boeing Airplane, Boeing Air Transport, and Pacific Air Transport ..."[10] It would not be surprising if Bill was beginning to feel that he, rather than the system of awarding airmail contracts, was the subject of the investigation.

Some weeks later, on the afternoon of Saturday, January 27, Bill Boeing, having returned to Seattle, received a telegram from Hugo Black asking him to appear before his Senate Committee at 10 a.m. on Wednesday the 31st. The telegram ended with a not-so-subtle threat: "Please wire if you will attend without service of process."[11] In other words, "If you decline to testify, I will subpoena you."

# 46. MONEY MATTERS
# 1934

Bill wasn't able to get away from Seattle as quickly as Black requested, so his testimony was delayed until February 6. Before heading to Washington, Bill spent a lot of time talking with his lawyers and studying his sixty-page list of answers. The long document painted a fascinating financial history of the evolution of Bill's interest in aviation.

From the summer of 1915, when Bill began to dabble in aviation, to July 15, 1916, when Pacific Aero Products was incorporated, Bill spent $87,236 pursuing his hobby. This included $11,863 for his Martin TA, $27,745 on materials to build the two B&W float planes, $42,516 on real estate, including the Oxbow plant and the Lake Union hangar, and $5,110 for miscellaneous tools and equipment. When he incorporated Pacific Aero Products Company (the business that would eventually become Boeing Airplane Company), he gave all $87,237 in assets to the new company, plus $12,763 in cash, for a total startup investment of $100,000. Then he issued himself 1,000 shares of stock at $100 per share.

Throughout 1916 and 1917, Bill loaned the company $245,000 dollars, and on January 2, 1918 he exchanged the debt for 2,450 more shares of stock valued at $100 per share. Later in 1918, when the company needed cash to tool up to build the fifty Curtiss flying boats, Bill loaned another $95,000, which he converted to 950 shares of stock. He was the sole owner of the Boeing Airplane Company, with 3,950 shares of stock, except for a few shares he gave to employees as bonuses and rewards.

In 1927, when Bill decided to get into the airmail business, he created Boeing Air Transport. His lawyers at Donworth & Todd advised him to use a more traditional method of financing, so he bought 7,250 preferred shares of BAT stock at $100 per share, for a total investment of $725,000. At the same time, he bought 4,319 common shares. The difference between common and preferred shares is significant.

The buyer of common stock is in fact purchasing a share of the company. As the value of the company goes up (or down) the value of the stock follows. A common stock also comes with a vote in how the company should be run.

In some ways a preferred share is more like a loan to the company. The company is obligated to pay the buyer back on a predetermined schedule regardless of how the company is performing. When a preferred share has been fully paid back, it is "retired" and ceases to exist. The main advantage of a preferred share is that it can pay a higher dividend than common stock. The big disadvantage of a preferred share is that unlike common stock, it doesn't come with a vote.

Bill had purchased 7,250 preferred shares in his new company. He knew that if he ever took the company public, he would need some common stock and the votes that came with it. The best time to buy the common stock was before the company had started doing business and the stock has no "par value." This literally means the stock has no stated value and can legally be sold for whatever price an investor is willing to pay. Since Bill was the only investor, he could pay whatever he wanted. His records indicate that he planned to buy 4,319 shares for $12,500, about $2.90 per share. For reasons that have not been discovered, the reports that were sent to Patterson show that he only paid $259.14 ($.06 per share) for this stock. There was nothing illegal in Bill selling "no par value" shares to himself at $.06 each, but the fact that at the same time he paid $100 each for preferred shares was about to become a public relations nightmare.

Bill's final major purchase of aviation stock came in 1928, when he paid $91,860 for 921 shares of common stock in Pacific Air Transport. Between

1916 and 1929, Bill had spent $1,212,119 on three different aviation companies, and he owned a combined total of 9,190 shares of common stock in those three companies.

When Boeing and Pratt & Whitney merged in 1929, Bill exchanged his 9,190 shares for 318,067 shares of UATC. When UATC was offered for sale on the New York Stock Exchange on January 2, 1930, it opened at $97 per share, making Boeing's investment worth $30,852,549.[1]

Bill was proud of his accomplishments; for almost two decades he had chased his dreams. To his way of thinking, he had taken huge risks, but now he was reaping huge rewards. He felt like he was a shining example of the American dream. Unfortunately for Bill, FDR and Hugo Black did not agree.

# 47. SENATE HEARING WASHINGTON DC, 1934

Hugo Black was a tarnished choice of a leader for an investigation into another man's ethics. He had been an active member of the Ku Klux Klan for almost three years, joining in September 1923 and only resigning in July 1926 when he decided to run for governor of Alabama.[1] According to his biographer Roger Newman,

> [Black] marched in parades and attended and spoke at meetings around the state. Dressed in full Klan regalia, he addressed a local Klavern in Greensborough, seventy-five miles southwest of Birmingham, and attended meetings in Tuscaloosa.
>
> But the highlight of his Klankraft was initiating new members into the Invisible Empire.
>
> In a stately ritual the initiates pledged their allegiance to the United States, its Constitution and flag, the Klan and its members and the Christian creed. Crossed swords lay on the Bible on the altar. Black read the oath from the Kloran book. "I swear that I will most zealously and valiantly shield and preserve by any and all justifiable means and methods ... white supremacy"[2]

Like a good politician, Black knew that he needed to build support for his cause. A few days before the airmail hearings began, he made the following address on the radio:

The control of aviation ha[s] been ruthlessly taken away from men who could fly and bestowed upon bankers, brokers, promoters, and politicians, sitting in their inner offices, allotting among themselves the taxpayers' monies.[3]

Based on Louis Fulton's inflated allegations and Black's damning radio address, newspaper reporters and radio announcers began to refer to the Air Mail Conference of 1930 between Postmaster General Brown and top airline executives as "The Spoils Conference." On January 26, 1934, Black went to the White House to meet with Roosevelt. Over lunch he told the President that "the whole system of airmail contracts emanating from the 1930 split was fraudulent and completely illegal."[4]

Flying with Bertha to the hearings, Bill kept the answers to Patterson's questions open on his lap, hoping to find the words that would give Black what he was looking for and defuse the brewing scandal. Bill was uncomfortable speaking in public, and the idea of having to testify about his personal finances in front of a Senate hearing was terrifying.

At 10:30 on the bitterly cold morning of February 6, with his stomach in knots from anxiety, Bill entered room 357 of the Senate Office Building and took his seat, alone, at a small mahogany table across from an imposing panel of five senators. Each was attended by a scurrying team of aides. Just before the hearing started, Black leaned to one of his aides and drawled, "Tell the boys in the press to come in. The show is about to begin."[5] After banging a gavel to quiet the room, Black swore in Bill Boeing.

History is full of examples of capable men being thrown into unfamiliar circumstances and rising to the occasion; this was not going to be one of those times. Bill's testimony to the committee was a disaster. He was nervous and unsure of himself. His lawyers were not allowed to join him at the table, so they had advised him in advance to give vague, noncommittal answers like "maybe," because firm definite answers like "yes or no," if they turned out to be wrong, could lead to contempt of Congress charges.

· Black, with twenty years of courtroom experience, began to question Boeing, skillfully leading him through the various stock purchases. It didn't take long to come to the formation of Boeing Air Transport.*

Chairman Black: When was the Boeing Air Transport Company incorporated …? Boeing: That was so far back, I do not remember any dates, Mr. Chairman, so I have to look for them in the questionnaire. Chairman Black: Mr. Boeing, perhaps I might simply refresh your recollection and you may remember it. I will ask you if the Boeing Air Transport was not organized and you received 4,319 shares at a consideration of 6 cents a share, making a total payment for the stock of $259.14?

Boeing: That is not exactly right, because there was $750,000[6] paid by me for preferred stock as well.[7]

Black ignored Boeing's answer and went on with his questions.

Chairman Black: You did receive 4,319 shares of the common stock at 6 cents a share in the Boeing Air Transport, Inc., March 2, 1927, did you not for a total price of $259.14?
Boeing: Yes, sir.

Boeing wanted to explain that he had invested much more than just $259 in BAT. He had invested $750,000 and bought twenty-five Model 40A mail planes, opened ten airmail depots, and hired dozens of pilots and mechanics. He had taken a huge risk, but Black barreled on.

Chairman Black: Now I will ask you to look and see if it is not a fact that for this investment of $259.14, which brought you 4,319 shares of Boeing Airplane & Transport stock, you received in exchange therefor 54,972 shares of United Aircraft & Transport Corporation stock?
Boeing: Yes sir.
Chairman Black: That is the stock for which you paid 6 cents a share?
Boeing: That is not the whole truth: We had invested money that went into the operation to finance it at first – the $750,000 in cash.
Chairman Black: ... You made an annual report to the Post Office Department did you not – a sworn statement – as to how much stock was out on this Boeing Air Transport Company?
Boeing: I'm not sure, I don't know ... I presume we did, although I did not handle it.
Chairman Black: I have, for instance, the report for the fiscal year 1930 showing capital stock of $750 and showing net income for that year of $1,488,306.09 ... or a net profit of over 200,000 percent.
Boeing: Yes sir; but it is not that percentage of profit ... because there was $750,000.[8]

Black refused to acknowledge the existence of Boeing's $750,000 investment. The lone Republican on the committee, Senator White of Maine, tried to come to Bill's aid:

---

* The transcripts of the Proceedings of the Senate Special Committee to Investigate Ocean Mail and Air Mail Contracts take up more than a dozen bound volumes, with more than 10,000 pages. For brevity's sake, only short excerpts are used here, but caution has been taken to ensure that these excerpts accurately represent the proceedings.

Senator White: I want to get this clear. I do not know just what the reorganizations were, but even if there were only $750 of common capital stock in the structure at the time, it is not suggested is it that there was not a great deal more money than that that went into the concern ...

Chairman Black: I might state, to make it clear, that this is my understanding that there was originally $750 put into that company ... and that not a single dollar from any source on earth ever went in to increase the assets, except what came from the U.S. Government.[9]

The whole argument was so absurd that Bill couldn't even think of how to refute it.

Chairman Black: I believe you have already testified that for these 4,319 shares of stock that you bought from Boeing Air Transport Company ... for 6 cents a share – you received in exchange 54,972 shares of United Aircraft and Transportation Corporation ... which opened on the market at $97, making a total value of $5,332,384.00.[10]

Black smugly added, "Please multiply that so we will be sure that it is right."

Boeing: That is quite possible ... but I was not to blame for that ... you see I've been in the business 19 years ... [11]

Black went right on, leading Bill through the history of UATC stock prices, pointing out that eventually Bill had over 318,000 shares.

Chairman Black: You do know that the stock went up to $162 a share don't you?
Boeing: Yes sir.
Chairman Black: All right, what was the value of that stock [318,000 shares] that reached $162?
Boeing: Well, the figures submitted here, which are not my own figures at all, state that it was $51,528,312."[12]

As the words "fifty-one million" left his mouth, Boeing could hear chairs scraping the floor all across the committee room as reporters jumped to their feet and rushed out of the building in a race to file their shocking headline.

The $51,528,312 amount infuriated Bill. He knew that Black was well aware that the price of $162 per share was several years old and had come at the height of the 1920s bull market. The actual price of UATC stock on the day of the hearing was $35 per share, making the current value of Bill's stock only $11,132,660. Bill also knew that Black's questionnaire showed that he had invested nineteen years of his life and over a million dollars, but Black seemed to unfairly focus the entire hearing on the $259.14 he had paid for the common shares of BAT. Bill tried to defend himself:

Boeing: Aviation is a new thing and it has been developed over these years. I feel that the men that have gone into it and have hazarded what they have and contributed what they have to the development are entitled to remuneration. Mr. Chairman, I am going to go back to my life in aviation. It goes back over a period of 19 years.
Chairman Black: All right.
Boeing: I had over $800,000 in it.
Chairman Black: You had what?
Boeing: At one point I had over $800,000 in it.
Chairman Black: Your answers to the questionnaire do not show it, Mr. Boeing.[13]

Bill felt the hearing slipping away. He turned to his notes, looking for the reassuring numbers that would make sense of what Black was saying. He flipped from page to page, searching for answers that would support him. Black kept hammering away with numbers that Bill thought were wrong: they didn't make sense. For the first time ever, the numbers failed Bill; he couldn't find what he needed. Finally he just sat, staring down at his notes until Black said "That is all, you may be excused, Mr. Boeing."

Bill got to his feet slowly and left the room. Feeling exhausted and defeated, he couldn't help but ponder the fact that almost all the questions had been focused on his personal finances, and virtually none dealt with airmail contracts.

Evening newspapers across the nation ran banner headlines that portrayed Bill as an unscrupulous profiteer. In his hometown, *The Seattle Daily Times* ran bold red-ink headlines declaring "Boeing's Profit $51,000,000."[14] *The Seattle Star* said, "Boeing Made Millions From $259 Investment."[25] Worst was *The Brooklyn Daily Eagle*, which ran an editorial with the following viewpoint:

It is impossible to imagine a more sordid picture of looting of the taxpayer's money which ought to be considered treason as much as communicating with the enemy during times of war. In Russia at least they take men that do things like these out, stand them against a wall and shoot them.[16]

# 48. NOT WORTH A NICKEL
# 1934

The massive profits reported in the airmail hearings were "paper profits" that only represented the fluctuations in the stock prices and hadn't been realized by Boeing because he hadn't sold much of his stock, but FDR was furious by what he saw as the airmail carriers taking advantage of the government. On February 8, two days after the hearing, he instructed Postmaster General Farley to cancel all airmail contracts and turn the routes over to the Army Air Corps. Farley asked if he could have until June 1 to make the transition, but Roosevelt said no: he wanted the contracts canceled immediately.

Roosevelt and Farley knew that the army had flown the mail for the Post Office from 1918 to 1926 and didn't think there would be any problem in giving the routes back to the military. Their confidence was buoyed when, in a cabinet meeting on February 9, George H. Dern, the secretary of war, told Roosevelt that the nation's air forces would be ready to take over the airmail by February 19.

A deflated and demoralized Bill Boeing headed back to Seattle. He arrived at Aldarra late in the evening on February 12. Boeing's butler, Mr. Clark, helped carry Bill and Bertha's luggage up to their room. Once the luggage was put away, Clark nervously approached Boeing and told him that there was an important matter requiring immediate attention. An exhausted Boeing asked if it could wait until morning. Clark shook his head saying it couldn't, and handed Boeing a plain, rumpled envelope, explaining that it had been left anonymously on the front porch earlier in the day.

Bill silently took the envelope, removed a folded piece of inexpensive tan newsprint and read:

Seattle, Washington
February 12, 1934

Mr. W. E. Boeing

You are a very rich man and we need money, if you don't put $5,000.00, Five Thousand in a gunney [*sic*] sack and put it on a large rock next to the side walk in front of 149 Melrose North at 12 o'clock midnight Thursday Night Feb 15th 1934 we will handle you our way and if you try to cause us any trouble it will just be to bad for you so be a good sport and don't notify the cop for we are all armed and can handle any force you may bring

to avoid any trouble or loss of live leave the 5 thousand and go away and
be quiet,

The Roben Hood Gang [*sic*][1]

The letter's grammatical errors and spelling mistakes were similar to the ones
in the Lindbergh kidnapping note. Boeing could not have doubted that the
letter was genuine and written by someone who was poor and desperate
enough to do anything. He wondered what new hell the extortionist was
threatening. Would it be a fire at the Oxbow plant, or another bomb in a
plane? Billy Jr. was still hiding in the gated confines of Pebble Beach, but what
if someone had seen the photo in the *Examiner*?

Coming on top of his humiliation by Black in the Senate hearings and his
public excoriation on the front pages of the nation's newspapers, the extortion
letter seems to have triggered a period of deep introspection in Bill. He had
often said that he would retire at fifty. He was now fifty-two and had more
money than he could possibly need. He had been motivated by the belief
that he was building something new and wonderful: "We are embarking as
pioneers upon a new science and industry," he had said.[2] And he had sincerely
believed that he was helping create something that the world wanted and
needed. But now his own government was telling him that what he had done
was wrong, perhaps even illegal. Newspapers were calling him a traitor and
suggesting that he "be put up against a wall and shot." Common criminals
were skulking around his home and threatening to harm him or his family.
Clearly something had to change.

While King County Sheriff Claude Bannick searched for the "Roben Hood
Gang" and Bill Boeing pondered his future, the army moved ahead with its
plans to take over the airmail. It didn't start well. On Saturday, February 17,
the front page of *The Seattle Daily Times* ran the headline "3 Army Airmen
Killed On Mail Test Flights."

> Salt Lake City-to-Seattle Plane Crashes in Idaho: Two Die in Utah Mountain
> Canyon: Visibility Poor.
>
> Tragedy today marked the entrance of the United States Army into the
> air mail service, with three Army flyers dead as the result of two airplane
> crashes in the rugged intermountain country last night.
>
> One of the pilots was burned to death when his craft plummeted to earth
> near Twin Falls, Idaho. The bodies of the other two were found in the cockpit
> of their plane, down in Weber Canyon, sixty miles east of Salt Lake City ...[3]

Two days later the Army Air Corps started actually flying the mail, and things
didn't get any better. "First Army Airmail Plane Crashed in Hedge at Airport,"
read one newspaper headline.

An hour and a half after leaving Atlanta with the Army's first airmail plane, Lieut. E.T.Gorman of Mitchell Field crashed at the Greenville Airport after attempting five landings.[4]

Three days later there were seven more airmail crashes, including two that were fatal. One of the fatalities was the stuff of nightmares. Lieutenant Durwood Lowry was flying a Curtiss Falcon biplane from Chicago to Toledo. He ran into engine trouble in a blinding snowstorm a few minutes before 5 a.m. over Deshler, Ohio. He attempted to bail out, but his parachute got caught on the tail of the plane and he was dragged to his death behind the plane as it crashed into a wooded area. The Associated Press reported that the plane bounced across the ground before coming to rest and that "Lowry's body was torn to bits."[5]

Roosevelt, Farley, and much of the country were caught off guard by the army's inability to fly the mail safely. A lot of things had changed since 1926, when the army had last handled the job. First, the army pilots in the 1920s were veterans of the Great War, with thousands of hours of flying experience in all kinds of weather. In the 1930s, the Army Air Corps, like the rest of the country, was digging out of the Depression and didn't have the money to fly more than a few hours a week. The training the army had given most of its pilots had been in nimble one-seater fighters in combat scenarios. The young pilots didn't have much experience with the all-weather, cross-country flying that the mail required. Second, in the 1920s, the mail routes had been much shorter, covering only about 12,000 miles. By 1934 the routes had grown to 27,000 miles and covered every type of terrain imaginable. Third, and most important, the majority of the 1920 routes had been daytime routes; by 1934 almost all the routes required night flying.

When Eddie Rickenbacker, America's number one combat ace, heard about the army's plan to take over the mail flights, he called it "legalized murder."[6] United and TWA had spent millions of dollars in developing modern mail planes with enclosed cockpits, twin engines, deicing boots, two-way radios, and copilots. The new planes also had modern electronic equipment like artificial horizons, directional gyroscopes, and radio direction finders to help the pilots know where they were in the night sky. The army took inexperienced pilots, placed them in biplanes with no radios or navigational equipment, and asked them to fly the same routes. By March 11, after less than three weeks of flying, the Army Air Corps had suffered sixty-six crashes and thirteen fatalities.

Roosevelt and Black agreed to give the airmail contracts back to the airlines, but they insisted that none of the companies that had had taken part in the "Spoils Conference" could bid on the new contracts. In a face-saving move, Farley convinced Black to write the new law in a way that allowed the old companies simply to change their names to become eligible to bid. So United

Air Transport became United Air Lines Transport Company; Transcontinental & Western Air became Trans World Airlines; and Eastern Air Transport became Eastern Airlines.

When the new bids were opened on May 4, 1934, United Air Lines had won back most of the same routes it had flown when it was called United Air Transport. Before the Black hearing, it had carried the mail across the continent from Newark to Oakland for 42.65 cents per pound. The new rate was 38 cents. The Seattle to San Diego rate dropped from 44 cents per pound to 39.5 cents. The United rate from Salt Lake City to Seattle went from 44.33 cents to 39.5 cents.[7] Roosevelt and Black made much of the rate reductions, claiming that over the years the reduction would add up to millions of dollars, but to the fliers who had risked their lives in the army's clumsy handling of the airmail service, the average rate reduction of less than five cents per pound caused a few pilots to quip that, to the government, their lives weren't worth a nickel.

# 49. PROJECT A
# SEATTLE, 1934

The news that United had won back many of its airmail routes was carried on the front page of the *Seattle Post-Intelligencer* on May 4, but that wasn't the only good news for Bill Boeing. Next to the United story was a headline announcing "Boeing Given Guggenheim Aviation Award."

The Guggenheim family had made its fortune in mining and was one of the wealthiest families in the United States. Daniel Guggenheim was enthralled with aviation. In 1928 he created the Daniel Guggenheim Medal with the intention that it would be the world's most prestigious aviation award, honoring a lifetime of work in aeronautics. The first winner had been Orville Wright, and successive winners were a who's who of early aviation. The winner for each year was chosen, in part, by a vote of the previous winners, and it was decided that Bill Boeing was going to be the sixth recipient.

The medal was to be awarded to Boeing at a dinner in San Francisco on June 20, 1934, and the timing seemed to be an attempt to soothe the hurt that Bill must have felt after his humiliation by Black. The famous award must have made Boeing feel proud, but he was still reevaluating his role in aviation and had not yet decided if he was going to stay on as the chairman of United Aircraft and Transport Corporation.[1]

A few weeks after Bill had testified at Senator Hugo Black's hearings, Claire Egtvedt received a surprising package from Brigadier-General Conger Pratt of the Army Air Corps. It contained details of the Air Corps' secret "Project A," with a request for Boeing to design a new long-range bomber. There wasn't any money to build the new plane, at least not right away, but the idea was to see what the engineers thought the outer limits of bomber capabilities were.

Pratt asked for a plane that seemed impossible: it needed to have a range of 5,000 miles, with a wingspan of 150 feet and a gross weight of 60,000 pounds. Boeing's biggest bomber was the B-9, with a range of 1,250 miles, a wingspan of 76 feet, and a weight of just 13,000 pounds.

Egtvedt put a team of his best engineers on the secret project. Boeing assigned this giant plane model number 294. Before long, the engineers settled on what was essentially a gigantic version of the Model 247, powered by four massive W-24 Allison engines. It would carry 8,000 pounds of bombs, with wings so thick that a flight engineer could crawl through them and service all the engines while the plane was in flight.

Thorp Hiscock was now in charge of technological development at United Air Lines. He believed that United needed a new transport plane, something bigger than the twin-engine 247. Egtvedt told Hiscock about the gigantic Project A bomber. Hiscock said that it was much too big for United's needs but suggested something halfway in between, with perhaps a 100-foot wingspan and four Pratt & Whitney Hornet engines. Egtvedt liked the idea.

On March 17, a few days after this significant conversation, which laid the groundwork for the plane that would eventually become the vaunted B-17, Thorp suffered a massive heart attack and died.[2] He was only forty-two. Grace was heartbroken, and the entire Boeing family was plunged into mourning.

In early May, the Air Corps announced a new competition for a mid-sized, multi-engine bomber.[3] Claire and Evelyn Egtvedt had been vacationing in California when the announcement was made. "We ... drove straight through," wrote Evelyn. "'Why' I asked, 'Do we have to drive so fast?' [Egtvedt] said, 'I want to get home in order to attend a meeting with Mr. Boeing.'"[4]

In the past, whenever the army had talked about multi-engine bombers, it was assumed that it meant two engines, but that limit wasn't written into the requirements. Boeing decided to roll the dice and see if the Air Corps would consider the mid-sized, four-engine plane with the 100-foot wingspan that Thorp had suggested before he died. Boeing assigned the new project model number 299. Its wingspan would be 103 feet 9 inches, and it would be designed to carry about 2,400 pounds of freight or bombs.

The preliminary drawings for the Project A bomber were completed, and the Air Corps named it the XB-15.[5] On June 28th the army gave Boeing approval to begin making plywood mockups of the gigantic plane. If all went well, actual construction was scheduled to begin sometime before the end of summer.

Throughout spring, while Boeing was designing its new planes and United Air Lines was working on getting its mail routes back in order, Senator Black's new Air Mail Act of 1934 was working its way through Congress. There was an aspect of the bill that seemed like a personal attack on Bill. It read:

> After December 31, 1934 it shall be unlawful for any person holding an air-mail contract to buy, acquire, hold, own, or control, directly or indirectly, any shares of stock or other interest in any other partnership, association, or corporation engaged directly or indirectly in any phase of the aviation industry... whether such buying, acquisition, holding, ownership, or control is done directly, or is accomplished indirectly, through an agent, subsidiary, associate, affiliate, or by any other device whatsoever ...[6]

If the bill passed, no company involved in any aspect of airplane manufacturing would be allowed to bid on an airmail contract. There was only one solution: Airmail was such a lucrative business that UATC would have to be broken up.

On May 24, Phil Johnson sent a letter to all of UATC stockholders detailing the company's plans to reorganize if the bill passed. The letter made it onto the front page of newspapers across the country.

> Philip G. Johnson, president of United Aircraft & Transport Corporation, in his communication to the stockholders, says: 'If the great air transport system which this corporation has created and developed is to be preserved for the stockholder, it appears to be essential, in view of the Government's expressed attitude, that the system shall become wholly independent of [its] equipment manufacturing affiliates. Reorganization is therefore, not so much a matter of choice as of necessity, and the sole consideration should be not whether a reorganization is desirable for on that point argument seems to be precluded, but how it can be best effected in the interest of the stockholders.'[7]

Johnson went on to explain that United Aircraft & Transportation Corporation would be divided into to three separate companies: All airline and airmail operations would be taken over by the new United Air Lines Transport Corporation, headed by William Patterson. All manufacturing in the eastern half of the U.S. would become The United Aircraft Corporation, with Donald L. Brown acting as president and treasurer. And manufacturing in the western half of the country would be brought together under the name Boeing Airplane Company with Claire L. Egtvedt as president.[8]

One of the most intriguing parts of the announcement speaks directly to Phil Johnson and Bill Boeing's plans to stay involved with the business:

Philip G. Johnson, now president of the United Aircraft & Transport Corporation will be one of the three voting trustees of United Air Lines ... William E. Boeing, chairman of the board of United Aircraft & Transport, will be a member of the board of directors of [the] Boeing Airplane Company.[9]

There was a special board meeting scheduled for June 20 in New York for the stockholders to vote on the reorganization plan. It happened to be the same night on which Bill was to receive the Guggenheim medal in San Francisco, so he gave his proxy to Phil Johnson and made plans to head to San Francisco.

The Air Mail Act of 1934 was finally passed and signed by Roosevelt on June 12. It was to take effect on July 1. It contained an unexpected five-year ban on government contracts for companies that still employed any executives who had taken part in the Spoils Conference. It would have been hard to see this as anything but an attack on Phil Johnson, who had been invited to the conference by Postmaster General Brown and never felt he had any choice but to attend. Now, if United Air Lines wanted to keep its newly recovered airmail routes it would have to fire Johnson, and if Johnson went back to Boeing Airplane Company, it would be barred from getting military contracts.

On June 18, six days after the Air Mail Act was signed into law, and two days before the special UATC meeting to discuss the breakup of the company, Boeing received permission from the Army Air Corps to go ahead with a prototype of the mid-sized four-engine model 299 bomber.[10]

At the special meeting in New York, the UATC board voted unanimously to dissolve the corporation, but dealing with Johnson's termination as well as implementing the dissolution of the massive company would take a while to sort out. Another meeting was set for July 20 to determine what to do next.

At the same time that the UATC board was making the crushing decision to dissolve the company, Bill was 3,000 miles away, wearing a tuxedo with a starched white shirt and being honored by a roomful of his peers at the University of California in Berkeley. The Guggenheim medal was presented to him at a dinner put on by the San Francisco chapter of the American Society of Mechanical Engineers. After dinner, Bill gave a jovial speech, saying, "It began with impatience," referring to the slow repair of his Martin, which prompted him to build a plane for himself.[11]

There is no firm record of when Bill finally decided to retire from Boeing, but it is clear that as late as May 24, 1934 he was planning to stay on the board of directors. After he had received the Guggenheim Award, he boarded the *Rover* and flew to Canada to meet up with the *Taconite* for a two-month cruise to Alaska. By the time he returned in mid-September, he was ready to retire.

There is an intriguing piece of evidence in the *Taconite*'s log, kept by Bertha. Not only did she note the weather and the ship's location, put she also commented on the fishing, the food, and who won the latest card games. If she and Bill had shared a particularly fine bottle of wine, she would paste the label in the book.

July 15, 1934 was the eighteenth anniversary of Bill's founding of the company. Five days later there were no guests on the *Taconite*. It was gray and rainy, with heavy fog. *Rover* had been flown back to Seattle and would not be returning with the next group until the following morning, yet for some reason after dinner, Bill opened an 1878 bottle of Berry Brothers Champagne.[12] The fifty-six-year-old bottle of Champagne must have been intended to celebrate an important occasion, but in the *Taconite* log, Bertha gives no indication of what it was.

Bill had always been especially loyal to his employees, and it is likely that the final straw to tip the scales toward retirement was the way in which Phil Johnson had been treated by the Air Mail Act. It seems that Bill made his decision alone with Bertha onboard the *Taconite* on the foggy evening of July 20. When Johnson left Boeing for the last time, he would be walking out side-by-side with Bill Boeing.

# 50. GONE FISHING
## CANADA, 1934

Born and raised in Seattle, Phil Johnson loved the Pacific Northwest. In the 1920s he built a home surrounded by tall fir trees on the bluff overlooking Puget Sound in the picturesque Woodway Park neighborhood, 10 miles north of Bill Boeing's Aldarra home. In 1931 Johnson moved to Chicago to run United's airmail operation, and then in 1933 he moved to New Jersey to oversee UATC. Now that he was leaving the company, he moved home to the sweeping views and pine-scented bridle trails of Woodway Park.

UATC was set to be officially dissolved on September 26, 1934. Bill Boeing and Phil Johnson's resignations were scheduled to take effect at the end of the day on September 17. Boeing invited Johnson to celebrate with a week-long fishing cruise in British Columbia onboard the *Taconite*. Clayton Scott would fly them in the *Rover* to catch up with the *Taconite*, sailing near the south end of Vancouver Island, and they were to meet the *Rover* at Lake Union, where it had all started so many years earlier.

Knowing how deeply Boeing and Johnson cared for their friends and co-workers at Boeing, it's hard to imagine that they met at Lake Union without making the short 8-mile drive to the Oxbow plant to say goodbye to Claire Egtvedt and other colleagues and to take a final walk through the factory.

Over the years, Boeing, Johnson, and Egtvedt had taken countless walks across the production floor. In the early days, the whir of band saws and clouds of spruce-scented sawdust had filled the air; now they walked to the sharp snap of rivets being driven into aluminum and the buzz of arc welders. On this speculated occasion, Egtvedt would certainly have shown Johnson and Boeing the massive mockups of the XB-15 and the new prototype B-17 just starting to take shape. Their feelings would have been deeply nostalgic, with more than a trace of bitterness, perhaps, that this closure of a great chapter in their lives had been forced upon them. Unbeknownst to both men, however, the greatest challenge was yet come, and in a few years they would be back, driving the company forward for the sake of their country and the same government that was now forcing them out.

When they arrived at Lake Union, Clayton Scott was waiting for them with the *Rover* warmed up and ready to go. He quickly helped load their baggage on board. The following is the entry in the *Taconite* log:

Monday September 17
The plane left Lake Union in a cloud of spray at 3:45 pm. The fog of the morning had cleared at Seattle but still held over the [Puget] Sound until we reached Point-no-Point. Then it was clear to the north and east. We passed over Port Ludlow and directly over Protection Island at the entrance to Discovery Bay. No wind and a calm sea, over the Straits of Juan [de Fuca]. The Government buildings and the Empress Hotel were directly below us as we passed over Victoria to Esquinalt Harbor where we were on the water at 4:20. At the landing we were met by a courteous Customs Inspector who, after a few words with Bill and without inspection of baggage, passed us and we were on our way at 4:45.

Telephone communication with the *Taconite* had told us she was anchored at Departure Bay where we landed at 5:45. On coming on board the *Taconite* we found the best of Scotland waiting for us (Scotch Whiskey), later toddies and dinner then early to bed.[1]

The following day was too windy for fishing, so the *Taconite* cruised up the eastern edge of Vancouver Island while Johnson, bundled against the wind, stood at the ship's rail in deep thought, watching the fall foliage slide past. They anchored for the night off Yellow Island. The next morning, Phil was up at dawn and took one of the *Taconite*'s tender boats to the nearby fishing grounds. Fog swirled around him as he headed toward a cluster of First Nation fishing boats. He stopped alongside a fisherman paddling a traditional dugout canoe and learned that the salmon were feeding on herring. He traded his hat for some live herring bait and began to fish. He didn't get a bite.

Around 7 a.m. Bill showed up in small tender with an electric motor. He had a knack for fishing and quickly caught several large salmon, impressing the First Nation fishermen with his intuition for where the fish were. As soon as Bill had enough salmon to feed everyone on the *Taconite*, he and Johnson headed back to the yacht. They had a breakfast of fresh orange juice spiked with gin and salmon steaks with fried potatoes.

After breakfast, Scotty fired up *Rover* and flew Bill and Phil to the interior of Vancouver Island for trout fishing on Buttle Lake. Bill, sitting in the copilot's seat, took the controls for a while to keep his flying skills current. Scotty set the plane down and taxied to a dock. While Bill and Phil were getting their gear out, a gust of wind pushed the plane into the pier, damaging its left aileron. Bill and Scotty spent the day repairing the plane while Phil tried his hand at trout fishing. By 5 p.m. the plane was fixed, and they all headed back to *Taconite* by way of a scenic flight over the wild Campbell River.

They enjoyed toddies, with roast duck for dinner, followed by bridge at a penny a point. Phil had a good sense of humor about being jobless. Every time he had to write his name, whether it was in the logbook, the score sheet for the bridge game, or even in an impromptu fishing tournament (fifty cents for the biggest fish) he wrote "Unemployed Johnson."[2]

For seven relaxing days the friends fished, played cards and let the wounds from their treatment at the hands of Roosevelt heal. To an outside observer, they looked like two old friends on a fishing trip; no one would have recognized them as titans of the aviation world. On September 24 they loaded into the *Rover* and flew back to Seattle, each to start new chapters in their lives.

# 51. FLYING FORTRESS
# 1935

In September 1934, a German immigrant named Bruno Richard Hauptmann bought gasoline with one of the uncommon $10 gold certificates that Charles Lindbergh had used to pay the ransom for his kidnapped child. A quick-thinking gas station attendant wrote down Hauptmann's license plate number and alerted the police, who placed a tail on Hauptmann. He was arrested when he ran a red light in an effort to lose the tail, and a subsequent search of his house discovered $14,660 of the ransom bills hidden in his garage.

Hauptmann was charged with the kidnapping and murder of Charles Lindbergh Jr., and his trial began in January 1935. Every detail of it was blazed across the front pages of the nation's newspapers, and an obsessed public waited impatiently for radio updates every afternoon. But there was other news too.

Monday, February 4 was the type of dreary day that Seattle was famous for. A heavy colorless overcast blocked out the sun, temperatures stayed in the low forties all day, and a light drizzle kept things wet without ever really being noticeable as rain. The front page of *The Seattle Daily Times* was dominated, as usual, by the Hauptmann trial, and the defense's effort to give Hauptmann an alibi. Buried deep in the newspaper was a two-inch-tall story out of Washington DC. It said "The District of Columbia Court of Appeals held today that Postmaster General Farley's cancelation of airmail contracts amounted to a breach of contract which gave the airlines the right to sue the government in the Court of Appeals."[1]

Bill and Phil Johnson were thrilled. It looked like the first small step toward exoneration had been taken. Neither man would be able to take part in the suit, but they would certainly be interested spectators as the case wound its way through the courts. The rest of the country was still focused on the Hauptmann trial. A week and a half later the defense rested, and after deliberating for eleven hours, the jury found Hauptmann guilty of murder. He was sentenced to death. The publicity the case received was unparalleled, and it soon spawned another copycat.

John Weyerhaeuser was the grandson of Tacoma-resident Frederick E. Weyerhaeuser, founder of the gigantic lumber company and a friend of Bill Boeing's. On May 24, Weyerhaeuser's nine-year-old son George disappeared while walking home from school. Later that night, a poorly typed ransom note was delivered to the Weyerhaeuser home.

According to the newspapers, police immediately suspected Annie Vermilia and John Thompson, "who participated three years ago in the attempted kidnapping of Bill Boeing, Jr."[2] However, Vermilia was living thousands of miles away in New Jersey and could not have been involved. The ransom note had been written with a typewriter that included a few special characters unique to the lumber industry, and so the police turned their attention to a group of unsavory characters in Hoquiam.

After Weyerhaeuser paid the $200,000 ransom, his son was released unharmed. A week later, a nineteen-year-old girl was arrested for trying to use one of the $20 bills from the ransom at a Woolworth Store in Salt Lake City, Utah. Later that night her twenty-four-year-old husband, Harmon Metz Waley, was arrested and confessed to the crime. Neither Waley nor his accomplice, William Dainard, who was arrested much later, had any connection to the lumber business; the use of the unique typewriter had been a coincidence.

For Bill, this was third time in four years in which he had found himself deeply concerned about his son's safety. Even though he knew that Billy was safe behind the gates of Pebble Beach, school would be ending soon, and Billy would come home for the summer. Bill wanted to find a better way to protect his only child.

The *Taconite* was ready to leave for its annual summer cruise. Once again, Billy would be taken on board and out of harm's way while the yacht sailed leisurely to Alaska; but when summer ended, Bill wanted to send his son as far away from danger as possible. He considered L'Institut Sillig Fréres in Switzerland, but decided against it; either his memories of Vevey were not pleasant or he was nervous about the tensions growing between Germany and its neighbors. For the second time in three years, Billy was to head out on the *Taconite*'s summer cruise with no idea of where he would be living when school started in the fall.

Billy and Jane arrived home from Pebble Beach on June 11. The yacht got underway at 3:15 p.m. for its first voyage of 1935. They sailed out of Vancouver Harbor and headed north "up the Gulf of Georgia under grey skies – very smooth and peaceful, in fact each and every one of us slept a good part of the afternoon."[3] The Boeing family quickly fell back into the rhythm of shipboard life, waking each morning to a steward's gentle rap on their cabin door with a chilled glass of fresh orange juice to let them know that breakfast was served. Then fishing or sightseeing as they cruised north toward a new anchorage in time for a fresh seafood lunch, followed by swimming, rowing, or sightseeing flights on the *Rover*. Then they dressed for dinner – often another seafood feast – followed by cards, puzzles, or reading, and then off to sleep as the waves lapped against the *Taconite*'s hull.

Sunday, July 28 was overcast and cold. The *Taconite* spent all day moored in a secluded cove halfway up the British Columbia coast on the way to Ketchikan. Five hundred miles to the south, at Boeing Field, the Boeing Company's brand-new four-engine bomber was rolled out of its hangar and prepared for its first flight.

The plane had been unveiled to the public eleven days earlier, and *The Seattle Daily Times* reporter Richard Williams, impressed by the bristling array of machine guns protruding from the plane's turrets, had described it as a "15-ton flying fortress." The name stuck. A few minutes after 6 a.m., test pilot Les Tower fired up the four Pratt & Whitney Hornets and taxied onto the flight line. Tower headed to the north end of the runway, ran the engines up to 2,250 rpm, released the brakes, and began to roll forward. *The Seattle Daily Times* took up the story:

As the sun shone over the top of Beacon Hill, the big ship's four, 750-horsepower motors howled raucously; its four three bladed propellers disappeared in gleaming arcs, and the plane lumbered forward.

Ten seconds later the big wheels were free of the earth. The bomber
climbed gently and soared away toward Tacoma. Silent groups on the field
began to laugh and talk.[4]

The plane spent an hour making slow, lazy laps between Seattle and Tacoma
with the morning sun glinting off its polished aluminum skin. At a few minutes
after 7 a.m., continued the *Times*,

> The big bomber made a perfect landing on the north end of Boeing Field ...
> It is equipped with wing flaps which increase the lift of its wings and allow
> slow landing speed. When Tower dropped the flaps as the ship came in it
> seemed to hover before settling to the ground.
>
> The bomber will be flown to Dayton Ohio for trials August 22 in
> competition with ships of other airplane companies.[5]

When Scotty returned in the *Rover* from a refueling trip on August 1, he must
have brought newspapers with coverage of the flight, but there is no reference
in the log to Bill's reaction. Meanwhile, the *Taconite* continued north, reaching
Alaskan waters on August 6.

Bill used the radio telephone and an occasional trip back to Seattle on the
*Rover* to search for a school for Billy. Eventually he and Bertha decided to
send him and his governess Ole to the Punahou School in Honolulu. Punahou
had been founded in 1841 as a missionary school on land that had belonged
to King Kamehameha I, the first king of Hawaii.[6] The school was located on
the outskirts of Honolulu, nestled among the banyan trees and palm groves of
the Manoa Valley, surrounding the fresh water of Ka Punahou (New Spring),
which gave the school its name.[7]

Punahou was virtually unknown on the mainland, and Bill and Bertha saw
it as the perfect solution for keeping Billy safe. Plans were quickly made for
Bertha and Grace to accompany Billy and Ole on their voyage from Victoria
to Honolulu. Bertha and Grace would stay a week to get them settled before
returning to Seattle.

The Alaskan cruise was cut short and the *Taconite* headed south to Victoria.
The *Rover* came and went with new friends and guests every few days. On
August 26, Phil Johnson was back for a three-week stay. He and Bill had
always been close, and now, with the constraints of an employee–employer
relationship removed, their friendship developed into an even deeper mutual
respect between equals.

On September 7, the *Taconite* was tied up to the long dock in front of
Victoria's elegant Empress Hotel, where Bill treated the "Honolulu Party" to
a bon-voyage luncheon with plenty of farewell toasts. The next day, Bertha,
Grace, Billy, and Ole boarded the *Empress of Canada*, sailing to Honolulu.

The *Taconite* cruised north through the Strait of Georgia on the lookout for more fishing opportunities. With his family on the high seas heading to Hawaii, Bill had plenty of free time to fish, play cards, and enjoy cocktails with Phil. They talked long into the night, moored in the dark waters of various quiet Canadian anchorages. It is very likely that Johnson told Bill about his new friend Harry Kent and his business problems.

Kent had partnered with Edgar Worthington in a truck manufacturing company named Gersix Trucks. Eventually the company dropped the Gersix name and took the first syllables from Kent and Worthington, renaming the company "Kenworth Trucks." Worthington had retired and Kent was now president, but the stock market crash and Depression had made life difficult for Kenworth, and Kent was facing a revolt among his stockholders. Johnson saw an opportunity at Kenworth. From his perspective, manufacturing was manufacturing, and the same principles that applied to airplanes ought to apply to trucks. Johnson explained that he was going to invest in Kenworth. Bill must have listened intently and offered his own opinion, but he declined to invest any of his own money.

Billy, Bertha, Grace, and Ole arrived in Honolulu on September 12 and checked into the Halekulani Hotel on Waikiki Beach, a low, rambling collection of beachfront bungalows nestled in a grove of coconut palms a few yards from the water. Each bungalow had a wide, shady porch with wicker furniture and magnificent views of Diamond Head and the crashing surf. Because Bill and Bertha had waited so long to decide where to send Billy, there were not any rooms available on campus, so Bill had booked one of the Halekulani's bungalows for the entire year, and Billy and Ole were to live at the hotel.

The Boeing party was greeted with traditional Hawaiian leis and a newspaper reporter with a camera. The next morning a quarter-page photo of Bertha in her lei appeared on the front page of the *Honolulu Advertiser*'s society section. The story went on to describe that she was in town to enroll Billy at the Punahou School. Bill and Bertha's carefully orchestrated plan to give Billy anonymity had lasted less than twenty-four hours. There was nothing that could be done, however. Bertha and Grace got everything arranged for Billy and sailed for home on September 22, promising to be back in time for Christmas.

# 52. ALOHA
# HAWAII, 1935

When people first saw Boeing's Model 299, with its sleek aluminum skin and Plexiglas turrets, they often said that it looked right – the way a plane was supposed to look. The 299 was introduced seven years after Boeing's Model 80, a tri-motor biplane with fabric-covered wings that had revolutionized the airline industry, but when the two planes were placed side by side, they looked like they were from different centuries.

Brigadier-General Hap Arnold, commander of the Army Air Corps on the Pacific Coast, inspected the new plane and told the army brass in Washington DC that the "plane has practically no limits as a bomber."[1] In late August, the new Model 299 flew from Seattle to Wright Field in Dayton, Ohio, setting a world record for the trip with an average speed of 252 mph. The Model 299 was taking part in a three-plane bomber competition to determine which company would get the next bomber contract from the army. With a top speed that was 35 mph faster than the next plane and a range of 3,000 miles, compared to the 1,200 miles of the other competitors, the Model 299 was a heavy favorite to win. The Air Corps was so impressed by the huge bomber that Boeing was promised a sixty-five-plane order right away, outside of the bomber competition.

Then, at 9 a.m. on the chilly overcast morning of October 30, the unthinkable happened: The new plane crashed and burned on takeoff, killing army test pilot Ployer P. Hill and burning Boeing's chief test pilot Les Tower so badly that he died from his injuries twenty-eight days later.

Immediately after the crash, the army withdrew its sixty-five-plane order and disqualified Boeing's plane from the bomber competition. The inferior Douglas XB-18 "Bolo" won the contract and a $6 million order for 133 planes. Two weeks later the Air Corps investigators released their report, saying that the crash was caused by pilot error. Hill had attempted to take off with a cockpit-located gust lock on the elevator controls still engaged, causing the plane to stall and crash.[2] A gust lock keeps the plane's control surfaces locked in place so they don't get damaged flapping back and forth in the wind while the plane is on the ground.

\* \* \*

On December 2, Bill and Bertha flew in the *Rover* from Seattle to Victoria to catch the *Empress of China* sailing to Honolulu. They were headed to Hawaii to celebrate Christmas and New Year's with Billy. After a quick four-day passage, the island chain appeared as a green smudge on the horizon, slowly coming into focus: black mountains rising above a green tangle of jungle, and next the white band of surf, followed by the brown strip of beach. As the *Empress* rounded Diamond Head, the pleasant scent of tropical flowers wafted across the deck. Once the ship was safely moored in Honolulu harbor, Bill and Bertha were greeted by native women in grass skirts who placed colorful leis around their necks. Hawaii was still twenty-four years from becoming a state and had an exotic quality to most mainlanders.

Bertha's sons, Nat and Cranston, arrived from San Francisco on the *President Hoover*, and they all checked into the Halekulani Hotel on December 6.[3] The Boeings had the beach almost to themselves. Even in December the water was warm and full of fish and shells.

On December 22, the entire Boeing party chartered a seaplane and flew to Hilo on the Big Island of Hawaii to go deep-sea fishing.[4] There are no photographs of the trip, but it is easy to imagine Bill fighting a big striped marlin that jumped and splashed while Bertha and Billy shouted encouragement. The next day they toured one of Hilo's giant sugar plantations and spent the afternoon relaxing on the plantation house's wide veranda beneath a slow-moving ceiling fan. Bill felt at home in Hawaii and found a sense of peace that he had previously only been able to find in Alaska.

On Christmas Eve, the family flew back to Honolulu to celebrate a tropical Christmas at Waikiki, where an outrigger canoe, pulled by plywood cutouts of dolphins, substituted for Santa's traditional sleigh. Sleigh bells gave way to ukuleles and the traditional turkey dinner with mashed potatoes and gravy was replaced by a pit-roasted Kalua pig with noodle soup.

Billy stayed at Punahou School for two years and lived at the Halekulani Hotel the entire time. During his second year, his cousin Jane came over to keep him company, and Bill and Bertha were frequent visitors. During one trip Bill was treated to a private tour of the island's military defenses by Major-General Hugh A. Drum, commander of the U.S. Army's Hawaiian Department.[5] At the time, the tour seemed like a pleasant diversion to while away a warm day. A few years later, when Hawaii was attacked by Japan, Bill's firsthand knowledge of Hickam Field, Ford Island, and Pearl Harbor, along with the officers defending them, amplified his feeling of outrage toward the Japanese.

\* \* \*

When Bill returned from Hawaii in January 1936, he learned that Phil Johnson had moved ahead with Kenworth Truck Company, buying 25 percent of the company's stock and becoming vice-president. Harry Kent was still president and owned about 35 percent of the stock. Kent's adversaries on the board of directors owned close to 35 percent too, and could be counted on to oppose just about any idea that Kent proposed. Johnson found that his 25-percent stake became the "swing vote," giving him almost total control of the company.

Bill Boeing never bought any shares of Kenworth, but he did use his position as one of the founding directors of Pacific National Bank to assist Phil Johnson with a $750,000 preferred-stock offering to help Kenworth retool and expand. The deal was similar to the $750,000 deal that Bill had arranged to launch BAT back in 1928. Boeing and Johnson were finding that even though they no longer worked together in the same company, there were still plenty of opportunities to help each other in the business world.

By the end of 1935, the Boeing Company was in a financial bind. The breakup with United had left it with very little cash, and it had gambled all of what it had on the new Model 299 bomber. When it crashed, the company lost a $500,000 airplane and millions of dollars in orders. Then, on December 22, 1935, Boeing caught a lucky break when the army offered a contract for thirteen new B-17s.

There wasn't room to build the big bombers at the old Oxbow plant, so Claire Egtvedt, the president, decided that a second plant was needed. He found land across East Marginal Way from Boeing Field. There was money coming down the pipeline from the army, but it was still a few months away, and the Boeing Company needed money to start construction on its second plant straight away. Egtvedt went to Pacific National Bank to see if it would underwrite another stock issue.

Bill Boeing had founded PNB in 1928 to assist the Boeing companies with their banking needs, and as one of PNB's founding directors, he could still exert considerable influence on the Boeing Company by opening or closing the purse strings. PNB led the syndicate that underwrote Boeing's new stock offer to pay for "Plant 2" and the startup of B-17 production. A short while later, on April 22, 1936, in what had all the appearances of a quid pro quo in exchange for the loan, the Boeing Company brought back Phil Johnson as an unpaid member of the board of directors.[6]

For the time being, Bill steered clear of direct contact with the Boeing Company, but he continued to socialize with both Johnson and Egtvedt, and it was only a matter of time before he would find his way back home. Phil Johnson, meanwhile, was in high demand; along with serving on the Boeing board of directors, he became president of Kenworth in 1937. A few months later was also elected to a two-year term as vice-president of the fledgling

Trans-Canada Air, based in Montreal. He left Seattle for Canada on August 10 but announced that he would be retaining his positions at Kenworth and Boeing.

A short while later, in a brilliant chess move by Bill Boeing, William M. Allen, the talented young lawyer from Boeing's corporate law firm, Donworth & Todd, was added to the PNB board of directors.

# 53. THE SPORT OF KINGS
# 1936-38

When the Depression started, state governments across the nation were faced with a dramatic loss of tax revenue. Many turned to pari-mutuel betting[1] on Thoroughbred horse racing[2] to make up the shortfall. By the mid-1930s, racing was legal in twenty-three states and generated more than $168 million annually in tax revenue.[3]

Perhaps it was a form of escapism; maybe it was the allure of a well-placed bet yielding a big payday, or in the words of Beryl Markham's memoir *West With the Night*, "Perhaps it is none of these. Perhaps it is the unrecognized expectation of holding for an instant what primordial sensations that can be born again in the free strength of flashing flanks and driving hoofs beating a challenge against the ground."[4]

Whatever the cause, horseracing was America's newest craze, and in the second half of the 1930s newsreels and newspapers were full of stories about great horses like War Admiral and Seabiscuit. Races such as the 100 Grander at Santa Anita, the Belmont Sweepstakes, and the Kentucky Derby drew the type of national attention that used to be reserved for a Jack Dempsey prize fight.

On August 3, 1933 a couple of Seattle sportsmen opened Longacres Racetrack in Renton, south of Seattle. Over 11,000 people crowded through the turnstiles that first day to watch the spectacle and try their luck at the betting windows. Each course had a season lasting between one and two months, allowing for a large field of professional stables with well-known horses to move in sequence from track to track. By 1936, after three popular seasons, Longacres was an established stop on the racing circuit.

Bill Boeing was retired from the airplane business and looking for his next endeavor. He remembered the tranquility that being around horses had brought him as a young man, and after the unpleasantness of the Black hearings, he longed to experience it again. Bill decided that he wanted to get into horse racing.

The 1936 racing season at Longacres was scheduled to open on July 3, but rain the day before had turned the carefully groomed dirt track into a sea of mud. Leg injuries are common in these conditions, and few trainers were willing to risk their horses on the first day of a two-month-long meet. The races were not filling up.

The harried racing secretary was massaging his temples with a half-burnt cigarette dangling from his lips. He tapped the ash into an overflowing ashtray and keyed the switch on the public address microphone: "I need three horses for the first race, four for the third, and two for the fifth," he announced.[5]

A few moments later a tall man with a square jaw and brown homburg hat walked in. "Well I just got in from Omaha," he said, "and I've got seventeen horses in my barn and I'll run my whole stable tomorrow if it will help you. That's what I came here for – to run."[6]

The stranger from Nebraska was named Earl Beezley, and for the next two months he and his horses dominated racing at Longacres. According to California turf writer Tom Gwynne, "He won some 32 purses, virtually all of the sweepstakes including the $10,000 Longacres Mile."[7] Beezley had an expert eye for horses and a generous portion of old-fashioned good luck: he picked up a beautiful bay mare named Blue Boot for $2,000 in a claiming race on August 12, and five days later earned it all back with a healthy profit when she won the $10,000 Longacres Mile. By the time Beezley had packed up his horses and headed south to San Francisco's Tanforan Racetrack, the nation's turf writers had nicknamed him "The Miracle Man."

Blue Boot and Beezley continued their winning streak in San Francisco: "He took Tanforan in his stride," wrote Gwynne, "and finished [the season as] the leading money winner."[8] After Tanforan, Beezley and his horses wintered at Santa Anita, near Los Angeles. His luck apparently changed, however, on January 1, 1937, when his wealthy partner, William Haynes, died suddenly of a heart attack just a week before the start of racing season at Santa Anita.

Beezley was a tremendous horse trainer, but he did not have the deep pockets needed to own a Thoroughbred stable. He needed a new partner and he needed one quickly. Word reached Bill Boeing, and he and Bertha set out for Santa Anita.[9] By January 29, Bill had formed a three-way partnership with Earl Beezley and Pasadena oil man Harry Hunt called the Hunt, Beezley, and Boeing Stables. When Bill Boeing walked into the Santa Anita clubhouse for the start of the 1937 racing season, there was a spring in his step and a gleam in his eyes. He joked with the waiting reporters, "I'd rather win a $10 bet on my own horse than see my stock go up two points."[10] He loved the spectacle, excitement, and glamour of racing. He invested money in the track and was rewarded with season tickets for eight box seats at the finish line. Santa Anita was visited by Hollywood royalty like Al Jolson, Olivia de Havilland, and Bette Davis. If Bill was enjoying a cocktail in the clubhouse, the stars always made it a point to stop at his table to pay their respects.

For the first two weeks things went perfectly. The Hunt, Beezley, and Boeing Stables won nine races and were ranked near the top of the track's money winners. By mid-February the team was making plans to head to races at Tanforan, but then on the morning February 19, the headlines declared "Tanforan Bars Beezley Stables."[11] Anonymous telegrams from Texas claimed that Beezley's horse Blue Boot was a fake, and that the real Blue Boot was heavy with a foal and living in comfortable retirement on a horse farm in Kentucky. In racing terms, Beezley's Blue Boot was a ringer.

The accusation was absolutely true. Paul Harvey, of Midland Texas, had had two bay-colored mares with almost identical markings. One was a slow three-year-old named Blue Boot that he had paid $300 for, and the other was a dynamic four-year-old racer named Exotude that had cost several thousand dollars. In January of 1936, Harvey ran the real Blue Boot several times at San Antonio, Texas, and established her as a second-rate horse.

Faster horses are worth more than slower horses, so to keep races close, horses are only raced against others of similar price. To make sure that an owner doesn't run an expensive horse against a field of cheap horses, races are run with a "claiming price." That means that all the horses in a given race are for sale for the same price, and anyone who wants to can pay the claiming price and buy any horse in the field. The size of the claiming price determines the quality of the horses in the race.

Harvey shipped Exotude to Kansas City's Riverside Park and entered her under the name Blue Boot. Based on her apparent lack of success in Texas, the fake Blue Boot was given high odds. For example, on May 31, the fake Blue Boot entered a $500 claiming race and was given 10 to 1 odds. She won easily and a $5,000 bet would have yielded a $50,000 payout.

Harvey's scheme was going so well that after a few weeks in Kansas City he decided to move on to Longacres. There he ran into Earl Beezley, whose keen eye immediately recognized that "Blue Boot" was a great horse that was racing well below her natural level. Beezley did not suspect that there was anything underhand going on; he just saw a horse that appeared to be undervalued. When Harvey entered "Blue Boot" in a $2,000 claiming race, Beezley snapped her up, and within a week he had collected $8,255 in winnings and taken his new horse south to Tanforan.

Eventually Paul Harvey confessed to his scheme and was banned from racing for life. Beezley was exonerated, but the whole episode left a bad taste in Bill's mouth, and he dissolved the partnership at the end of the 1937 season.

In the breakup, Bill ended up with eighteen racehorses, which he sent to Santa Anita. He hired the talented Ted Horning to be his trainer, and Horning soon expanded his stables to include more than forty horses. By mid-January 1938, Boeing Stables was considered to be the largest racing stable on the West Coast.[12]

Bill also hired Basil James, a skinny eighteen-year-old boy from Sunnyside, Washington, to be his main jockey. James had learned to race at the Pendleton Round Up, and even though Bill had no memory of seeing him race there during his many trips to Pendleton, the idea that James was a Northwest boy appealed to him. It also didn't hurt that in 1937, aged only sixteen, James had been crowned America's Champion Rider with 245 wins at twelve different tracks.

In 1938 America's fascination with horse racing grew into a full-blown obsession. The previous year, War Admiral, a three-year-old son of the legendary Man-o-War, became the fourth horse to win the Triple Crown (the Kentucky Derby, The Preakness Stakes, and the Belmont Stakes). War Admiral, voted horse of the year in 1937, was a magnificent dark brown horse, big and proud in the way one would expect a Triple Crown winner to look.

One of Bill's fellow Santa Anita racers, Charles Howard, had a large stable of magnificent horses, the best of which was a small five-year-old bay with crooked legs named Seabiscuit. She was the fastest horse on the West Coast. All through the 1937 and '38 seasons, Howard tried to arrange a race between Seabiscuit and War Admiral. At first, War Admiral's owner, Glenn Riddle, dismissed the idea as pointless, thinking there was no way that a West Coast horse, especially a small, awkward one like Seabiscuit, could compete with his mighty War Admiral. But racing fans clamored for the matchup, and toward the end of the 1938 season, Riddle gave in. The two horses met in a match race at Pimlico in Baltimore. War Admiral was a four to one favorite, but Seabiscuit shocked the racing world with an upset victory and was named 1938 Horse of the Year.

The Seabiscuit–War Admiral rivalry was a legendary David *vs.* Goliath contest. It stoked America's passion for horse racing, and attendance records were shattered from one end of the country to the other. Bill raced his horses at over a dozen different tracks in 1938 and won sixty-four races. When the season ended, Charles Howard's stable was the nation's top money winner, but Boeing Stables, with $146,625 in purses, was number five, prompting the *Oakland Tribune* to declare that "The Boeing Stable is one of those rare things in horse-racing – a rich man's stable – that has shown a substantial profit."[13]

# PART VI

# The War Years and After
# 1939-1956

# 54. THE FAILURE OF PEACE
# 1939

When the Great War ended in 1918, people were calling it "The War to End All Wars." Unfortunately, far from ending all war, the harsh and punitive Treaty of Versailles lit the fuse that would start a new and even larger war. When the treaty was drafted, President Wilson had expected the United States to act as an umpire in Europe and keep things in line, but Congress, tired of Wilson's involvement overseas, rejected the U.S. role in Europe and passed strict neutrality laws intended to keep the U.S. out of future wars.

The crippling worldwide Depression brought on by the 1929 collapse of the stock market devastated the German economy. This financial crisis helped fuel the rise of Adolf Hitler's nationalistic Nazi movement, and in 1935 Hitler began rebuilding Germany's military. The Allies turned a blind eye toward the treaty violations, hoping that a stronger Germany would stop the spread of Soviet communism.

By March 7, 1936, Hitler had sent armed forces into the Rhineland. The Allies did nothing. Two years later, Hitler annexed Austria into his expanding Third Reich. Again, the Allies did nothing. Emboldened by the Allies' lack of response, Hitler turned his attention to Czechoslovakia, threatening that unless the Sudetenland, a mountainous region on the border between Germany and Czechoslovakia, was given to Germany, he would take it by force.

The British prime minister, Neville Chamberlain, flew to an emergency meeting in Munich. Hitler told Chamberlain that if the Allies would grant him the Sudetenland, his ambitions in Europe would be met. Chamberlain approved Hitler's request and returned to England, declaring, "We have secured peace in our time!" Six months later, Hitler's troops swept out of the Sudetenland and took over all of Czechoslovakia. The Allies wrote sternly worded letters but did nothing to stop Hitler. Then, on September 1, 1939, when Hitler's armies overran Poland, England and France finally reached their breaking point. On September 3, they declared war on Germany.

On September 8, President Roosevelt declared a "Limited State of Emergency" and asked the U.S. military to begin beefing up its defensive capabilities. The Boeing Company was in no position to respond to Roosevelt's declaration. It had lost $500,000 in 1938 and was struggling to survive. The B-17 had just not panned out. Even though Brigadier-General Hap Arnold was a great admirer of the plane, the expected flood of orders had not materialized.

After Boeing had built the thirteen planes ordered in 1936, the army asked for one more with new General Electric turbochargers on the engines. The turbos brought the B-17 to life, boosting its top speed to 295 mph. The modified plane was offered under the name B-17B, and the army ordered thirty-nine.[1] However, the army did not want Boeing to produce all of the bombers in Seattle; in the advent of a war, a single enemy attack could destroy the entire U.S. ability to produce bombers. It was highly ironic, of course, that a few years earlier the Roosevelt administration had forced Boeing to give up its production facilities in the rest of the country. In the event, Boeing was instructed to split the order with Consolidated Aircraft of San Diego.[2]

While preparing for the B-17 job, Consolidated sent a delegation to Seattle to inspect the B-17 and Boeing's production technique. There was a familiar face in the delegation: Ed Gott, the former president of Boeing Airplane Company and cousin to Bill Boeing, was now vice-president of Consolidated and in charge of its bomber program.[3]

Consolidated told the army that both the B-17 and Boeing's production process were obsolete and declined the job, asking instead for a chance to offer a new plane of its own design. Gott worked with the brilliant aerodynamicist David R. Davis to design Consolidated's own four-engine long-range bomber, to be called the B-24. Gott claimed that it would have a longer range and higher ceiling and carry a heavier payload than the B-17. The army returned production of all the B-17Bs to Boeing, and before Gott's new B-24 prototype was even finished and his boasts about its superior performance could be tested, the army combined with Britain and France to order 320 of the new B-24s.[4]

Boeing was struggling to find an airplane it could sell. It had married the big 103-foot B-17 wing to a brand-new pressurized body to create the first high-altitude airliner, capable of flying over the weather in comfort. The new plane, called the Stratoliner, first flew on the last day of 1938, and Boeing immediately received orders for nine planes. For ten brief weeks things were looking up for the Boeing Company, but on March 18, 1939 the Stratoliner crashed on a test flight near Mt. Rainier, killing everyone on board. Eventually an investigation determined that the plane was blameless. An inexperienced pilot visiting on behalf of KLM Airlines had allowed the plane to stall and then nose over into a spin. The panicked pilot had then attempted to pull too quickly out of the 350-mph dive and had caused the wings to break off the plane.

Boeing was in a terrible position. Orders dried up and there would be no more cash coming in until the company could start delivering some planes. Between the B-17s that Consolidated had refused to build and the nine Stratoliners that had been ordered before the crash, Boeing had over $14 million in orders, but only $4 million in cash to pay wages and buy materials. Worse yet, it had already outgrown Plant 2 and needed to double its size before it could set up production lines.[5] By September, Boeing was running $2.6 million in the red.[6]

Egtvedt went back to Pacific National Bank and asked for underwriting on another issue of Boeing stock. He was shocked by the answer he received. William Allen, still only in his thirties and one of the youngest members on the board, answered with such frankness that one has to wonder if he was speaking on behalf PNB founder Bill Boeing. Phil Johnson's five-year "ban" had expired, so he was free to work wherever he wanted. Allen suggested, "Why don't you try to get Phil Johnson back in the company? The need now is production, and that is Phil's long suit."[7]

Next, Egtvedt reached out to Joseph Ripley, now part owner of Harriman Ripley Company, one of the largest investment banks in New York.[8] Egtvedt asked if he would consider underwriting another Boeing stock issue. According to *The Seattle Daily Times*, Ripley agreed with Allen, saying that he would "underwrite a $5,000,000 issue of stock ... but only on the condition that Johnson be put at the helm."[9]

Egtvedt would have to have been blind not to see Bill's fingerprints all over this. Bill believed that Johnson had been wronged by Roosevelt. It seems entirely consistent with his sense of right and wrong, as well as the profound loyalty he felt for Johnson, that he would use his influence to "correct" Roosevelt's mistake and place Johnson back at the head of the company. The message was clear: find a way to bring back Johnson or find a way to get along without any more money.

Egtvedt wrestled with the idea for a while and eventually decided that Allen and Ripley were right: Phil Johnson had what the company needed. When he contacted Johnson, Egtvedt was in for another surprise. Before he would consider coming back, Johnson said he needed to hear directly from President Roosevelt himself. Early in September 1939, there was apparently a call from Washington DC and "Mr. Johnson was invited back at Mr. Roosevelt's urgent request to become President of Boeing again."[10]

On September 10, a rare Sunday meeting of the Boeing board of directors made it official. Claire Egtvedt moved up to become chairman of the board and on the next day Phil Johnson walked back into Boeing as the once and future president.

# 55. IN GOD'S GOOD TIME
# 1940

When Great Britain and France declared war on Germany after Hitler's invasion of Poland, a strange calm descended over Europe. Britain and France began moving their great armies into place while Germany consolidated its gains and plotted its next move. For nine months life on the continent seemed almost normal; hardly a shot was fired and pundits began to talk of a "Phony War."

The mood in America was changing. At the end of the Great War, the majority of Americans believed firmly in isolationism. As Hitler began to flex his muscles with troop movements into the Rhineland and Austria, the politicians who had backed America's neutrality laws patted each other on the back, confident that they had saved the country from another war. But by the time Germany invaded Poland, many Americans were beginning to see Hitler as the clear villain of the story. Still, they believed that France and Britain, with two of the most powerful militaries in the world, were capable of handling the threat.

May 10, 1940 dawned clear and sunny across most of northern Europe. It could have been one of those late spring mornings that promised a beautiful summer, but as the first rays of daylight touched the earth, thousands of Panzer tanks, with machine guns blasting, poured across the German border into neutral Holland, Belgium and Luxemburg. With deadly precision, Stuka dive bombers shrieked out of the sky and blew apart all the defenses, clearing the way for the tanks. The Wehrmacht raced across the Low Countries, overcoming their hapless armies. This was a brand-new type of war: the Germans called it "Blitzkrieg," meaning "Lightning War," and the Allies had no defense against it.[1]

Across the English Channel, Neville Chamberlain's Conservative government, which had spent years trying to appease Hitler, crumbled. It was replaced by a coalition government headed by Winston Churchill. Short, heavy, and in his mid-sixties by the time of his appointment as prime minister,

Churchill was viewed by many as an old-fashioned, obsolete politician. He was, however, an unquestionably good orator, and he electrified Parliament and the nation from the start with his rousing words, "I have nothing to offer but blood, toil, tears, and sweat."[2]

By May 16 the Nazi conquest of the Low Countries was nearly complete, and the German army had turned toward France. In Washington DC, Roosevelt called a joint session of Congress. As he headed to the podium at the front of the House chamber, he was struck by the parallels to April 2, 1917, when Woodrow Wilson had climbed the same stairs to ask Congress to declare war on Germany. But Roosevelt did not intend to declare war.

"These are ominous days," he said, "days whose swift and shocking developments force every neutral nation to look to its defenses in the light of new factors."

The brutal force of modern offensive war has been loosed in all its horror.

New powers of destruction, incredibly swift and ready, have been developed; and those who wield them are ruthless and daring.

No old defense is so strong that it requires no further strengthening and no attack is so unlikely or impossible that it may be ignored.[3]

Roosevelt called for a massive military buildup at a cost of $1,182,000,000. His goal was to ensure that America was strong enough to deter Nazi aggression. A key element of the plan was the construction of 50,000 new war planes. Congress approved the plan and by the end of the year, Boeing had orders for 520 B-17s.

The war raged on in Europe. The collapse and surrender of the Belgian army on May 28 had left the entire British Expeditionary Force in Europe, approximately 400,000 soldiers, trapped and facing annihilation near the French town of Dunkirk, surrounded by more than 800,000 German troops. A hastily assembled armada of almost 900 vessels, many of which were privately owned trawlers and pleasure boats with civilian crews, sailing from tiny ports and fishing villages on England's southern coast, worked day and night for over a week, "under an almost ceaseless hail of bombs and an increasing barrage of artillery fire," to evacuate 338,226 soldiers to safety in England.[4] Priority was given to soldiers over equipment, so virtually all of the massive army's weapons and supplies were left behind, including "680 of the 700 tanks it had sent to France, 82,000 scout cars and motorcycles, 8,000 field telephones, 90,000 rifles, and an even greater number of machine guns."[5]

On June 4 Churchill went to Parliament to report on Dunkirk. Even though he was standing in front of the House of Commons, the real target of his speech was 3,000 miles away, across the Atlantic. He started with some words of caution:

We must be very careful not to assign to this deliverance the attributes of a victory. Wars are not won by evacuations.[6]

Churchill knew that the only way he could replace the thousands of tons of abandoned equipment that would be desperately needed if the Nazis were to invade, was to beg, borrow and buy from the U.S. But strict U.S. neutrality laws stood in his way. With an instinctive understanding of America's love of the underdog, Churchill described the crisis:

> Even though large tracts of Europe and many old and famous States have fallen or may fall into the grip of the Gestapo and all the odious apparatus of Nazi rule, we shall not flag or fail. We shall go on to the end. We shall fight in France, we shall fight on the seas and oceans, we shall fight with growing confidence and growing strength in the air, we shall defend our island, whatever the cost may be. We shall fight on the beaches, we shall fight on the landing grounds, we shall fight in the fields and in the streets, we shall fight in the hills; we shall never surrender, and if, which I do not for a moment believe, this island or a large part of it were subjugated and starving, then our Empire beyond the seas, armed and guarded by the British Fleet, would carry on the struggle, until, in God's good time, the New World, with all its power and might, steps forth to the rescue and the liberation of the old.[7]

As he left the rostrum, well aware that without resupply from America, Britain was doomed, Churchill quipped to one of his aides,

> ... and we shall fight them with the butt ends of broken beer bottles because that is bloody well all we've got.[8]

Churchill's carefully crafted message hit the mark. An opinion poll taken the week after the speech showed a 43 percent increase in the number of Americans who favored selling planes to the Allies, but it was going to take time to get Congress to change the laws.

As was often the case, FDR was ahead of the country and had already begun searching for ways to get more aid to Churchill. The administration determined that it could declare military equipment surplus and sell it to a private corporation, and the corporation could then sell directly to the British. U.S. Steel agreed to be the intermediary,[9] and Churchill sent over a long wish list, which included "93 bomber planes, 500,000 Enfield rifles, 184 tanks, 76,000 machine guns."[10] Included in the request for the bombers were several B-17s. By mid-1940 the U.S. Army had taken delivery of thirty-eight B-17s, and it agreed to divert twenty of them to the British.[11]

Bill Boeing, like most Americans, watched the situation in Europe with growing concern. He was still a firm believer in military preparedness, and just as in the years leading up to World War I, he believed that war with Germany was inevitable. But for the time being, his anger at the Roosevelt administration kept him on the sidelines. In the meantime he continued to race horses (winning thirty-four races in 1939 and twenty-two in 1940) and cruise the Northwest Pacific Coast in the *Taconite*. He also caused a stir on June 6, 1940 when he bought a custom-outfitted DC-5 twin-engine transport from Douglas aircraft. Newspapers called the plane "a luxury yacht of the sky."[12] Many people were tempted to read an implied message into this purchase – one regarding Bill's feelings toward his former company. In truth, however, Bill had bought the plane on the advice of his stepson, twenty-seven-year-old Nathaniel Paschall Jr. Nat Paschall had been hired by Donald Douglas as a salesman for Douglas Aircraft and Bill respected his judgment.

# 56. BOEING BOMBERS BLAST BATTLESHIP! 1941

General Henry "Hap" Arnold, who had been an early advocate for the B-17, was now chief of the Army Air Corps. He called Phil Johnson at home on the night of May 7, 1941. Six months earlier, Franklin Roosevelt had promised the beleaguered British that the United States would become "the great arsenal of democracy," and Arnold was working on turning this noble phrase into a tangible thing. He told Johnson that there were huge orders coming: "What is the fastest way to get mass production of planes?" he asked. "Think about it and call me back in the morning."[1]

Johnson spent a sleepless night wrestling with the problem, and came up with four basic principles:

1  Only build one or two proven models.
2  Repurpose existing factories so that time and money are not wasted building new factories, and all resources can go straight into building planes.
3  Give the factories priority for materials and machine tools.
4  Continue research and development so that when a better plane is developed it can slide into production, replacing one of the existing models.

The next morning, cradling a cup of coffee in his hands, Johnson reread his notes. They looked good. He set down the coffee and picked up the phone.

It was a surprisingly brief conversation. Johnson presented his ideas to General Arnold. The general listened and then said, "That's what we're going to do."[2] Next, Arnold announced that he was ordering 350 B-17s, and that he needed them right away. In keeping with Johnson's second point regarding the repurposing of existing plants, Arnold set about ordering a Douglas plant in Los Angeles and a Lockheed Vega Plant in Burbank to work with Boeing on producing Flying Fortresses.

Again, the irony of it all must have struck Phil Johnson powerfully. In 1934 he had been head of one of the largest aircraft manufacturers in the world, but Roosevelt had demanded that it be broken up. Now, just seven years later, one of Roosevelt's generals was telling him that his company was too small, and he had to partner with his rivals to build the planes the army wanted. Johnson had the sense not to say anything to Arnold, but it's likely he called Bill Boeing and let him know.

The friendship between Bill Boeing and Phil Johnson continued to grow. Johnson and his wife, Katie, were frequent guests at Aldarra for Bill's Bohemian parties and they often went on cruises together aboard the *Taconite*. The Johnsons had a beautiful house and enjoyed entertaining too. There is a scratchy black-and-white home movie of Bill and Bertha arriving at a costume party at the Johnsons'. Bertha is dressed as a flapper and Bill as a bootlegger with a fake nose. With an impish twinkle in his eyes, he strikes a dramatic pose, places his hands on the lapels of his long overcoat, and suddenly flashes it open to reveal dozens of inside pockets, each containing a bottle of booze.

In July 1941, Bill and Bertha headed to Los Angeles. Boeing Stables had a promising three-year-old colt named Welcome Pass racing at Hollywood Park in Inglewood. The colt was being groomed for the $75,000 Hollywood Gold Cup and, as Ted Horning prepared the spirited horse for its first big race, Bill wanted to share in the excitement.

There were several other celebrity owners with horses in the field, including Charles Howard, the owner of Seabiscuit, and Louie B. Mayer, co-founder of MGM Studios. A few days before the race, Ted Horning pulled Welcome Pass out of the competition because of a disappointing seventh-place finish in a warm-up event, but Bill and Bertha stayed in Los Angeles to watch the race anyway. It meant that Bill was not in Seattle to see the headlines on July 25. W. L. White of *The Saturday Evening Post* reported:

> The funny thing about it, that afternoon in Seattle, was the way people would forget to count their change. When they saw the headlines, BOEING BOMBERS IN ACTION: BLAST NAZI BATTLESHIP, they would walk up to the newsstands, staring like sleepwalkers, take a paper in one hand and

put the other out with the money. Never taking their eyes off the type, they would fumble the handful of change back into their pocket and stumble off down the street, still reading that story.[3]

On July 24, Britain's Royal Air Force had attacked the German battleship *Gneisenau* with Boeing-built B-17s, scoring seven direct hits.[4] As far as anyone in Seattle knew, this was the first time "their" planes had been used in live combat.[5]

> All over Seattle's business district they were reading it. On the busses coming in from the Boeing plant ... the assembly men who riveted the aluminum skin onto the big bomber's ... wing were reading it, then turning around in their seats to talk about it with the other guys who handle the jigs, stamps, saws, and dies which turn out the Flying Fortress.[6]

A few months earlier, twenty B-17s had rolled out of Boeing's Plant 2 and across a temporarily closed East Marginal Way to Boeing Field. The planes had rumbled into the sky, heading south toward Mt. Rainier, but they didn't go far, landing only 34 miles away at the newly opened McChord Field. There, U.S. Air Corps crews painted the red, white, blue, and yellow roundels of the RAF on the wings, while American pilots trained RAF pilots to fly the big plane and use its complex Sperry bombsight.[7] When the training was complete, the B-17s left McChord to hopscotch their way across North America and the Atlantic, to their new home in England. The U.S., while still technically neutral, was now 100 percent behind Britain and her Allies, and Americans were spoiling for a fight with Hitler. All across Seattle, people were proud of Boeing and the way Boeing's planes had struck a blow for liberty.

No one was prouder of that first raid than Phil Johnson. "He sits in the president's office of the Boeing Plant, overlooking the airport from which he has watched the Fortresses ... thunder into the air on the first leg of the trip to England," wrote W. L. White for the *Post*. "Phil's most striking feature is his small, narrow blue eyes which ... twinkle as he reads the praise lavished on his Flying Fortress by the British pilots. It means a job well done and an even bigger job beginning for himself."[8]

The job ahead for Johnson was huge. The army would soon be asking for 12,000 B-17s. It was to prove too great a task for one man to handle, but Johnson would give it his all right up to his death in little more than three years.

Bill Boeing may have missed out on the excitement in Seattle over the RAF raid, but he was there on November 17, 1941 when another big story broke. The headlines read, "Air-Mail 'Scandal' Charges Held Groundless."[9] After a three-year investigation, Richard H. Akers, the commissioner of the

United States Court of Claims, released a 40,000-word, 116-page report that concluded: "The contracts involved in these proceedings were secured through open, competitive bidding and route certificates were issued under the governing statutes in effect at the time of their issuance." The report also cut "the ground out from under the charges the Government made ... and ruled that the Government had no counter claim," opening the door to a $3 million suit for damages brought by former UATC divisions Boeing Air Transport, Pacific Air Transport, and United Airlines.[10]

Phil Johnson got the news from Boeing's attorneys in Washington DC, hours before the newspapers came out. It is likely that he called Bill with the good news right away. Both of them must have been thrilled at being fully exonerated. In the joy of the moment, Phil may have taken the opportunity to invite his friend to assist him in the monumental task ahead. If he did so, Bill declined the offer; he was still too angry at Roosevelt to consider it. However, in less than three weeks, events sweeping across the Pacific were to change everything.

# 57. A Day That Will Live in Infamy
## December 7, 1941

At 8 p.m. on December 6, eight brand-new B-17s from the 88th Reconnaissance Squadron were lined up, engines rumbling, on a taxiway at Hamilton Field, north of San Francisco, awaiting tower clearance to take off. Most of the planes had just arrived the day before from the Boeing plant in Seattle. They were heading to Clark Island in the Philippines to work with the 19th Bomb Group, already in the Philippines.

The tower gave permission and the big aluminum birds began to fly off into the darkness. Pilot Robert E. Thacker described it: "We roared down the runway of Hamilton toward the lights of San Francisco over the Golden Gate Bridge and into the starry night."[1] One plane had to abort because of a faulty generator, but the remaining seven met up with six additional B-17s from the 38th Reconnaissance Squadron. Thirteen strong, the planes headed into the night and across the Pacific Ocean. They were planning to stop and refuel at Hickam Field at Pearl Harbor, Hawaii, where they were scheduled to arrive at 8 a.m. on Sunday, December 7.

A short while into the flight, another one of the planes turned back with a mechanical problem, but the twelve remaining Fortresses continued into the darkness – except they could hardly be called Fortresses. At 2,500 miles from San Francisco, Hawaii was at the far outer limit of the B-17's range, so everything that was not essential was removed from the planes, and since the U.S. was not at war, that included the twenty-two cases of .50-caliber machine gun ammunition, weighing almost 3,000 pounds, that was normally carried by each B-17. Without ammunition, there was no point in mounting the guns, so they stayed neatly packed in their wooden cases as the planes flew toward an ambush.

It was Saturday night in Honolulu, and that meant date night. On the terrace of the Royal Hawaiian Hotel, young lovers swayed to the music of radio station KGMB, while warm breezes ruffled their hair and the hotel's neon sign cast a pink glow on the surf. Typically, KGMB signed off at midnight, but the U.S. Army had agreed to pay the station to stay on all night so that the bombers flying from California could home in on the radio signal.[2] Unfortunately, the B-17 pilots were not the only ones homing in on the music.

A Japanese taskforce of thirty-one warships, including six aircraft carriers, was 275 miles away, heading for Hawaii. They too were following KGMB's signal. At 6 a.m., an hour before sunrise, the carriers turned into the wind and launched the first wave of 189 planes carrying bombs and torpedoes.

Japan's leaders dreamed of turning their country into a world power. Having built a formidable military, they had taken over large parts of China in the 1930s. In 1940 they allied themselves with fascist Germany and Italy to create the Tripartite Alliance.

Natural resources were scarce in Japan, and the Japanese imported most of the steel they used to build their weapons and the oil they used to power them from the U.S. In July 1941, their access to these essential resources came under threat when they attacked and overran much of Southeast Asia, prompting Roosevelt to seize all Japanese assets in the U.S. and place an embargo on the country, demanding its withdrawal from the invaded territories. Japan refused and instead pursued an aggressive strategy based on extracting the resources they needed from their conquered neighbors. To start with, they set their sights on the Philippines, Singapore, Hong Kong, and Thailand. The only force strong enough to stand in their way was the U.S. Pacific Fleet, based at Pearl Harbor, and the Japanese goal on December 7 was to destroy that fleet.

At 7:55 a.m. an army radar operator picked up a large formation of inbound aircraft. He notified an Air Corps officer. The incoming planes were on almost the exact heading that the B-17s were expected to take, and only five minutes ahead of schedule. The Air Corps officer figured the radar contact was the flight of B-17s and did not alert anyone. It was a fatal mistake: in minutes Pearl Harbor was a scene of chaos and destruction.

At 8:00 a.m., fourteen hours and 2,500 miles after taking off, the unarmed B-17s arrived over Pearl Harbor. One of the pilots saw a large plume of black smoke and asked his co-pilot if he thought it was a farmer burning his cane fields. Another saw the brief tall splashes of spent anti-aircraft shells falling into the sea and asked if they might be whales spouting. The lead B-17 called the tower for permission to land. No answer. The pilot didn't know what was going on, but he was low on fuel after his flight across the ocean and needed to get his plane on the ground. Without permission, he lined up with the runway, extended his flaps, lowered and locked his landing gear, and descended toward the field.

All of a sudden "4 or 5 U.S. Navy destroyers shot at us," pilot Frank Bostrom recalled.[3] Finally the tower answered with the shocking news: Pearl Harbor was being attacked! The tower told the B-17 not to land. It banked away and escaped to the other side of Oahu, landing on the fairway of the Kahuku golf course. The next plane wasn't so lucky. "As we passed Diamond Head, I noticed a few bursts of [anti-aircraft] fire ... off to our right," recalled co-pilot Ernest Reid. "I thought some American ... unit was practicing. Then I saw a flight of six pursuit ships apparently flying through a bunch of ack-ack bursts. I recall thinking that somebody on the ground was getting a little careless about where he was shooting."

There was too much ack-ack around, and I began to feel that something was wrong, although I still had no idea what it was.

We had made the flight under radio silence, but we were cleared to contact the tower. They had not answered any of our calls.

We had to continue our approach; our gas supply would soon become a problem. We were now at 600 feet and turned to our final approach. I got my first clear look at Hickam Field.

What I saw shocked me. At least six planes were burning fiercely on the ground. Gone was any doubt in my mind as to what had happened. Unbelievable as it seemed, I knew we were now in a war. As if to dispel any lingering doubts, two Japanese fighters came from our rear and opened fire.

A tremendous stream of tracer bullets poured by our wings and began to ricochet inside the ship. It began to look as though I would probably have the dubious distinction of being aboard the first Army ship shot down ... smoke began to pour into the cockpit. The smoke was caused by some of their tracer bullets hitting our pyrotechnics,[4] which were stored amidships ... There was now no choice but to try to land. The captain yanked the throttles off, and I popped the landing gear switch to the down position.

Seconds later, we hit the ground. Because of the smoke inside the cockpit, we couldn't see outside very well, and the plane bounced hard. It took both of us on the controls to get the wings level after that first bounce. Then the tail came down. Almost immediately, the plane began to buckle and collapse, breaking in the middle where the fire had burned through. When that happened, we stopped very quickly.[5]

The United States was now at war with Japan, and Reid's B-17, serial number 40-2074, is claimed by many to be the first of 22,948 American planes shot down during the war.[6]

# 58. BACK IN THE FIGHT
# SEATTLE, 1942

The attack on Pearl Harbor left 2,403 Americans dead, 1,143 wounded, 347 planes damaged or destroyed, four battleships sunk, and the whole of the U.S. clamoring for revenge. The next day Roosevelt addressed a joint session of Congress. He began:

> Yesterday, December 7, 1941 – a date which will live in infamy – the United States of America was suddenly and deliberately attacked by naval and air forces of the Empire of Japan.

He then listed the other places Japan had attacked: Malaya, Guam, the Philippines, Wake Island, and Midway Island. He ended by saying:

> With confidence in our armed forces – with the unbounding determination of our people – we will gain the inevitable triumph – so help us God.
> I ask that the Congress declare that since the unprovoked and dastardly attack by Japan on Sunday, December 7, 1941, a state of war has existed between the United States and the Japanese Empire.

After a brief debate, Congress passed a resolution declaring war on Japan. Two days later Hitler declared war on the U.S. and twenty-three years of isolationism came to an end. Once more, the U.S. found itself leading the Allies in a war against Germany.

Congress directed Roosevelt "to prosecute the war to its successful conclusions" while promising "all of the resources of the country." The defense budget in 1941 had been $6.4 billion. In 1942 it increased to $25.7 billion. In 1943 it went up further to $66.7 billion, then $79.1 billion in 1944, and it topped out at $83 billion in 1945. Much of that money was earmarked for Boeing bombers.

Bill must have been struggling with conflicting emotions. He was extremely patriotic. Prior to World War I he had strongly advocated for airplanes to play a major role in the nation's defense, and during the 1920s and '30s he had built a company that had become America's largest manufacturer of fighter aircraft. He knew that airplanes would be the key to victory in this new war, and that few people knew more about building them than he did. His country needed him, yet his loathing for Franklin Roosevelt was not something he could easily ignore. In Bill's eyes, Roosevelt was the smug bureaucrat who had blocked Westervelt's resignation in 1916; the rash leader who had unjustly canceled the airmail contracts and carelessly sent more than a dozen army fliers to their deaths; and the tyrant who had held Bill's mighty UATC in his hands and broken it to pieces.

Bill spent several sleepless nights wrestling with his conscience. Christmas was approaching, and as the decorated fir trees and lighted reindeer displays began to pop up around Seattle, Bill was reminded of the Christmases he had spent in Honolulu when Billy was at school there. Now, beside the graceful coconut palms wrapped in twinkling white lights he imagined the fresh graves of his countrymen. Like most Americans, Bill hated the Japanese for their surprise attack on Pearl Harbor, but his feelings about Germany were naturally more complicated.

In the years since World War I, Bill had corresponded with his German family in the Ruhr Valley, exchanging holiday cards and birthday greetings. He felt connected. He had also admired the work of German innovators like Willie Messerschmitt and Claude Dornier and praised their contributions to the science of aviation. Like many Americans of German descent, Bill made the distinction between Hitler and the people of Germany; he had no difficulty condemning Hitler's aggression while still embracing his family's heritage. But he was enough of a realist to know that the German people would be the ones who would pay the heaviest price for a war with the U.S.

Eventually Bill's patriotism won out, and he returned to Boeing as an unpaid consultant. Even though the Boeing Company would receive billions of dollars in government contracts, it was important to Bill that he was not paid; he did not want to appear to be profiting from doing what he saw as his patriotic duty.[1]

The exact date of Bill's return is difficult to pin down. On April 5, 1942 *The Seattle Daily Times* announced that Bill was back to work at the company, and Phil Johnson confirmed it, saying, "Mr. Boeing ... has offered his services to the company for the duration of the war" and "the company more than welcomes the return of the man who gave the plant its birth."[2] The Boeing family archives provide more insight into Bill's return. They contain thousands of Boeing Company documents dating from the birth of the company until Bill's retirement at the end of 1934. From January 1935 to December 1941, there is not a single company document in those archives, but on December 26, 1941, Boeing Company memos start showing up again, indicating that Bill may have been active for several months before the *Times* announcement.

Phil Johnson gave Bill positions on three committees: management, engineering and technical, and staffing. Each committee met at least once a week, and Bill attended at least 200 committee meetings between December 26, 1941 and April 24, 1946.[3] Executive Order No. 1, from June 19, 1942, provides insight into how highly Bill's opinion was valued. The order provided a list of seventy-nine executives who should receive documents that were addressed to "All Supervisors." The directory appears to be arranged by order of importance, with Phil Johnson, president, being number one on the list and H. C. West, vice-president, number two. Number three was Bill Boeing.

The size of the management committee varied between twelve and sixteen members, who typically met at 10 a.m. on Fridays for one hour to deal with both weighty matters, such as air-raid precautions in the event of an enemy attack and progress reports on government contracts, and more mundane topics like the availability of "Boeing Slacks" for female employees and the design of the coat hangers used in the Renton plant.[4] Bill rarely spoke up in the management meetings, but he shined in the engineering and technical committee (ETC) meetings.

As soon as the management committee meeting ended, Bill would hurry to chief engineer Wellwood Beall's office for the ETC meeting, which met on Fridays at 11 a.m. The ETC was a much smaller group, with only five members, plus Bill. All were close friends from before the UATC breakup. They were: Bill Boeing, company founder; Claire Egtvedt, chairman of the board; Phil Johnson, president; Eddie Allen, director of research and development and chief test pilot; W. E. Beall, chief engineer; and E. C. Well, assistant chief engineer.

The ETC was a hands-on group that often took field trips to the factory. In a carryover from the early days at the Oxbow plant, Bill, Johnson, and Egtvedt, followed closely by the others, would walk the plant floor, asking questions, looking at parts, and working to understand every aspect of the planes they were building.

On July 3 they visited Plant 1 and toured the Engineering Test Lab to inspect B-17 brake parts and flap assemblies for the top-secret B-29 "Super Bomber." Then they stopped at the model shop to look at mocks-ups and observe aerodynamic tests on the B-29's engine nacelle. After that they went to the Static Test Building to check on the ground tests of the Wright Cyclone B-29 engines. July 17 was another inspection day: they went to Plant 2 to inspect the "Blue Print and Photo Units," and later to Plant 3 to check out the X-Ray Unit and Visual Education Unit.[5] And on it went, all through 1942; every fortnight, the "Big Three" – Boeing, Johnson, and Egtvedt, – popped up somewhere in the company to watch, learn, and inspect.

At other companies, executives sat in padded chairs in remote offices and issued edicts like would-be sovereigns; they were not expected to show up at aerodynamic tests (August 14), get their knees dirty crawling through mockups (September 4 and September 25), or shiver in the cold while touring a large hangar open to the wind (October 16).[6] But this was Bill Boeing's way. He wasn't getting paid a penny and he didn't own a single share of stock, but his name was going on these planes and he wanted to make sure that they were the best planes ever made.

Bill was tall and easy to spot. At first the workers would look up with silent awe when they saw the company's namesake walk past. Eventually they got used to his presence and were occasionally comfortable enough to throw him a friendly wave and shout "Hello, Mr. Boeing." Bill, shy and proper, never answered, but would nod his head in self-conscious acknowledgment.

Bill was often struck by how different Plant 2 was from his old Oxbow plant. This new plant was made of steel and cement and echoed with the constant rattle of rivet guns and the buzz of arc welders. Another change was the workforce: of Boeing's 50,000 Seattle-based employees, more than 30,000 were women. Most were young, in their twenties and thirties, the same age as the men they were replacing. They wore overalls over cotton shirts with their hair tucked up under colorful scarves, and they were skilled and capable. Across the nation these trail-blazing women were given the nickname "Rosie the Riveter." Bertha often told Bill that had she been younger, she could have been a "Rosie," and as Bill watched the thousands of confident women building planes, he had no doubt that Bertha would have fitted in just fine.

B-17s were being built in huge quantities and the prototype XB-29 was also heading into production, but there were many new projects to discuss. One that caught Bill's attention was known as the Model 376, a transport version of the B-29. Bill thought the plane had tremendous potential for a civilian application when the war ended. During an August 7, 1942 ETC meeting, there was a spirited debate about how best to load heavy equipment like tanks and guns into the plane, which, due to its size, sat higher than most. Bill suggested "mechanical jacks or a cargo elevator that could lift the freight up to the plane." The army eventually vetoed this idea, but it is worth noting that after the war, the powered cargo elevator was patented by an engineer for Lockheed Aircraft and is still in use at airports around the world today.

## 59. THIS TERRIBLE GAME OF WAR
## ENGLAND, 1942

At 7:15 p.m. on February 23, 1942, a Japanese submarine surfaced in the dark water a mile off the coast of Ellwood, California. It fired sixteen 5.5-inch shells from its deck gun at the rich Santa Barbara oil fields.[1] The attack made headlines all across the U.S. and Bill began to worry that his Aldarra estate, perched on the edge of Puget Sound, was vulnerable to a similar attack.

Bill knew that airplanes carrying his name would soon be dropping thousands of tons of bombs on Europe and Japan and that his celebrity might put his family at risk. Aldarra would be an easy target for a seaplane launched from a big Japanese B1 submarine in the Strait of Juan de Fuca. An enemy plane skimming the waves to avoid radar could come straight down Puget Sound some night and target Bill's well-known house without anyone knowing what was going on until the first bomb hit. Aldarra might not have been a legitimate military target, but it would be a gigantic propaganda victory if the Japanese could announce that they had "Bombed Bill Boeing." Bill decided it would be safer to move to a more secluded home in a rural community.

Ten days after *The Seattle Daily Times* announced that Bill Boeing had gone back to work for the Boeing Company, it carried another story saying that he had purchased a 500-acre piece of property called Duthie Farms in the foothills of the Cascade Mountains, near the tiny logging community of Fall City. "The farm," said the article, "one of the showplaces of King County, is highly improved. It was established by J. F. Duthie, Seattle shipbuilder, after the first World War."[2]

Duthie Farms was as close to a "Gentlemen's Farm" as could be found anywhere west of Virginia. The main house was a two-story Dutch Colonial with stone columns supporting a portico over the entryway. More stone columns flanked a wrought-iron gate at the main road. Past the gate, the driveway curved gently uphill to the house. There were tennis courts, a swimming pool, a huge manicured lawn, an apple orchard, a large vegetable garden, and a greenhouse to supply the kitchen with fresh vegetables year-round. But Duthie Farms was also a real working farm with cattle, hogs, and chickens.

The property needed upgrading and remodeling before it could meet the Boeings' needs. It also needed a name change. Bill and Bertha decided to call their new home "Aldarra Farms" and Bertha took over supervising the remodeling.

* * *

Early in 1942, the U.S. Army Air Corps created the Eighth Air Force, made up of three major units: Bomber Command, Fighter Command, and Ground Air Services Command. Its purpose was to oversee U.S. air operations in Europe. About the same time that Bill was regaining his bearings by taking walking tours around Boeing, Bomber Command decided that it was time to send U.S.-operated B-17s to Europe. Starting on June 18, B-17s from the 340th Squadron of the 97th Bomb Group began lifting off from Bangor, Maine, to make the first of several hops to take them 3,500 miles to RAF Polebrook, northwest of London.

The commander of the 340th was a twenty-seven-year-old major named Paul Tibbets. Arriving in England, Tibbets' first challenge had nothing to do with fighting Germans. Polebrook was built on land belonging to the estate of the Rothschild family, which maintained a well-stocked mansion nearby. After two years of fighting the Nazis virtually alone, the people of Britain were grateful for American help, and the Rothschilds had the resources to express their gratitude with generous cocktail parties that started in the afternoon and often ran until the next morning. More than once, Tibbets had to pull his men out of fancy parties where expensive Scotch flowed like water, to get them back to base and into bed so they would be sober enough to fly the next day.

Tibbets' first exposure to aerial bombing had come when he was twelve years old. His family lived in Miami, where his father ran a candy and confection distributor. Among his father's biggest customers was the Curtiss Candy Company, whose most popular candy bar was the Baby Ruth. Curtiss hired barnstorming pilot Doug Davis to fly his red, white, and blue WACO-9 biplane, across the U.S. dropping candy bars on tiny parachutes over county fairs, baseball games, and anywhere else he could find a crowd.

The young Tibbets was visiting his father's office when Davis stopped by to map out his candy bombing missions in Miami, and Davis casually mentioned that he needed an assistant to tie the parachutes to the candy bars and toss them out of the plane. Paul begged his father until he finally said yes. For the better part of a week, young Tibbets and Davis flew across Miami at rooftop level, tossing candy to the crowds at the Hialeah Racetrack and sunbathers at Miami Beach.

It didn't take long for Tibbets to learn that he had to "lead" the target and toss out the bars long before he was over the crowd, so that by the time they reached the ground they were on target. The basic bomber mechanics that fascinated Paul during his candy-bombing missions directly contributed to him enlisting in the air force and choosing to fly bombers.

On August 9, after weeks of training, Tibbets and the 340th Squadron were ordered to prepare for a mission over occupied France. Bad weather kept them grounded for eight days until August 17, when the rain stopped, the skies turned blue, and the mission moved ahead. By mid-afternoon eighteen B-17s, each loaded with about 3,000 pounds of bombs, sat idling on the taxiways. At 15:30 a bright green flare arced into the sky, signaling to the waiting planes that they could take off. (Radio commands risked being intercepted by German spies who would then warn the Luftwaffe, so missions were launched by flare guns.)[3]

By 15:39 all the planes had climbed to 22,000 feet and were arranged in their attack formations, heading south toward the English Channel. As they crossed the water, they were joined by a flight of British Spitfires that flew protectively above them as they headed toward enemy territory. When they reached the coast of France six of the bombers turned west to create a diversion, while the remaining twelve B-17s, led by Paul Tibbets in a plane named *Butcher Shop*,[4] flew inland to the rail yards at Sotteville, near Rouen, France, where RAF reconnaissance had found a concentration of 2,000 freight cars. Tibbets described the mission:

> We caught the Germans by surprise. They hadn't expected a daytime attack, so we had clear sailing to the target. Visibility was unlimited and all 12 planes dropped their bomb load – 36,900 pounds in all.
>
> A feeling of elation took hold of us as we winged back over the Channel. All the tension was gone. We were no longer novices at this terrible game of war. We had braved the enemy in his own skies and were alive to tell about it.[5]

Years later, a reporter asked Tibbets to describe his emotions:

> The first time I dropped bombs on a target … I watched them go down. Then I watched those black puffs of smoke and fires in some instances. I said to myself, "People are getting killed down there that don't have any business getting killed. Those are not soldiers."[6]

Tibbets reflected on General Sherman's famous "War is Hell" quote, that he hadn't invented war or started this one.

> Let it be understood that I feel a sense of shame for the whole human race, which through all history has accepted the shedding of human blood as a means of settling differences between nations.[7]
>
> My one driving interest was to do the best job I could so that we could end the killing as quickly as possible.[8]
>
> I made up my mind then that the morality of dropping that bomb was not my business. I was instructed to perform a military mission to drop the bomb. That was the thing that I was going to do [to] the best of my ability.

Morality? There is no such thing in warfare. I don't care whether you are dropping atom bombs, or 100-pound bombs, or shooting a rifle. You have got to leave the moral issue out of it.[9]

In a twist of fate straight out of a dime-store novel, Tibbets had the distinction of being lead pilot on the first Eighth Air Force heavy bomber mission of World War II in Europe, and thirty-two months later he piloted the plane that dropped the world's first atomic bomb on Hiroshima, Japan.

# 60. SUPERFORTRESS
# 1942

In the early days of World War II, when France fell to Germany and Britain was fighting for its life, U.S. generals faced the possibility that they might have to fight Germany alone. They realized that they needed a long-range bomber capable of attacking targets in Europe from bases in Greenland and Canada. Boeing was already working on Model 345, its own idea for a "Super bomber"; it would be bigger and faster than the B-17, with a range above 4,500 miles. In August 1940, the army ordered two prototypes and labeled them XB-29s. Britain survived the "Battle of Britain," but the war in Asia caught fire and as the island-hopping nature of the conflict with Japan became apparent, the army realized that the long-range B-29 was exactly the plane it needed. Even before the first B-29 had flown, the army ordered more than 1,500 of them[1] and committed roughly $3 billion to the program.[2]

The journey from preliminary drawings to completed prototype is rarely smooth, and the B-29's journey was rougher than most. The army had a lot of questions. In the bluntest of terms, it worried that the plane couldn't fly. Army engineers operated under a long-standing aerodynamic theory that the maximum amount of lift a plane's wing could develop was 54 pounds per square foot. The B-29 was using a new, high-aspect wing with large "Fowler Flaps" that Boeing claimed would provide 69 pounds of lift per square foot. If Boeing's calculations were wrong, the plane would be too heavy for its wings and would not fly. With a price tag of $639,000 per plane and 1,500 on order, there was a lot riding on whether the plane could get off the ground.

Seattle was suffering through a long drought in September 1942. The grass around Boeing field was brown when the huge B-29 was rolled out on September 21 for its first flight. As the polished aluminum skin of the plane's 141-foot wings glinted in the sunshine, Bill and four other members of Boeing's engineering and technical committee shaded their eyes from the glare. The ETC's sixth member, Eddie Allen, was busy going through his preflight checklist from the pilot's seat.

This was Allen's big day. He was not only the brains behind the super bomber, he was Boeing's chief test pilot. He was forty-six, balding, with a trim pencil-thin mustache. Contrary to the dashing test-pilot image promoted by Hollywood, Allen was a vegetarian who loved poetry and practiced yoga.[3] He had been called "a scientist at heart."[4] The men he worked with said that "he loved the search for a fundamental principle, not so much with his hands as with thought; not so much his own findings as the findings of his group."[5] He once said, "For me to sit here and make design decisions would be the worst kind of folly. This is a group effort."[6]

Allen brought a huge advantage to the job of an engineer. Most had to stand on the ground and watch "their" planes fly, and then quiz the pilots about what it was doing once they landed. Allen was his own test pilot. He took "his" planes up and could diagnose what was going on in real time. And he was such a well-respected test pilot that even though he was a long-time Boeing employee, other manufacturers would hire him to make the first flight in their new planes.[7]

The B-29 moved into position at the north end of the runway. Because the plane was top secret, there were only few spectators and none of the normal fanfare that usually accompanied a first flight. Allen set the brakes. His back was to the city of Seattle and the big bomber's Plexiglas nose was pointed almost directly at Mt. Rainier.

The plane was powered by four gigantic Wright Cyclone Duplexes at 3,350 cubic inches each. One at a time, Allen ran the Cyclones up to full power. When all four engines were howling, he released the brake and began to roll forward. The plane picked up speed, lifting easily. Johnson, Boeing, and Egtvedt cheered as they watched the plane climb into the hazy fall sky and curve west over Puget Sound. After several comfortable circles around the Sound, the plane came back to a perfect landing. Allen climbed out and joyously announced, "She flies!"[8] By the broad smile on his face, it was clear that he loved this plane, but in under a year it would cost him his life.

At the exact time that Eddie Allen was bringing the enormous B-29 back to earth at Boeing Field, an old-fashioned steam locomotive was chugging across Eastern Washington at the sedate speed of 35 mph, heading for Puget Sound. It was pulling a top-secret string of ten rail cars, and at the tail end of the train was an olive-green Pullman coach, 84 feet long, 15 feet tall, and 10 feet wide. It was trimmed with gold paint and featured bullet-proof armor. Stenciled on the rear corner of the coach were the inconspicuous letters: "U.S. N°. 1." The letters were small, only a few inches tall, but they were important. U.S. N°.

1 meant that this car got priority over every other train car in the U.S. The reason was that this car carried Franklin D. Roosevelt, the President of the United States.

While all the U.S. thought that Roosevelt was taking a well-deserved late summer vacation, he was actually on a twenty-four-state mission to visit the country's major defense plants and military facilities.[9] At Boeing, only Phil Johnson and perhaps Bill Boeing knew of his scheduled visit. He arrived at Fort Lewis on the morning of September 22 to observe combat maneuvers by the 33rd Infantry Division. After he had watched a noisy demonstration of armored cars and tanks from the front seat of a DeSoto convertible, the Secret Service drove him through Tacoma. They then crossed the Tacoma Narrows by ferry to the shipyards in Bremerton. Roosevelt spent several hours touring the shipyards before he and his entourage caught another ferry, this time to Seattle. From the water, the typically beautiful view of Seattle and Mt. Rainier was obscured by a smoky haze, the result of late-season forest fires.

Roosevelt arrived at Boeing's Plant 2 late in the afternoon. Before entering the factory, the President's car stopped to take in Arthur B. Langlie, governor of Washington, and Boeing's president, Phil Johnson. Boeing was now turning out twenty-five B-17s per week. Roosevelt's convertible cruised slowly beneath the wings of the big four-engine bombers. According to *The Seattle Post Intelligencer*, "Expressions of amazement flooded the faces of hundreds of workers as they looked up from their jobs and saw the President. He waved. They cheered and then with scarcely a pause they were [back] at work."[10]

The President asked that everyone keep his visit a secret until he could get back to Washington DC on October 1. The newspapers and radio stations all cooperated, as did most of the Boeing employees, but a few rumors inevitably leaked out. A particularly intriguing one is that, at the beginning of Roosevelt's tour, in a special restricted area of the plant where the top-secret B-29 was being worked on, the President found a moment to have a brief conversation with Bill Boeing, although there is nothing in the archives to confirm it.

When Roosevelt left the factory, he drove underneath six completed B-17s waiting to head across the ocean to war. He then spent the night visiting his daughter Anna Roosevelt Boettiger and her husband John Boettiger, who lived on nearby Mercer Island, and the next morning he was back on his secret train, continuing his journey.

September 23, the day after Roosevelt's visit, Bill was back at Boeing for a special meeting of the ETC. The U.S. had only been at war for nine months, and Boeing was in line for billions in government contracts, but three of the principals of the ETC, Johnson, Egtvedt, and Bill Boeing, recalled working at the company when World War I ended. Bill called it "the hard struggle," when government contracts were canceled, employees were laid off, and Boeing had to build bedroom furniture to survive.

The end of the war was years in the future, but no one wanted to repeat the post-war struggles, so the topic of this day's meeting was, "Planning for the Future." W. E. Beall, the chief engineer, presented a report outlining the challenges and opportunities that the company might face in a post-war economy. His report also included a million-dollar engineering research budget to make sure that when the war ended, Boeing would know what type of planes the world would need and be ready to build them. Johnson, Egtvedt, and Boeing approved the budget and thus ensured that the transition from war to peace would not become another "hard struggle."[11]

Two weeks later, on October 16, Bill received a certified letter from the Boeing Company. He carefully opened the envelope to find another envelope enclosed within. The inner envelope was stamped "LIMITED" four times on the front. Turning the envelope over, Bill saw a large red wax seal and the word "LIMITED" stamped three more times. He used a letter opener to slice open the second envelope and slipped out a few typewritten pages. They were revised pages to replace four of the original pages of W. E. Beall's "Planning for the Future" research program. The first two pages only included some minor clerical corrections, but the third page shocked Bill. It included a new area of research: "Installation of Jet Propulsive Systems in Aircraft." Boeing was going to be building jets.

# 61. FARM LIFE
## FALL CITY, 1942

Bill and Bertha moved into their new home in rural Washington on September 23, 1942. At the same time they announced that they would be donating their Aldarra estate in the Highlands to Seattle's Children's Orthopedic Hospital.

"Our official move into our beautiful new house," wrote Bertha in her diary. "A magnificent warm, clear sunny day, the valley below gay with autumn foliage."[1] The move was more than just a change of address; it was a wholesale change of lifestyle. To be sure, the farm was a showpiece and offered an opportunity for Bill and Bertha to entertain their wealthy friends, but it was also a real working farm with tractors, plows, and all the backbreaking work one might expect. There was a staff to handle much of the day-to-day work, but Bill and Bertha wanted to do more than just live on the farm; they wanted to embrace the lifestyle and learn how to run the farm themselves.

In many ways, Bill's desire to have his feet planted firmly in two worlds harkened back to his early days in Hoquiam, when he spent weeks slogging through the damp woods cruising his own timberland and then returned to Virginia and the privileged lifestyle of a Gilded Age gentleman. And just as Bill had always reveled in serving his *Taconite* guests the salmon or halibut that he had caught himself, he enjoyed providing food he had produced with his own hands on his farm. With wartime food rationing being imposed across the country, the idea of being self-sufficient was irresistibly attractive to Bill.

Bertha's diary illustrates the complete change in lifestyle brought by living on the farm:

February 5ᵗʰ, 1943, About 3:30 we began to churn butter. It took us hours for the cream was too thick but eventually the job was done, and the result was excellent, about 7 ½ lbs of butter from 2 ½ gallons of cream. Dinner was late, but we did enjoy it – steak – broccoli and carrots and frozen strawberries. Then Jack Knight – Butcher [from] "Pleased to Meat You" arrived [to] bring us our steer all neatly packaged – and we stored it away in our cold freeze box.

February 6ᵗʰ, 1943, we had a delicious supper of hamburgers from our <u>own</u> steer.

February 9ᵗʰ, 1943, Cold, gray and overcast. To Issaquah in the Farm Truck with Bill [driving] to put part of our steer meat in the locker at the Grange Mercantile Store.

February 13, 1943, Foggy all day and damp. The two WEBs [Bill and Bill Jr.] drove over to Wally Moore's and picked up a hundred or so week-old New Hampshire chickens.[2]

Bill was enjoying his new role as gentleman farmer. "Dutch" Abbot, the farm manager, was good about keeping the farm supplied with everything it needed, but Bill wanted to be involved in all aspects of farming. If there was something that needed picking up on a day that he was already heading to town for a Boeing meeting, Bill would take the farm's dark blue Ford pick-up truck and stop by one of the farm supply stores south of the plant on his way home after his meetings.

February 18, 1943 was a cold gray day that threatened rain. There was a Boeing management committee meeting scheduled for 11:30 a.m., so Bill had to leave Aldarra by 10:00 to make it to the office on time. Around 10:30 a.m. he paid the 45-cent toll on the Lake Washington Floating Bridge and headed across the lake toward town. After crossing the lake, the bridge fed into a tunnel underneath the Mt. Baker neighborhood and let out onto Rainier Avenue. A quick right on Rainier, followed by a left on Dearborn and another left onto Airport Way, and he had a 3-mile run straight to Boeing Field. On the right side of Airport Way was a large red-brick building with 4-foot-tall white lettering spelling out "FRYE'S DELICIOUS BRAND HAM AND BACON." Before Bill had become a farmer, he had probably never given this meat-packing plant a moment's thought, but now, driving by, he might have thought about it in connection to cutting and packing some of the dozen or so Duroc hogs he had at the farm. By the end of the day, and for the most tragic reasons, this building would be forever seared into his memory.

Bill was chatting casually with Claire Egtvedt and chief engineer Ed Wells at 11:30 when Phil Johnson called the management committee meeting to order. The first piece of business was a report on B-17 production by executive vice-president Oliver West, who proudly announced that they were expecting to deliver 176 B-17s in February and hoped to be up to 200 per month soon. Harold Mansfield was at the meeting and described what happened next:

> The telephone rang in the anteroom. Ed Wells slipped out to get it. He reappeared at the door, face ashen. "The tower just got a message from Eddie [chief B-29 test pilot Eddie Allen], they're coming in with a wing on fire."[3]

There was a flurry of activity as the meeting broke up and everyone rushed across Marginal Way to the field. Allen wasn't alone in the plane; along with him was a crew of ten Boeing engineers and aerodynamicists.

Bill had no difficulty imagining the scene on the flight deck as Allen struggled to save the plane. Two weeks earlier, Eddie Allen had given Bill a tour of the B-29's cockpit mockup.[4] His confident voice still echoed in Bill's mind, pointing out gauges and switches on the B-29's complicated control panel. There were two B-29 prototypes; on this day, Allen was flying the second plane. He had already had one scare when a runaway propeller had caused an engine fire; Allen had been lucky to save the plane that day. Everyone on the ground was hoping he could do it again.

> [On the flight deck of the plane] Eddie turned to the flight engineer, "Feather Number [one]! Fire extinguisher!" Smoke and sparks were streaking from the exhaust stack ... the fire was getting worse, globs of oil streaming through the cowl flaps. "Give it another $CO_2$ bottle."
> The extinguisher had no effect. Smoke began pouring into the cockpit through the bomb bay. Crew members were coughing and choking, their eyes smarting. Flames were trailing in long fingers from the nacelle access door.[5]

The plane was a few miles south of the field and heading back at about 135 mph. Allen was prepared to declare an emergency and land from the south, flying against the pattern. "When they were a half mile from the field, the last $CO_2$ bottle was fired into the nacelle," wrote Mansfield. "This one seemed to smother the fire, but smoke and carbon dioxide fumes grew denser in the cabin."[6]

With no flames visible and the fire apparently under control, Allen decided that a landing from the north, the correct direction, would be safer. He flew past the field, banked to the left to get on the base leg of the pattern, then one more left and he was on final approach. Suddenly one of the fuel tanks erupted in an explosion of flames.

Bill, Phil, and the other worried executives gathered on the field, waiting for Eddie to come sailing over the end of the runway and set the big plane down with a screeching of brakes. It wasn't to be. A huge plume of black smoke swirled into the sky north of the runway.

When the fuel tank caught fire, the B-29 lost altitude, narrowly missing a hospital, and slammed into the side of the Frye & Company packing plant.[7] It exploded into a raging inferno that killed Eddie Allen and the entire crew. The fire also killed twenty-one employees of the packing plant and a Seattle firefighter, making it the deadliest airplane crash in the history of Seattle. Adding to the hellish scene of the crash, the plant was full of hogs waiting to be slaughtered; the awful shrieking as eighty of the hogs burned to death, while dozens more of the panicked animals raced through the flaming rubble, turned the crash site into a scene from an awful nightmare.

# 62. AFTERMATH
## SEATTLE, 1943

At 2 p.m. on February 23, the rivet guns and drill presses fell silent at all of Boeing's plants. Every man and woman stood with heads bowed, wiping tears from their eyes as the slow mournful sound of "Taps" was played over the loudspeakers. The music was being piped in live from the Masonic Temple's Shrine Auditorium on East Pine, where the eleven flag-draped, flower-strewn coffins of Eddie Allen and his crew were being honored. When the music ended each casket was carried to its waiting hearse by a military honor guard comprised of army officers assigned to the Boeing Company. *The Seattle Daily Times* described the service as Boeing's farewell to eleven comrades "who as surely as the men of Bataan and Guadalcanal had laid down their lives so that their country might live."[1]

According to Bertha's diary, her son Cranston Paschall, who was a test pilot on the B-29 program, drove out to the farm with his wife and daughter Jane a week after the accident.[2] Jane, who was only five at the time, remembers sitting with her mother and "Mother Bee" (Bertha), while her father and "Grandpa YoYo" (her childhood name for Bill) talked quietly in private. Neither Bertha's diary nor Jane's childhood memories shed any light on the conversation, but it is impossible to imagine that they talked about anything other than the accident. Jane does remember that her father and "YoYo" talked about planes whenever they got a chance and that Bill "never lost his love of aviation."[3]

Sunday, February 28 was, in the words of Bertha's diary, "a beautiful, warm and sunny day!" It was only ten days after the accident. Claire Egtvedt and his wife Evelyn came by Aldarra Farms for Sunday lunch. It was the Egtvedts' first visit to the farm. Taking advantage of the nice weather, Bill gave Claire a walking tour; it must have been a good opportunity for both men to talk privately about the crash and how much their dear friend Eddie would be missed.

The farm was a peaceful sanctuary to be enjoyed between friends. For the next several years, at least twice a month, Egtvedt and his wife, often joined by Phil and Katie Johnson, found the time to come to Aldarra for Sunday dinners. While strolling around the farm on these quiet Sundays, Bill, Claire, and Phil had the chance to talk openly about company issues without the risk of being overheard, to relive shared memories and to indulge in whatever conversations that came to mind, whether regarding their health, the war, politics or how to keep building the best planes they could.

At 11:30 a.m. on March 4, Phil Johnson called the management committee to order. He began by reminding everyone about the correct way to handle confidential data. The reason for the reminder became obvious as soon as Henry West stood up and announced that he was about to make a full report on the causes of the B-29 crash.[4] Bill had sat through many accident investigations before, but never one in which so many of the victims were people he had known. He tried to concentrate on West's flat, factual delivery in the hope that it might make it more bearable.

Eddie Allen and the B-29 took off from Boeing Field at 12:09 on February 18 with 5,410 gallons of fuel onboard. At eight minutes after takeoff, as the plane was climbing past 5,000 feet, a fuel supply line on engine number one began leaking. The fuel ignited when it came into contact with hot portions of the engine. Allen immediately shut down the engine, feathered the propeller, and activated the onboard $CO_2$ fire extinguisher. He then notified the tower that he was descending to 2,400 feet and returning to the field.

The first extinguisher did not keep the fire from spreading. As the plane approached the field a second extinguisher was discharged, which knocked down all visible flames, but smoke continuing to come from the nacelle indicated that the fire was not completely out. Allen elected to make a normal landing, from the north, so he flew past the field and over the city. The plane was so low that witnesses in the upper floors of Seattle's Smith Tower reported looking down on the plane. Allen banked to the left to enter the landing pattern in the normal fashion. Suddenly fire erupted again; perhaps fuel that had pooled up in the nacelle splashed onto the hot engine when the plane banked.

With the fire extinguishers exhausted, Allen had no choice but to proceed with landing as quickly as possible. The fire then ignited the magnesium valves for the wing deicing system. Magnesium burns at over 5,000 degrees Fahrenheit and its flames quickly reached a fuel tank in the wing, causing a massive explosion. Two crewmen attempted to bail out, but the plane was too low. Their parachutes didn't open and they died upon impact with the ground. At 12:26 the plane struck two power lines near the intersection of Walker Street and Airport Way, and then slammed into the Frye & Company packing plant.

So much had gone wrong, but the one piece of good news in the heartbreaking report was that because the plane hit the plant in the middle of the noon lunch hour, most of the employees were away eating lunch, so the loss of life was not as horrific as it might have been.

The army's review of the crash resulted in the flight test operations being withdrawn from Boeing and given to the Air Corps. The first test pilot that the Air Corps assigned to the B-29 program was the newly promoted Colonel Paul W. Tibbets.[5] The army was also concerned that Seattle was too close to the Pacific Ocean and therefore vulnerable to a Pearl Harbor-style attack from aircraft carriers. The army insisted that Boeing move a large portion of its B-29 production inland to Wichita, Kansas.[6]

Even with all the interest being given to the B-29, Boeing's main focus was still the B-17 program. In 1942 Boeing had received orders for 6,785 B-17s. Production was divided, with an order of 1,350 going to Douglas, 1,400 to Lockheed, and 4,035 staying in Seattle. Most of the 1942 orders were delivered in 1943, and soon Boeing's Plant 2 was turning out twelve planes per day.

Whenever possible, Bill would stop and watch as a new flight of bombers lifted off from Boeing Field to join the war. As satisfying as it was to see planes bearing his name flying away to do their part in defeating Hitler, it was poignant too. Bill knew that the B-17s he was watching take off and fly south were heading into combat and would run a tremendous risk of being shot down. With crews of ten men for each of the twelve new planes leaving each day, Bill knew that, day after day, his planes were carrying off dozens of boys who would never be coming home.

# 63. Run for the Roses
## Fall City, 1943

You can do your best to prepare for the hard knocks and difficult shocks of life. One can stay strong in the face of adversity, but sometimes a small thing can sneak under your defenses and cause incredible pain.

Bill was doing well in dealing with Eddie's death and the general worry over B-17 combat losses and production stresses. He even coped admirably when, on March 7, less than a month after the B-29 catastrophe, he and Bertha received a call from the emergency room at Harborview Hospital saying that their son Billy, twenty years old by 1943, had been involved in a motorcycle accident and was seriously hurt.[1]

When Bill and Bertha arrived at the hospital, they were relieved to learn that Billy's injuries were not life threatening. He had a compound fracture of his right leg and would need to be transferred to Virginia Mason Hospital for surgery.[2] He was going to be all right, but the shock and anxiety inevitably took a toll on his parents, especially his father.

Bill and Bertha had a couple of dogs at the farm, and they were a comfort to Bill. There was a young Airedale terrier named Tag-a-log and a brown and black Pomeranian with a tiny white beard named Lilly-Pups, who acted like she owned the farm. Dogs tend to choose "their person," and there is little doubt that Lilly-Pups had chosen Bill.[3]

March 18 was a clear day that started with temperatures in the teens, with the heavy freeze causing puddles to turn into miniature skating rinks. The sun shone bright but never warmed up enough to melt the frost in the shade of the barns. Bill let the dogs out. For a while they barked and played and chased leaves. It wasn't long before Tag-a-long was scratching to come in. Bill opened the door and Tag rushed in, but the little Pomeranian stayed out to keep playing.

The ETC was meeting that afternoon to discuss changes to the B-29 based on the accident investigation. Bill couldn't miss it and didn't wait for Lilly-Pups to come in; Bertha would be home all day and she could let the dog in later. Bill got in his car and left. Unbeknownst to him, the loyal little dog chased his car for a while and got lost when she gave up and tried to head home.

The meeting turned out to be fascinating. Before addressing the B-29, there was a report on a "mockup conference" held earlier that morning with a delegation of army personnel who had toured plywood mockups of the Model 367 (which the army was now calling the XC-97). Plywood mockups were inexpensive to build and allowed the army to see exactly what a plane would look like in different configurations before making a final selection.

That day the army brass had toured and approved a mockup of the XC-97 cockpit layout. Next, they compared two different loading options. One consisted of large side doors, much like the waist gun openings on a B-17, and the other was a rear loading ramp that swung down beneath the tail, allowing freight and even small vehicles like jeeps to be loaded straight in. The army chose the drive-up ramp.

The meeting then turned to the B-29 accident. Boeing engineering already had eighteen safety modifications to recommend. The changes included increased fire extinguisher capacity and a simplification of the fuel system to eliminate hose joints (thereby reducing the chance of leaks). The engineers also called for external drains anywhere that leaked fuel could pool. Additional fire stops were recommended, and the engineers called for flammable materials (like the magnesium deicer valves) to be replaced.[4]

Bill returned from the meeting with a lot on his mind. He sat in his study reading for a while. Eventually it was time for dinner. He filled the dogs' bowls and put one down for Tag, who came skidding across the linoleum with a clatter of claws. Then he opened the back door and called for Lilly-Pups. She never showed. After a while he let the door swing closed, thinking she would come in when she got hungry.

It was dark by 7:30 and still no sign of Lilly-Pups. It gets cold fast in the foothills. By 10 p.m. the temperature had dropped to the 20s. Bill stood at the back door one more time, whistling and calling for the missing dog before heading to bed. He couldn't sleep. Every few hours he would put on his robe and slippers, head to the back door and call.

Bill had been a rock all though the B-29 crash and the follow-up ETC meetings. He had held Bertha's hand and talked reassuringly at the hospital after Billy's accident. Now he was undone by his missing dog.

At 3 a.m. he whispered to Bertha that he was going out to find her. Bertha insisted that they go together. They bundled up in coats and scarves, each grabbed a flashlight and headed into the frosty night for what Bertha described as "a lugubrious search" of the farm "in very cold moonlight at 3AM." They didn't find anything. Chilled to the bone and depressed, they came back to the house to warm up and try to sleep. Bertha's diary called it "a bad night followed by a worse morning. But at noon – Baldwin [one of the farm hands] found our prodigal pup in Issaquah."[5]

Bill was overjoyed. Lily-Pups raced up to him, wagging her tail and jumping up. Bill knelt down and hugged her long and tight, as if by hugging her he could undo all the pain he had experienced in the past month.

\* \* \*

Bill was still deeply involved in horse racing. When his two-year-old chestnut stallion Slide Rule was an unexpected winner in the Babylon Handicap at New York's Aqueduct Racetrack in 1942, sports writers across the nation began to tout the horse as a favorite for 1943's Kentucky Derby.

Wartime travel restrictions dramatically changed the way the 1943 Derby would look. The ability to wage modern mechanized warfare successfully depended on the availability of gas, oil, and rubber, and to ensure that the U.S. military had these supplies in the quantities it needed, the Roosevelt administration created the Office of Defense Transportation, charged with "coordinating all domestic transportation for the successful prosecution of the war."[6] The ODT had broad powers, which included rationing all American households to 3 gallons of gasoline per week, canceling motorsports like the Indianapolis 500, and requiring the World Series to be played in a "4-3" format so that the teams would only travel once during the competition.

On February 6, 1943, Joseph Eastman, director of the ODT, announced that "because of the heavy demands on railroads and inter-city bus lines for the movement of troops and other necessary passenger traffic ... it would be better, from a transportation standpoint, if the Kentucky Derby were not run."[7]

Matt Winn, president of Churchill Downs, the racetrack where the Derby was held, immediately made Eastman an intriguing offer: he promised to host a "Street Car Derby" whereby no out-of-town tickets would be sold, no special trains would be run, and locals wishing to attend the race would not be allowed to drive their own cars but would have to come via streetcars. Eastman accepted the compromise and the sixty-ninth "Run for the Roses" was scheduled to go ahead on Saturday, May 1, with no out-of-town attendees and the traditional box seats reserved for the horse owners turned over to Louisville servicemen home on leave.

Two of Bill's horses, Slide Rule and Twose, were selected for the race, but with the out-of-state travel ban, he and Bertha were unable to attend. The race was to be carried live on CBS radio, so they invited friends to a "Derby Party" at Aldarra, where they would serve traditional mint juleps and gather around the radio to listen to the race.

The broadcast began at 1:30 Seattle time, with the race starting at 2:40. Earlier in the morning, trainer Cecil Williams had called from Louisville to let Bill know he was scratching Twoese, but Slide Rule was in great spirits. Bertha made sure that everyone was gathered around the big mahogany Zenith console radio by post time with a mint julep in hand.

As the gravelly voice of Clem McCarthy came out of the speakers, Bill shushed the crowd. McCarthy described the horses being loaded into the starting gate. Blue Swords was on the rail, Slide Rule was in lane two. The race favorite, Count Fleet, owned by Fannie Hertz, wife of the rental-car company founder John Hertz, was in lane five. Gold Shower, another favorite, was in lane ten. Bill turned up the radio and McCarthy's rapid-fire call filled the room:

Steady … Steady … AND THEY'RE OFF! And they get away together … it's Gold Shower on the outside, he's stepping to the front, he's got a half a length lead … Blue Swords on the inside is second. Burnt Cork is lying in third. Count Fleet with Johnny Longden is driving … through the middle, [and] is now in third place! They're going to the turn and it's Gold Shower in the lead by three quarters of a length, Count Fleet is in second place, Longden taking no chances with him. Burnt Cork is third on the outside and Blue Swords just two lengths away in fourth place and right after them we've got Amber Light in fifth place, so far being out run …

Bill looked questioningly at Bertha as if to say, "Where is our horse?"

… and while I'm talking to you Count Fleet is going up and challenging Gold Shower for the lead! … And now Slide Rule is moving through on the inside, going up to get third place and going up very fast on Count Fleet.

Aldarra erupted in cheers. Bertha was jumping up and down and Bill was shushing everyone so he could hear.

Count Fleet is now only two lengths in front, … Slide Rule cut that corner, driving hard on the inside to get to second place … but that Blue Swords is a game horse; he's making one more challenge … but Count Fleet is safe. COUNT FLEET IS HOME FOR THE KENTUCKY DERBY! It's Count Fleet by three lengths, Blue Swords is second by five lengths and Slide Rule is third.[9]

The crowd at Aldarra cheered. The vast majority of Thoroughbred owners never even get a chance to run a horse in the Derby, so a third-place finish was well worth celebrating.

The race gained in significance when Count Fleet followed up his Kentucky Derby win with wins at the Preakness Stakes and the Belmont Stakes to become only the sixth horse in history to claim the Triple Crown.

# 64. THE BOEING BRAND
## ALDARRA, 1943

With his involvement in Thoroughbred racing, Bill had developed an interest in horse breeding. It fascinated him how the right combination of mare and stallion, neither with any great history, could produce a champion, and likewise, the careless pairing of two notable champions could easily produce unexceptional offspring. Bill was determined to make Aldarra Farms a successful working farm, and his interest in breeding racehorses triggered his decision to pursue cattle breeding.

In April 1943 Bill bought twenty-nine pregnant Guernsey dairy cows. They became the foundation of his new herd and his first step toward creating one of the Pacific Northwest's most successful cattle ranches.

With Aldarra soon to be home to dozens of head of cattle, Bill needed to come up with a "brand" to identify his livestock.[1] It turned out that there was already a simple pairing of numbers and a letter that people associated with Bill Boeing: B17. In August, the state approved, registered and published the brand, and from then on Bill's livestock was branded B17.[2]

Many historians, unaware of Bill's role at the company during World War II, have concluded that he did not have any input on the B-17. However, it would have been uncharacteristic of Bill to have so personally identified himself with the name had he not felt closely associated with the plane's development.

* * *

In 1943, the Department of War revived a program of 1906 named "The Army-Navy Production Award." The World War II version was named "The Army – Navy E," with the "E" standing for "Excellence in Production." It was an exclusive award, given to "plants which have achieved outstanding performance."[3] Of the 85,000 manufacturing businesses involved in the war effort, only 5 percent had received an E by the end of the war.

Boeing Flying Fortress School (a training school for B-17 flight crews and mechanics) was given the award on May 21, 1943, making Boeing the first business on the West Coast to win an E. Fourteen hundred students showed up to stomp and cheer while Phil Johnson and Bill Boeing accepted the award from Brigadier-General Claude E. Duncan of the Army Air Corps. "Our task is not finished," said Johnson in his acceptance speech. "The enemy is far from broken. We give our solemn pledge not to relent in our efforts until the enemy lays down his arms."[4]

The dignitaries sat on a raised platform at Boeing Field while brand-new B-17s rumbled into the air. Both *The Seattle Daily Times* and the *Post-Intelligencer* carried photos showing Bill and Phil on the stage, providing concrete evidence of Bill's ongoing involvement in the company.

The B-29s were flying again and on May 30, Bill's stepson, B-29 test pilot Cranston Paschall (known in the family as "Boo"), buzzed the farm: Bertha noted in her diary, "Boo paid an aerial call about 1:30 PM today."[5]

Bill was now balancing his commitments at both the farm and the company. He was learning that farming was ruled tyrannically by the weather, and that he literally had to make hay when the sun was shining. The first two weeks of June were warm and sunny, and Bill spent the time in the fields helping harvest the hay before the weather turned wet. Bertha's diary kept track:

Tuesday June 8th, Hayed all day!

June 9th Haying Continues, thanks to our neighbor Hanson who operated the hay loader today, 17 loads went into the small silo.

June 12th Haying continues to go into the silos, the big silo is almost finished.

June 14th Hay stacked for silage near the barn WEB [Bertha's shorthand for William E. Boeing] reported for supper with hay seeds in his hair.

June 15th The outdoor stack of hay grows hourly – WEB has put in a good day's work.[6]

Bill still took his corporate responsibilities very seriously, and on a morning in early June 1943, in the middle of haying, he brushed off his clothes, hurried to his car, and rushed to the plant to make sure he was in Wellwood Beall's office by 12:30 for an important ETC meeting.

The committee was deciding how to move forward on a classified directive from the Army Materiel Command to begin preliminary design work on the first United States jet-engine bomber.[7] Germany, Britain, and the U.S. had all been experimenting with jet fighters since the late 1930s and early 1940s, and disturbing new intelligence coming out of Germany indicated that Messerschmitt was preparing to mass produce a twin-engine jet fighter capable of speeds of over 550 mph. The army worried that Boeing's 200-mph B-17 would be helpless against such a fearsome weapon. While brushing seeds and grass clippings off his pants from his morning's haying, Bill Boeing discussed with Phil Johnson and Claire Egtvedt whether they should try to add jet engines to the B-29 airframe or build a completely new plane.

In the security-conscious era of World War II, sometimes a document is more important for what it doesn't say than what it does. On September 9, 1943, the ETC's agenda was cryptically described as "General Discussion."[8] E. C. Wells' official minutes of the meeting don't offer much more information than a statement of its attendees – only Bill Boeing, Phil Johnson, Claire Egtvedt, and himself – and a nebulous topic of discussion: "Army and Navy projects including relative priority of projects."[9] The details of the meeting begin to emerge, however, when one analyzes the list of Boeing models. The military jet, which had only been a theory when Bill had met with the ETC after cutting hay in June, was coming to life. It was assigned Model 424, and serious design work began in early September 1943.[10] Boeing had entered the jet age.

# 65. Bombing the Stadium (Again)
# 1943

Bertha's foster sister, Amy Burnett,[1] had inherited a large hay farm on the south end of Lake Washington, in the small town of Renton. The land turned out to be too swampy for farming, so in 1936 she deeded it to the State of Washington. At the start of World War II, the U.S. Navy ordered fifty-seven Boeing PBB-1 Sea Ranger flying boats, and because Boeing's Plant 2 was overcrowded with B-17s, the navy bought the vacant farmland and built an airplane factory to give Boeing a place to build the flying boats. Then, in 1943 the War Department determined that B-29s were the priority, so it canceled the order of flying boats and converted the factory to B-29 production.

According to Bertha's diaries, Bill soon found himself spending one day a week at the Renton plant and another at Boeing Plant No. 2. Even in the early days of the company, Bill hadn't gone to the plant very often, preferring to work from his office on Second Avenue. Back then, if Johnson or Egtvedt had questions, they would visit him at the Hoge Building. It is likely that the two days a week Bill spent shuttling between plants during the war was the most time he had ever spent working on site at company property.

Bill and Bertha still found time to host the Johnsons and Egtvedts for dinner a couple of times a month, and during the summer of 1943 the Boeings entertained other luminaries as well, including Harold Lobdell, manager of personnel for MIT's Division of Industrial Cooperation and Research, and Admiral Jack Fletcher of the U.S. Navy.

Fletcher had been the operational commander at the critical battles of the Coral Sea and Midway, the first two victories for the U.S. Navy after Pearl Harbor. He used his U.S. carrier task force to attack and destroy five out of six Japanese aircraft carriers and to clear the way for the U.S. to go on the offensive in the Pacific. He was hailed as a hero and awarded the Distinguished Service Medal, but his public image suffered a month later when he was put in charge of supporting the amphibious assault on Guadalcanal with a carrier task force.

After the marines had secured their beachhead, Fletcher withdrew his ships for the evening to protect them from night attacks from land-based torpedo bombers. While Fletcher was steaming back to Guadalcanal the next morning, a U.S. supply convoy was attacked and savaged by Japanese cruisers. The convoy was unable to resupply the marines and Fletcher was criticized by civilians in the Roosevelt Administration who accused him of caring more about protecting his ships than the marines on the beachhead. He was relieved of his command and reassigned to a desk job in Seattle.

When Bill and Admiral Fletcher met, they immediately bonded, perhaps over their mutual experiences of being (in their minds) mistreated by the Roosevelt administration. During the summer of 1943, the Fletchers were dinner guests at Aldarra at least five times.

Bill and Bertha continued to enjoy their role as genteel farmers. Bertha, with help from the kitchen staff, was learning the ins and outs of canning and preserving, and Bill enjoyed providing Bertha with the raw ingredients, as shown in her diary:

July 10, 1943: Big day preparing cherries (Picked by WEB) for freezer, 10 quarts 28 pints – result of our day's work.
August 2, 1943: Prepared plums for freezing (Picked by WEB on old Foster Place)[2]

October 1 was Bill's sixty-second birthday, a day that would normally be marked with parties, cocktails, and rich foods, but Bill spent the day in bed with stomach troubles and was served a bland diet of milk, eggs, and ice cream. Unbeknownst to him, while he was flat on his back observing an inglorious birthday, the residents of his father's hometown, including several of the cousins he had visited in 1903, were enduring hell on earth.

When the Allies devised their round-the-clock bombing strategy for Europe, the RAF took the nighttime hours and the U.S. took the daytime. October 1 was the day the strategy went into effect. U.S. B-17s, flying out of northwest Africa, made the 1,800-mile round trip to hit Munich. It was the first time American bombers had hit targets inside the borders of Germany.

As darkness settled over Europe and the U.S. planes departed to safety, heading over the Mediterranean back to Africa, thirty-eight Lancaster bombers, following eight Mosquito Pathfinders, left England to fly up the Ruhr Valley to Hagen. They dropped a thousand tons of high explosives on the steel manufacturing plants near Wilhelm Böing's hometown.

The next day, October 2, was an important one for Bill, and he needed to be on his feet. He was expected at Boeing Field to meet General Hap Arnold of the U.S. Air Corps and Field Marshal Sir John Greer Dill, head of the British Joint Staff Mission. Arnold and Dill were coming to Seattle to a take part in massive War Bond promotion called "Seattle Attacks." The program included a military parade through the city, capped off that evening by a mock battle held at the University of Washington Stadium. The battle was to feature an amphibious attack with 2,000 marines storming ashore from Lake Washington, followed by Boeing B-17s staging a fake bombing run on the stadium. Patriotic music was provided by four military bands, with the whole spectacle narrated by popular comedian Bob Hope.

The morning's fog and haze lingered. Bill was feeling better and began to dress for his meeting. He was still one of the wealthiest men in Washington State, but Bertha couldn't help bragging in her diary that he had found a shop in Renton where he could get his hair cut for only a dollar. When he arrived at Boeing Field, flashbulbs popped as if he was a movie star and photographers clamored to take pictures of him and General Arnold for the next day's newspapers.[3]

Seattle felt a strong connection to Boeing and the B-17. A full-page advertisement for the Bon Marche department store on the day Arnold arrived expressed it well:

To us in Seattle and the Northwest our Flying Fortresses are no novelty. Indeed like the high Olympics, the Cascades, the lofty trees and lakes, and the [Puget] Sound, these mighty planes have long been part of our daily surroundings. We admire them as they swing down over us, giving out a comfortable feeling of security and pleasant sense of pride. Relatively few of us have ever glimpsed the complicated interior and the men at all their stations. Not many of us have scaled the heights of Mt. Rainier either. But now somewhat suddenly, we are made to realize that our familiar Flying Fortress is the greatest weapon in the world, the terror of the Axis, and the champion of quick Victory.[4]

The same advertisement heaped praise on General Arnold too:

General Arnold, next to Angel Gabriel himself, has charge of more winged folk than any man on earth today or yesterday. At the end of 1942 his force numbered one and a half million. By the end of 1943 he will have well over two million. He has been a pilot since 1910. He was one of the first five Army officers trained to fly by the Wright Brothers. It means something in the Air Forces that the first pilot should survive as boss. He has ... long fought for the establishment and maintenance of the world's strongest air force which he now directs. He has recently flown to all war theaters. From Britain he came back with the conviction that overwhelming air power would play a major role in breaking the back of the German resistance and smash their war industries.[5]

Bill's stomach troubles kept him from attending the parade and the bomber exhibition, but he must have taken great pleasure from the fact that the army's staged attack on the University of Washington football field was an oversized re-creation of his own mock stadium bombing with a fragile biplane back in 1915.

Over 40,000 people showed up to watch "Seattle Attacks." There were many thrilling moments in the program, but the biggest cheers of the night came when General Arnold talked glowingly about Boeing's B-17.

Seattle is where that wonderful bomber, the Flying Fortress, was conceived, born, and developed – a piece of machinery that is so effective in its destructive power that many would not believe its capabilities. There were countless military men among the doubters.

But now it has more than proved itself in hundreds of battles – time and again it has done the impossible. You the people of Seattle should be proud of it and prouder still of those men and women who produce it. You should do everything in your power to help the Boeing Company to bring them out of the factory doors in ever increasing numbers.

In that plane you find a war machine – praised to the skies by our Allies and damned to hell by our enemies – and well they may, for the Fortress is mighty near to sweeping the German fighters from the sky over Europe."[6]

# 66. "FESTUNG EUROPA" 1944

In 1944 the war in Europe was heading toward a climax. Hitler bragged that Nazi-occupied Europe was "Festung Europa" – Fortress Europe. He believed it was impregnable to an Allied invasion. In order to win the war, the Allies would eventually have to land troops in Hitler's fortress.

General Dwight D. Eisenhower, supreme commander of the Allied forces, knew that an amphibious attack across the English Channel would be suicidal unless the Luftwaffe was neutralized. He gave Hap Arnold and the "Mighty Eighth" the unenviable task of destroying Germany's ability to manufacture weapons while gaining control of the skies over Europe.

The Eighth Air Force sent huge armadas of a thousand or more bombers at a time across the Channel, escorted by hundreds of single-engine fighters, to attack Germany's airplane plants. The Flying Fortresses rained thousands of tons of high explosives onto Germany's industrial centers, dramatically disrupting the Nazis' ability to manufacture planes.

To defend the factories, the Luftwaffe launched wave after wave of fighters to meet the B-17s. The bombers, each bristling with thirteen 50-caliber machine guns, were effective at protecting themselves, and shot down more than 6,700 enemy planes during the war.[1] The fighters that escorted the bombers were even deadlier, accounting for another 10,000 enemy kills.[2] Just when the Luftwaffe's need for fighters reached the point of desperation, the ability of Germany's industries to supply new planes was being destroyed.

By spring of 1944, Eisenhower felt that the Luftwaffe was crippled enough for the Allies to make a cross-Channel invasion. The success of the Eighth Air Force, however, had been costly. The U.S. lost 18,418 airplanes (almost 3,000 of which were B-17s) in combat missions over Europe, and more than 40,000 airmen.[3] Unlike in Germany, where lost airplanes were becoming more and more difficult to replace, U.S. manufacturers like Boeing, Douglas, and Consolidated were flooding England with close to a dozen new planes for every one shot down. America held its collective breath, waiting for the invasion.

June 5 was just another night at Boeing's Plant 2 in Seattle. Rivet guns clattered against the polished aluminum skins of dozens of Flying Fortresses. *The Seattle Daily Times* set the scene as the night turned into June 6.

Hammers, handled with the deft touch of sure, skilled hands, clanged artfully against metal.

The night workers of the graveyard shift were on the job–as they had been for years of nights–relentlessly turning out bombers for the destruction of Hitler's crumbling empire.

Then at 1 AM, loudspeakers came to life all over the plant.

"Confirmation has just been received," came a solemn voice, with an undertone of excitement and jubilation, "that the invasion of France has started."

The guns, the drills, and hammers were stilled. A hush like that of a cathedral descended over the thousands of overall-clad men and slacks clad women. For a moment they stood, in spontaneous recognition of the solemnity of the moment. Then breaking the spell, men and women shook hands, slapped each other on the backs as if to say: "Let's get on with it!"

They picked up their tools [and] the workers of the graveyard shift were [back] on the job.[4]

The war in Europe was far from over, but the eventual outcome was a foregone conclusion to everyone but Hitler. At Boeing, the emphasis shifted away from production of B-17s toward B-29s. The long stretches of open ocean in the Pacific made the B-29, with its 5,592-mile range, the plane of choice for the war against Japan.

With almost 9,000 planes on order, the Air Corps took a high-stakes gamble and rushed the plane into production before testing and development was finished.[5] The plan was to start building the basic airframe while the modern fire-control system, which automatically aimed and fired the plane's 50-caliber machine guns, the radar bombsight, and several other high-tech components were still being perfected. The hope was that these elements could be sorted out quickly and added later at "Modification Centers." The plan became even more complicated when production was split between four different plants: Boeing in Renton and Wichita; Bell Aircraft in Marietta, Georgia; and Glenn L. Martin Company in Omaha.

Bill's stepson Cranston Paschall was transferred to Wichita to work with Colonel Tibbets in the B-29 test-flying program. On October 29, Bill and Bertha received a long-distance phone call from a rattled but unhurt Cranston, who had just landed a B-29 with its landing gear jammed in the up position. He wanted to let his family know he was safe before Bill heard any internal company rumors about the crash landing.

The air force's modification center in Kansas couldn't keep up with the output from the plants. When General Arnold discovered in January 1944 that of the ninety-seven planes delivered by the Wichita Plant, only sixteen were ready to fly, he threw a fit, saying that the planes had to be ready in two months. When he returned two months later he found that not only had the original planes not been finished, but that there were now 175 unfinished planes sitting outside in the Kansas winter, waiting for parts. Arnold was livid and demanded that the B-29 plants around the country immediately send 600 of their most experienced workers to finish the planes. There was no place big enough to work on 175 B-29s inside, so all the work had to be done outside during one of the coldest winters in memory. Within the Air Corps, the struggle to get the B-29s finished was known as "The Battle of Kansas." It took a herculean effort, but by April 15, all the planes were finished and headed toward bases in China, where they could launch bombing missions against Japan.

# 67. ANOTHER EMPTY CHAIR
# SEATTLE, 1944

The last time Bill Boeing saw his good friend Phil Johnson alive was at the August 24 ETC meeting in chief engineer Wellwood Beall's office. It was a typical business meeting, with most of their attention given to a detailed discussion of the budget process. As the meeting broke up, Johnson reminded everyone that he was heading to Washington DC and would miss the next two meetings. Bill wished him a safe trip and said that he would look forward to having him and Katie out to Aldarra for dinner when he got back.

The main purpose of Johnson's trip was to attend a three-day conference of the Aeronautical Chamber of Commerce, where the heads of seventeen major aviation businesses were gathering to discuss how to survive in the post-war economy. When the war ended, production of aircraft would have to drop considerably, perhaps even to the pre-war level. Boeing built thirty-five planes a year before the war,[1] while in 1944, between the B-17s from Plant 2 and the B-29s in Renton and Wichita, the company was building almost that many a day. It was the same for other companies too. At the meeting, Glenn Martin, president of the Glenn L. Martin Company, described a "nightmare filled with thousands of DC-3 military transports ... available after the war for use as commercial transports at prices so low that no one can afford to buy a new plane."[2] But plans were made to make the transition as painless as possible. At the end of the meeting, on September 9, Eugene Wilson, chairman of the Aeronautical Chamber of Commerce, issued a vague but optimistic statement saying that the aviation executives were confident that they could shrink their companies by 75 percent without damaging the economy.

Rather than coming straight back to Seattle, Johnson flew to Wichita to check on the B-29 production issues. On Tuesday night, September 12, he called Earl Schaffer, the Wichita plant manager, to complain that he wasn't feeling well. Later that night he was admitted to St Francis Hospital in Wichita with a cerebral hemorrhage. His wife, Katie, and his two teenage children immediately flew to Wichita to be with him.[3] He never regained consciousness, and he died on the morning of September 14.[4]

The news rocked Seattle. Not only was Boeing the city's largest employer, but it was also a huge source of civic pride. Virtually everyone in Seattle felt a deep connection to the company and its charismatic young president. Claire Egtvedt sent a Boeing-owned B-17 to Wichita to bring Johnson's body and his family home to Seattle. The bomber, carrying the remains of the man most responsible for its success, touched down at Boeing Field in the rain late on the night of the 14th.[5]

The funeral was set for Monday, September 18. In the meantime, tributes began to pour in from around the country. The following was written by the New York financial columnist Merryle Stanley Rukeyser:

> The late Phillip G. Johnson, president of Boeing Aircraft Company, though a civilian, may be put down as a war casualty. He spent his energies lavishly in converting his relatively small manufacturing company into a giant-sized manufacturer of Flying Fortresses. And, in view of the havoc wrought in Germany and Japan by bombers which he built, Phil Johnson doubtless did not feel that he was paying too high a price for his contribution to the successful prosecution of the war.

When the funeral started, the altar was surrounded with flowers and the church was so packed with mourners that they "overflowed from the building."[6] Claire Egtvedt, Governor Langlie, and several other prominent men were named as pallbearers. Bill Boeing and the financier Joseph Ripley were honorary pallbearers. They sat in the second row, behind a red-eyed Katie Johnson, and walked together in front of the coffin as it was carried to the hearse.

Phil's death was painful for Bill, but it also served to bring him even closer to Egtvedt. In the early days of the company, Ed Gott, Phil Johnson, Claire Egtvedt, and Bill had all chased a common dream. Now Claire and Bill were the last survivors of this small band who had worked together to keep the company going through two world wars, the Spanish Flu, the Great Depression, and the Roosevelt-mandated breakup.

Throughout the early 1940s, Bertha's diaries recorded the frequent dinners that she and Bill hosted for Phil and Katie Johnson and Claire and Evelyn Egtvedt. Unfortunately, there is a gap in Bertha's diaries from 1943 to 1953 (perhaps there is a stack of them in a mislabeled box in some relative's basement), but as soon as the diaries pick up again in October 1953, they mention visits from the Egtvedts and from Phil's widow Katie. There is every reason to believe that the powerful friendship that Bill and Claire had forged continued through those undocumented years and the rest of Bill's life.

On September 24, the Boeing Aircraft Company announced that its board of directors had approved Claire Egtvedt to serve as acting president until a new one could be named. It was entirely for Egtvedt and the Boeing board of directors to decide on who that new president would be, but after almost thirty years of friendship, Bill Boeing had tremendous influence with Claire, and he had a favorite candidate for the job.

From the first time Bill had met William M. Allen, he had known that he was destined for great things. In 1927, as a junior partner at Donworth, Todd & Holman, Allen was assigned to draw up the articles of incorporation for Bill's new Boeing Air Transport. It was the beginning of Allen's lifelong connection with Boeing. In the spring of 1928 Bill and Allen drew up the legal paperwork to create Pacific National Bank; in October of that same year, Allen assisted Bill with consolidating all the Boeing companies' stocks to prepare for the merger with Pratt & Whitney; in 1930, Bill nominated Allen for a position on the Boeing board of directors; and in 1934, Allen helped Bill prepare his testimony for the Hugo Black airmail hearings. Soon after that, Bill arranged for Allen to join the board of Pacific National Bank. Outside business, in 1936, Bill nominated Allen for residency in the exclusive Highlands Country Club (upon approval, Allen bought a home less than a mile from Bill's Aldarra mansion), and he saw to it that Allen was accepted into the Rainier Club and the Seattle Golf Club. In the end, however, it did not matter how highly Bill recommended William M. Allen for the role of Boeing president; when Egtvedt offered it to him, he surprisingly turned it down.

Around the time of Johnson's death, the years of flying in loud open-cockpit airplanes began to take their toll on Bill's hearing. It became difficult for him to follow what was being said in the large, twelve-to-twenty-person management committee meetings, so he stopped attending them, although he continued to be an avid participant in the smaller ETC meetings.

After Phil's death the ETC felt different to Bill. There were new faces replacing his old friends, but the board still had important work to do. On August 31, 1944, in a meeting that was attended only by Bill, Egtvedt, assistant chief engineer Ed Wells, and director of sales F. B. Collins, the specifications for a "new bombardment type airplane" requested by the U.S. Army Materiel Command were introduced. They were:

A high speed (550 mph) at tactical operating altitude;
A tactical operating ceiling of 40,000 feet;
A range of 3,500 miles.[7]

These requirements would be difficult to achieve with a traditional propeller-driven plane, but one requirement made it obvious what the army was asking for: "Fuel System – The design must provide for kerosene."[8] The army wanted its first large jet bomber. The proposal was assigned Boeing Model 450 and would eventually mature into the B-47.

Throughout the rest of 1944, the ETC meetings seemed to deal with three main issues:

1. Production problems on the B-29.
2. Final decision and early flight tests on the XC-97.
3. Early design work on the Model 450 and the new experimental engines.

As an indication of how well the secret of this new jet bomber was being guarded, the minutes are scrupulously crafted to avoid using the word "jet". Instead "power unit" was used wherever one would have expected to read "jet."[9]

In mid-fall of 1944, a request came in from the Second Air Force to strip at least 7,000 lbs. from each of its fifteen B-29s. Even with its production problems, the B-29 could still fly faster and higher and carry more weight than just about any other bomber of the era; but that, apparently, was not good enough. At first, the engineers balked at the request, saying it was impossible, but eventually word came back from the air force saying that the request was not debatable; the modifications were required for a top-secret project called "Silverplate" and Boeing needed to send its answers right away.

Within a few days, a twenty-eight-page report made its way to Bill, Egtvedt, and the rest of the ETC. The report started with ten pages of typical dry narrative, followed by an eighteen-page chart that listed in one column every possible change that could be made to the B-29, an estimated weight saving from that change, and another estimate that converted the saved weight into increased range and speed. Some changes were significant:

> Replace 4-gun turret and restructure to 2-gun turret; weight saving 883 [pounds]; range increase 194 [miles]; speed increase 4.7 [knots per hour].

And:

> Eliminate central fire control system except tail turret; weight saving 7,520 [pounds]; range increase 1,502 [miles], speed increase 29.9 [knots per hour].

Other changes were not as dramatic:

> Change oak inner tank ribs to spruce or light pine; weight saving, 50 [pounds]; range increase 7 [miles]; speed increase [negligible].[10]

The report finished with a tabulation showing that if all the changes were made, the weight of the plane could be reduced by 13,341 pounds, its top speed could be increased to almost 400 knots per hour, and its range could be extended by 2,460 miles. Each change had a check box next to it that indicated whether the changes were approved by Boeing.

After an hour of ETC debate, the completed report was forwarded to the army. In a short while, it came back to Boeing marked with the required changes. Sent with it was an order for fifteen new B-29s modified to the new specifications, with two additional changes. The B-29 had two bomb bays. The air force asked that the front bay be modified to accept one large 10,000-pound bomb, and that the second bay be filled with an extra 600-gallon fuel tank. Clearly there was something special planned for the Silverplate B-29s.

# 68. SILVERPLATE
# 1944

From a distance, history appears to be a straight line connecting one event to another. Closer examination reveals that it is much more like a string of dominoes, where each event is independent, but if fate topples it in the right direction that domino will knock over the next one in line.

The chain of "dominoes" that led to the creation of the Silverplate B-29s started on August 2, 1939, when Albert Einstein sent a letter to Franklin Roosevelt telling him that "the element uranium may be turned into a new and important source of energy in the immediate future," and that "extremely powerful bombs of this type may thus be constructed."[1] Einstein also pointed out that Nazi-occupied Czechoslovakia had large uranium mines.

In October 1939, Roosevelt formed the Advisory Committee on Uranium. The committee went through a few name changes, eventually being called the S-1 Committee. By November 1941 it had determined that it would be possible to build a bomb. Roosevelt approved the project, and the job was assigned to the Army Corps of Engineers, which created the Manhattan Engineering Department to oversee the job.

Robert Oppenheimer, a professor at the University of California in Berkeley, was one of the top nuclear physicists in the U.S. at the time. In mid-September 1942, six members of the S-1 Committee headed to the Bay Area to try to convince him to take over the bomb-making program. Secrecy and security were major concerns, so the September 12-13 meeting was moved off campus to the secluded Bohemian Grove, north of Berkeley, on the Russian River.[2] The summer encampment had ended in July, and nobody but the S-1 Committee and a few Bohemian Club employees were there; it must have felt an empty and primitive place. It seems ironic that the decision to build the deadliest weapon of the twentieth century was made in a secluded log cabin in front of a stone fireplace in the middle of a Californian forest.

Oppenheimer agreed to take on the job of building the new bomb, but he suffered from a mild case of tuberculosis, which was eased by frequent vacations to the desert. The need for secrecy and Oppenheimer's preference for a desert location sent the S-1 Committee to New Mexico in search of a location for the bomb-making laboratory. It did not take long to locate the Los Alamos Ranch School in New Mexico. It was perfect. It was isolated, with dormitories for the scientists to sleep in, cooking facilities and a cafeteria, and classrooms and lecture halls. And to top it off, it had the Wilhelm Böing shop that Bill's sister Caroline had left for the school in her will. Oppenheimer and the rest of his team began work in early 1943.

The U.S. Army Air Corps was tasked with delivering the bomb. It determined that the B-29 was best suited for the job. It also determined that the most qualified pilot in the Air Corps to develop the first atomic strike force was Paul Tibbets. The combination of his bombing experience in B-17s over Europe and his time as a B-29 test pilot in Wichita made him ideal for the job.

On September 1, 1944 Tibbets was given command of his "own secret Air Force consisting of 15 B-29s and 1,800 men."[3] One of the first problems he had to address was how to drop the big bomb and then get the plane far enough away to survive the explosion. Preliminary estimates showed that the bomb would weigh 10,000 pounds and would knock down any airplane within 8 miles of the blast. A stock B-29 was not fast enough to get to safety in time. When he was a test pilot in Wichita, Tibbets occasionally flew empty B-29s before all their guns and armor had been installed. He was convinced that a stripped-down B-29 could do the job; the massive weight reduction that the Boeing ETC had wrestled with, as well as the request for fifteen modified B-29s, had come directly from Tibbets.

The army gave Tibbets a code word to use whenever he ran up against any kind of bureaucratic obstacle. Everyone in the government, military, and all weapons manufacturers was warned that a request accompanied by the code word "Silverplate" had to be honored instantly. Tibbets' B-29s were eventually known as the "Silverplate B-29s."

# 69. VE-DAY AND VJ-DAY
## SEATTLE, 1945

On Sunday, May 6, 1945, the Eighth Air Force launched Mission 982. Fifteen B-17s took off from Suffolk and headed east across the North Sea, where they were met by a flight of eight P-51 Mustangs. They crossed into German air space and dropped leaflets quoting President Roosevelt: "...The rights of every nation, large or small, must be respected and guarded as carefully as are the rights of every individual within the United States of America." Turning west, the planes dropped similar leaflets over France. They then turned to the north, flying over the English Channel and the white cliffs of Dover, landing safely back in England.

A few hours later, Dwight Eisenhower, supreme commander of the Allied forces, announced that Germany had surrendered unconditionally at Reims, France, and that "the Mission of this Allied force has been fulfilled at 0241 local time, May 7, 1945." With that announcement, Mission 982 became the last official Eighth Air Force combat mission flown by B-17s over Europe.[1]

In Seattle, the front page of *The Seattle Times* was dominated by a photo of General Josef Jodl, chief of the operations staff of the German High Command, signing the surrender documents, under the headline "Now Japan! City Works on V.E. Day."[2] Claire Egtvedt issued the following statement to all Boeing staff:

To all of us at Boeing the fall of Germany has a double significance, for it represents achievement of our first objective ... the destruction of Nazi

Germany, and a challenge to continue our efforts unslackened until final victory over Japan.

It means that at long last the forces of tyranny in Europe have fallen to the armed might of America and her Allies, of which a major tool was our B-17 Flying Fortress. The Flying Fortress in fact, has come to be a symbol of the air war against the Nazis. So this is a day of supreme achievement for the men and women of Boeing and the thousands of individuals with whom we have been associated in the B-17 program.

This day also carries a clear challenge from the far Pacific. Just as the B-17 has dominated the air over Europe, so must our B-29 Superfortress darken the skies of Japan. We have made a good start. Radio Tokyo has described the B-29 as the most effective weapon of the war.

Yet the job before us remains great ... we must continue to meet our schedules for B-29s, to speed the day when Japan, too, will be forced into unconditional surrender.[3]

Speaking from the Oval Office, Harry Truman, who had succeeded to the presidency upon Roosevelt's death three weeks earlier, said, "Our victory is only half won."[4] He then reminded the Japanese that the defeat of the Nazis would free up millions of Allied soldiers as well as thousands of planes and ships, and that all would soon be headed for Japan. Truman ended the address by telling the Japanese that they had a choice "between unconditional surrender and utter destruction."[5]

The B-29 production lines in Renton and Wichita continued to turn out bombers, while at Plant 2 in Seattle, B-29 construction jigs were brought in and placed between the rows of B-17s to support the various components that would make up the new bomber. As the last Flying Fortresses passed through the plant, the B-17 jigs were pulled down and replaced with new ones for the Superfortresses.

Bill's routine did not change with victory in Europe. He continued to come to the plant and sit in on the ETC meetings. The minutes from May 24 show that Egtvedt, Bill, and the rest of the committee were on hand to hear a special report from Boeing engineer Robert H. Jewett about the new "Special Power Plant Development." The new jet power plant was so important that it was the only topic addressed during the entire meeting. Jewett brought "several sample parts" to show to the committee.[6] Parts that were small enough were passed by hand from one committee member to another. While there are no records of how Bill reacted to Jewett's presentation, the fact that he was at the meeting provides indisputable proof that he was aware of and involved in Boeing Aircraft's development of jet-powered airplanes.

The war in the Pacific had dramatically turned against the Japanese, who were falling back on all sides, but their code of honor required them to fight to a "glorious death in honor of the Emperor." This led to the deployment of Japanese kamikaze pilots, who went into battle planning to die by crashing their planes into U.S. ships.

In June of 1945 the Japanese government began a propaganda campaign aimed at the civilian population called "The Glorious Death of One Hundred Million."[7] The purpose of the campaign was to promote the idea that civilians should give their lives for the emperor, and that every man, woman, and child should prepare to die when the Allied invasion started. This dramatically altered the way in which the Allies planned for the invasion.

By the summer of 1945, the Allies had prepared a detailed plan for attacking Japan. Named "Operation Downfall," it called for a force of 5 million U.S. troops and 1 million British. Truman's Joint Chiefs of Staff estimated that the Allies would suffer 1.2 million casualties, including 267,000 deaths,[8] and the Department of the navy estimated that Japanese casualties could be as high as 10 million.[9]

Modern historians question the accuracy of these numbers, but two pieces of evidence point to the fact that U.S. military leaders genuinely believed them. First is a 1945 memo from General George C. Marshall of the U.S. Army to President Truman stating, "The Army must provide 600,000 replacements for overseas theater before June 30th and together with the Navy will require a total of 900,000 inductions by June 30th."[10] Second is the War Department's order for the manufacture of 500,000 Purple Heart medals (in addition to the 700,000 already on hand) in the summer of 1945, to be awarded to the anticipated casualties of Operation Downfall. The U.S. ended the war with such a large surplus of Purple Hearts that almost all those awarded to U.S. servicemen from the conflicts in Korea, Vietnam, the Persian Gulf, and Afghanistan have been drawn from this surplus left over from Operation Downfall.[11]

By the early hours of July 16, 1945, the U.S. government had spent over $2 billion on developing the atomic bomb, and no one knew if the idea was going to work. That all changed at 5:29 a.m. when a test bomb nicknamed "Gadget" exploded in the middle of the New Mexico desert with the force of 20,000 tons of TNT. When Oppenheimer saw the size of the explosion his new bomb had made, he famously quoted a passage of Hindu scripture, "Now I am become Death, the destroyer of worlds."[12]

The atomic bomb program was so secret that even President Truman was not told about it in full until April 24, twelve days after he had been sworn in. Now, after being in office for just over ninety days, Truman was faced with one of the most difficult decisions any leader would ever have to make. To make matters worse, Truman was not in Washington DC, but at the Potsdam Conference in Germany for a two-week meeting with Stalin and Churchill to discuss the order of the post-war world.

Truman learned about the successful test on July 17 and immediately let Churchill in on the secret. After a week of deliberation, he decided to tell Stalin about it:

> On the evening of July 24th Truman approached Stalin without an interpreter and as casually as he could, told him that the United States had a 'new weapon of unusual destructive force.' Stalin showed little interest, replying only that he hoped the United States would make 'good use of it against the Japanese.' The reasons for Stalin's composure became clear later: Soviet Intelligence had been receiving information about the U.S. Atomic bomb program since fall 1941.[13]

Truman, Churchill, and Chiang Kai-shek, President of the Republic of China, issued a joint statement on July 25, 1945:

> We call upon the government of Japan to proclaim now the unconditional surrender of all Japanese armed forces, and to provide proper and adequate assurances of their good faith in such action. The alternative for Japan is complete and utter destruction.[14]

On July 28, *Asahi Shimbun*, a national newspaper in Japan, published the government's official response: "The Japanese government ignores this, and we are determined to continue our fight to the end."[15]

The Potsdam Conference ended on August 2, and Truman boarded the cruiser U.S.S. *Augusta* to head back to the States. Before he left, he authorized the Air Corps to proceed with delivering "its first special bomb as soon as weather will permit visual bombing after about 3 August 1945 on one of the targets: Hiroshima, Kokura, Niigata, and Nagasaki."[16] Tibbets and the Silverplate B-29s had been given the green light.

On August 6, Truman was eating lunch on board the *Augusta* in the middle of the Atlantic Ocean when Captain Frank Graham rushed in with a message: "Hiroshima Bombed ... No Flak no fighter opposition ... Results clear cut and successful in all respects. Visible effects greater than in any test."

Truman issued another ultimatum to the Japanese: "Let there be no mistake; we shall completely destroy Japan's power to make war ... If they do not now accept our terms, they may expect a rain of ruin from the air, the likes of which has never been seen on this earth."[17] Reeling from the shock of the Hiroshima attack, Japan's Supreme War Council could not agree on how to respond and failed to issue any official response. On August 8, Tibbets' team of Silverplate B-29s dropped a second atomic bomb on Nagasaki.[18]

By August 9, Emperor Hirohito and his prime minister, Kantaro Suzuki, agreed that, in spite of continued strong opposition from many in the military,

Japan should accept the Potsdam Declaration and surrender. On August 14 there was an attempted coup d'état led by Major Kenji Hatanaka aimed at assassinating Suzuki and kidnapping the emperor in order to keep the war going. It failed, and on August 15 Japan publicly accepted the surrender terms. Because Japan was on the other side of the international date line, the news was announced in Seattle at 4 p.m. on August 14.[19]

The war was won, and to the people of Seattle it felt like Boeing, their hometown's biggest company, had played a major role in winning it. Tens of thousands of Seattleites poured into the streets for a joyous celebration that lasted all night. In the midst of it, the Truman administration announced the cancellation of $25 billion in defense orders. Claire Egtvedt issued a statement aimed at reassuring his tens of thousands of employees by announcing that there would be "no immediate heavy cut-back in employment, although personnel will be reduced during the next two months."[20]

# 70. BLUE SKIES AND TAILWINDS SEATTLE, 1945-56

Saturday, September 1, 1945 started out foggy. By 10 a.m. the fog had burned off to reveal a clear day that hinted at the beautiful autumn ahead. It was William Allen's forty-fifth birthday and it seemed to him like a good day to make a big change. He resigned his position at Donworth & Todd (which by then was known as Holman, Sprague & Allen) and called Claire Egtvedt to say he would take the president's job at Boeing. Boeing's board of directors met on September 5 and voted unanimously to hire him.

Though the war had been over since August 1945, Bill stayed on the ETC until April 1946 to help his friends Egtvedt and Allen steer the company through the post-war challenges. The eight extra months Bill spent on the ETC turned out to be one of the most revolutionary periods in aviation history; it was during this period that the American military began moving away from straight-winged propeller planes towards swept-wing jets. At the same time, Boeing finished design work on its nuclear-capable B-47 swept-wing jet bomber and took first orders for the plane; it started designing the Model 462 heavy bomber, which eventually became known as the B-52; and Boeing's Ground-to-Air Pilotless Aircraft (GAPA) program was begun, leading to the U.S Air Force's first surface-to-air guided missiles.

All these programs were discussed in detail by the ETC while Bill was still a member, and his name is included on all the agendas and minutes. W. E. Boeing's name is also found on documents discussing the weight, speed, and range of the Model 462, the eventual B-52, which is still an important workhorse in today's air force.[1]

When the B-47 Stratojet bomber was finished, Bill's stepson Cranston Paschall became one of the test pilots on the program. Occasionally he would invite Bill and Bertha to dinner at his home on Lake Washington, and it was on one of those warm summer's evenings, sipping cocktails on the patio that Bill first met a confident new test pilot named Alvin "Tex" Johnson, whose name would soon become inexorably linked to the Boeing Company.[2]

One of the disappointing planes of the post-war transition was the Model 367. The army bought a few under the name C-97 and Bill had been hopeful that a civilian version of the plane would be popular with airlines, but it wasn't. There were, however, to be great things ahead for this model.

\* \* \*

Bill left the ETC at the end of April 1946 and his career at Boeing ended. He divided his time between Aldarra and the *Taconite*, which had spent the war years tied up in Lake Union. The slow-moving yacht would have been a tempting target for the Japanese submarines that prowled the West Coast during World War II, but as soon as the war had ended, Bill was back out cruising and fishing between Seattle and Alaska.

When he wasn't aboard his yacht, Bill was traveling to cattle auctions with a crew of farmhands led by the farm's foreman, Dutch Abbot, buying and selling blue-ribbon Hereford bulls. Bill didn't show the cattle himself – that was left up to his trusted employee Dutch – but he took great pride in the quality of cattle bred at Aldarra. He was soon a familiar face at livestock shows on the county fair circuit in Washington, Oregon, Idaho, and Montana, and a reporter for *The Seattle Daily Times* was surprised one September afternoon when he took his family to the Western Washington State Fair in Puyallup and recognized Bill and Bertha Boeing strolling casually down the midway, past popcorn stands and scone booths as they headed toward the livestock arena to watch the bull judging. With the rise of his interest in cattle, Bill's passion for horseracing waned, and by the end of 1946 he had sold his entire stable.

\* \* \*

In September 1947, Boeing Aircraft rolled out the first of what would eventually be more than 2,000 B-47 jet bombers. The air force wanted to extend the range of the B-47 with aerial refueling, and Boeing had been working on installing a "flying boom" that could be lowered from the belly of a converted B-29 tanker. The boom carried a refueling hose and had stubby wing-like control surfaces that could be controlled by an operator in the rear of the B-29. The operator would "fly" the boom to connect to a receptacle in the nose of a following B-47, and fuel could then be pumped from the tanker to the jet bomber. The idea worked well, and the air force ordered 116 B-29s converted to tankers and fitted with flying booms. Boeing suggested that the C-97 was better suited to the tanker role; the air force agreed and ended up ordering 800 KC-97 tankers.

As the new long-range high-speed B-52s entered production, it became obvious that a 650-mph jet bomber would have trouble refueling from a 400-mph propeller-driven tanker. Boeing began to make plans for a jet tanker. The military had not asked for a one, so this was a Boeing-financed gamble with no guarantee of a payoff. Rather than starting from scratch, Boeing engineers pulled out their old drawings of the Model 367, which was already the basis of the KC-97 tanker, and began making revisions: the Wright Radial Cyclone engines were replaced with new Pratt & Whitney jets; the design was redrawn with a swept wing; the shape of the control surfaces was changed; and a more streamlined fuselage was added. When the engineers were finished, they had made eighty revisions to the 367, so the final plane became known as the 367-80, and eventually just the "Dash 80."

William Allen thought the basic Dash 80 airframe could also be used for a passenger jet. The jet age was dawning and the entire aviation world was at a crossroads, but the question was, would passengers accept a jet-powered airliner? If he timed it right, Boeing would dominate aviation for years to come, but if he launched the new jet airliner too soon, before the public was ready, the company could be bankrupt within a year.

Allen needed $15 million to begin producing a passenger version of the Dash 80. He would have to issue another batch of stock, and having helped Bill do this several times before, he followed the same path that Bill had blazed in 1927. Back then Bill had used Pacific National Bank to underwrite the stock to raise money for a revolutionary new plane with a ground-breaking new Pratt & Whitney engine. Twenty-five years on, with another revolutionary plane in mind, Allen approached the same Pacific National Bank.

By this stage Bill had turned his position on the board of PNB over to son, Bill Boeing Jr., and when the time came for the board to approve PNB's role as lead bank in the syndicate underwriting Allen's gamble on the Dash 80, the younger Boeing, undoubtedly with his father's approval, voted for it.

The prototype was finished and ready for rollout on May 15, 1954. In 1927, when the Model 40A was completed thanks to financing via the first PNB stock deal, Bertha Boeing had christened the brand-new plane with orange juice, it being Prohibition. When it was time to roll out the Dash

80, Bertha was again asked to do the christening, and this time she got to swing a real bottle of Champagne. "I christen thee the plane of the future!" she said, as Champagne cascaded down from the nose of the modern jet. The next day, both *The Seattle Daily Times* and the *Post-Intelligencer* carried large photographs of William Allen and Bertha Boeing smiling broadly.[3]

Without a doubt, the Dash 80's most famous public appearance came on Sunday, August 8, 1955. The prototype was scheduled to do a flyover at the Gold Cup hydroplane race on Lake Washington. Test pilot Tex Johnson was impressed with the new plane's capabilities and took it upon himself to put it through a barrel roll in front of hundreds of thousands of spectators. At 490 knots and only 1,500 feet above the lake, Johnson rolled the 160,000-pound plane with its 130-foot wingspan as smoothly as if it had been a tiny stunt plane. And for good measure, he did it again on his return pass over the racecourse.

The next morning Bill Allen called Johnson into his office. "What do you think you were doing yesterday?" he yelled.

"Selling airplanes," Johnson calmly replied.

Two days later there was a meeting at Seattle's Olympic Hotel of the International Air Transit Association, including over 600 delegates from the world's major airlines. Many of the delegates had witnessed the two Dash 80 rolls and could talk of little else. Soon orders started to flood in and Johnson's place in Boeing history was secure. When the passenger version of the Dash 80 entered production it was renamed the 707. Between 1956 and 1979 1,010 were built, making it one of the most successful commercial airliners of all time.

\* \* \*

On September 27, 1956, Bill and Bertha celebrated their thirty-fifth anniversary aboard the *Taconite* at the Seattle Yacht Club in Portage Bay, Lake Union. Bill Jr. and his wife Marcy, along with their children Susie and Bill III, came on board with bouquets of flowers just before noon. After a brief celebration, Billy and his family went ashore and the *Taconite* cast off for a romantic anniversary cruise to Canada. The big yacht made it through the Ballard Locks and almost all the way to Deception Pass by nightfall. The pass has a strong current and lots of rocks, so they anchored at Hope Island to watch a spectacular sunset and spend the night. They planned to try the pass with the slack tide at 10 a.m. on the 28th.

When he awoke the next morning, Bill wasn't feeling well, and at 9:32 a.m. the *Taconite* turned around and headed back towards Seattle. At 12:05 p.m. Captain McIntyre used the radio telephone to notify Billy that his father had suffered a heart attack. Billy quickly got hold of Bill's personal physician, Dr.

Bauwick. Bill Jr.'s personal pilot, Miroslav Slovak, flew Dr. Bauwick and Billy by float plane to intercept the *Taconite* on her way back. They reached the yacht off Edmonds at 1:52 p.m. but were too late. The entry in the boat's log in Bertha's handwriting says simply, "WEB died at 1:08 PM."[4] The *Taconite* arrived back at the Seattle Yacht Club at 3:50, and the news was released to the local papers and TV stations. Bill Boeing was dead, just four days shy of his seventy-fifth birthday.

The next day, Claire Egtvedt was quoted in *The Seattle Daily Times*:

> The death of Mr. Boeing marks the passing of a pioneer in aviation; a man of great vision ... He was a friend who extended opportunity and stood by us when the path was rough and the future was insecure. It has been a rare privilege to have been associated with Mr. Boeing [for] ... over 40 years.[5]

Arrangements were quickly made for Bill's body to be cremated. By October 5 the *Taconite* was moored in Queen Charlotte Sound, north of Vancouver. Bill's entire family was on board. In a quiet ceremony, his ashes were sprinkled into the water that he loved so much.

When Bertha returned from Canada, she found a letter waiting for her from Bill Allen. It read,

> The death of Bill was a shock to all of us. Somehow although not actually with us he seemed always in the background – exerting a solid and forthright influence. Although he has left us, that influence will continue. As I told our management people, our job is to see that the company continues as a living memorial to Bill and in all aspects worthy of him. We will do our best to see that it is that way.[6]

# Epilogue

There is an interesting character of speech in Seattle that falls along generational lines. If you ask someone born after World War II for the name of the big airplane manufacturer on the Duwamish River, the answer they will give is "Boeing." But if you ask old timers who worked for the company in the 1930s or '40s, invariably they will say "Boeing's." That possessive "s" at the end of the name reveals much about how the people of Seattle felt toward the company. Workers hired in the 1930s and '40s felt like they were working at "Bill Boeing's Airplane Company."

Bill was respected by the community and admired by his workers. The way he treated his employees was based on a philosophy born that blustery autumn night in 1918 when he knew that he should close the business, but he could not bring himself to hurt "that splendid and loyal group of men."[1] Bill passed his philosophy on to Claire Egtvedt, whose wife, Evelyn, expressed it many years later when talking about the men who built the company: "They were not an employee of the company from a standpoint of an employee, boss or whatever. They were ... friends working together on a common project, which was the betterment of aircraft."[1]

Bertha was heartbroken when Bill died. She had planned on a long happy retirement with the man who was the love of her life. She continued to support Seattle's Children's Orthopedic Hospital and a number of other Seattle charities, and she was a devoted grandmother. For the rest of her life, on her wedding anniversary, she would put on her most beautiful dress and travel to one of Seattle's finest restaurants. There she would sit by herself at a candlelit table and eat an elegant meal, alone with her memories of her husband. Bertha died on June 27, 1977.

**William Allen** spent twenty-seven years leading the Boeing Company, first as president and then as CEO. He successfully steered it into the jet age and made good on his promise to Bertha, running the company as a living memorial to Bill and making sure it was worthy of him in all aspects. He retired in 1972 and passed away in 1985.

**William E. Boeing, Jr.** never went to work for his father's company. Instead he blazed his own trail in aviation, founding a company named AeroCopter, which ran a fleet of helicopters that served the timber and mining industries on the U.S. West Coast and up into Alaska. Bill Jr. was also well known for being one of the first and largest importers of Volkswagen cars into the United States. He served on the board of several banks and was active in real estate development. He was a generous philanthropist, continuing his parents' support of the Children's Hospital as well as donating frequently to Seattle's Museum of Flight. Bill Jr. was instrumental in moving Boeing's original Plant 1 (The Red Barn) from the Duwamish Oxbow to Boeing Field, where the building has been restored and is now an important part of the museum. Bill Jr. was married twice and had four children with his first wife Marcella (Marci) Cech. They were Gretchen, Mary, Susan, and Bill the 3rd. After Marci died, Bill married June Tinkham. With both Bill and June well into their sixties, there were no children from this union. Bill passed away in 2015 at the age of ninety-two.

**Claire Egtvedt** stayed on as CEO until he retired in 1966. He died in 1975.

**James A. Farley,** who had been postmaster general at the time of the air mail hearings that had forced the breakup of UATC, had his own falling out with Roosevelt. He resigned from the administration in 1940 and became chairman of the board of the Coca Cola Export Corporation, a position that he held until 1973. After Bill's death, Farley sent Bertha a heartfelt letter saying, "Like all Americans I highly esteemed and admired your husband; his contributions to air transport will live on always in our country's history of progress." Farley died in 1976.

**Edgar Gott** was eventually promoted to president at Consolidated Aircraft, but his tenure was short-lived. Consolidated merged with Vultee Aircraft to form Convair in 1943, and Gott retired soon afterward. In late 1946 he was diagnosed with a terminal illness and reached out to Bill in an effort to repair their damaged relationship. Gott apologized for any wrongdoings and hurt he had caused, and he asked if Bill would do the same. If Bill responded, there are no copies of his letter in the family archives. Gott died July 17, 1947. He was sixty years old.

**Eddie Hubbard** never had a chance to see how big Boeing's airmail business would become. He passed away in December of 1929 from complications after an operation on his stomach. He was only thirty-seven years old.

**Terah Maroney** continued to make a living out of flying until January 12, 1929, when he died after he slipped and fell into the propeller blades of his own plane.

**Herb Munter** started a charter service to Alaska in 1930 and flew for the U.S. Navy during World War II. After the war he helped found West Coast Airlines and served as its vice-president until he retired in 1958. He died on May 14, 1970.

*Rover.* Between 1929 and 1956, Bill owned four private airplanes named *Rover.* The first was a four-passenger Boeing 204A flying boat built in 1929. The second was a Douglas Dolphin twin-engine flying boat that Bill bought used from the Vanderbilt family in 1934, shortly before his resignation from the Boeing Company. The third *Rover* was the DC-5 that Bill bought in June 1940 (it was not a flying boat), and the fourth was a Grumman G-73 Mallard, bought in 1947. The only confirmed surviving plane is the Grumman Mallard, which is privately owned and kept in storage in Texas.

**Roy Olmstead** served four years in prison and was pardoned by President Roosevelt when Prohibition ended. While in prison he discovered religion, and after his release he began teaching Sunday school and working with prisoners around the Seattle area on an anti-alcoholism agenda. He died in 1966.

*Taconite* stayed in the Boeing family until Bertha's death in 1977, when it was sold to a wealthy Canadian named Daryl Brown. The yacht has been restored and has changed hands several times. Until recently, it was available for charters out of Vancouver, Canada, for $48,000 per week. Its most recent owner is planning on moving it to the Bahamas.

**Wong Tsoo** returned to China at the start of World War I and helped establish the Mah-Wei Airplane Company in Shanghai. In 1928 he became the chief engineer of the China National Aviation Corporation. In 1930 he partnered with Conrad Westervelt, who was then working for Curtiss-Wright on a joint venture flying mail and passengers from Shanghai to several destinations in China, including Beijing and Nanjing. After the joint venture ended, Wong Tsoo took on a number of aviation-related jobs, and when the Communists took control of China in 1949, he fled to Taiwan with the Nationalist government and became a college professor at the National Cheng-Kung University. He died on March 4, 1965.

**Conrad Westervelt** retired from the U.S. Navy in 1927 and took a job as vice-president of Curtiss-Wright. In 1930 the company sent him to China to partner with his long-time friend Wong Tsoo on a joint venture with China National Aviation Corporation. After his retirement from aviation he devoted his attention to writing. He completed twenty-seven plays, most of which were comedies, and had at least four produced on Broadway. (None ran for more than fifty performances.) He also wrote several unpublished novels. He died a few months before Bill Boeing, on March 15, 1956.

# Bill Boeing and Race

Revelations made several years after Bill's death showed that real estate he owned north of Seattle had been developed using harsh racially restrictive covenants. The deeds stipulated that the property could not be "sold, conveyed, rented, or leased in whole or in part to any person not of the White or Caucasian race." Non-whites could only occupy a property on the land if they were employed as domestic servants. It is indisputable that these covenants were used and that they are racist. However, any historian wishing to draw a conclusion about Bill Boeing's views on race is advised to consider the following points:

First, from its inception in 1934 until 1949, when it was mandated to change by the Supreme Court, the Federal Housing Administration (FHA) refused to provide mortgage insurance on property that did not include a racially restrictive covenant. The FHA's 1934 manual required that "no person of African descent be allowed to live in a FHA-insured property except as a domestic servant or labor[er]."[1]

By 1938 the FHA manual had been updated to include detailed instructions on how to create the exclusionary clauses, even to the point of providing the specific language to be used.[2] Banks were unwilling to offer mortgages that could not be insured, so any large real estate developer had to utilize the FHA-authored racial covenants. Many other Seattle-area developments, including Ballard, Broadmoor, Capitol Hill, Green Lake, Madrona, and White Center, included similar restrictions.

Secondly, Boeing retired in 1934 and turned the day-to-day operation of his real estate holdings over to an agent named Hugh Russell. The racial covenants on the Boeing property so closely follow the form outlined in the 1938 FHA manual that it is highly likely they were written in 1938. The historical record is mute on whether or not Bill was aware of changes that were made to sales contracts four years after he retired.

# Endnotes

Prologue
1. In the statement Boeing sent to *Flying Magazine* for their December, 1915 issue, he said that the purpose of the stunt was to "awaken the people of the northwest …"
2. Denny Field was replaced by Husky Stadium on November 27, 1920. That same year the Sun Dodgers changed their name to the "Huskies".
3. Dobie never lost a game during his nine-year stay at UW. His string of sixty-two games without a loss is still the record for NCAA football.
4. "Aero Club's Head Sounds Warning From Sky," *The Seattle Daily Times*, November 12, 1915, p. 1.
5. "New Aero Club will prepare for service," *Oakland Tribune*, September 1, 1915, p. 2.
6. "Seaplane Soars Above Seattle," *The Tacoma Times*, October 22, 1915.
7. "Dr Sydney Gives Strong Warning to Aero Club," *The Seattle Post-Intelligencer*, November 15, 1915, p. 1.
8. Personal interview with Mary Boeing, May 13, 2016. She had heard this story from "Grandma Bee" (Bertha Boeing).
9. "Warplane Falls Taking Two Into Lake," *The Seattle Post-Intelligencer*, November 15, 1915, p. 1.
10. "Aero Club's Plane Drops Into Lake, Pilot Is Injured," *The Seattle Daily Times*, November 15, 1915, p. 1.
11. Young, "Notes on Old Day," *Douglas Retirees Newsletter*. Excerpted in Museum of Flight Archives, Boeing Box #1.
12. F. Taylor, *High Horizons*, 1951, p. 25. A new float arrived from Martin the following week and some people have cited this as proof that Martin did not drag his feet on the replacement parts. However, the float had been ordered a month previously. Most Martin floatplanes were delivered with a float with a single step in the bottom. Boeing's had an experimental double step. Boeing did not like the way it performed, complaining that it slowed the plane down, so a few weeks before the crash, Martin had agreed to ship a replacement float.
13. H. Mansfield, *Vision*, 1956, p. 10.

**Chapter 1**

1   Barbara Hiscock Spaeth, *Fast Forward: Bertha Potter Boeing, From Tod's Point to the Jet Age,* https:/youtu.be/.OC_aNylJuv8

2   Personal letter from Wilhelm Böing to his parents, October 6, 1873. Boeing family archives.

3   Marie Ortmann's exact age is difficult to pin down. Her birth year is listed variously as 1853, 1859, 1862, and 1863.

4   Bill was born at home at a time when birth certificates were not required for home births. When Bill tried to apply for a passport in 1936, he searched across Michigan for a record of his birth certificate and couldn't find one. Eventually his aunt, Blanche Ortmann, had to sign an affidavit certifying that Bill had been born in Detroit on October 1, 1881. Her affidavit became his only record of birth. The affidavit lists his name at the time of his birth as William Edward Boeing. Boeing family archives.

5   Personal letter from Wilhelm Böing to his sister Emma, April 18, 1883. Boeing family archives.

6   W. Van Brunt, *Duluth and St. Louis County, Minnesota,* 1921.

7   Bornefield, Dr. P., "The Böings," *Genealogy of a Hohenlimburg Family of Entrepreneurs,* 1967, p. 14.

8   "William Boeing Dead," *Detroit Free Press,* January 11, 1890, p. 8.

9   Johannes Wolfgang Von Goethe: "Es ist nicht genug zu wissen – man muß auch anwenden. Es ist not nicht genug zu wallen – man muß auch tun."

10  Personal letter from Wilhelm Böing to M. H. Alworth, February 11, 1886. Boeing family archives.

11  "William Boeing Dead," *Detroit Free Press,* January 11, 1890, p. 8.

12  *Ibid.*

13  "In the Halls of Justice," *Detroit Free Press,* February 12, 1890, p. 3.


**Chapter 2**

1   *The Spectator,* February 11, 1890, p. 211.

2   Collected letters from Marie Boeing to Bill Boeing, 1893-1896. Boeing family archives.

3   *Ibid.*

4   Boeing Company, "Executive Biography of William E. Boeing" www.boeing.com/history/pioneers/william-e-boeing.page

5   "Balloon Captif Diplone." Boeing family archives.

6   Baillargeon, J. *Selections From the Library of William E. Boeing,* 2011, p. 165.

7   "Glooston Manor, Fine Virginia Home of Dr. and Mrs. F. D. Owsley," *Detroit Free Press,* May 27, 1900, p. 35.

8   "Last Will and Testament of Wilhelm Constantin Julius Johannes Böing."


**Chapter 3**

1   Yale did not begin accepting women until 1969.

2   *Yale Yearbook,* 1902.

3   "Yale: For God, Country and Success," *The Harvard Crimson,* November 25, 1950.

4   *Ibid.*

5   Yale was founded by Eli Yale, so students were often referred to as "Elis."

6   M. Wortman, *The Millionaires' Unit,* 2007, p. 16.

7   "In the Superior Court of the State of Washington," *Aberdeen Herald,* March 13, 1902, p. 10.

8   "Guardianship Discharged," *Aberdeen Herald,* Grays Harbor, October 30, 1902, p. 8.

9   Albemarle County Deeds 126:198, 132:102.

## Chapter 4

1 R. A. Weinstein, *Grays Harbor 1885-1913*, 1978.
2 *Ibid.*
3 *Ibid.*
4 *Ibid.*
5 "Richmond Horse Show," *The Old Dominion*, October 9, 1913, p. 1.
6 "Fair Sex Brave Rain For Ending," *The Times Dispatch,* October 18, 1903, p. 15.
7 "A Fall Sustained By Miss Skelton," *The Times Dispatch,* October 15, 1903, p. 1.

## Chapter 5

1 John D. Daniels, Kill Devil Hills Life-Saving Station crew member. http://www.smithsonianeducation.org/educators/lesson_plans/wright/group_d.html
2 A typographical error in transmission changed fifty-nine seconds to fifty-seven.
3 A typographical error in transmission changed Orville to Orevelle.
4 F. C. Kelly, *Miracle at Kitty Hawk*, 1951, p. 431.

## Chapter 6

1 "Iron at Elma," *The Aberdeen Herald,"* July 24, 1905, p. 8.
2 Gordon T. *The San Francisco Earthquake Minute by Minute.* 2014 Kindle location – 1000.
3 *Ibid.*
4 R. L. Polk & Co., *Directory of Aberdeen, Washington*, 1908 p-24.

## Chapter 7

1 "Fine Boat Launched," *Aberdeen Herald*, July 25, 1907, p. 4.
2 A widgeon is a type of duck.
3 Albemarle County Deeds 126:198, 132:102.
4 Poole, "Boeing Military Wedding at Fine Old Virginia Home," *Evening Star*, Washington DC, December 24, 1907, p. 7.
5 *Decennial Record of Yale 1904*, Yale University, 1914, pp. 207-8.
6 *Ibid.*
7 Personal interview with Barbara Hiscock Spaeth, January 23, 2021.
8 1910 U.S. Census.
9 *The Menasha Record*, May 14, 1908, p. 2.
10 S. Andrews, *The University Club of Seattle Centennial*, 2005, p. 6.
11 "Big Timber Deal Closed," *Morning Oregonian*, December 11, 1908, p. 1.
12 *Ibid.*
13 The Rainier Club, the College Club, the Washington Athletic Club, the Arctic Club, the Seattle Golf and Country Club, the Olympic Tennis Club, and the University Club.
14 S. Andrews, *The University Club of Seattle Centennial*, 2005, p. 6.

## Chapter 8

1 Decoration Day has been renamed Memorial Day and is now celebrated on the last Monday of May.
2 "Chased Wrong Man Across the Continent – Long Hunt Ends in Joke," *The Seattle Star*, June 11, 1908.
3 *Ibid.*
4 *Ibid.*
5 *Ibid.*

6  *Ibid.*
7  *Ibid.*
8  "New Officers For Wishkah Company," *Aberdeen Herald,* September 27, 1909, p. 8.

## Chapter 9

1  https://www.legendsofamerica.com/wa-seattleklondike/
2  One prospector, a Swedish immigrant named John Nordstrom, returned from the gold fields with $13,000. He had seen that the miners who made it to Alaska needed good warm boots, so he invested in a shoe store in Seattle. The store grew to become the upscale Nordstrom department store chain.
3  E. David & S Ellis, *Seattle's Commercial Aviation 1908-1941,* 2009, p. 11.
4  *Los Angeles Times,* January 5, 1910.
5  Shortly after Poole had married Caroline, he was promoted from lieutenant to captain.
6  Both Harold Mansfield's and Dewitt Poole's accounts of the Los Angeles Aviation Meet describe Boeing arriving there by automobile. Since Highway 99 from Seattle to Los Angeles was not built for another sixteen years and there weren't any car rental businesses in California until 1918, it is likely that Boeing had his car shipped from Seattle by train.
7  "Paulhan is the Star Aviator," *The Tulare Advance Register,* January 11, 1910, p. 1.
8  *Ibid.*
9  H. Mansfield, *Vision,* 1956, pp. 7-8.
10 D. C. Poole, *American Cavalcade,* 1997, pp. 350-52.
11 "First Flights This Morning," *Los Angeles Daily Times,* January 11, 1910, p. 4.
12 P. Braud, "Famous French Aviator Has Great Hopes for the Future," *Los Angeles Daily Times,* January 11, 1910, p. 4.

## Chapter 10

1  E. W. Heath Bill of Sale. Boeing family archives.
2  "Children Seek Court's Aid in Enforcing Their Mother's Wish," *Evening Star,* Washington DC, May 24, 1911, p. 20.
3  *Ibid.*
4  Undated letter from William E. Boeing to Mr. Perkins of Charlottesville, VA. Boeing family archives.
5  "Will Take Extended Alaskan Coast Trip," *Aberdeen Herald*, August 8, 1912, p. 6.
6  Undated letter from William E. Boeing to Mr. Perkins of Charlottesville, VA. Boeing family archives.
7  *Chicago Tribune*, November 30, 1913, p. 30.
8  "Homes in Artistic District," *The Seattle Daily Times,* July 20, 1930, p. 29.
9  "South Dakota Girl Lionized In Europe," *The Daily Deadwood Pioneer Times,* March 20, 1912, p. 2.
10 "Attractive Program Given by Orchestra" *The Seattle Daily Times,* December 11, 1912, p. 10.
11 By 1912 Bill had replaced his Packard with a new Rolls Royce Silver Ghost.
12 W. Leary, "George Conrad Westervelt Capt., U.S.N.," *AAHS Journal,* Summer 1972, p. 92.
13 H. Mansfield, *Vision,* 1956, p. 10.

14 W. Leary, "George Conrad Westervelt, Capt. U.S.N.," *AAHS Journal*, summer 1972, p. 92.
15 P. Spitzer, "Westervelt Girdled Globe In Can-Do Career," *Boeing News* February 5, 1988, p. 6.

## Chapter 11

1 D. Catchpole, "Boeing Founder's First Pilot: Terah T. Maroney," *Everett Herald*, July 2, 2014.
2 The Kla-How-Yah Festival, named after a native word for "welcome," has become the Kla-Ha-Ya Days festival and continues to be held each summer in Everett.
3 D. Catchpole, "Boeing Founder's First Pilot: Terah T. Maroney," *Everett Herald*, July 2, 2014.
4 "Two Airships in Flight Over Lake," *Seattle Post-Intelligencer*, July 18, 1914, p. 2.
5 H. Mansfield, *Vision,* 1956, pp. 11-12.
6 Interview with Conrad Westervelt by Harold Mansfield, "Westy Trip Notes" Boeing Company archives, Box 1-A-2.
7 *Ibid.*
8 *Ibid.*
9 "France and Germany Will Fight It Out in Clouds If War Comes," *The Seattle Star,* July 30, 1914, p. 1.
10 *Ibid.*
11 M. Wortman, *The Millionaires' Unit,* 2007, p. 41.

## Chapter 12

1 H. Mansfield, *Vision,* 1956, p. 13.
2 *Ibid.*
3 Gott's mother was Stephanie Ortmann, the younger sister of Bill's mother, Marie Ortmann.
4 D. E. Schmidt, *The Folly of War,* 2005, p. 7.
5 Personal letters of William E. Boeing, April 22, 1916. Boeing family archives.
6 *The Seattle Daily Times,* August 3, 1915.
7 *Aerial Age Weekly,* May 31, 1915, p. 252.
8 "Millionaire Turns Aviator for Sport," *San Francisco Examiner*, August 11, 1915, p. 1.
9 "New Aero Club Will Prepare for Service," *Oakland Tribune*, September 1, 1915, p. 2.

## Chapter 13

1 "Big Military Aeroplane Makes First Flight Here," *The Seattle Star*, October 22, 1915, p. 1.
2 "Seaplane Soars Above Seattle," *The Tacoma Times*, October 22, 1915, p. 5.
3 "Aero Clubs Head Sounds Warning From Sky," *The Seattle Daily Times,* November 12, 1915, p. 1.
4 "Flight to Tacoma," *The Seattle Star*, November 13, 1915, p. 5.
5 *The Navy and Marine Corps Register*, January 1916, p. 116.
6 *Aerial Age Weekly,* January 31, 1916, p. 473.

## Chapter 14

1 Washington State granted women the right to vote in 1910, almost a decade before the 19th Amendment was ratified giving all American women the right to vote.

2  "Liquor Seized in Fine Homes," *San Francisco Chronicle*, January 20, 1916, p. 4.

3  "Not Safe at Home. Rich Men's Palaces Invaded," *Los Angeles Times*, January 20, 1916, p. 1.

4  *Ibid.*

5  "Wife Hodge Cast Off Was Bread Winner," *The Seattle Post-Intelligencer*, October 21, 1912, p. 1.

6  https://www.olyblog.net/newWP/ungovernor-1920-robert-bridges/

7  "Officers Seize Liquor Found In Boeing Cellar," *The Seattle Star*, January 19, 1916, p. 1.

8  "Liquor Seized in Seattle Homes," *San Francisco Chronicle*, January 20, 1916, p. 4.

9  "Seize All The Liquors At Home of Rich Lumberman," *Anaconda Standard*, January 20, 1916, p. 1.

10 "Not Safe at Home. Rich Men's Palaces Invaded," *Los Angeles Times*, January 20, 1916, p. 1.

11 Museum of Flight, William E. Boeing Collection. Box 2, Folder 42, Box 2, letter from W. E. B. to Westervelt, March 17, 1916.

12 "Bob Hodge Tells What He's Going To Do Under Search Law – And Why," *The Seattle Star* January 21, 1916, p. 1.

13 *Ibid.*

14 *Ibid.*

15 *Ibid.*

16 "Boeing Pays High," *The Seattle Star*, February 7, 1919, p. 4.

## Chapter 15

1  "Boeing Sues to Determine Sheriff's Dry Law Rights," *The Seattle Star*, January 29, 1916, p. 6.

2  "Curt Reply is Made by Sheriff to Matthews," *The Seattle Star*, January 31, 1916, p. 1.

3  "Right To Search Homes Upheld," *The Seattle Daily Times*, February 20, 1916, pp. 1-2

4  "Unruly Wind Plunges Air Flyer into Lake Union," *The Seattle Daily Times*, February 20, 1916, p. 1.

5  Museum of Flight, William E. Boeing Collection. Box 2, Folder 83, letter from Davies to Daniels, June 2, 1916.

6  Museum of Flight, William E. Boeing Collection. Box 2, Folder 84, letter from Davies to Franklin Roosevelt, June 2, 1916.

## Chapter 16

1  Personal letter from Bill Boeing to Conrad Westervelt, March 17, 1916. Boeing family archives.

2  Personal letter from Bill Boeing to Conrad Westervelt, April 22, 1916. Boeing family archives.

3  Personal letter from Bill Boeing to Conrad Westervelt, May 19, 1916. Boeing family archives.

4  Museum of Flight, William E. Boeing Collection. Box 2, Folder 93, telegram from W. E. B. to Westervelt, June 12, 1916.

5  "Hydroaeroplane Made in Seattle Undergoes Tests," *Seattle Post-Intelligencer*, June 16, 1916.

6  *Ibid.*

7  *Ibid.*

8   "Supreme Court Plays Hob With Dry Law, He Says," *The Seattle Star,* July 6, 1916, p. 1.

9   "Hodge Will Fly to Bellingham," *The Seattle Star*, August 11, 1916, p. 10.

## Chapter 17

1   Museum of Flight, "Facilities 1916." Plant 1, Archives, Box 1, Folder 131.

2   Personal interview with Michael Froese, director of the University Club.

3   *Ibid.*

4   H. Mansfield, *Vision*, 1956, p. 17.

5   *Ibid.*

6   "Borden's Arctic Expedition Now Weeks Overdue," *Minneapolis Star Tribune,* August 24, 1916, p. 4.

7   Personal telegram from Bill Boeing to Mrs. John Borden, August 27, 1916. Boeing family archives.

8   "Borden Safe," *San Francisco Examiner*, August 27, 1916, p. 3.

## Chapter 18

1   Personal letter from Bill Boeing to Conrad Westervelt, September 27, 1916. Boeing family archives.

2   Personal letter from Bill Boeing to Conrad Westervelt, September 29, 1916. Boeing family archives.

3   "Short News," *The Seattle Star,* October 2, 1916, p. 6.

4   H. Mansfield, *Vision,* 1956, pp. 18-19.

5   *Ibid.*

6   *Ibid.*

7   *Ibid.*

8   *Ibid.*

9   *Ibid.*

10  "Boeing Airplane Company, Report and Accounts as at December 31, 1918," Price Waterhouse Inc. The Boeing family archives.

11  Museum of Flight, William E. Boeing Collection. Box 3, Folder 129, letter from W. E. B. to Westervelt, September 26, 1916.

12  *Fast Forward Bertha Potter Boeing from Tod's Point to the Jet Age.* Video by Barbara Hiscock Spaeth. https://www.youtube.com/watch?v=OX_aNyIJuv8

13  Seattle socialite and philanthropist Emma Stimson took credit for introducing Bill and Bertha at one of her elegant parties in the early 1920s, after Bertha and Nathaniel were divorced. Bill and Bertha never disputed Emma's claims, but there is significant evidence that they had met well before her party.

## Chapter 19

1   Alex Roland, *Model Research, Volume 1*, 1983.

2   Personal letter from Westervelt to Boeing, February 22, 1917. Boeing family archives.

3   *Ibid.*

4   *Ibid.*

5   *Ibid.*

6   *Ibid.*

7   *Ibid.*

8   "Offers Treatment for Tuberculosis," *New York Times*, February 29, 1920, p. 4.

9   *Ibid.*

10  *Ibid.*

11  Telegram from Bill Boeing to Conrad Westervelt, September 4, 1917. Boeing family archives.
12  Letter from Conrad Westervelt to Bill Boeing, February 22, 1917. Boeing family archives.
13  Letter from Conrad Westervelt to Bill Boeing February 26, 1917. Boeing family archives.
14  Letter from Bill Boeing to Conrad Westervelt, December 1917. Boeing family archives.
15  https://trademarks.justia.com/712/90/mycoleum-71290847.html


## Chapter 20
1  "Wilson Foils Kaiser," *The Seattle Star,* March 1, 1917, p. 1.
2  "Pass Giant Naval Bill – $535,000,000," *The Seattle Star,* March 2, 1917, p. 1.
3  "Kaiser Confesses Plot Against US," *The Seattle Star*, March 3, 1917, p. 1.
4  "Wilson Warns of War as He Pleads Peace," *The Seattle Star*, March 5, 1917, p. 1.
5  "Try To Bomb Wilson," *The Seattle Star,* March 5, 1917, p. 1.
6  *Ibid.*
7  "Kaiser Speed 'U' Boats to the United States," *The Seattle Star,* March 12, 1917, p. 1.
8  *Ibid.*
9  "American Crew of 27 All Safe," *The Seattle Star,* March 14, 1917, p. 1.
10  "Germany Making War on U.S.," *Washington Post*, April 3, 1917, p. 1.
11  "McAdoo Asks for Billions," *The Seattle Star*, April 5, 1917, p. 1.
12  *Ibid.*
13  Personal telegram from Conrad Westervelt to Bill Boeing, June 1, 1917. Boeing family archives.
14  U.S. Naval Report, May 24, 1917. Boeing family archives.
15  Personal letter from Conrad Westervelt to Bill Boeing, June 6, 1916. Boeing family archives.
16  H. Mansfield, *Visions*, 1956, p. 22.
17  "Scrappy at First, Boeing grew into a company built to last" https://www.heraldnet.com/news/scrappy-at-first-boeing-grew-into-a-company-built-to-last/


## Chapter 21
1  "War Dulls Campus," *The Seattle Star*, June 12, 1917 p. 2. With a graduating class of only about 350, the absence of sixty-seven graduates was noticeable. (*University of Washington Program of Exercises for the Forty Second Commencement.* June 9, 1917.)
2  Interview of C. L. Egtvedt by H. Mansfield February 11, 1955. Boeing Company archives, Box E-1.
3  Boeing had become close friends with UW president Henry Suzzallo since their negotiation for the wind tunnel. When Wong Tsoo left to return to China, Boeing knew he needed to get some engineering help, so he asked Suzzallo to recommend a couple of good engineering students. Suzzallo passed the request on to the dean of the engineering department, who sent over Egtvedt and Johnson.
4  Personal letters from Bill Boeing to Conrad Westervelt, June 9, 1917. Boeing family archives.
5  *U.S., Navy and Marine Corps Registries, 1814-1992,* pp. 438 and 2762.
6  Personal letter from Conrad Westervelt to Bill Boeing, August 27, 1917. Boeing family archives.

7 *Ibid.*
8 *Ibid.*
9 *Ibid.*
10 *Ibid.*

**Chapter 22**

1 Personal letter from Boeing to Westervelt, October 16, 1917. Boeing family archives.
2 H. Mansfield, *Vision*, 1956, p. 25.
3 *Ibid.* p. 27.
4 *Ibid.*
5 *Ibid.*
6 *Ibid.*
7 Personal letter from Boeing to Westervelt, October 16, 1917. Boeing family archives.
8 "Boeing Airplane Company, Report and Accounts As At December 31, 1918," Price Waterhouse Inc. The Boeing family archives.
9 At this point in the war there had been about 45,000 combat fatalities and 55,000 deaths from illness, particularly from the Spanish flu.
10 "Big War Pageant to Launch Phila's Forth Loan Drive," *Philadelphia Inquirer*, September 28, 1918, p. 1.
11 "Yesterday's Gripping Liberty Sing," *Philadelphia Inquirer*, September 2, 1918, p. 26.
12 "Flu epidemic hits Seattle on October 3,1918," www.HistoryLink.org
13 "Spanish Flu Takes First Victims Here," *The Seattle Star*, October 4, 1918, p. 1.
14 "Flu Grips 984 Seattle Victims," *The Seattle Star*, October 8, 1918, p. 1.
15 "Flu epidemic hits Seattle on October 3,1918," www.HistoryLink.org
16 "Ban Lift Will Soon Be Here Says McBride," *The Seattle Star,* November 9, 1918, p. 1.
17 "Holiday is Proclaimed," *The Seattle Star*, November 11, 1918, p. 1.

**Chapter 23**

1 H. Mansfield, *Vision*, 1956, p. 34.
2 The B-1 has been restored and donated to Seattle's Museum of History and Industry and is currently on display at that museum.
3 "Would Fly With Mail To Alaska," *Spokane Chronicle*, January 8, 1919, p. 5.
4 Ralph Valies, "The History of the Seattle to Victoria Air Mail from 1919 to 1937," *Airpost Journal*, August 1989.
5 The plane was Boeing's personal CL-4S, a Model C that had been refitted with a more powerful Hall-Scott L-4 engine.
6 "Waves and Wind Delay Airplane," *The Seattle Daily Times*, February17, 1919, p. 14.
7 H. Mansfield, *Vision*, 1956, p. 32.
8 "Anacortes Proves Boeing's Waterloo," *The Vancouver Sun*, February 28, 1919, p. 14.
9 "Seattle Flyer Arrives in City," *Vancouver Daily World*, February 28, 1919, p. 1.
10 "William E. Boeing and the Little Airplane Company That Grew," *The Seattle Post-Intelligencer*, June 6, 1976, p. 189.

**Chapter 24**
1   P. Garnett, *The Bohemian Jinks: A Treatise*, 1908, p. 8.
2   "Urge of Life Pulses in Brescia Music," *The San Francisco Examiner*, June 29, 1919, p. 79.
3   Lazarus was a large department store chain in the Midwest from 1850 to 1986. It had a popular restaurant, and in the teens and twenties it was considered chic to cook recipes from Lazarus.

**Chapter 25**
1   Memo from Gott to Boeing, July 17, 1919. Boeing family archives.
2   Letter from Gott to Boeing, November 26, 1919, p. 4. Boeing family archives.
3   "Sea-Sled ordered off Lake Union," *The Seattle Star*, August 30, 1919 p-9.
4   G. R. Newell, *Ready All!* 1987, p. 60.
5   Letter from Gott to Egtvedt, September 17, 1919, p. 2. Boeing family archives.
6   Letter from Gott to Boeing, August 27, 1919, p. 1. Boeing family archives.
7   Letter from Gott to Boeing, October 1, 1919, p. 1. Boeing family archives.
8   "Weekly Report of Sales Dept. Boeing Company, October 16, 1919." Boeing family archive p-1.
9   *Ibid.*
10  H. Mansfield, *Vision*, 1956, p. 37.
11  Draft for speech on the dedication of Boeing Field, 1927, p. 1. Boeing family archives.
12  *Ibid.*
13  "Seattle Wins Big Army Airplane Job," *The Seattle Daily Times*, November 19, 1919, p. 5.

**Chapter 26**
1   H. Mansfield, *Vision*, 1956, p. 34.
2   *Ibid.* pp. 34-35.
3   R. Valles, "The History of the Seattle to Victoria Air Mail from 1919 to 1937, Part III," *Airpost,* October 1989.

**Chapter 27**
1   "50 Shots Fired, $14,000 Worth Of Booze Taken," *The Seattle Star,* March 22,1920, p. 1.
2   N. Clark, *The Dry Years,* 1965, pp. 163 & 165.
3   *Ibid.,* p. 165-66.
4   *Ibid.,* p. 166.
5   B. Holden, *Seattle Prohibition,* 2019, p. 59.
6   F. L. Allen, *Only Yesterday,* 1931, p. 86.

**Chapter 28**
1   H. Mansfield, *Vision*, 1956, p. 38.
2   *Ibid.*
3   *Ibid.*
4   *Ibid.*
5   R. Valles, "The History of the Seattle to Victoria Air Mail from 1919 to 1937, Part III," *Airpost,* October 1989.
6   Hubbard's contract was the second airmail contract issued by the Post Office and therefore designated FAM 2. FAM 1, a contract signed in August for mail between Florida and the West Indies, was not yet operational, making Hubbard's service the first fully operational U.S. foreign airmail service.

7   "Mail Plane Makes Record Trip In Heavy S.E. Gale," *Victoria Daily Times*, October 16, 1920.
8   "Aerial Post Is Commercial Success," *Victoria Daily Times*. September 3, 1921.
9   H. Mansfield, *Vision*, 1956, p. 43.
10  R. Serling, *Legend & Legacy*, 1992, p. 7.

## Chapter 29

1   F. L. Allen, *Only Yesterday*, 1931, p. 90.
2   Undated notebook of Bertha Boeing. Boeing family archives.
3   *Ibid.*
4   Copy of wedding ceremony, September 27, 1925. Boeing family archive
5   https://www.boeing.com/news/frontiers/archive/2009/august/i_history.pdf
6   H. Mansfield, *Vision*, 1956, p. 47.
7   *Ibid.*, p. 48.
8   *Ibid.*
9   The "P" stood for pursuit, the "W" stood for water-cooled engine, and the "9" was added because the PW-9 was the ninth pursuit designed for the army.
10  H. Mansfield, *Vision*, 1956, p. 50.
11  "Harry John A. Weyerhaeuser," *The Chehalis Bee Nugget*, April 7, 1922, p. 12.
12  Bertha Boeing's diary, June 12, 1922.
13  Doctor's bills. Boeing family archives.
14  R. Serling, *Legend & Legacy*, 1992, p. 7.

## Chapter 30

1   P. Bowers, *Boeing Aircraft Since 1916*, 1956, p. 83.
2   "Roy Olmstead Arrested in Federal Booze Raid," *The Seattle Daily Times*, November 18, 1924, p. 4.
3   "Noblesse Oblige in Bootlegging," *The Seattle Daily Times*, April 9, 1989, p. 9.
4   "New Name on Rum Buying List Given by Fryant," *The Seattle Daily Times*, January 29, 1926, p. 1.
5   P. Metcalfe, *Whispering Wires*, 2007.
6   "Olmsted Recovers Seized Papers," *The Seattle Daily Times*, February 2, 1926, p. 8.
7   *Ibid.*
8   *Ibid.*
9   *Ibid.*
10  *Ibid.*
11  *Ibid.*
12  "Olmstead Tells Of Rum Running Plot," *The Arizona Republic*, August 23, 1930.
13  The dissenting opinion written by Justice Brandeis spoke eloquently about a citizen's right to privacy and laid the ground for future Supreme Court battles over the right to privacy that eventually culminated in the Roe *vs.* Wade decision, that a woman has the right of privacy regarding her own reproductive choices.
14  Philadelphia, *The Iron Age*, October 7, 1926, p. 1646

## Chapter 31

1   One of the unexpected results of the Kelly Act was to prompt the new airmail carriers operating scheduled flights between major cities to offer passengers seats on their flights. It is a sad irony that the railroad lobby's efforts to level

the playing field on airmail actually spawned an airline industry that would contribute to no fewer than eight railroad bankruptcies in the next ten years.

2 Bertha Boeing's diary, June 26, 1925 – November 27, 1925.

3 *Ibid.*

4 *Ibid.*

5 *Ibid.*

6 "Hoover and New Ask Civil Flying Aid," *New York Times*, September 24, 1925, p. 1.

7 *Ibid.*

8 Hash was a "working man's" food in the 1900s. Bill had discovered it in the timber camps of Hoquiam, and if became one of his favorite breakfasts. Bertha's diary often gives the menu for their meals, and Bill ate hash for breakfast several times a week.

## Chapter 32

1 H. Mansfield, *Vision*, 1956, pp. 70, 72-73.

2 *Ibid.*

3 *Ibid.*

4 *Ibid.*

5 *Ibid.*

6 *Ibid.*

7 *Ibid.*

8 Bertha Boeing's diary, January 17, 1927 – June 30, 1927.

## Chapter 33

1 Bertha Boeing's diary, June 26, 1925 – November 27, 1925.

2 *Ibid.*

3 *Ibid.*

4 *Ibid.*

5 R. Van der Linden, *Airlines and Air Mail,* 2015, p. 33.

6 Bertha Boeing's diary, June 26, 1925 – November 27, 1925.

7 *Ibid.*

## Chapter 34

1 Bertha Boeing's diary, June 26, 1925 – November 27, 1925.

2 *Ibid.*

3 H. Mansfield, *Vision*, 1956, p. 74.

4 F. L. Allen, *Only Yesterday*, 1931, p. 189.

5 "Boeing Factory Reorganizes to Handle Airmail," *The Seattle Daily Times*, June 13, 1927, p. 3.

6 "S.F.-to-Chicago Air Passenger Service At $200 Fare to Be Opened July 2," *The San Francisco Examiner,* June 29, 1927, p. 19.

7 "10,000 See Boeing Plane at Store, Interest in Airmail Service Runs High," *The Seattle Daily Times*, June 21, 1927, p. 3.

8 Bertha Boeing's diary, June 26, 1925 – November 27, 1925.

9 *Ibid.*

10 H. Mansfield, *Vision,* 1956, p. 74.

11 *Ibid.*, pp.75-76

## Chapter 35

1 Bertha Boeing's diary, September 20, 1927 – August 10, 1928.

2 *Ibid.*

3  *Ibid.*
4  *Ibid.*
5  "Nerve of Flyer Averts Tragedy," *Spokesman Review*, September 22, 1927, p. 1.
6  Bertha Boeing's diary, September 20, 1927 – August 10, 1928.
7  *Ibid.*
8  "Nerve of Flyer Averts Tragedy," *Spokesman Review*, September 22, 1927, p. 1.
9  Bertha Boeing's diary, September 20, 1927 – August 10, 1928.
10 R. Serling, *Legend & Legacy*, 1992, p. 11.
11 F. Taylor, *High Horizons*, 1951, p. 21.

**Chapter 36**

1  "Plane Passenger is Sunday Victim," *Lincoln Journal* Star, February 27, 1928, p. 2.
2  F. Taylor, *High Horizons*, 1951, p. 61.
3  H. Mansfield, *Vision*, 1956, p. 77.
4  F. Taylor, *High Horizons*, 1951, p. 61.
5  "New Mystery Plane Phone To Be Tried Here," *Seattle Post-Intelligencer*, August 16, 1928, p. 2.
6  Any car, boat, or plane that uses an internal combustion engine and is also fitted with a radio owes its ability to receive radio signals to Thorp Hiscock's shielded spark plugs and his original patent, # 2,113,590.

**Chapter 37**

1  "Program for Dedication of Boeing Field, July 26, 1928." Boeing family archives.
2  "Mr. Boeing's Remarks at Boeing Field Dedication, July 26, 1929." Boeing family archives.
3  *Ibid.*
4  *Ibid.*
5  *Ibid.*
6  "City Put on Map by Opening of Boeing Field," *The Seattle Daily Times*, July 27, 1929, p. 10.
7  Bertha Boeing's diary, September 20, 1927 – August 10, 1928.
8  *Ibid.*

**Chapter 38**

1  Personal letter from Rentschler to Boeing, June 28, 1927. Boeing family archives.
2  Bertha Boeing's diary, September 20,1927 – August 10, 1928.
3  Personal letter from Boeing to Rentschler, July 15, 1927. Boeing family archives.
4  "Minutes of the First Meeting of the Board of Directors of Boeing Airplane & Transport Corporation, October 31, 1928." Boeing family archives.
5  "Minutes of the Board of Directors of Boeing Airplane & Transport Corporation, December 22, 1928." Boeing family archives.
6  *Ibid.*
7  *Ibid.*
8  *Ibid.*
9  *Ibid.*
10 "United Aircraft & Transport, First Annual Report to the Stockholders. December 31, 1929." p-8.

11 *Ibid.*
12 Information with respect to certain lumber and logging companies, October 14, 1929. Boeing family archives.
13 Personal letter from William Carson to William E. Boeing, December 28, 1929. Boeing family archives.

**Chapter 39**
1 W. B. Maynard, *Woodrow Wilson*, 2008, p. 322.
2 W. Wilson, "The Pueblo Speech," September 25, 1919.
3 F. W. Allen, *Since Yesterday*, 1939, pp. 11 & 22.
4 *Ibid.*, p. 26.
5 *Ibid.*, p. 38.
6 *Ibid.*, p. 39.
7 Medical records, February,1930. Boeing family archives.
8 Letter from John Hudson Poole to William E. Boeing, June 24, 1930. Boeing family archives.
9 Letter from Boeing to Poole, July 2, 1930. Boeing family archives.
10 "Memorandum for Mr. Boeing outlining recent conservation with Mr. Ortmann, July 8, 1930." Boeing family archives.
11 "Down the banks" was a slang expression in the 1920s and '30s for someone who is in trouble and lost their way. Imagine a path alongside a river with steep banks. A traveler who wanders off the path and slips "down the banks" might have a difficult time getting back to the path.
12 Letter from Poole to Boeing, June 24, 1930. Boeing family archives.

**Chapter 40**
1 F. Taylor, *High Horizons*, 1951, p. 87.
2 The McNary-Watres Act, April 29, 1930, p. 1.
3 F. Taylor, *High Horizons*, 1951, p. 87.
4 Letter from Phil Johnson to James Farley, February 16, 1934. Boeing family archives.
5 "United Aircraft & Transport, First Annual Report to the Stockholders, December 31, 1929," p. 11.
6 Interview with Bill Boeing Jr., February 2014.
7 The first female airline pilot was Emily Howell Warner, who flew for Clinton Aviation in 1973.
8 F. Taylor, *High Horizons*, 1951, p. 70.

**Chapter 41**
1 Some sources claim that this first plane was built in 1914, but in an interview with Frank Ellis, published in the May 1955 edition of *Canadian Aviation*, Hoffar gave the year as 1917.
2 "Inbred Timidity is Handicap to Women," *The Seattle Daily Times*, July 15, 1930, p. 14.
3 *Taconite* Log, Vol. I: June 11, 1930 to August 5, 1931.
4 Handwritten inscription in Bertha Boeing's copy of *20 Hrs., 40 Min.* Boeing family archives.
5 J. Farley, *Jim Farley's Story*, 1948, p. 177

**Chapter 42**
1 Letter from P. B. Battey, MD, superintendent of New York State Reformatory for Women, to Claude G. Bannick, King County sheriff, August 20, 1932. Boeing family archives.

2   Letter from R. A. Allingham, chief criminal detective, King County Sheriff's Office, to William E. Boeing, October 4, 1932. The Boeing family archives.
3   *Ibid.*
4   *Taconite* Log, Vol. III: July 14, 1932 to June 14, 1933, p. 86.
5   *Ibid.*
6   C. Wilson, *The Weekly*, April 22, 1981.
7   Jane Hiscock's diary, p. 105.
8   *Ibid.*, p. 106.

## Chapter 43

1   "Mrs. Caroline Boeing Poole," *The Santa Fe New Mexican*, January 11, 1931, p. 6.
2   *The Pasadena Post*, February 25, 1932, p. 4.
3   "Mrs. Poole Leaves Large Estate and Love in Her Will," *The Pasadena Post*, January 27, 1932, p. 3.
4   R. J. Serling, *Legend & Legacy*, 1992, p. 26.
5   Taped interview with Mrs. Claire Egtvedt by Howard Lovering and John Italiane, November 1, 1984. Museum of Flight, Seattle, Washington.
6   F. D. Roosevelt's acceptance speech to the 1932 Democratic Convention: https://www.presidency.ucsb.edu/documents/address-accepting-the-presidential-nomination-the-democratic-national-convention-chicago-1.
7   *"No, the System Worked,"* Washington Post*, November 9, 2000 (retrieved January 9, 2021).
8   "Farley Admits Ignorance, Haste In Airmail Action," *The San Francisco Bulletin*, February 28, 1934, p. 2.

## Chapter 44

1   H. Mansfield, *Vision*, 1956, p. 106.
2   T. Brady, *American Aviation Experience,* 2000, p. 177.
3   https://about.usps.com/who-we-are/postal-history/airmail-route-maps.pdf
4   Eugene Vidal was the father of author Gore Vidal.
5   https://www.salon.com/2005/05/26/fulton_lewis_connection/
6   R. K. Newman, *Hugo Black*, 1994, p. 3.
7   https://www.senate.gov/artandhistory/history/common/investigations/MailContracts.htm
8   "500,000 In Street Cheer Roosevelt," *The New York Times*, March 4, 1933, p. 1.
9   Franklin D. Roosevelt's inaugural address: https://avalon.law.yale.edu/20th_century/froos1.asp

## Chapter 45

1   Two Model 247s were sold to Lufthansa (s/n 1944 and s/n 1945) and delivered in late 1933 and early 1934. War with the U.S. was seven years in the future and Hindenburg was still president of Germany. The planes were eventually turned over to the Luftwaffe for inspection, but reports that Boeing sold them directly to the Luftwaffe are clearly false as Hitler created the Luftwaffe in 1935, two years after the sale of the 247s.
2   "Seven Die As Plane Crashes In Flames," *The New York Times*, October 11,1933, p. 15.
3   *Ibid.*
4   "Plane Wreck Laid to Nitroglycerine," *The New York Times*, October 15, 1933, p. 31.

5 Purvis was moved off the Chesterton crash by orders from his boss, J. Edger Hoover, to head up the successful manhunt for the notorious bank robber John Dillinger.

6 Letter from A. G. Patterson to Boeing, November 6, 1933. Boeing family archives.

7 William E. Boeing's handwritten answers to the Senate Committee Investigating Ocean and Airmail, November, 1933. Boeing family archives.

8 Registered airmail receipt signed by A. G. Paterson, December 12, 1933. Boeing family archives.

9 "Christmas Pageant Presented by Children," *San Francisco Examiner*, December 31, 1933, p. 23.

10 Telegram from A. G. Paterson to William E. Boeing, December 27, 1933. Boeing family archives.

11 Telegram from Hugo Black to William E. Boeing, January 27, 1933. Boeing family archives.

## Chapter 46

1 William Boeing's answers to questions enumerated in a letter from the Special Senate Committee to Investigate Foreign and Domestic, Ocean and Air Mail Contracts, November 29, 1933. The Boeing family archives.

## Chapter 47

1 R. Newman, *Hugo Black*, 1994, p. 94. Regardless of Hugo Black's early involvement with the Klan, he turned out to be very a progressive judge. When he was appointed to the U.S. Supreme Court he sided with the majority and ruled against school segregation in the 1954 landmark case Brown *vs.* Board Education.

2 *Ibid.*

3 R. F. Van der Linden, *Airlines and Air Mail*, 2002, p. 261.

4 C. S. Dewitt, *A Few Great Captains*, 1989, p. 1.

5 G. T. Dunne, *Hugo Black and the Judicial Revolution*, 1977, p. 152.

6 Transcripts show that during the hearing Bill gave the amount he invested in BAT as $350,000, $700,000 and $750,000. It is unclear if these discrepancies are errors in the transcripts or mistakes made by Bill, but according to records in the Boeing family archive, the correct number is $750,000, and for clarity's sake, this number is used throughout.

7 "Report of Proceedings, Special Committee to Investigate Ocean Mail and Air Mail Contracts," February 6, 1932, p. 2251.

8 *Ibid.*, p. 2253.

9 *Ibid.*, p. 2254.

10 *Ibid.*, p. 2255.

11 *Ibid.*

12 *Ibid.*, p. 2261.

13 *Ibid.*, p. 2266.

14 "Boeing's Profit $51,000,000," *The Seattle Daily Times*, February 6, 1934, p. 1.

15 "Boeing Made Millions from $259 Investment," *The Seattle Star*, February 6, 1934, p. 1.

16 "The Sunday Review," *The Brooklyn Daily Eagle*, March 25, 1934, p. 70.

## Chapter 48

1 Letter from the "Roben Hood Gang" to W. E. Boeing. Boeing family archives.

2 https://www.boeing.com/news/frontiers/archive/2005/may/i_history.html

3 "3 Army Airmen Killed on Mail Test Flights," *The Seattle Daily Times,* February 17, 1934, p. 1.

4 "Bad Break Given New Mail Fliers," *The Record*, February 20, 1934, p. 1.

5 "Army Air Mail Pilot Dies As Plane Crashes – Flier Saves Part of Mail Before Falling; Others Are Forced Down," *The Columbia Record*, 22 February 1934, p. 9.

6 J. Duffy, *Lindberg vs Roosevelt,* 2010, p. 8.

7 "U.S. Restores Air Mails to Private Firms; United wins Seattle Routes," *Seattle Post-Intelligencer*, May 4, 1934, p. 4.

## Chapter 49

1 A. E. Magnell, "United Aircraft Plan For Reorganization Is Sent To Stockholders," *Hartford Courant,* May 24, 1934, p. 1.

2 https://www.nytimes.com/1934/03/18/archives/thorp-hiscock-dies-officer-of-air-line-vice-president-of-united.html

3 P. M. Bowers, *Boeing Aircraft since 1916-1966*, p. 283.

4 Taped interview with Mrs. Claire Egtvedt by Howard Lovering and John Italiane, November 1, 1984. Museum of Flight, Seattle, Washington.

5 H. Mansfield, https://www.loc.gov/law/help/statutes-at-large/73rd-congress/session-2/c73s2ch466 1956 p-115

6 https://www.loc.gov/law/help/statutes-at-large/73rd-congress/session-2/c73s2ch466

7 A. E. Magnell, "United Aircraft Plan For Reorganization Is Sent To Stockholders," *Hartford Courant,* May 24, 1934, p. 1.

8 *Ibid.*

9 *Ibid.*

10 P. M. Bowers, *Boeing Aircraft since 1916 -1966*, p. 284.

11 "It Began with Impatience," *San Francisco Examiner*, June 21, 1934, p. 6.

12 *Taconite* Log, Vol. V, August 27, 1933 to August 5, 1934.

## Chapter 50

1 *Taconite* Log, Vol. VI, August 6, 1934 to August 8, 1935.

2 *Ibid.*

## Chapter 51

1 "To Sue on Mail Contracts O.K.'D," *The Seattle Daily Times*, February 4, 1935, p. 18.

2 "Break in Kidnap," *Akron Beacon Journal*, May 29, 2020, p. 9.

3 *Taconite* Log, Vol. VI, August 6, 1934 to August 8, 1935.

4 "Rose With Sun," *The Seattle Daily Times,* July 29, 1925.

5 *Ibid.*

6 Hawaii would not become a state until August 21, 1959.

7 The Punahou School has had a number of famous alumni, but none so famous as the forty-fourth President of the United States, Barack Obama, who graduated from Punahou in 1979.

## Chapter 52

1 "Gen Arnold Gives 'Mystery Bomber' Entire Approval," *The Seattle Daily Times*, August 10, 1935, p. 9.

2 The 299 crash spawned two significant safety innovations. First, gust locks on most planes (designed to keep the control surfaces from being damaged by strong winds when the plane is on the ground) were removed from the cockpit

and replaced with external locks that are now marked with bright red streamers that say "Remove before flight." Second, all Boeing and military pilots began using preflight check lists to make sure that the planes were ready to fly.

3   "Landing Passengers," *Honolulu Advertiser*, December 6, 1935, p. 17.

4   "Visiting Here," *Hawaiian Tribune Herald,* December 22, 1935, p. 8.

5   "Steel, Aircraft Leaders Visit General Drum," *Honolulu Advertiser*, December 2, 1936, p. 3.

6   The Boeing board believed that since the clause in the Black Air Mail Act of 1934 prohibited contracts from going to any company that employed an executive who had taken part in the Spoils Conference, allowing Johnson to sit on the board as an unpaid member did not violate the statue.

### Chapter 53

1   Pari-mutuel is a system of betting invented in France in 1867 that places all bets of a specific type together in a pool. Taxes and the house take are subtracted from the pool and the payoff odds are calculated by sharing the remaining pool between all winning bets.

2   Thoroughbred is the name for a specific breed of horse. All Thoroughbred horses can trace their lineage back to three foundational sires brought to England from the Middle East around the turn of the seventeenth century. The goal was to breed the fast and fiery Arabians with the strong, sturdy English breeds to create strong, fast horses bred specifically for racing.

3   T. R. Underwood, *Thoroughbred Racing & Breeding*, 1945, p. 219.

4   B. Markham, *West With the Night*, 1942.

5   T. Gwynne, "Hoof Beats," *Monrovia News-Post*, January 13, 1937, p. 5.

6   *Ibid.*

7   *Ibid.*

8   *Ibid.*

9   Santa Anita Park had been founded in 1934 by movie producer Hal Roach and dentist Charles Strub. Rumor had it that Roach and Strub met at the Bohemian Club and that a group of Bill Boeing's well-heeled friends convinced them to join forces to build the track at Santa Anita.

10  "Beezley, Horses Will Fly Now," *Los Angeles Times*, January 29, 1937.

11  "Tanforan Bars Church and Beezley Stables," *Los Angeles Times*, February 17, 1937, p. 33.

12  "Boeing Stables Become Largest in the West," *Daily News*, Los Angeles, California, January 19, 1938, p. 15.

13  "East Coast is Forced To Recognize Three West Coast Trainers," *Oakland Tribune*, October 13, 1938, p. 26.

### Chapter 54

1   P. M. Bowers, *Boeing Aircraft since 1916*, 1966, p. 294.

2   "Biography of Liberator Bomber is a Tale of Achievement," *Tucson Daily Citizen*, February 22, 1943, p. 6.

3   *Ibid.*

4   https://en.wikipedia.org/wiki/Consolidated_B-24_Liberator#Prototypes_and_service_evaluation

5   H. Mansfield, *Vision,* 1956, p. 150.

6   "Out of the Dog House," *Saturday Evening Post*, November 15, 1941, p. 126.

7   H. Mansfield, *Vision,* 1956, p. 162.

8   W. L. White, "Out of the Dog House," *Saturday Evening Post*, November 15, 1941, p. 126.

9   *Ibid.*
10  F. E. Holman, *The Life and Times of a Western Lawyer 1886-1961*, 1963, p. 279.

## Chapter 55

1   The demand made in the Treaty of Versailles that the German military be disbanded at the end of World War I had an unexpected consequence: all the equipment in the Third Reich's rebuilt arsenal – everything from guns, to tanks, to planes – was brand new and often far superior to the antiquated equipment used by the Allies in Europe.
2   "Churchill's Speech to Commons," *The New York Times*, May 14, 1940, p. 6.
3   "The President's Address," *The New York Times*, May 17, 1940, p. 10.
4   D. K. Goodwin, *No Ordinary Time*, 1994, p. 63.
5   *Ibid.*
6   https://winstonchurchill.org/resources/speeches/1940-the-finest-hour/fight-them-on-beaches/
7   *Ibid.*
8   *Ibid.*
9   D. K. Goodwin, *No Ordinary Time*, 1994, p. 66.
10  *Ibid.*
11  http://www.aviation-history.com/boeing/b17.html
12  "W. E. Boeing Buys Douglas Plane," *The Honolulu Advertiser*, June 7, 1940, p. 9.

## Chapter 56

1   H. Mansfield, *Vision*, 1956, p. 183.
2   *Ibid.*
3   W. L. White, "Out of the Doghouse," *Saturday Evening Post*, November 15, 1941, p. 14.
4   "Seven Hits Scored on *Gneisenau* By British," *Seattle Post-Intelligencer*, July 25, 1941, p. 1.
5   Three RAF B-17s had flown a bombing mission against the German city of Wilhelmshavem, but the news of that raid had not been released yet.
6   W. L. White, "Out of the Doghouse," *Saturday Evening Post*, November 15, 1941, p. 14.
7   "Brest Raid Had Made in U.S. Label," *Seattle Post-Intelligencer*, July 25, 1941, p. 2. Both the Sperry and Norden bombsights were used on the B-17. The Sperry had been approved for export to the RAF in 1940, but the more advanced Norden bombsight was still top secret and was held back for U.S. use only at the time.
8   W. L. White, "Out of the Doghouse," *Saturday Evening Post*, November 15, 1941, p. 14.
9   "Air-Mail Charges Held Groundless," *The Evening Sun*, Baltimore, Maryland, November 17, 1941, p. 1.
10  *Ibid.*

## Chapter 57

1   R. F. Dorr, *7th Bombardment Group/Wing*, 1997, p. 48.
2   *Ibid.*
3   *Ibid.*
4   U.S. bombers carried flare guns and colored flares so that when planes approached their home fields, the flight crews could alert the ground crews to emergencies on board without using radios.

5 E. L. Reid, "Shot Down at Pearl Harbor," *Air Force Magazine*, December 1, 1991. https://www.airforcemag.com/article/1291pearl/
6 *Ibid.*

**Chapter 58**
1 Personal interviews with Bill Boeing Jr., February 2014.
2 "Wm. E. Boeing Founder Will Return To Firm," *The Seattle Daily Times*, April 5, 1942, p. 9.
3 This total is based on over 800 pages of World War II-era Boeing Company documents in the family archives, as well as Bertha's diaries, which frequently mention Bill's trips to "the plant."
4 Boeing Aircraft Company, Renton Division, Management Committee Minutes, June 2, 1942; June 12, 1942; June 26, 1942. Boeing family archives.
5 *Ibid.*, July 17, 1942.
6 *Ibid.*, August 14, 1942; September 4, 1942; September 25, 1942; October 16, 1942; August 7, 1942.

**Chapter 59**
1 "Submarine Shells Southland Oilfield," *Los Angeles Times*, February 24, 1942, p. 1.
2 "Big Duthie Farm Sold to Boeing," *The Seattle Daily Times*, April 15, 1942, p. 15.
3 P. W. Tibbets, *The Tibbets Story*, 1978, p. 75 & 78.
4 "The plane that is best remembered for the first attack was Yankee Doodle, which lead the second formation of six B-17s. On board this plane was Brigadier General Ira Eaker, head of the Eighth Bomber Command. The official war histories will record that General Eaker led the first American daylight raid on occupied Europe. This is a matter of military protocol, for although I [Paul Tibbets] led the attacking formation – the highest-ranking officer on the flight is officially credited with being the leader." P. W. Tibbets, *The Tibbets Story*, 1978, p. 82.
5 *Ibid*
6 https://www.manhattanprojectvoices.org/oral-histories/general-paul-tibbets---reflections-hiroshima
7 P. W. Tibbets, *The Tibbets Story*, 1978, p. 75.
8 *M. Harden, "Still No regrets for Frail Enola Gay Pilot," Columbus Dispatch, August 6, 2005, p. 21.*
9 https://www.manhattanprojectvoices.org/oral-histories/general-paul-tibbets---reflections-hiroshima

**Chapter 60**
1 W. J. Boyne, "The B-29's Battle of Kansas," *Air Force Magazine*, February 1, 2012. https://www.airforcemag.com/article/0212b29/
2 H. Mansfield, *Vision*, 1956, p. 205.
3 J. Broom, "How a top-secret tragedy helped give rise to the popular Frye Art Museum," *The Seattle Times*. October 24, 2002.
4 Bertha Boeing's diary, January 1, 1943 – March 22, 1943.
5 *Ibid.*
6 H. Mansfield, *Vision*, 1956, p. 205.
7 Lockheed hired Eddie Allen to pilot the first flight of their huge Constellation. "New Super Transport Plane Makes Debut In First 1943 Flying Sensation," *Los Angeles Times*, January 10, 1942, p. 2.

8  *Ibid.*
9  https://mynorthwest.com/404023/presidents-secret-visit-to-puget-sound/
10 "Roosevelt's Visit Here Described By Writers," *Seattle Post-Intelligencer*, October 2, 1942 p. 4.
11 "Planning For The Future," The Boeing Company, September 23, 1942, MPF 2,745.

## Chapter 61

1  Bertha Boeing's diary, October 27, 1953 – January 30 1954. This quotation actually describes the move from the original farmhouse to a new farmhouse built in 1953. This book does not cover that time period, so I ask the reader's forgiveness in allowing me use it to describe the move into the first home in 1942.
2  Bertha Boeing's diary, January 1, 1943 – March 22, 1943.
3  H. Mansfield, *Vision*, 1956, p. 211.
4  Boeing Aircraft Company, Engineering Technical Committee, Minutes, February 4, 1943. Boeing family archives.
5  H. Mansfield, *Vision*, 1956, p. 206. There were no survivors of the February 18 B-29 crash, and as it happened years before cockpit data records were invented, there is no way to know exactly what took place. I have used the description of the action in the B-29 cockpit during the December 30 fire to illustrate what probably took place during the fatal fire.
6  *Ibid.*
7  Charles Frye, owner of Frye & Company, had been an avid art collector. When he died in 1940 and his heirs decided to sell his home, his extensive collection of 240 paintings was moved to the office of the packing plant. None of the paintings were lost in the fire. His heirs soon created the Frye Art Museum to house and protect the collection.

## Chapter 62

1  "Boeing Men, Women Pause In Tribute to Dead Comrades," *The Seattle Daily Times*, February 24, 1943, p. 14.
2  Bertha Boeing's diary, January 1, 1943 – March 22, 1943.
3  Personal interview with Jane Paschall, January 9, 2021.
4  Boeing Aircraft Company, Management Committee Minutes, March 4, 1943. The Boeing family archives.
5  P. W. Tibbets, *The Tibbets Story*, 1978, p. 147.
6  *Ibid.*

## Chapter 63

1  On January 30, 1943 Bill Boeing Jr. had bought a bright red Indian Chief motorcycle with a 1,210-cc engine that could rocket the bike along at 85 mph.
2  The injury was the start of a lifelong ordeal; Billy's leg did not heal correctly and had to be re-broken and reset, which resulted in his right leg being shorter than his left. He ended up having to wear a brace and he walked with a limp for the rest of his life. During a personal interview in February 2014, Bill Boeing Jr. said that he suspected that this accident reinforced his father's opinion that he was a ne'er-do-well who would not amount to much.
3  Bertha Boeing's diary, January 1, 1943 – March 22, 1943.
4  Interview with Bobby Hiscock.
5  Bertha Boeing's diary, January 1, 1943 – March 22, 1943.

6  B. Flamm, "Putting the Brakes On Non Essential Travel," *Journal of Transport History, March 2006*, p. 17.

7  "Downs May Attempt Street Car Derby," *West Palm Beach Post,* February 9, 1943, p. 9.

8  https://archive.org/details/KentuckyDerbyBroadcasts/1943-05-01-WHAS-1943-Kentucky-Derby-Clem-McCarthy.mp3

**Chapter 64**

1  For a brand to be official in Washington, it has to be registered with the State Department of Agriculture and published in its official livestock brand book.

2  Official Livestock Brand Book for the State of Washington, August 1943.

3  https://www.history.navy.mil/research/library/online-reading-room/title-list-alphabetically/a/army-navy-e-award.htm

4  "Fort School Given Banner," *The Seattle Post-Intelligencer*, May 21, 1943, p. 19.

5  Bertha Boeing's diary, May 18, 1943 – November 22, 1943.

6  *Ibid.*

7  A. Pelletier, *Boeing*, 2010, p. 110.

8  Boeing Aircraft Company Engineering Technical Committee, Agenda, September 9, 1943. Boeing family archive

9  *Ibid.*

10  H. Mansfield, *Vision,* 1956, p. 254.

**Chapter 65**

1  Amy Louis Burnett was the daughter of Renton coal magnate Charles H. Burnett. When her mother died, she was sent to live with Alice and Howard Potter (Bertha's mother and father), and Amy was raised as Bertha's foster sister. http://www.wikiwand.com/en/Boeing_Renton_Factory.

2  Bertha Boeing's diary, May 18, 1943 – November 22, 1943.

3  "Boeing Greets Arnold," *The Seattle Daily Times*, October 3, 1943, p. 12.

4  "The Bon Marche," *The Seattle Daily Times*, October 3, 1943, p. 8.

5  *Ibid.*

6  "U.S. Planes Won Salerno," *The Seattle Post-Intelligencer*, October 4, 1943, p. 5.

**Chapter 66**

1  *Boeing B-17, Flying Fortress 1935-2010,* 2010, p. 38. The book, published by the Museum of Flight, states that the Eighth Air Force's B-17 "racked up a kill score of 23 enemy aircraft per 1,000 sorties" and flew 291,508 sorties. The math works out to 6,704 enemy planes downed.

2  Eighth Air Force Fighter Command credited its pilots with 5,280 enemy aircraft shot down and 4,100 destroyed on the ground: https://en.wikipedia.org/wiki/VIII_Fighter_Command

3  Spitfire Association, Horrific WWII Statistics: http://www.pippaettore.com/horrific_WWII_Statistics.html

4  "Boeing Silent Moment, Then Work Resumes," *The Seattle Daily Times*, June 6, 1944, p. 5.

5  Orders for more than 5,000 B-29s were canceled when the war ended and only 3,970 B-29s were actually produced. https://www.b29-superfortress.com/b29-superfortress-production-assembly-plants.htm

## Chapter 67

1  R. Serling, *Legend & Legacy*, 1992, p. 56.
2  N. S. Finney, "Airplane Industry Hopeful to Face X-Day Deflation," *Minneapolis Star Tribune.* September 11, 1944, p. 4.
3  "P.G. Johnson Stricken in Wichita," *Seattle Post-Intelligencer*, September 14, 1944, p. 1.
4  "Johnson of Boeing Dies of Stroke," *The Seattle Daily Times*, September 14, 1944, p. 1.
5  "Phil Johnson's Death War Casualty," *The Seattle Post-Intelligencer*, September 19, 1944, p. 14.
6  "Phil Johnson Eulogized By His Boyhood Pastor," *The Seattle Post-Intelligencer,* September 19, 1944, p. 9.
7  Summary of information on new bombardment-type airplane obtained from Materiel Command, August 31, 1944. Boeing family archives.
8  *Ibid.*
9  Boeing Aircraft Company, Engineering Technical Committee Minutes, August 31, 1944. Boeing family archives.
10  "Report on results of meeting of weight reduction board on B-29 airplane." Boeing family archives.

## Chapter 68

1  https://www.atomicheritage.org/key-documents/einstein-szilard-letter
2  https://www.osti.gov/opennet/manhattan-project-history/Events/1942/final_approval_build.htm
3  P. W. Tibbets, *The Tibbets Story*, 1978, p. 155.

## Chapter 69

1  This author's father, 2nd Lieutenant Richard Williams, was a bombardier on Mission 982.
2  "Now Japan! City Works On VE Day," *The Seattle Daily Times*, May 8, 1945, p. 1.
3  "Accomplishment and a Challenge," *The Seattle Daily Times*, May 8, 1945, p. 4.
4  "President Asks Prayer For Victory," *The Seattle Daily Times*, May 8, 1945, p. 1.
5  *Ibid.*
6  Boeing Aircraft Company, Engineering Technical Committee Minutes, May 24, 1945. Boeing family archives.
7  https://m.andalusiastarnews.com/2020/07/31/the-invasion-of-japan-nov-1-1945/
8  https://www.historylearningsite.co.uk/world-war-two/the-pacific-war-1941-to-1945/operation-downfall/
9  *Ibid.*
10  "Adopt Job Draft Law In Hurry, F.D.R. Plea," *New York Daily News*, January 18, 1945, p. 1.
11  https://www.stripes.com/blogs-archive/the-rumor-doctor/the-rumor-doctor-1.104348/are-purple-hearts-from-1945-still-being-awarded-1.116756#.YDv1O_c74os
12  https://www.atomicarchive.com/media/videos/oppenheimer.html
13  https://www.osti.gov/opennet/manhattan-project-history/Events/1945/potsdam_decision.htm
14  https://www.atomicarchive.com/resources/documents/hiroshima-nagasaki/potsdam.html

15  K. Torikai, *Voices of the Invisible Presence,* 2009, p. 33.
16  https://www.osti.gov/opennet/manhattan-project-history/Resources/order_drop.htm
17  https://www.history.com/.amp/news/the-inside-story-of-harry-truman-and-hiroshima
18  Post-war critics have speculated that Truman must have known that Japan would surrender after Hiroshima and only allowed Nagasaki to be bombed in an attempt to send a message to Stalin. This theory is undercut by two facts: 1. The Japanese government's response to the Potsdam ultimatum was that they were "determined to continue our fight to the end." They made no statement that contradicted their Potsdam response until August 15, after both bombs had been dropped. 2. Stalin already knew about the bomb and had told Truman to go ahead and use it.
19  D. Magnuson, "Seattle Exhausted by Victory Bedlam. Finds Joy In Peace," *The Seattle Daily Times*, August 15, 1945, p.1 & 14.
20  *Ibid.*

## Chapter 70

1  Boeing Aircraft Company, Engineering Technical Committee Minutes, February 19, 1946. Boeing family archives.
2  Personal interview with Jane Paschall, December 26, 2020.
3  "Boeing's New Jet Tanker – Transport Christened," *Seattle Daily Times*, May 15, 1954, p. 20.
4  *Taconite* Log, Vol. XX, May 7, 1956 to October 30, 1956.
5  "Associates Pay Tribute to Vision of William Boeing," *Seattle Daily Times*, September 29, 1956, p. 4.
6  Personal letter from William M. Allen to Bertha Boeing, October 22, 1956. Boeing family archives.

## Epilogue

1  Tape interview with Mrs. Claire Egtvedt by Howard Lovering and John Italiane, November 1, 1984. Museum of Flight, Seattle, Washington.

## Appendix

1  https://www.inquirer.com/philly/opinion/20070830_Letters_FHA_rules_not_Levitt_kept_blacks_away.html
2  http://wbhsi.net/~wendyplotkin/DeedsWeb/fha38.html
3  https://depts.washington.edu/civilr/boeing_battle.htm such story

# Bibliography

Aeronautical Chamber of Commerce, *The Aircraft Year Book, 1930* (New York, NY, D. Van Nostrand Co., 1930)

Alaspa, B., *Sabotage: A Chronicle of the Chesterton Crash* (Chicago, IL, Bryan W. Alaspa, 2012)

Alef, D., *William Edward Boeing: Sky King* (Santa Barbara, CA, Meta4, 2009)

Alexander, D., *A Sound of Horses* (New York, NY, Bobbs-Merrill Company, 1966)

Allen, F. W., *Lords of Creation: The History of America's 1 Percent* (New York, NY, Open Road Media, 1935)

Allen, F. W., *Only Yesterday: An Informal History of the 1920s* (New York, NY, Open Road Media, 1931)

Allen, F. W., *Since Yesterday: The 1930s in America* (New York, NY, Open Road Media, 1939)

Andrews, S., *The University Club of Seattle Centennial* (Seattle, WA, Sasquatch Books, 2005)

Astor, G., *The Mighty Eight* (New York, NY, Dutton Books, 1997)

Baillargeon, J., *Selections from the Library of William E. Boeing, Part I* (Seattle, WA, Restoration Books, 2007)

Baillargeon, J., *Selections from the Library of William E. Boeing, Part II* (Seattle, WA, Restoration Books, 2007)

Benitez, Major N., *World War II War Production* (Montgomery, AL, Air Command and Staff College, 1997)

Bogle, L., *The Highlands* (Seattle, WA, The Highlands, 1938)

Bolcer, J. & Wills A., *University of Washington* (Charleston, SC, Arcadia, 2014)

Bowers, P., *Boeing Aircraft since 1916* (Annapolis, MD, Naval Institute Press, 1966)

Bowers, P., *Boeing B-17* (Seattle, WA, Museum of Flight, 2010)

Cable, M., *Top Drawer* (New York, NY, Athenaeum, 1984)

Christopher, G. I., *Enola Gay and Bockscar: Atomic Bomb Missions in Japan* (Kindle Unlimited, 2020)

Clark, N., *The Dry Years Prohibition & Social Change in Washington* (Seattle, WA, University of Washington Press, 1965)

Collison, T., *Flying Fortress The Story of The Boeing Bomber* (New York, NY, Charles Scribner's Sons, 1943)

Craff, C., *Boeing Field* (Charleston, SC, Arcadia, 2008)

Churchill W. L. S., *The History of the Second World War: Volume 1 – The Gathering Storm* (Boston, MA, Houghton Mifflin, 1948)

Daniel, J., *Aircraft World Wars I & II* (Stanford, CT, Chevprime Ltd, 1988)

Davies, E. & Ellis, S., *Seattle's Commercial Aviation 1908-1941* (Charleston, SC, Arcadia 2009)

Dice, M., *The Bohemian Grove* (Mark Dice, 2015)

Duffy, J., *Lindbergh Vs Roosevelt: The Rivalry that Divided America* (Washington DC, Regency Publishing, Inc., 2010)

Farley, J., *Jim Farley's Story: The Roosevelt Years* (New York, NY, McGraw Hill Book Company, 1948)

Ficken, R., *Lumber and Politics* (Seattle, WA, University of Washington Press, 1979)

Fredrickson, J., *Boeing* (Charleston, SC, Arcadia, 2016)

Goodwin, D. K., *No Ordinary Time* (New York, NY, Simon & Schuster, 1994)

Gordon T., *The San Francisco Earthquake: A Minute by Minute Account* (New York, NY, Open Road Media, 2014)

Groves, L., *Now It Can Be Told* (New York, NY, De Capo Press, 1962)

Grun, B., *The Timetables of History* (New York, NY, Simon & Schuster, 1982)

*Hearings Before a Special Committee On Investigation of Air Mail* (Washington DC, United States Govt. Printing Office, 1934)

Hillenbrand, L., *Seabiscuit* (New York, NY, Random House, 2001)

Holden, B., *Seattle Prohibition* (Charleston, SC, History Press, 2019)

Holden, H., *The Boeing 247 – The First Modern Commercial Airplane* (Seattle, WA, Tab Books, 1991)

Holman, F., *The Life and Career of a Western Lawyer 1886-1961* (Baltimore, MD , Port City Press, Inc., 1963)

Hourly History, *The Great Depression* (2018)

Johnson, A. M., *Tex Johnson: Jet-Age Test Pilot* (Washington DC, Smithsonian Institute Press, 1991)

Johnson, O., *Stover at Yale* (New York, NY, Frederick A. Stokes Company, 1912)

Jones, J. (ed.), *A History of the B-24 Liberator* (Jeffrey Frank Jones, 2015)

Larson, E., *The Splendid and the Vile.* (New York, NY, Crown, 2020)

Lehrer, H., *Flying the Beam: Navigating the Early U.S. Airmail Airways 1917-1941* (West Lafayette, IN, Purdue University Press, 2014)

Lukoff, B., *Seattle, Then and Now* (San Diego, CA, Thunderbay Press, 2010)

Mansfield. H., *Vision: The Story of Boeing* (New York, NY, Duell, Sloan and Pearce, 1956)

Markham, B., *West with the Night* (New York, Open Road, 1942)

McCullough, D., *Truman* (New York, NY, Simon & Schuster, 1992)

McCullough, D., *The Wright Brothers* (New York, NY, Simon & Schuster, 2015)

Metcalfe, P., *Whispering Wires* (Portland, OR, Ink Water Press, 2007)

Muirhead, J., *Those Who Fall* (New York, NY, Random House, 1986)

Nelson, T., *William Boeing Builder of Planes* (New York, NY, Children's Press, 1999)

Newell, G. R., *Ready All! George Yeoman Pocock and Crew Racing* (Seattle, WA, University of Washington Press, 1987)

Newman, R., *Hugo Black: A Biography* (New York, NY, Pantheon Books, 1994)

Miller, D. L., *Masters of the Air* (New York, NY, Simon and Schuster, 2007)

O'Donnell, E., *America In The Gilded Age* (Chantilly, VA, The Great Courses, 2015)

Okrent, D., *Last Call* (New York, NY, Scribner, 2011)

Pelletier, P., *Boeing, The Complete Story* (Sparkford, UK, Haynes Publishing, 2010)

Rand McNalley & Co., *Deluxe Road Atlas* (Chicago, IL, Rand McNally, 1990)

Serling. R., *Legend & Legacy: The Story of Boeing and Its People* (New York, NY, St Martin's Press, 1992)

Siefkes, D., *Kenworth: The First 75 Years* (Seattle, WA, Documentary Books, 1998)

Smith, H., *Airways: The History of Commercial Aviation in the United States* (Washington DC, Smithsonian Institute Press, 1941)

Spector, R., *Family Trees: Simpson's Centennial Story* (Bellevue, WA, Documentary Books, 1990)

Stout, J. A., *Hell's Angels* (New York, NY, Penguin, 2015)

Taylor, F., *High Horizons* (New York, NY, McGraw-Hill Book Company, 1951)

Torikai, K., *Voices of the Invisible Presence: Diplomatic Interpreters in post-World War II Japan,* (Philadelphia, PA, John Benjamin's Publishing Company, 2009)

Tuchman, B. W., *The Guns of August* (New York, NY, Macmillan, 1962)

Tuchman, B. W., *The Zimmermann Telegram* (New York, NY, Viking Press, 1958)

Tibbets. P., *The Tibbets Story* (New York, NY, Stein and Day, 1978)

Underwood, T., *Call me Horse* (New York, NY, Coward, McCann, Inc., 1946)

Underwood, T., *Thoroughbred Racing & Breeding* (New York, NY, Coward, McCann, Inc., 1946)

Van Brunt, W., *Duluth and St. Louis County, Minnesota: Their Story and People* (Chicago, American Historical Society, 1921)

Weinstein, R., *Grays Harbor 1885-1913* (New York, NY, Penguin Books, 1978)

Woodwick, B. & G., *Logging in Grays Harbor* (Charleston, SC, Arcadia, 2014)

Wortman, M., *The Millionaires Unit* (New York, NY, Public Affairs, 2007)